Experiential Learning

THIRD EDITION

Experiential Learning

A handbook for education, training and coaching

Colin Beard
John P Wilson

KoganPage

LONDON PHILADELPHIA NEW DELHI

First published in Great Britain and the United States in 2002 by Kogan Page Limited entitled *The Power of Experiential Learning*
Second edition 2006 entitled *Experiential Learning*
Third edition 2013
Reprinted 2014

2nd Floor, 45 Gee Street
London EC1V 3RS
United Kingdom

1518 Walnut Street, Suite 1100
Philadelphia PA 19102
USA

4737/23 Ansari Road
Daryaganj
New Delhi 110002
India

www.koganpage.com

© Colin Beard and John P Wilson

The right of Colin Beard and John P Wilson to be identified as the authors of this work has been asserted by them in accordance with the Copyright, Designs and Patents Act 1988.

ISBN 978 0 7494 6765 4
E-ISBN 978 0 7494 6766 1

British Library Cataloguing-in-Publication Data

A CIP record for this book is available from the British Library.

Library of Congress Cataloging-in-Publication Data

Beard, Colin (Colin M.)
    Experiential learning : a handbook for education, training and coaching / Colin Beard, John P. Wilson. – Third edition.
        pages cm
    Includes bibliographical references and index.
    ISBN 978-0-7494-6765-4 – ISBN 978-0-7494-6766-1 (eISBN) 1. Experiential learning–Handbooks, manuals, etc. 2. Active learning–Handbooks, manuals, etc. 3. Employees–Training of–Handbooks, manuals, etc. I. Wilson, John P. (John Peter), 1955 Aug. 11- II. Title.
    BF318.5.B43 2013
    153.1'52–dc23
                                    2013011418

Typeset by AMNET
Printed and bound by 4edge Limited, UK

CONTENTS

PART TWO The learning combination lock model 91

04   Learning environments: spaces and places 93 (The belonging dimension)

05   Experiential learning activities 123 (The doing dimension)

06 Sensory experience and sensory intelligence (SI) 165 (The sensing dimension)

07 Experience and emotions 189 (The feeling dimension)

08   Experience, knowing and intelligence 223 (The knowing dimension)

09   Experience, learning and change 251 (The being dimension)

PART THREE Experiential learning and the future 277

10 Imagining and experiencing the future 279

PART ONE
Experiential learning: foundations and fundamentals

Unlocking powerful learning – a new model

> *Experience is the child of Thought, and Thought is the child of Action – we cannot learn men from books.*
>
> **BENJAMIN DISRAELI, 1826**

Introduction

If you followed the advice of Benjamin Disraeli's quotation above, you would not proceed any further than the first page of this book before returning it to the shelf! However, don't go away; bear with us as we explain how this book will offer a new way of thinking about and organizing the development and delivery of experiential learning.

Disraeli was using his skills as a political orator to polarize the debate about theory and practice and draw attention to the need to think and learn through experience. The argument that 'we cannot learn men through books' is an unsustainable one but Disraeli's underlying message has a kernel of truth. Traditional learning, with the teacher or trainer spouting facts and figures and with pupils or participants regurgitating the information without deeper involvement, is a very ineffective form of learning. A much more effective and long-lasting form of learning is to involve the learner by creating a meaningful learning experience.

This handbook will enable you to see new opportunities to unleash some of the more potent opportunities for learning through experience. In order to free the spirit of learning, whether it be in management education, corporate training, youth development work, therapy, higher education or life coaching, it is necessary to explore in much greater detail the interconnected nature of the learning 'experience'. We explore the meaning of experiential learning in Chapter 2, but to provide greater clarity from the beginning we present a definition that embraces the notion of a whole person approach to learning, and we embrace thinking derived from different disciplines, including biology, neurophysiology, psychology, and social and environmental sciences. Experiential learning was defined in our second-edition book as a sense-making process of active engagement between the inner world of the person and the outer world of the environment. Here we introduce a balanced, connective approach to learning as:

> a sense making process involving significant experiences that, to varying degrees, act as the source of learning. These experiences actively immerse and reflectively engage the inner world of the learner, as a whole person (including physical-bodily, intellectually, emotionally and spiritually) with their intricate 'outer world' of the learning environment (including belonging and doing – in places, spaces, within social, cultural, political context etc) to create memorable, rich and effective experiences for and of learning.

> (Beard, 2010: 17)

This is of course a very broad and rudimentary definition. Edward Cell in his book *Learning to Learn from Experience*, referred to a definition offered by Keeton and Tate way back in 1978. Cell was highlighting the differences between academic learning and experiential learning, and the definition quoted referred to experiential learning as:

> learning in which the learner is directly in touch with the realities being studied. It is contrasted with learning in which the learner only reads about, hears about, talks about, or writes about these realities but never comes into contact with them as part of the learning process.

> (Keeton and Tate, 1978, in Cell, 1984: viii).

Interestingly, the Keeton and Tate text was titled *Learning by Experience – what, why and how*. The immersion in, and contact with, the experience is thus perceived as very important. The 'experience' takes centre stage: it is the foundation of, and the stimulus for, learning. This is the core argument in much theoretical work on experiential learning. That is why several core dimensions of the experience of learning form the focus of this book.

Although there are no easy answers to the creation of learning experiences, whether they be by deliberate programme design or by emergent opportunity, there are significant areas of knowledge about many of the main ingredients that can be used to create new and innovative learning experiences. In this first chapter we illustrate this with a model, presented initially and for practical understanding in the form of a combination lock, which comprises a series of tumblers each designed to illustrate the almost infinite range of ingredients that can be altered in order to enhance learning. Many participants on our programmes are given six polystyrene cups that fit together and rotate to form a copy of the combination lock model. Using this visual metaphor of a combination lock with six tumblers, the potential number of learning permutations is more than 15 million and it can be further expanded to an almost infinite number. Although we are on our guard to avoid simplistic mechanistic thinking, we do believe it is robust material and we discuss the theoretical basis of our thinking, as well as offering many practical examples to illustrate the value of learning from experience. Learning specialists are required to understand the very complex processes involved in experiential learning, and that is where this model can help unpick some of the complexity. We have also used other visual interpretations of the model to aid initial understanding and memory retention: a tennis court in Malaysia, where the net represented the senses, large pebbles on a beach in Greece, and a large yellow circle that was found painted on concrete flooring on Pulau Ubin off the coast of Singapore where Outward Bound is based. The yellow circle was used as the sensory interface between the inner and outer worlds and we added coloured plastic hoops to facilitate discussion of other key dimensions involved in experiential learning.

Experience, in its many guises, pervades all forms of learning; however, its value is frequently not recognized or is even disregarded. Active engagement is one of the basic tenets of experiential learning: experiential learning undoubtedly involves the 'whole person', through thoughts, feelings and physical activity. The recognition of this 'whole environment', both internally and externally, is important. Experiential learning can take on many appearances in life, such as recreational or leisure activities, exhilarating journeys or adventures, experimentation or play. It can also take the form of painful events. Indeed Mälkki (2011) demonstrates how transformation often results from powerful negative emotional experiences that take us from our *comfort zone* into *edge emotions*. Heron (2000: 316), in writing about the facilitation of learning using 'whole person' approaches suggests we recognize that the perfect life web is never complete, but often torn and damaged. People, he said, were engaging in a form of action enquiry throughout their everyday life: 'This consciousness-in-action involves, intentionally, both participatory and individuating functions: feeling and emotion, intuition and imagery, reflection and discrimination, intention and action.'

This handbook explores both the theory and practice of experiential learning. It offers an exciting range of illustrative case material from around the world in an attempt to 'ground' this contribution to contemporary theory. It provides numerous signposts leading to other sources to draw upon, and we, like other professionals, have ventured into, borrowed and learnt from many other disciplines in order to facilitate learning and change. We include ideas and integrating concepts from fields such as psychotherapy, psychology, education and training, people development, adventure and leisure. The book suggests numerous ways to work with human emotional intelligence (EQ) and sensory intelligence (SI), to improve deeper thinking and learning. We offer methods that help people to see and understand things as if for the first time, even though they may have undergone the experience before. We also offer experiential techniques that revisit past experiences and allow learners to view them in a new light: these methods we call retrospective learning. Moving from the past to the present, we consider methods to improve immediate learning, which we call concurrent learning. Finally, we investigate the possibilities of learning through imagination and projecting ideas into the future; we call this prospective learning.

The book offers techniques that help learners make sense of their experience, as well as methods to develop and practise new behaviours. The techniques include mood setting, drama, creative writing, art, meditation, environmental modification and routine rituals. Much more detailed accounts covering over 30 practical experiences are found in the sister book *The Experiential Learning Toolkit* (Beard, 2010). We seek to help you as a coach, developer, educator or trainer, to focus on new ideas and we explore ways to improve professional practice and ethical responsibility through self-monitoring and feedback techniques. Many of the theories and practical methods presented in this book apply equally to providers and learners; indeed as practitioners, we too are learners, and good practice emanates from our ability to learn from our own experiences.

In building the model called the learning combination lock, we first explore simple dichotomies and the notion of balance in learning activities. In rejecting the classical dualisms we call for balance: of energy–tension, challenge–support, task–process, male–female, indoor–outdoor, natural–artificial environments and real–simulated activities. These themes illustrate some of the key factors that present countless opportunities in the design of experiential learning.

We develop many simple models that take the form of waves or circles, and these are important in our thinking throughout the book. Waves of energy underpin the daily experience and these waves of activity influence the basis of experiential programmes. We nurture and prepare people, energize and engage people, help to support, provide for or create their experience and then encourage relaxation. There are surface waves and deeper ones, short ones and long ones.

> A novel can be likened to an ocean. The little waves we see lapping the shore are in fact carried on the waves that are nine ordinary waves long. These waves are themselves carried by waves that carry nine of them and these larger waves are similarly carried by waves that carry nine of them. Some waves in the ocean are miles long.
>
> (Buzan, 2000: 200)

So let us now look at the learning combination lock as a new conceptual framework (see Figure 1.1).

For the first time ever, to our knowledge, all the core ingredients of the learning equation have been brought together in the learning combination lock. This model was initially theoretically grounded in a concept of cognitive processing, including contemporary theories of embodied cognition (linked with bodily learning) and embedded cognition (linked to the environment). Both are discussed in more detail later in the book. In the past, only some of the elements have been discussed in the literature, and then often in isolation, which therefore gives only a partial picture of human learning. The chapters that follow this one will address in sequence the tumblers (as key dimensions of learning) that make up the learning combination lock; however, we will briefly discuss each of these main categories here in

FIGURE 1.1 A simple diagnostic tool – the learning combination lock

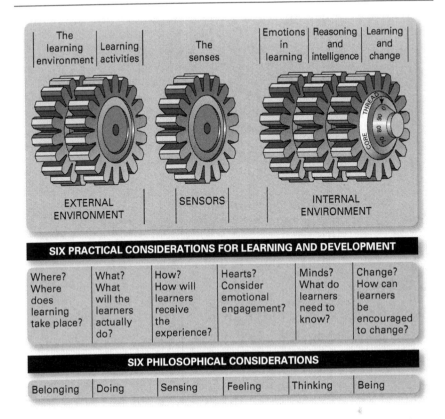

The learning environment	Learning activities	The senses	Emotions in learning	Reasoning and intelligence	Learning and change

EXTERNAL ENVIRONMENT		SENSORS		INTERNAL ENVIRONMENT	

SIX PRACTICAL CONSIDERATIONS FOR LEARNING AND DEVELOPMENT

Where? Where does learning take place?	What? What will the learners actually do?	How? How will learners receive the experience?	Hearts? Consider emotional engagement?	Minds? What do learners need to know?	Change? How can learners be encouraged to change?

SIX PHILOSOPHICAL CONSIDERATIONS

Belonging	Doing	Sensing	Feeling	Thinking	Being

order to provide an overview that will enable you to dip in and out of the book in order to find strategies and answers that apply to the circumstances in which you find yourself.

The learning combination lock in its elementary sense is based on the notion that the person interacts with the external environment through the senses. It is presented as a visual metaphor of six tumblers that represent the complexity of the many possible experiential choices. Beginning on the left of the learning combination lock, the first tumbler involves the question of *where, and with whom?* The environment consists of the people, place and space in which learning takes place, providing the location, external stimuli and ambience for the experience. The next tumbler represents the *what* of the experience; *what is it that people are going to do?* Many possible learning activities present themselves in practice; for example, a journey or a challenge. The next group of tumblers are concerned with the *how*. How is the learning actually received? This tumbler represents the senses through which we receive the various forms of stimuli. The fourth tumbler involves engaging the emotions (*heart*) where we perceive, interpret and emotionally respond to the stimuli from the external environment; in other words we internalize the external learning experience. The fifth tumbler focuses on the scope and form of intelligence (*mind*). The final tumbler concerns change and transformation. Each of these six tumblers should inform practice; choices, and selection of other tumbler options, so as to avoid a random, one-armed bandit approach to selecting the possible components for experiential activities for learning.

As you read through the book, you may well identify new elements to add to the contents of individual tumblers, and perhaps even add completely new categories of tumblers. We strongly encourage you to create your own personalized learning combination lock to answer and respond to your own obstacles and challenges.

The tumblers: representing the core dimensions of learning

Tumbler 1

The learning environment: *where and with whom?*

The learning environment of places and people can strongly influence the experience. Space and place and the spatial ecology involved in the experience of learning are relatively unexplored territory in most other texts on experiential learning. Learning is literally and metaphorically breaking out of the traditional venues. The redesign of learning spaces, and the understanding of the milieu of spaces best suited for different aspects of a learning experience, is contributing to the emergence of a new pedagogy of space. The learning experience is related to and dependent on environmental features. For example, involving the participants in an orienteering or treasure-hunt exercise over windswept moorland in winter will produce a very different atmosphere from one that involves people sitting around a log fire, on a warm beach watching the sun setting. Similarly, learning about boiler-making through a long bullet-point screen presentation in a hotel boardroom layout will be a very different experience from reading about organizational development sitting by a log fire with coffee and croissants by your side. Outdoors, the primal elements of earth, air, fire and water may also be incorporated within the learning activity to help learners explore within themselves, discover new things and create personal enlightenment. Elements, such as darkness and silence, tend to be less commonly used within education, training and development exercises but can prove to be very powerful channels to encourage learning. People construct learning together and this is an important consideration for this first tumbler. Many exciting dimensions of this tumbler in the model are explored in Chapter 4.

Tumbler 2

Learning activities: *what* experiences will people have, what are they going to actually do?

What might people do in order to learn? Doing does not necessarily mean physically active! In the design of deliberate indoor and outdoor learning activities there appears to always be a number of basic ingredients in which the participants are involved. These normally have some aspect of *physical*, *emotional* and *intellectual* involvement that may provide a challenge that engages the whole person: eg designing a website, tall ship sailing, the building of a raft, or the operation of a virtual organization. Sometimes the activity involves a *journey*, which may be geographical, imaginary, chronological or even the life cycle of a company. Most, if not all, activities involve *obstacles* and *problems* that must be overcome by the participants. These may be *real* or *imaginary*, and require those involved to operate within an agreed set of *rules*. New obstacles may be introduced, rules altered and *targets* changed depending upon the *learning aims and objectives*. But these apply more to planned learning experiences, not the emergent opportunistic ones. These basic ingredients and other more emergent learning experiences are discussed and explored in detail in Chapter 5. The degree to which a learning activity is real or perceived as real, and the extent to which this reality is manipulated by educators or facilitators will be a key consideration for the design and delivery of planned experiential learning. The degree of reality is an important theoretical and practical consideration in learner engagement and it is also explored in depth in Chapter 5. Perceptions of reality will apply to many dimensions of the experience, including the learning process, the activities provided and the location in which they take place. So-called 'real' projects or activities might include environmental or community work.

Tumbler 3

The senses: *how* will the experience be received initially through the senses?

Sensory Intelligence (SI) is particularly important in experiential learning. The senses, including bodily senses, are pivotal in the communicating relationship between our inner and outer world experiences. The senses directly communicate with our brains: the senses connect rapidly with what is said to be our primitive 'feeling brain', and more slowly to our 'thinking brain'. The more senses we use in an activity the more memorable the learning experience will become because it increases the neural connections in our brains and therefore will be more accessible. Habituation is a problem for learning: often the skilled application of *sensory variation* in the learning experience increases greatly the levels of engagement and learning. The optimization of sensual learning and the nature of sensory intelligence (SI) and sensory awareness are discussed in Chapter 6.

Tumbler 4

The emotions: *hearts* – how will the emotional self be engaged?

All experiences have an emotional fast response – it cannot be avoided as we shall highlight in this book. In any learning experience emotions can act as the gatekeeper: the emotions are fast-wired to the brain as part of our 'fast, System 1' mode of thinking (see Kahneman, 2011). Positive and negative emotions are pervasive in the roller-coaster events of life, yet so often aspects of society seek to disinfect our lives from the emotional realities. We cannot totally avoid bringing emotional baggage into our everyday experiences, and a range of emotions continually surface as any learning experience progresses. Much theoretical and practical literature now exists that focuses on working with human emotional experiences. Goleman (1996), in his book *Emotional Intelligence*, argues that, although intelligence or IQ is important, it is emotional intelligence (EQ) that is more likely to determine a person's achievements in life. Chapter 7 will investigate the influence of emotions on the learning experience, and explore techniques to work with and surface the *feeling* dimension of the self.

Tumbler 5

Intelligence: *mind* – what do people need to know?

In the section above we mentioned the concept of emotional intelligence, which, to a considerable extent, developed from the work of Howard Gardner. Gardner's (1983) book *Frames of Mind* proposed that there were several forms of intelligence including: linguistic; logical/mathematical/scientific; visual/spatial; musical; bodily/physical/kinaesthetic; interpersonal; and intra-personal. He maintained that there were other forms of intelligence. Significantly, he argued that we should spend less time ranking children and more time helping them to identify and cultivate their natural competencies and life gifts. There are, he argues, hundreds of ways to succeed, and many different abilities that will help people get there (Gardner, 1986). Another form of intelligence is that of spiritual intelligence (SQ). Zohar and Marshall (2001: 9) suggest that Gardner's forms of intelligence are basically composed of IQ, EQ and SQ, and that SQ is 'an internal, innate ability of the human brain and psyche, drawing its deepest resources from the heart of the universe... Spiritual intelligence is the soul's intelligence. It is the intelligence with which we heal ourselves and with which we make ourselves whole.' This tumbler, looking at notions of knowledge, knowing, intelligence and higher forms of learning, including wisdom, will be explored in Chapter 8.

Tumbler 6

Learning and change – developing *change* in
the self, and our being state?

Some of us learn better in the morning, others in the dark hours of the night, and if we are aware of our preferences we tend to use this insight to plan how to organize our learning. In effect, this is personal learning theory and it can be very influential on our behaviour. More general theories of learning have developed over the millennia, and a vast array now exist that would require several volumes in order to give justice to their importance in influencing learning strategies. The three main types are behaviourist, cognitivist and humanist, and these are included in a table in Chapter 9, which identifies and briefly describes the main aspects of key learning theories. One of the main theories that we discuss is Kolb's learning cycle, which led to Honey and Mumford's (1992) learning styles inventory, which focused attention on the manner in which people learn; ie activist, pragmatist, theorist and reflector. There are also numerous other theories about the manner in which people learn. Three of these – retrospective, concurrent and prospective learning – are developed and discussed in Chapter 2. In addition, action learning, developed by Revans, and reflective practice (Argyris and Schön) are brought together in Chapter 9 to illustrate the practical value of taking time out from busy schedules to think and reflect about work patterns and behaviour and thus lead to improvements in performance.

An overview of the chapters

Few books other than novels are designed to be read from cover to cover, and this book is based on the pick-and-mix principle. You will have your own particular requirements and should, therefore, dip in and out to select the areas that have most value to yourself. The book is in three parts: the first part introduces and defines experiential learning and the role of the coach, facilitator and educator. The second part of the book has a chapter for each of the six tumblers in the model; ie chapters devoted to *belonging, doing, sensing, feeling, knowing,* and *being.* The final part of the book considers experiential learning and the future.

Below we provide a brief description of each of the chapters, to help guide you through the book and to support your personal learning and topic investigations.

Chapter 2: Exploring experiential learning

Experiential learning, while superficially a relatively simple concept, becomes more complex as we probe the subject more deeply. Through this investigation the various dimensions of experience are revealed, and one of the most fundamental is that experience can be considered as a synonym for learning. We look at how to create positive learning environments and also how even negative experiences can have a powerful impact on learning. We explore the core definitions of experiential learning and the distinction between formal learning and experiential learning. A number of the basic models of learning are provided to illustrate how experiential learning has evolved, and we also consider experiential learning from the perspectives of the past, present and future. Finally, to provide balance, we critique the notion of experiential learning and Kolb's learning cycle.

Chapter 3: Coaching and facilitation, good practice and ethics

At the start of the chapter we explore what is meant by good practice for people involved in designing and providing experiences for learning and we take a close look at the process of facilitation, training and coaching and some of the responsibilities within the professional domain. Real codes of practice are presented for scrutiny, and we examine the vast range of ethical dilemmas that face experiential providers. In so doing we create a hierarchy of responsibility involving individual, organizational, professional and governmental roles. We offer case studies addressing incompetence, bad behaviour and lack of awareness, and pose ethical questions such as, 'What would you do in this situation?' We explore the ethics of emotional engineering as well as the provision of emotional scenarios. Last, we look at principle ethics and virtue ethics, and offer a step-by-step approach to the resolution of ethical dilemmas. We also guide you to further reading that presents even more case material on ethical dilemmas for discussion.

The next section of the book has chapters covering each of the six dimensions of the Combination Lock Model.

Chapter 4: Learning environments: spaces and places

The belonging dimension

Experiential learning can take place indoors or outdoors, and in natural or artificially created environments. Learning is also about interacting with other people, even reaching out into communities, and this chapter explores people, and the more-than-human world of places and spaces for learning. We examine the empathetic and combative use of space and location for experiential learning and show how the design and use of artificial and natural learning environments can maximize learning. Sheds, tall ships, school classrooms, artificial caves, ski-slopes, climbing walls, concrete whitewater rafting courses and many other places are offered as illustrative case examples. A greater understanding of the rich and varied spatial ecology is emerging: many different spaces are being utilized for the many different functions involved in the experience of learning.

Chapter 5: Experiential learning activities

The doing dimension

Doing what? Doing less or more? This chapter guides you through a range of design ideas for particular forms of planned experiential learning. We recognize that much learning occurs in an unplanned way, and that outcomes are often unanticipated. The chapter explores what it is that people 'do' in order to learn. By systematically analysing many experiential learning activities we have created a basic design typology or checklist. Each of the 17 elements of the typology is covered, and a very extensive range of practical examples and case studies are provided. The chapter examines stories and journeys, planned and unplanned learning, real versus simulated learning, the use of objects to help or to act as obstacles, sequencing and pacing, and the degree of challenge and support. The main theme of this chapter is that there are many new and emerging trends that provide endless possibilities for experiential providers to enhance the delivery of any experience for educational, training or developmental purposes. In this chapter we also consider the way in which the degree of 'reality' can be altered to benefit learning. Learner perceptions of reality can be applied to many aspects of experiential learning, including the learning process itself, the perceived reality of the activities and the perceived reality of the location in which the experience takes place. We show examples where reality can be manipulated as a key consideration in the design and delivery of experiential learning, including the alteration of elements of realness in a negotiating training programme, as well as the altering of reality in play, drama, sculpture, art and fantasy.

Chapter 6: Sensory experience and sensory intelligence

The sensing dimension

Educators, facilitators and coaches acknowledge that the senses are the means through which information or stimuli reach our bodies and brains – they are the conduits which connect the outer world with the inner world experience and the means by which we communicate in its raw sense. This chapter acknowledges that the more senses that are used during experiential learning the stronger the possibility that learning will be deeper. For this reason, the various senses are considered one by one and strategies for enhancing and enriching them are addressed. The chapter also recognizes that the senses can be overwhelmed by data and we provide advice on the benefits of solitude or silence, or by reducing sensory input through, for example, the use of blindfolds.

But it is not as simple as that: the senses can be viewed as basic data, or profoundly important for learning. In compassionate communication (Rosenberg, 2003) and in other complex communication dynamics, learning to develop pure observation skills without emotional judging means developing a strong sensory awareness focus. Excessive feeling and thinking are to some extent suspended. In this chapter we also offer many practical examples where the senses can be used to enhance learning, including activities that awaken the senses, as well as ideas for sensory enhancement and reduction, sensory stepping, solitude, the use of masks, and the applications of sensory work to higher mind states, for working with people with learning difficulties, and for therapeutic work. Sensory data significantly influence the learning experience and there is a need for more research into sensory intelligence for learning.

Chapter 7: Experience and emotions

The feeling dimension

Emotional experiences and emotional intelligence underpin learning, yet many educators and trainers have only recently given more attention to emotional capability. Emotional intelligence is at the core of all success according to Goleman. Emotions are played out in the theatre of the body, and experiential learning will always have an emotional dynamic as part of the experience. This chapter begins with an examination of how emotions and moods underpin experiential learning. The concept of emotional intelligence is examined and set in context with other types of intelligence. The chapter examines the nature of emotional waves, including the troughs, with balance as a central theme: different waves, different sizes and different frequencies all create the essential roller coasters that form the emotional self. Emotions also form the root to our identity, and we examine the role of emotional blocks to learning such as fear and risk taking. The positive and negative aspects of emotional engineering are also considered. In this chapter the learning combination lock shows how the senses form the basic conduit for an external experience to be translated into an internal stimulation. The stimulation of the senses creates a parallel affective response, one that is a powerful determinant of subsequent learning. Helping people to be conscious of this emotional experience can allow people to manage and intensify their own learning. The chapter offers ways to read and work with key emotional signs and to understand the emotional nature of unfulfilled need within conflict. We suggest methods to access the roots of emotion and ways to surface feelings and challenge emotions, and we further explore how humour, metaphors, trilogies and storytelling can be used to access and influence the emotional connection to learning. Helping learners to sense, surface and express both positive and negative feelings rather than to deny or censor them requires great skill and care in group work. It enables the colour and richness of the feelings of learners to be expressed and considered in a controlled way so as to maximize learners' understanding of the learning processes.

Chapter 8: Experience, knowing and intelligence

The knowing dimension

Which is best: thinking slowly or thinking fast, thinking superficially or thinking with depth, thinking too little or thinking too much? How important is the human body in the process of thinking? We address many of these core issues in this chapter. We explore the historical period when computational processing by the brain was the dominant view of human learning, and we consider new developments. Howard Gardner's book *Frames of Mind* drew attention to the validity and importance of multiple intelligences (MI), eg musical, linguistic. This chapter considers the range of intelligences, including the difficult areas of spiritual intelligence, naturalistic intelligence, and creative intelligence. Each of the three intelligences – spiritual, naturalistic and creative – is theoretically discussed and descriptions of skills are listed. As with the rest of the book, there are frequent illustrations of practical examples that link theory and practice, thus applying the essence of experiential learning.

Chapter 9: Experience, learning and change

The being dimension

To select the most appropriate elements from each of the tumblers in the learning combination lock requires that we have an understanding of the basic theories of learning. The final tumbler provides a brief description of the main theories, all of which are linked through the notion of experience. The fundamental message of this book is the importance of linking action with thought or reflection. This is a key element in the work of Kolb (1984) and is equally seen in Revans' (1982) action learning. This chapter demonstrates how action learning can be used within organizations to improve performance for individuals and groups. It also investigates the strategies employed in reflective practice (Schön, 1983), which are increasingly being used to develop the performance of people involved in professional practice. Practical case studies are used to illustrate the value of encouraging effective learning through practice and theory.

The final section of the book contains a single closing chapter.

Chapter 10: Imagining and experiencing the future

It is not only through considering past and present experiences that we can learn. It is also possible to imagine multiple futures and rehearse alternative scenarios in our minds. This gives us the possibility to minimize the potential for failure and increase the chance of success. Thinking about future possibilities tends to develop the neural connections in the brain and further increase the likelihood of success. Furthermore, we look at how the conscious part of our brains can interfere with the subconscious to undermine our performance, and use the game of tennis as an example.

> To find that point, that reason for our doing and our being, it helps to build on three senses – a sense of continuity, a sense of connection and a sense of direction. Without these senses we can feel disoriented, adrift and rudderless... We shall need all the help we can find to recognise our place and role in it. These senses are the best antidote I know to the feelings of impotence which rapid change induces in us all.

(Handy, 1994: 239)

Conclusion

This handbook, in linking theory and practice, offers practical tools that address the main factors to consider when developing and delivering learning experiences, whether it be for yourself, for employees, youth groups, schoolchildren, or indeed for anyone who wishes to learn in a way that engages the self as a whole person. Experiences for learning can of course occur anywhere: outdoors, within classrooms, training rooms, hotels or residential centres. Also, much learning will occur in ways that were not planned.

As we develop many core principles throughout the book for each of the dimensions of learning (tumblers), it becomes clear that the number of permutations for designing or creating learning experiences is almost limitless. While we present you with some of the main concepts, we also strongly encourage you to add to the learning combination lock model, or to develop your own personal learning models as experience develops through practice. We wish you every success with this process and we hope this book is a small contribution towards helping you to find new connections, and a new direction for experiential learning.

Exploring experiential learning

> *The only source of knowledge is experience.* ALBERT EINSTEIN

Introduction

Learning from experience is one of the most fundamental and natural means of learning available to everyone. It need not be expensive, nor does it require vast amounts of technological hardware and software to support the learning process. Instead, in the majority of cases, all it requires is the opportunity to reflect and think, either alone or in the company of other people. This natural form of learning has become increasingly popular whether it operates at the individual, group, organizational or societal levels and for this reason it deserves close examination.

All too often theories of learning, education, training and development are produced in isolation from one another and thus there is no overall coherence. The great strength of experiential learning is that it provides an underpinning philosophy that acts as a thread joining many of the learning theories together in a more unified whole. Yet, this philosophy, while appearing relatively straightforward, is in actual fact rather complex and forces us to consider the nature of who we are and what we mean by experience.

In this chapter we will investigate experience in more detail and we encourage you to relate what you read to your own personal experiences so that your learning becomes deeper and more applicable. The more we understand what experiential learning is the more it can be harnessed to enhance learning opportunities and so a considerable focus will be on exploring what is meant by experiential learning and providing a definition. It will also examine why learning from experience does not always happen and some of its limitations.

Experiential learning's expanding horizons

The impact of David Kolb's (1984) book *Experiential Learning: Experience as the source of learning and development* has been quite extraordinary and far-reaching. An Experiential Learning Theory bibliography assembled by Kolb *et al* (2001) contained 1,004 entries across a range of disciplines: management (207); education (430); information science (104); psychology (101); medicine (72); nursing (63); accounting (22); and law (5). The bibliography was subsequently updated (Kolb and Kolb, 2008a, 2008b) and the original figure had expanded to 2,453 entries (Kolb and Kolb, 2009).

It is evident that the application of experiential learning is growing and is being applied in a breadth of subjects and locations including education and other occupational sectors. This widespread use illustrates the value and benefits that are perceived to accrue from its use and in some professional areas, such as medicine, it is the foundation of the learning philosophy, as Dunn and Chaput de Saintonge (1997: 25) state:

> Medical education in the UK differs from that in many other European countries in its emphasis on clinical experience as a means of learning... Experiential learning is therefore at the centre of the education of the pre-registration house officer.

Experiential learning is also commonly utilized in work-related learning, which, according to Smith and Betts (2000: 591), can be divided into three main forms which are interrelated:

- Learning *about* work which is *informational*;
- Learning *at* work which is *locational*;
- Learning *through* work that is *experiential*.

The experience society

And, it is not just at the individual and occupational levels that experience has become important. The concept of the experience society was largely introduced by Schultz (1992) in *Die Erlebnisgesellschaft*, and Pine and Gilmore's (2011) *The Experience Economy*.

Pine and Gilmore (2011) contend that societies have progressed through a number of stages, ie agricultural, industrial, service, knowledge, and are now predominantly experience economies. They also argue that although the other economic factors are still present the experience economy is the main active force.

Although they briefly mention the importance of experience in educational settings, the arguments presented by Pine and Gilmore are predominantly economic ones. They emphasize the financial benefits and state:

> Relying on the manufacturing of goods and the delivery of services remains the mindset of too many executives (and politicians), prohibiting the shift to more vibrant enterprise offering experiences (and thus more robust national economies). So let us be clear: goods and services are no longer enough to foster economic growth, create new jobs, and maintain economic prosperity. To realise revenue growth and increased employment, the staging of experiences must be pursued as a distinct form of economic output. Indeed, in a world saturated

with largely undifferentiated goods and services the greatest opportunity for value creation resides in staging experiences.

(Pine and Gilmore, 2011: ix)

The importance of experience

A few years ago I was driving across the high-level Pennine hills on the M62, the UK's main west-east highway, when there was a sudden torrential downpour. The rain was so heavy that it was very difficult to see through the windscreen and so I slowed down by gently applying the brakes. As I put my foot on the brake pedal I noticed that I slid sideways a little and then realized that I had been aquaplaning. In effect, my tyres were not in proper contact with the road but had a layer of water underneath them, thus reducing the tyre's grip with the road's surface and increasing the danger due to an increased risk of skidding uncontrollably. Gently, I pulled over to the slow lane together with many other careful and cautious drivers.

Yet, as I cautiously drove along the motorway in the dreadful conditions I noticed that there were still motorists who were racing along in the fast lane seemingly oblivious to the danger they were in. Later, on arriving at my destination, I described their suicidal tendencies to a colleague and commented that I couldn't understand this behaviour that brought danger to other road users and not just themselves. The colleague responded, 'You knew what the true road conditions were like, the drivers who were racing along in the fast lane probably had no experience of the dangers they were playing with.'

Although having experience can be valuable, it also can be a two-edged sword. People who have experience are often older and may take more things into consideration, thus making them more cautious and therefore, possibly, more accepting of the status quo. Younger people are often more active in seeking change hence the predominance of young people during the Arab Spring. Similarly, Wang Dan, one of the student leaders during the Tiananmen Square demonstrations in Beijing in 1989, was jailed for his involvement and later jailed again for criticizing the government until he was given 'medical parole' and studied in exile at Harvard and Oxford. He commented,

> We hoped we could have freedom – not necessarily the right to vote, but a free life. That was our understanding… It was the first time when the government told people not to go on the streets and they went anyway. We were making history. [Yet] I don't think we were brave. We didn't have the experience to feel fear.

(Hilton, 2009)

Experience and finance

> Experience keeps a dear school, but fools will learn in no other.

(Benjamin Franklin)

The value of experience in society would also seem very applicable to the financial sector, where hard lessons tend to be learned again and again by each succeeding generation. The great financial crisis has been preceded by numerous crises over the centuries yet people often need to learn directly for themselves before it has an impact on behaviour. Of course, people do not need personal experience of an event they can learn in other ways – for example, from observing the experiences of others through social learning (Bandura, 1977) or reading books etc – however, the impact of these forms of indirect 'secondary' learning is much less intense and therefore less likely to influence behaviour. This would appear to be the case with the highly educated whizz-kids in the financial sector. Greenwood and Nagel (2008) investigated the behaviour of experienced and inexperienced fund managers during the technology dot-com bubble of the late 1990s and discovered differences in behaviour between the older and younger employees.

The duration from the beginnings of a bubble to its crash can take years and this process might not happen again for decades. The consequence of this was that younger traders who had never experienced a financial bubble had nothing to compare it with and thus over-invested in technology stock. Older investors tended to take a longer view and be more cautious. Greenwood and Nagel (2008: 4) observed:

> Our results fit well with models of adaptive learning. According to our interpretation, the trend-chasing behaviour of young managers reflects their attempts to learn and extrapolate from the little data they have experienced in their careers. Such extrapolation may be excessive if young managers don't properly adjust for the small sample of data at hand (eg as in Rabin, 2002), or use simple models to forecast returns (eg as in Hong *et al* 2007). More broadly, our results are consistent with evidence that people learn how to solve decision problems primarily through learning-by-doing.

Experience and education

When John Dewey wrote his book *Experience and Education* he could hardly have imagined the possibilities that are now available in the digital world. A number of the US Ivy League universities including Berkeley, Harvard, MIT and Princeton have trialled open-access online courses attracting tens of thousands of students. These massive open online courses (moocs) have been highly popular and organizations such as Coursera (2012) proclaim their view of the future:

> We are a social entrepreneurship company that partners with the top universities in the world to offer courses online for anyone to take, for free. We envision a future where the top universities are educating not only thousands of students, but millions. Our technology enables the best professors to teach tens or hundreds of thousands of students.

Coursera also challenge the view that online learning isn't as effective as face-to-face instruction and cite a US Department of Education meta-analysis of online learning by Means *et al* (2010), which concluded that online instruction is as effective as traditional forms. The threat to existing traditional institutions will be to prove that the courses they offer are value for money compared to the cut-rate online ones. Darmer and Sundbo (2008: 3) state:

> Experiences have a high value for consumers and the demand for experiences is increasing. Consumers are therefore willing to pay a high price for experiences and experience production becomes very profitable.

Thus universities, colleges, schools, training providers, etc will have to demonstrate that the experiences they offer outweigh the cheaper virtual offerings elsewhere. The argument about educational experience will become increasingly important as more and more educational programmes become available online.

Of course there may be some people who prefer to keep economics and learning far apart, but the financial argument cannot be ignored. Pine and Gilmore (2011: xiii) explained that: 'More goods and services get sold because of experiential marketing.' Indeed, education, training and development programmes are forms of service and frequently differentiate themselves based on the types of experience that they offer. The more involving an experience the more memorable it will become and Pine and Gilmore (2011: xxi) stated:

> In envisioning engaging experiences, you can and should consider a multiplicity of dimensions. These include, but are not limited to, the multisensory nature of experiences, their level of personal meaningfulness, the way the experience is shared with others (if at all), the intensity and duration of various experiential elements, complexity (or simplicity), and untold other characteristics of how people spend time. Cultural considerations and national and local sensitivities, as well as the prior life experiences of guests all impact how people perceive experiences. Our belief is that no matter how it's viewed, any dimension of enjoyment usually translates into the experience being more memorable – even if few or no details can be recollected.

Learning and experiential learning are 'slippery' concepts

Learning plays such an important role in our societies that it might easily be assumed that we know exactly what it involves and how it might be best applied. Yet, even though we spend many years of our lives in compulsory education and continue to learn new things every day, close scrutiny of learning reveals numerous dimensions and a distinct lack of agreement among writers on the subject.

Six main perspectives on learning were identified by Wilson (2012a): behaviourism, cognitivism, constructivism, social learning, humanism and cognitive neuroscience. The consequence of these multiple perspectives is that there is no complete agreement among the numerous definitions of learning, with some writers placing emphasis on behavioural change, others cognition, and others experience. Drawing from a number of definitions Wilson (2012a: 47) provided the following definition:

> Learning is a relatively permanent change of knowledge, attitude or behaviour occurring as a result of formal education, training or development, or as a result of informal experiences.

Defining experiential learning also presents numerous challenges, many of which are similar to those described above for learning. When a word or concept is examined in order to write a definition, it soon becomes apparent how elusive its meaning is, and the closer we look, the more indistinct and vague it can become. The word 'experience' is no different in this respect; however, reaching for a dictionary can provide some assistance, and the *Oxford Dictionary* describes experience as:

> The fact of being consciously the subject of a state or condition; of being consciously affected by an event; a state or condition viewed subjectively; an event by which one is affected; and, knowledge resulting from actual observation or from what one has undergone.

Yet, in which ways do we experience something? Plato, for instance, discussed the difficulty of accurately explaining what was meant by the word 'bed', and Dewey (1925: 4–5) explored the different ways we experience a chair:

> When I look at a chair, I say I experience it. But what I actually experience is only a very few of the elements that go to make up the chair, namely, that colour that belongs to the chair under these particular conditions of light, the shape which the chair displays when viewed from this angle, etc. The man who has the experience, as distinct from a philosopher theorizing about it would probably say that he experienced the chair most fully not when looking at it but when meaning to sit down in it precisely because his experience is not limited to colour under specific conditions of light, and angular shape.

These perspectives provide a starting point, yet Dewey (1925: 1), who also gave us a well-known library classification system, stated that: 'experience is a weasel word. Its slipperiness is evident in an inconsistency characteristic of many thinkers.' An indication of this 'slipperiness' can be illustrated by looking at our own experiences. Take an incident that jointly happened to you and another person, eg a road accident or perhaps a memorable event, and describe to the other person what happened in detail. Next, get the person to describe the event as he or she saw it. Although many things will be very similar, there will be parts that either of you or perhaps both do not remember at all, and there may be interpretations of the events that you both see differently. You would both agree that although the event was experienced by both of you, its impact was in many respects different. Indeed, your understanding of the event will probably be influenced and co-constructed by dialogue with the other person (Baker *et al*, 2002).

From the road accident example above, it is evident that no two people experience the same event exactly the same way. More startlingly, and perhaps disturbingly, this casts doubt not only on the accuracy of our memory but also on what we mean when we say we experience something. If the accident happened to someone else without our involvement, ie had an existence beyond ours, then we can only assume that the various interpretations we can put on the accident are mental constructions and only interpretations of the event. This line of reasoning is called social constructivism and this helps us to appreciate the complexity of experience.

Each time we revisit a memory there is the possibility of interpreting it differently from the previous time. This is because during the intervening period we have new experiences and our brains alter their shape through neuroplasticity. Memories of experiences are not fixed but are dynamic (Baddeley *et al*, 2009) and, therefore, these new cognitive structures may influence the way in which we view the experience on revisiting it. In other words, as Heraclitus said: 'You cannot step in the same river twice.' This difficulty in accurately and precisely pinning down the meaning of experience is discussed by Boud *et al* (1993: 7) who commented:

> For the sake of simplicity in discussing learning from experience, experience is sometimes referred to as if it were singular and unlimited by time or place. Much experience, however, is multifaceted, multi-layered and so inextricably connected with other experiences that it is impossible to locate temporally or spatially. It almost defies analysis as the act of analysis inevitably alters the experience and the learning that flows from it.

Experience and learning

Experience and learning would appear to be closely intertwined and almost inseparable. Indeed, Kolb (1984: 38) explained that: 'Learning is the process whereby knowledge is created through the transformation of experience.' Similarly, Boud *et al* (1993: 8), stated:

> We found it to be meaningless to talk about learning in isolation from experience. Experience cannot be bypassed; it is the central consideration of all learning. Learning builds on and flows from experience: no matter what external prompts to learning there might be – teachers, materials, interesting opportunities – learning can only occur if the experience of the learner is engaged, at least at some level. These external influences can act only by transforming the experience of the learner.

It would also appear that experience can be applied to each of the dimensions of learning, ie behaviourism, cognitivism, constructivism, social learning, humanism and cognitive neuroscience; and Fenwick (2000: 244) stated:

> Experiential learning means a process of human cognition. The root of the word cognition in fact means 'to learn' and thus the two terms are used

interchangeably following standard usage within each perspective. I do not believe that the dimension of experience, broadly understood, is defensible as a classificatory signifier in cognition: What manner of learning can be conceived that is not experiential, whether the context be clearly educational or not?

Other writers express similar views, for example, Rogers (1996: 107) stated that: 'There is a growing consensus that experience forms the basis of all learning.' And, Moon (2004: 119) maintained: 'As indicated several times... all learning is based on experience.'

Yet, it is not entirely evident that all learning is experiential since it would appear that we possess some pre-wired responses. A brief consideration of infant and child development illustrates that when a baby is born they have the natural ability to strongly grip, and even hang from, the fingers of the midwife or parent. The infant also possesses the sucking reflex and will make stepping movements if their feet touch the floor even though they are unable to support their own weight (Siegler *et al*, 2006).

It would appear that many of our inner biological functions are already hard-wired while other dimensions develop and grow as a result of our experiences, eg the growth of the hippocampus among taxi-drivers (Maguire *et al*, 2000). In summary, we are saying that the foundation of much learning is the interaction between self and the external environment, in other words the experience. Whatever the exact relation between experience and learning there is little doubt that experience probably provides the most coherent theory of learning.

Defining experiential learning

The preceding discussion has demonstrated some of the dimensions of complexity associated with experience and learning, and Malinen (2000: 15) in attempting to identify the essence of experiential learning concluded that:

> Adult experiential learning is a complex, vague and ambiguous phenomenon, which is still inadequately defined, conceptually suspect – and even poorly researched... on the other hand, its theoretical and philosophical foundations are fragmented and confusing.... There are too many interpretations and priorities among the theorists and practitioners that no single, clear definition of these foundations could be constructed.

In spite of these shortcomings Warner Weil and McGill (1989: 27) approached the issue from the opposite perspective and stated:

> Both the experiential theorist and educational practitioner seem to agree on what experiential learning is not. It is definitely not the mere memorizing of abstract theoretical knowledge, especially if taught by traditional formal methods of instruction such as lecturing and reading from books.

These difficulties should not stop us from attempting to construct a definition since, without one, there can be little understanding about what is being discussed. Perhaps a consideration of some definitions might provide more clarity:

> Experiential learning... is synonymous with 'meaningful-discovery' learning... which involves the learner in sorting things out for himself by restructuring his perceptions of what is happening.
>
> (Boydell, 1976: 19, 20)

> The contrast between non-experiential and experiential learning is one between more and less abstract and more and less linguistic sets of symbols that are employed in the transactions in which learning takes place.
>
> (Tumin, 1976: 41)

> Experiential learning means that learning that occurs when changes in judgement, feelings or skills result for a particular person from living through an event or events.
>
> (Chickering, 1977: 63)

> [Experiential learning is] the process whereby knowledge is created through the transformation of experience. Knowledge results from the combination of grasping and transforming experience.
>
> (Kolb, 1984: 41)

> Experiential learning is learning that is rooted in our doing and our experience. It is learning which illuminates that experience and provides direction for the making of judgements as a guide to choice and action.
>
> (Hutton, 1989: 51)

> Experiential learning is a process in which an experience is reflected upon and then translated into concepts which in turn become guidelines for new experiences.
>
> (Saddington, 1992: 44)

> Experiential education refers to learning activities that engage the learner directly in the phenomena being studied.
>
> (Cantor, 1997: 1)

> [Experiential learning is] learning that begins with experience and transforms it into knowledge, skill, attitude, emotions, values, beliefs, senses.
>
> (Jarvis, 1999: 65)

> Adult experiential learning, broadly speaking [is] a process of re-construction performed by an individual learner.
>
> (Malinen, 2000: 85)

> The insight gained through the conscious or unconscious internalization of our own or observed experiences which build upon our past experiences or knowledge.
>
> (Beard and Wilson, 2002: 16)

The definition by Beard and Wilson (2002) was revised for the second edition of this book (Beard and Wilson, 2006) because we believe that we can also learn from the future not just the past or immediate present (see Chapter 10). We feel that this second definition still has broad applicability:

> Experiential learning is the sense-making process of active engagement between the inner world of the person and the outer world of the environment.

A more detailed interpretation of this definition is offered at the start of this book:

> a sense making process involving significant experiences that, to varying degrees, act as the source of learning. These experiences actively immerse and reflectively engage the inner world of the learner, as a whole person (including physical-bodily, intellectually, emotionally and spiritually) with their intricate 'outer world' of the learning environment (including belonging and doing – in places, spaces, within social, cultural, political context etc) to create memorable, rich and effective experiences for and of learning.

(Beard, 2010: 17)

These musings about the nature of experience are not merely an academic exercise with no real application in the learning environment. It is only by considering what we mean by experience that as trainers, educators and developers of human potential we can gain insight into one of the most powerful means to learning that currently exists. Why we are attempting to get closer to the term 'experience' and by relating our experiences to these discussions is to create a more coherent understanding where theory and practice relate to each other. And, although we might never reach the absolute truth about a person, an experience or a chair, we can at least try to understand and achieve a degree of enlightenment.

Experience: a bridging concept

The concept of experience is the bridge that connects the person and the object involved in an interaction, and this can be observed in some of the definitions above where there is reflection on the process involving a person and their external environment. Indeed, Cuffaro (1995: 62) emphasized: 'Action and thought are not two discrete aspects of experience. It is not to undertake an activity and then at its end to contemplate the results. What is stressed is that the two must not be separated, for each informs the other.'

Dewey is, arguably, the foremost exponent of the use of experience for learning, and the word occurs in a number of titles of his books, including *Experience and Nature* (1925), *Art as Experience* (1934) and *Experience and Education* (1938). Cuffaro (1995) explained that Dewey used experience as a lens through which he could analyse the interactions of people and their environments and it becomes clear that experiencing something is a linking process between action and thought (Figure 2.2). Dewey (1916: 144–45) argued:

FIGURE 2.1 The relationship between theory and practice

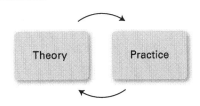

FIGURE 2.2 Experience: a unifying concept

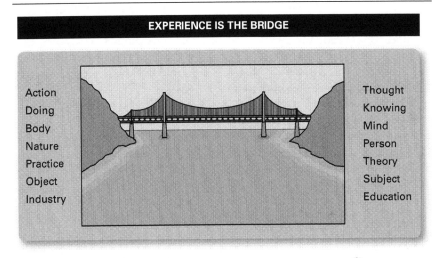

> Thinking, in other words, is the intentional endeavour to discover specific connections between something which we do and the consequences which result, so that the two become continuous. Their isolation, and consequently their purely arbitrary going together, is cancelled; a unified, developing situation takes place.

Figure 2.1 represents the relation between theory and practice. Our theories are abstract conceptualizations of how thoughts and external objects relate to one another in a consistent manner. They inform and guide us in our practice, and enable us to gain insights into the various events in which we are involved. If our practical experience does not match our theory of how we think things should be, then we often revise our theories or sometimes revisit the experience in order to see if it can be fitted into our weltanschauung – our way of seeing the world. Thus there is a continual interaction of theory and practice in which each informs the other.

In this way Dewey was able to connect opposites or dualities, eg person and nature, subject and object, knowing and doing, mind and body, etc.

These polarities become connected and the concept of experience creates an organic whole of continuity, process and situation.

Do we always learn from experience?

Nothing ever becomes real 'til it is experienced.

(John Keats)

The short answer to the question above is, 'No!' There are numerous circumstances in which experiences do not result in learning; for example, experience has little impact unless a child has reached a certain stage of development. Piaget (1950) observed the development of children and identified four main stages of cognitive development: sensori-motor (0–2 years), pre-operational thought (2–7 years), concrete operations (7–11 years) and formal operations (11–15 years). He argued that if a child has not reached the developmental capability then no amount of experience will induce them to respond in the desired manner.

When we undergo an experience, this does not always lead to new insights and new learning. For example, if the experience only serves to confirm some already-held beliefs it will be interpreted as supporting the existing cognitive status quo and little attention will be paid to it. If we do not pay attention to it the opportunity for new learning will not happen. Dewey (1933: 78) maintained that: 'We do not learn from experience. We learn from reflecting on experience.' Moreover, regarding the use of portfolios, the Royal College of General Practitioners (1993: 4) stated: 'The collection of experiential evidence by the individual learner is relevant as a potential source of learning, but the critical intellectual task is that of moving from a description of an experience to the identification of the learning derived from experience.' In effect, as Michelson (1996: 444) commented: 'Reflection allows a kind of scientific management over the messiness and unreliability of experience because it allows reason to take control.'

We have to engage with the experience and reflect on what happened, how it happened and why. Without this, the experience will tend to merge with the background of all the stimulants that assail our senses every day. There are stimulants around us all the time but our awareness of them and our sensitivity to them is dependent on how 'loud' they are, our degree of interest in them, what other stimulants are also competing for our attention, etc. Moreover, it is very easy to become habituated to something, eg a continuous noise, and eventually become unaware of its existence.

With the almost infinite number of stimulants around and within us, there is the possibility that we could become overwhelmed with the avalanche of information. Our brain, like a computer, might shut down as a result of overloading. Take just a minute to look out of the window and see the variety of objects and interactions happening between people. You can interpret each item you see at different levels of involvement in order to understand it. Through the use of a mental magnifying glass we are able to bring into focus varying levels of detail. However, to look at everything at this level of intensity would be overpowering and our brains would not be able to cope; in other words, there would be paralysis through analysis.

In order to prevent this overloading, the brain filters these stimulants to allow only those elements that are perceived to be of relevance to be mentally processed either consciously or unconsciously. Thus, we selectively choose what we believe to be of importance and, consciously or unconsciously, ignore other elements. It is these cognitive filters, which are part of our mindset and disposition, which can create mental blind spots. For this reason we may not be able to see things even when they are right in front of our eyes.

Despite cognitive blind spots our brains are always scanning the environment in what might be called the 'cocktail party phenomenon' (Bronkhorst, 2000). For example, at a party we might be talking to a person and concentrating on what is being said, oblivious to everything happening around us. However, this focus may only be happening at a very conscious level; subconsciously, we would appear to be taking in other things that are happening. For instance, despite high levels of noise we may suddenly pick out from the cacophony the sound of our name being spoken and then immediately tune into that frequency to hear what people are saying about us! Thus, perception and interaction are insufficient in themselves, we must interact in a meaningful way with external stimulants if we are to learn.

At a broader level Senge (1993: 23) described what he called the 'delusion of learning from experience'. He acknowledged the importance of learning from direct experience but then went on argue that this was limited because of the extended timescales which may elapse before the impact of behaviour can be observed:

> But what happens when we can no longer observe the consequences of our actions? What happens if the primary consequences of our actions are in the distant future or in a distant part of the larger system within which we operate? We each have a 'learning horizon,' a breadth of vision in time and space within which we assess our effectiveness. When our actions have consequences beyond our learning horizon, it becomes impossible to learn from direct experience.

> Herein lies the core *learning dilemma* that confronts organizations: *we learn best from experience but we never directly experience the consequences of many of our most important decisions.* The most critical decisions made in organisations have systemwide consequences that stretch over years and decades.

Learning is personal

> I do not think, sir, you have any right to command me, merely because you are older than I, or because you have seen more of the world than I have; your claim to superiority depends on the use you have made of your time and experience.

> (Charlotte Brontë, *Jane Eyre*)

We all have our own theoretical frameworks with which we interpret and cast illumination on our interaction with the world. Our own genetic make-up, experiences and disposition play a significant role in making each experience we undergo unique to ourselves. No one else sees the event in exactly the same way as we do ourselves; no one possesses the same experiences that influence our interaction with the event; and no one else perceives and processes the information in quite the same way.

All learning experiences are personal and unique to us. Boud *et al* (1993: 10) explained, 'Each experience is influenced by the unique past of the learner.' They maintained that a person is aware of some elements of the world and is oblivious to others. Furthermore, much of this process occurs without us being remotely conscious of what we choose to pay attention to and what we do not.

Perception is learning

When we perceive a stimulus, either external to us or even within ourselves, this can be regarded as a form of learning from experience. Figure 2.3 represents the complex process of perception and how we interpret and respond to an external or internal stimulus. It is based upon Gibson *et al*'s (1985) perception process model and the information/cognitive processing models of Massaro and Cowan (1993). Working from the left-hand side of the model there are five main elements:

1 stimuli;
2 our senses;
3 the filtering process;
4 interpretation; and
5 responses.

First, through our senses we register the stimulus at a conscious and/or subconscious level. At a conscious level we may see or hear something; alternatively, at a subconscious level our senses are continuously scanning the environment but we may not be consciously aware of external stimuli – for example, the cocktail party phenomenon. We are also consciously and subconsciously aware of internal stimuli such as feelings of hunger, cold, a migraine, a cut on our hand, etc and take steps, where possible, to resolve the discomfort.

Once we have become aware of this stimulus at a conscious and/or unconscious level it is 'filtered' and interpreted. This is dependent on a variety of factors, including previous knowledge, previous experience, emotions, our concept of self, choice, the 'loudness' of the stimulus, location and personal needs.

The next stage then involves us making sense of the stimulus to assess whether it matches our existing mental constructs. If the experience happens as was generally predicted there is no change to our mental schema

FIGURE 2.3 The process of perception and experiential learning

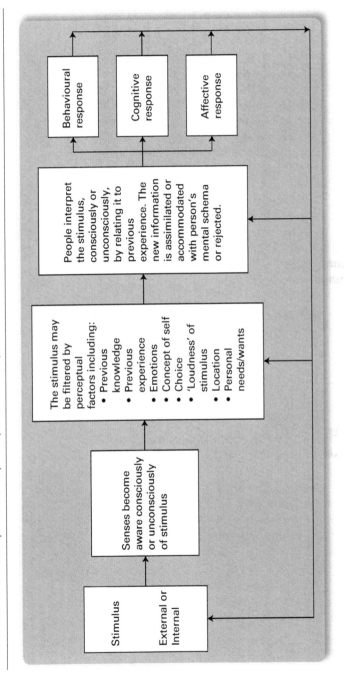

and we assimilate it. If the experience was different from our expectations we may choose to modify our mental frameworks and accommodate the new information and experience. Alternatively, if the experience is so alien to our expectations and ways of seeing the world, we may reject it as being atypical, biased or incorrect (Piaget, 1950).

The final three stages involve cognitive, affective and behavioural responses to the stimulus (Bloom *et al*, 1956). For example, we may think about how we respond to what our boss or partner might say (cognitive). We may decide that we like or don't like the pressure we are being put under at work or perhaps within the outdoor training exercise (affective). And last, we may physically respond by stepping back on to the pavement when we notice the truck speeding towards us (behavioural).

All the time these analyses and responses are being recycled to evaluate the stimulus further. This process can happen very quickly and when we are in immediate danger, for instance from being hit by the truck, the process may be short-circuited and we instinctively leap out of the way.

It is essential, however, to recognize that although two people may receive the same stimulus they do not necessarily respond in the same way. If we find ourselves on the edge of a cliff we may be terrified or exhilarated depending on past experience and attitudes. Similarly, if faced by a bully at work we may choose to avoid the situation, aggressively challenge the bully or act assertively. Kuhn (1970) explained that two people may look at the same object and receive the same stimuli but the sensations may be very different owing to differences caused by education, experience, etc. Indeed, people who come from different societies sometimes respond in quite different ways to the same stimulus. Kuhn (1970: 198) maintained: 'In the metaphorical no less than in the literal use of "seeing", interpretation begins where perception ends. The two processes are not the same, and what perception leaves for interpretation to complete depends drastically on the nature and amount of prior experience and training.'

At a very immediate level we may perceive, in other words learn, while carrying a full mug of coffee. Our senses are continually giving us feedback about how close to the brim of the mug the swirling coffee is and thus adjust how quickly we walk, how we control the muscles in our arm and what attention we pay to other people walking nearby. Furthermore, our awareness that the colour of the mug is white represents a very temporary learning experience. We possess an understanding of what 'white' means and we thus respond to the visual stimulus of the mug. This level of learning is very fleeting but it is a response to stimuli.

Bateson (2000: 293) developed a model of five levels of learning that represent how we develop learned behaviours in response to stimuli:

Level 0   Learning occurs as a response to stimuli and is 'not subject to correction'.

Level 1   Learning involves 'change of specificity of response' by correction of errors of choice within a set of alternatives.

Level 2   Is a 'change in the process of Learning 1', eg a change in the set of alternatives. This learning is deutero learning (double loop learning) or learning how to learn.

Level 3   Is a change in the process of Learning 2, eg a corrective change in the system of alternatives from which choice is made.

Level 4   Involves change in Learning 3, which is probably unlikely in any human being.

The interrelationship between an experience and previous experiences and perceptions is summed up in the following quotation from Boud *et al* (1993: 8):

> Learning always relates, in one way or another, to what has gone before. There is never a clean slate on which to begin; unless new ideas and new experience link to previous experience, they exist as abstractions, isolated and without meaning. The effects of experience influence all learning. What we are attracted towards, what we avoid and how we go about the task, is dependent on how we have responded in the past. Earlier experiences that had positive or negative effect stimulate or suppress new learning. They encourage us to take risks and enter into new territory for exploration, or alternatively, they may inhibit our range of operation or ability to respond to opportunities.

Cognition, memory and learning

The deeper one delves into the area of learning the more complex the issue becomes. As we saw in the previous section, perception may be regarded as a form of learning. And, if we continue down this line of reasoning, it can be argued that when an amoeba responds to an external stimulus it is learning in a similar way to a houseplant that tends to turn towards the light from a window. To what extent our learning as humans is the same or different to that of the amoeba is partly addressed by Bateson above; but, we will leave you to answer it further since it is beyond the scope of this book.

It would be remiss not to draw attention briefly to the areas of cognition and memory. Crowder (1976) connected both learning and memory together. Similarly, both cognition and memory may be regarded as forms of learning, and Newell (1990) attempted to unify numerous theories of cognition and described the similarities of memory, learning, cognition and perception. He discussed various forms of memory: short-term, long-term, episodic, procedural, declarative and semantic, and questioned whether they were similar or separate functions of the brain.

What research in these areas of cognition illustrates is that the distance between philosophy, sociology, education, psychology, cognitive neuroscience, etc is much closer than they would first appear. Whether a grand unified theory will emerge is yet to be seen, but for the time being and the purposes of this book we will continue to view the world through the lens of experiential learning that integrates theory and practice.

Painful learning

> Experience is the name everyone gives to their mistakes.
>
> (Oscar Wilde, *Lady Windermere's Fan*)

Learning from experience has its challenges since not all the circumstances we face in life can be said to be enjoyable. Although many learning opportunities can be satisfying, not all learning experiences would be chosen by the individual as a route to learning. Life is often unpredictable and as a result presents many opportunities for learning – as long as our minds are open to their potential.

It is the case that many painful experiences remain with us for the rest of our lives and become reference points that we take into account before acting again in a similar manner. Indeed, these painful experiences may act as blocks to learning through preventing us from acting in a particular way. This attitude can be a valuable survival mechanism but it can also lead to our own extinction through inhibiting our behaviour.

Snell (1992) investigated experiential learning at work and asked: 'Why can't it be painless?' He concluded that hard knocks and psychological blows are inevitable in the work situation and that these shocks provide the opportunity for moral lessons and character building. Snell (1992: 15) categorized these challenges, which are detailed in Table 2.1.

Snell emphasized that for people to learn from hard knocks they had to see them as a learning opportunity. He also drew attention to the fact that if people continued to experience a series of hard knocks then they were likely to be numbed and overloaded by their effects. In cases such as this, a person may withdraw physically and/or emotionally from whatever is causing the challenges and thus limit the potential for learning. It is therefore important to identify optimal learning experiences and Palethorpe and Wilson (2011: 423) stated: 'The management of anxiety is a central concern for learning providers who, if the correct balance is not struck, risk leaving delegates bored and unmotivated or paralysed with fear and anxiety.

Detrimental experiential learning

So far our discussion has been to illustrate how valuable and integral experiences are to learning. On the other hand, experience also has disadvantages when it comes to influencing our attitudes to learning. First of all, think of one of your favourite teachers or trainers and how he or she encouraged you to learn in a positive and supportive environment. Next, think about your least favourite teacher or trainer and the negative effect he or she had on your learning. Tim Martin, the founder of the extensive chain of public houses, J D Wetherspoon, named his pubs after one of his teachers who said that Martin would never be successful as a businessman. We will never know to what extent this negative comment spurred Martin on to achieve his objectives.

TABLE 2.1   Learning from distress

Source of distress	Suggested method of coping	Means of learning
(In general this is a psychological blow, shock or jolt.)	(In general this is to resist responding impulsively, and to find breathing space or seek counselling, if possible.)	(In general this is drawing lessons.)
A big mistake	Discharge anger or hurt in a private place.	Admit the mistake and look for causes.
Being overloaded/ feeling incompetent	Reduce the load and avoid dwelling on one's inadequacy.	Focus on specific improvement.
Being pressurized to violate one's principles	Come to terms with there being no easy resolution.	Identify what one *really* wants and values.
Impasse	Discharge frustration in a private place.	Listen to the arguments from opponents.
Injustice	Avoid self-blame and resist taking impulsive revenge.	Identify the values offended and adopt them.
Losing out	Discharge one's disappointment in a private place.	Admit that the defeat was fair and study the victor's approach.
Being attacked	Respond assertively.	Study the mentality of one's opponents.

Dewey (1938: 25) recognized that experience can also have a detrimental effect on learning and remarked:

> The belief that all genuine education comes about through experience does not mean that all experiences are genuinely or equally educative.... Any experience is miseducation that has the effect of arresting or distorting the growth of further experience.

As trainers and educators, we often come across people saying that something cannot be done. On further enquiry, it is sometimes the case that the person has had a negative experience and does not wish to repeat it. A variety of factors may have a negative effect on learning, and a number have been identified by Boud and Walker (1993: 79):

- Presuppositions about what is and is not possible for us to do.
- Not being in touch with one's own assumptions and what one is able to do.
- Past negative experiences.
- Expectations of others: society, peer group, figures of authority, family.
- Threats to the self, one's own world view, or to ways of behaving.
- Lack of self-awareness of one's place in the world.
- Inadequate preparation.
- Hostile or impoverished environments.
- Lack of time.
- External pressures and demands.
- Lack of support from others.
- Lack of skills: in noticing, intervening.
- Intent that is unclear or unfocused.
- Established patterns of thought and behaviour.
- Inability to conceive of the possibility of learning from experience: 'this is not learning', 'this is not possible'.
- Obstructive feelings: lack of confidence or self-esteem, fear of failure or the response of others, unexpressed grief about lost opportunities.

It is clear that learning processes can negatively affect a person; fortunately, however, human capabilities can be remarkably resilient. Einstein maintained: 'It is in fact nothing short of a miracle that the modern methods of instruction have not yet entirely strangled the holy curiosity of inquiry.'

If we can avoid or reduce these barriers when we are supporting our learning and that of others, then we can dramatically increase the chances of success. The dimension of attitude or emotion is a key factor in the learning process and we ignore it at our peril – not to mention its effect on our continued employment as teachers, trainers and developers of people!

Learning from mistakes

James Dyson is the successful industrialist and inventor of the bagless vacuum cleaner, the twin-cylinder washing machine and the Ballbarrow (a type of wheelbarrow with a ball instead of a wheel). While he was renovating his house he conceived the notion of a bagless vacuum cleaner and spent the next five years refining the concept, during which time he produced 5,127 prototypes and patented many of his ideas. The lesson that can be learnt from Dyson's experiences is that making mistakes enables us to find and identify information and knowledge that can help chart courses of action that will lead to the optimum solution. Similarly, Thomas Edison expended a great amount of energy, and not a little frustration, in identifying a suitable filament that would last when he invented the electric light bulb.

The important thing is that we learn from our mistakes. Peter Honey and Michael Pearn at the CIPD's Human Resource Development Conference in London looked at the nature of mistakes and stated that there were three types of people:

- those who make a mistake once and learn from it so as not to make the mistake again;
- those who make a mistake once and are so traumatized that they do not venture to that territory again; and lastly
- those people who continue to make the same mistake over and over again, never learning from the previous episodes in their experience.

Only the first of the three types of people above can be said to have truly learned. This scenario about learning was repeated by Akio Morita, former CEO of Sony, who stated to his workers, 'It's OK to make a mistake, but don't make the same mistake twice.'

It is when we move from the familiar to the unfamiliar that we are likely to make mistakes and this causes most of us to remain within our comfort zones. However, the environment in which we normally operate also tends to diminish our awareness of other areas and methods of operating. This occurs through continual reinforcement, which suggests that the habitual ways of seeing and operating are the only, or the best, means of behaving and feeling. We thus become blind to other options and can constrain ourselves unnecessarily. Later in the book we will examine the implications of exploring beyond our comfort zones into more challenging terrains of experiential learning.

Formal versus experiential learning

It is very difficult to become knowledgeable in a passive way. Actively experiencing something is considerably more valuable than having it described.

(Schank and Childers, 1988: 9)

Before the establishment of mass state schooling the provision of education was inadequate, restricted and not serving the needs of the general population nor the nation as a whole. With the arrival of compulsory education, the process of formal or traditional education has proved to be relatively successful in educating children and ensuring that the vast majority are literate and numerate (Wilson, 2011). However, while this factory system of learning achieved some successes, there were still a number of reservations.

Integrating theory and practice was a preoccupation of Dewey (1938) who drew attention to the limitations of formal education and the fact that much of what we were supposed to learn in school was no longer accessible. He considered that when learning occurred in isolation it was disconnected from the rest of the child's experience. Thus, because it was segregated and not linked through experience to the child's memory it became difficult to retrieve.

Examples of the power of impactful experiences are provided by Macala (1986: 57), who observed:

> If you were to ask a group of adults to talk about their most interesting and exciting learning experience, chances are good that instead of describing a classroom scenario, many of them will talk about a self-directed learning experience that enabled them to learn new information, a skill, theory, or process on their own. Their experiences might have included discovering how a city really works by serving on the Human Rights Commission, learning how to sail a boat by trial and error, or developing leadership or fund-raising skills through committee work. These adults learned by doing, and they probably remember well the how of the doing: They observed (what a 'luffing' sail looks like, how an alderman's body language belied his words); they asked questions, got feedback, did research, took risks, made mistakes, found mentors, informants, helpers, tried out and checked their progress, accuracy, skill; and they grew and changed as they were challenged.

The limited value of attempting to pour knowledge into the heads of young people without relating it to their experience was held not only by Dewey. This view was forcibly repeated some decades later by Freire (1982: 45–46) in his book *The Pedagogy of the Oppressed* where he advocated less state intervention in the learning process of children and argued:

> Education thus becomes an act of depositing, in which the students are the depositories and the teacher is the depositor. Instead of communicating, the teacher issues communiqués and makes deposits, which the students patiently receive, memorize, and repeat. This is the 'banking' concept of education, in which the scope of action allowed to the students extends only as far as receiving, filing, and storing the deposits. They do, it is true, have the opportunity to become collectors or cataloguers of the things they store. But in the last analysis, it is men themselves who are filed away through the lack of creativity, transformation, and knowledge in this (at best) misguided system. For apart from inquiry, apart from the praxis, men cannot be truly human. Knowledge emerges only through invention and reinvention, through the restless, impatient, continuing, hopeful inquiry men pursue in the world, with the world, and with each other.

Freire is damning about the role of schools in separating learning from the world in which it is to be used. And this view is also strongly maintained by Illich (1973) in his book *De-schooling Society*. Yet even learning in schools is not in total isolation from what already exists in the brains of the pupils. Thus, the challenge for educators, trainers and developers is to find the right type of experience that is immediately appealing to the learner and also has a longer-term impact.

It is important to stress here that this book is not a diatribe against formal schooling. There is a substantial volume of schooling that combines theory and

FIGURE 2.4 The formal learning and experiential learning authenticity continuum

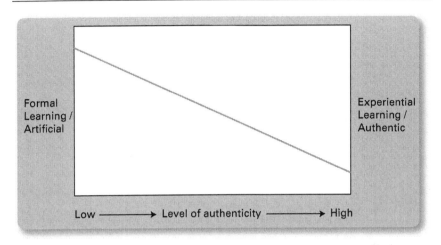

practice and also develops core skills such as the development of interpersonal skills and group working. Equally, the areas of training and development are less susceptible to criticism because they are linked to practical applications of knowledge. It is the area of traditional education in which the delivery of abstract theoretical knowledge is delivered through a teacher, lecturer, trainer or developer standing at the front and speaking or reading from a book that causes us most concern, together with some restricted forms of computer-mediated learning. What we are advocating here is the case that most aspects of learning will benefit from being linked to some form of experience.

On the whole, formal learning and experiential learning both contain elements of the other, eg formal classroom learning is likely to contain applied activities and consideration of the practical application of concepts (Figure 2.4). Likewise, experiential learning often has formalized processes where people take time out to reflect on what has happened during an activity and even have didactic direction from a team leader or trainer. In effect, formal and experiential learning processes have varying elements of each other and learning might be considered more of a continuum of authenticity.

The lineage of experiential learning

One of the most influential writers on the subject is David Kolb (1984: 3–4), who wrote *Experiential Learning*, in which he stressed its importance and stated:

> Experiential learning theory offers... the foundation for an approach to education and learning as a lifelong process that is soundly based in intellectual traditions of social psychology, philosophy, and cognitive psychology.

FIGURE 2.5   Dewey's learning process

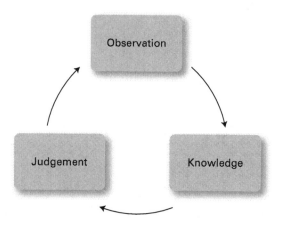

The experiential learning model pursues a framework for examining and strengthening the critical linkages among education, work, and personal development. It offers a system of competencies for describing job demands and corresponding educational objectives and emphasizes the critical linkages that can be developed between the classroom and the 'real world' with experiential learning methods. It pictures the workplace as a learning environment that can enhance and supplement formal education and can foster personal development through meaningful work and career development opportunities. And it stresses the role of formal education in lifelong learning and the development of individuals to their full potential as citizens, family members, and human beings.

The development of philosophical thought about the meaning of experience can be traced back to the Greeks, other philosophers such as John Locke (Adamson, 1911) and onwards to the present day (see also Chapter 5). Similarly, the development of understanding about experiential learning is grounded in philosophical thought, and numerous writers draw upon this heritage, including Dewey, Lewin, Revans and Kolb. Kolb, himself, looked at the process of experiential learning and drew on the legacy of the perspectives provided by Lewin, Dewey and Piaget. Kolb (1984) asserted that Lewin's description of the learning process is relatively similar to that of Dewey, which involved observation, knowledge and judgement (see Figure 2.5).

Kolb also described how Lewin's action research and T-group training in laboratories was influenced by the concept of feedback that was used by electrical engineers. This feedback process involved concrete experience; observations and reflections; formation of abstract concepts and generalizations; and testing implications of concepts in new situations (see Figure 2.6). The similarities with Kolb's learning cycle in Figure 2.7 may be seen.

FIGURE 2.6 Lewin's feedback process

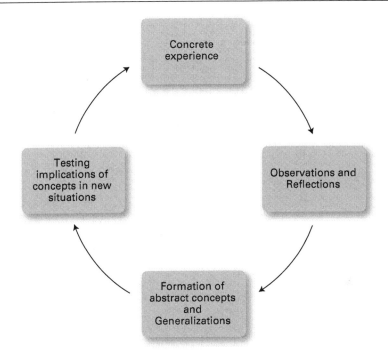

FIGURE 2.7 Kolb's experiential learning cycle

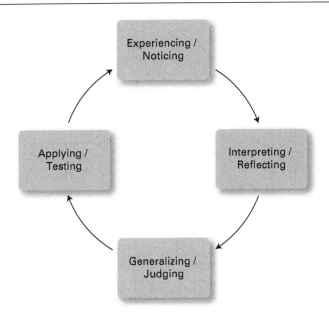

Experience and learning styles

The change in emphasis from teaching to learning has resulted, quite rightly, in a greater consideration being given to personal learning preferences. If a person finds it easier to learn in a particular way then consideration should be given to this although, of course, larger numbers of people can make individualized learning more challenging. In 1971, Kolb (1971) investigated learning styles and identified four learning styles: diverging, assimilating, converging and accommodating and later a learning styles inventory was published based around the four stages of the learning cycle (Kolb, 1976). The LSI has been subsequently revised a number of times and it is now composed of nine learning styles (Learning from Experience, 2012).

Learning styles inventories and questionnaires have proliferated and Cofield *et al* (2004) identified 71 different theories of learning styles. A popular questionnaire, based upon Kolb's learning cycle, was developed by Honey and Mumford who stated that, 'The term learning styles is used as a description of the attitudes and behaviours which determine an individual's preferred way of learning' (Honey and Mumford, 1992: 1). They argued that two people of similar intelligence and background who undergo a learning opportunity may be affected in very different ways, eg one is enthusiastic while the second person is disaffected. They maintain that the reason for this is that people have particular styles of learning that influence their attitudes and abilities towards learning opportunities. According to Honey and Mumford, people learn in two ways. The first is through teaching, and the second is through experience.

Honey and Mumford described four stages of learning and explained that a person may begin anywhere in the cycle and does not have to begin at Stage 1, eg the person may receive some information and review it (Stage 2), and then draw some tentative conclusions (Stage 3), and then plan a course of action (Stage 4) and finally undertake the course of action (Stage 1). The process is an iterative one and allows people to join the cycle at any point, the main proviso being that they complete the cycle; otherwise, the learning process is incomplete, eg they may review the experience that using a hammer to drive in a nail is a painful process to their thumb when they miss the nail, and never learn to use the hammer correctly. They need to complete the cycle by testing the theory and confirming it. Honey and Mumford (1992: 7) used the term 'experience' in three of the four stages, as can be seen in Figure 2.8.

Honey and Mumford explained that there are four types of people with preferences for each stage of the learning cycle. Although it was recognized that people's learning styles can alter when they change jobs and are therefore not fixed, there is value in taking into account the preferred learning style of a person. This is not only from the point of view of the teacher or trainer but also from that of the learner who can become more aware of his or her personal process of learning. The various styles are:

FIGURE 2.8 Honey and Mumford's learning styles

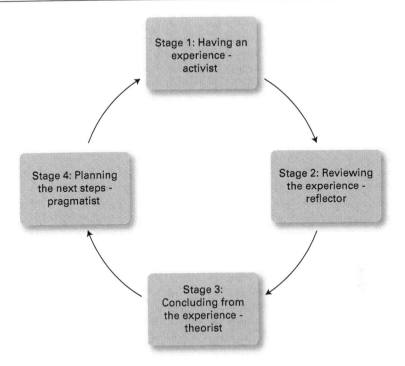

- **Activists:** prefer to involve themselves in an experience and do so in an open-minded manner. They involve themselves with the activity first and then weigh up the implications of their actions afterwards.

- **Reflectors:** prefer to gather information and carefully consider it before reaching a conclusion. They are thoughtful and cautious, and tend to reserve judgement in meetings until they are reasonably sure about their conclusions.

- **Theorists:** tend to be systems people who gather information and attempt to develop a coherent theory about the experience. They are logical and prefer to analyse information and produce an encompassing theory.

- **Pragmatists:** prefer to apply theories and techniques to investigate whether they work. Pragmatists are realistic people who seek out improved methods of operating.

Honey and Mumford explained that this cyclical process is a fundamental one, which is similar to the scientific method upon which Revans also based his model. It is also similar to problem-solving and decision-making approaches, as well as the quality cycle. W Edwards Deming was a physicist who used statistical methods to improve the quality of production in Japan

FIGURE 2.9 The Shewhart/Deming cycle of continuous improvement

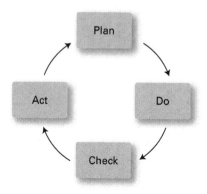

after the Second World War. He was a disciple of Shewhart, a statistician at Bell Laboratories, and he developed the Deming or Shewhart cycle of continuous improvement, which involved a systematic approach to problem solving and was a cyclical process of plan, do, check, act (see Figure 2.9).

That people prefer to learn in different ways is little doubted but whether these closely match the stages in the learning cycle is open to debate. Cofield *et al* (2004) investigated some of the main learning styles theories and concluded that they had not been sufficiently validated by independent research. In our experience, the value of these questionnaires/inventories is not in their diagnostic capabilities but in using them with learners to encourage self-reflection about different personal learning strategies.

We saw in Figure 2.1 the linking of theory and practice, which has a strong similarity to the various cycles of Lewin, Kolb, Honey and Mumford, and Deming/Shewhart. While they are all interlinked and have influenced one another, there would appear to be a fundamental principle at work here in which we need to combine thinking with doing or applying in order to create an effective learning process.

A chronology of experiential learning

It is also possible to consider the nature of experiential learning from a chronological perspective (see Figure 2.10). We can undertake this analysis of experience retrospectively, concurrently or prospectively, ie with reference to the past, the present or the future. When we undergo an event it is possible to learn from that experience at different times, ie:

- learning from an event at the time it occurs;
- learning from the past event when reflecting on it later;

FIGURE 2.10 A chronological perspective of experiential learning

| Past experiences shaped by cognitive, affective and behavioural involvement | Present experiences shaped by cognitive, affective and behavioural involvement | Multiple future experiences shaped by cognitive, affective and behavioural imagination |

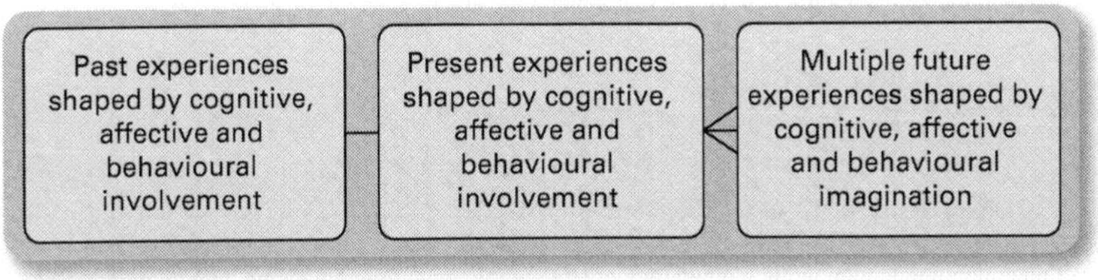

- learning more about a past event when thinking about it further;
- reinterpreting the past event differently in the light of further experience(s);
- analysing future scenarios.

Retrospective learning

Much experiential learning involves looking back at an event and analysing it (what Schön, 1983, termed reflection-on-action). Often when we are undergoing an experience there is insufficient time and/or we are too close – physically, chronologically or emotionally – to have the ability to make sense of what is happening. These processes of thinking about a past event may be illustrated when we say, 'If only I had...'. What we are doing is reflecting about the experience and making sense of it in our own mind – in effect we are attempting to fit the experience into our mental schema, adjust the schema or replace them altogether.

Another form of retrospective learning is to look back at an event and recollect even more closely what happened and thus learn in even greater depth. For instance, we may rewind the mental tape of a conversation we had to try to get more detailed insights into why another person behaved in a particular way.

Yet a further way of learning retrospectively is when an event can be reinterpreted in the light of subsequent experiences and there is the potential for its meaning to be considerably different to that at the time. One example is a parent rapidly lifting a child to safety before the child burns him- or herself on a stove. The child may be shocked and cry as a result of the sudden action or the frustration at not being allowed to do what he or she wants, but when the child is older the interpretation is much different, particularly so if the child has subsequently burnt him- or herself.

Not only can we learn from a new experience as we relate that experience to our existing ones, but we can also find new meanings hidden in old experiences. These old experiences may be drawn from any time in our history and although we may have incorporated them within a particular mindset we may change them as a result of our new experience.

It is possible to use learners' previous experiences to add depth, colour and a concrete reality to the more abstract environment of learning of the classroom or training room. This may involve revisiting a past experience in light of the theoretical and structured learning that has just been delivered.

Concurrent learning

We discussed above in the section 'Perception is learning' that we are able to learn almost concurrently as we interact with external stimuli. So, for example, as we are driving in a car and slowing down for some traffic lights ahead we will continuously adjust the pressure on the brake pedal to ensure that we come to a halt just behind the car in front rather than crashing into it. This learning is almost instantaneous.

Many of our physical actions, as well as our mental ones, are in a continual process of assessment and change. In the classroom, training room and workplace we often learn immediately from the experience and this may involve adjusting our tone of voice or demeanour so that the person responds in the desired manner. The next time you reach for that cup of tea or coffee just think about how your movements are finely coordinated to allow you to grasp the mug and drink from it without spilling the contents.

Similarly, if we notice that there is frost on the ground we may drive more carefully to avoid skidding and having an accident. Alternatively, we may adjust the pressure that we exert with our fingers on a new computer keyboard. Both these adaptations to the external environment are a form of learning, albeit short-term; as soon as the temperature rises above freezing or we return to our old keyboard we are likely to return to our previous behaviour.

The quality of the immediate learning in formal situations may be enhanced by coaching the learner to stand back from the experience he or she is undergoing and consider what is happening. This form of activity and reflection is common in team and management development activities where the participants are encouraged not only to succeed in the task but also to consider their own and others' behaviours and interactions. This behaviour was termed by Schön (1983) as reflection-in-action, and will be discussed further in Chapter 9.

Prospective learning

Although it is not possible to reflect on concrete experiences that have yet to happen, it is possible to analyse and reflect on the experiences of others who have been involved with an activity that we are contemplating in the future. This is known as social learning theory (Bandura, 1977). Through placing ourselves in the shoes of others we can have a reasonable expectation about what might happen and how we might respond. Unlike the past, which cannot be changed, only reinterpreted, it is possible to have a variety of futures. There is not, as many people subconsciously believe, only one future but there are many possible alternatives unless you are a believer in destiny.

The process of investigating possible futures involves a similar process to that of learning from past and present experience. This process is often called imagining, dreaming or visualizing and we often undertake it when we make plans, perhaps for a holiday or a business project (Wilson, 2012b). This process is increasingly being used for athletes and other people trying to achieve high levels of performance where they positively visualize a successful outcome so that they are prepared when the event happens. Another example of this is when we rehearse what we will say to a boss or some such figure when he or she asks us to explain a specific event.

This area of visualization, imagining and mental rehearsal is growing very rapidly, and will be discussed further in Chapter 10.

Challenging the concept of experiential learning

We have argued throughout this chapter, and indeed will do so throughout this book, that from a practical and philosophical perspective the interaction of experience and reflection is probably the most encompassing, clarifying and relevant approach to learning that we have come across. However, despite its many strengths it has not been immune to criticism, eg Malinen (2000), and in the cause of balance we will investigate three of the main criticisms below. The criticisms are based on 1) the lack of direction attributed to experiential learning; 2) the subjectivity of experiential learning; and 3) limitations that have been directed at Kolb's learning cycle.

Student-centredness leads to a lack of direction

Experiential learning has its critics who argue that there is too great an emphasis on experience to the detriment of the classical curriculum where subjects are taught in traditional and formal classrooms. Wildemeersch (1989: 61) referred to Jarvis's term 'the romantic curriculum' and stated that experiential learning 'emphasises elements like student-centredness, creativity, experience, discovery, awareness, originality and freedom'. Allowing students to determine the direction of their learning might lead to a neutering of the curriculum. Wildemeersch (1989: 62) cautioned that experiential learning 'might turn adult education into an apolitical, acurricular, reactive and consumer-orientated enterprise which casts the educator in the role of marketing expert and technician of the teaching–learning machinery' and also that 'the concept of self-direction may simultaneously lead to isolation, individualism and poor learning'.

The argument that adult learning is purely about supporting learners to grow in whatever direction they may choose is an incorrect one. Although people should have the opportunity to choose and follow their own interests, how many classes in adult education have no title, no syllabus or no clear direction in which they intend to proceed? For example, most programmes have clear specifications about their syllabus content. Students sign up for the various programmes and are guided in their learning; individual areas of learning are catered for within clearly defined and negotiated projects. Students enrolled to study botanical illustration will not progress far if they then propose to the tutor that they wish to learn more about the theory of music!

Experiential learning and technology

One of the more robust arguments aligned against experiential learning is the difficulty of linking it to complex areas of technology or, for example, theoretical physics. Wildemeersch (1989: 62) suggested that the incorporation of experience and technological frameworks was 'puzzling'. Indeed, trying to link experience to Stephen Hawking's (1988) string theory, or the development of drug treatments to counteract HIV and Aids, for all but the specialist is problematical.

However, even at these advanced levels of mental activity there are elements with which we can connect. The notion of a string is used by Hawking to address much more complicated issues and the term 'string' provides a metaphor with which ordinary people can at least grasp elements of the concept. Moreover, when explanations of drug treatments are described it is often in the form of the chemical jigsaw piece attaching itself to a matching receptor.

The subjectivity of experience

One regularly repeated criticism of experiential learning is that it is very subjective since it is based on what the learner has undergone and thus does not have wider applicability. In addition, the event lacks the scientific objectivity that would otherwise accrue from an external event. Dewey (1925: 1) described the reasoning of his critics:

> On the one hand they eagerly claim an empirical method; they forswear the *a priori* and transcendent; they are sensitive to the charge that they employ data unwarranted by experience. On the other hand, they are given to deprecating the conception of experience; experience it is said, is purely subjective, and whoever takes experience for his subject-matter is logically bound to land in the most secluded of idealisms.

Dewey (1925: 1) continued:

> When the notion of experiences is introduced, who is not familiar with the query, uttered with a crushingly triumphant tone, 'Whose experience?' The implication is that experience is not only always somebody's, but that the peculiar nature of 'somebody' infects experience so pervasively that experience is merely somebody's and hence of nobody and nothing else.

The value of introspection was discredited in the early days of psychology and it is only in more recent times that it has been given more consideration. One approach used to capture inner experience is Descriptive Experience

Sampling in which experimental subjects wear a beeper that randomly gives out a beep. The subject then pays close attention to what they were thinking about when the beeper sounded. In this way inner thoughts and experiences can be more precisely captured and given more objective credibility (Hurlburt and Heavey, 2006).

We all create our own reality and in that respect it is socially constructed (Berger and Luckmann, 1985). Alternatively, external events, eg an earthquake, can be argued to have their own independent existence and objectivity. However, the very act of observing or measuring such phenomena and using socially constructed measures such as language and measurement creates a shared social meaning and thus, it can be maintained, do not possess pure objectivity.

Limitations of the learning cycle

The learning cycle as developed by Kolb has become strongly established and is an almost taken-for-granted theory of learning. However, it has been challenged by some writers and we will now investigate some of the criticisms to assess their relevance. Miettinen (2000) argued that philosophical studies suggest experiential learning is inadequate as a means of providing new knowledge about the world. He maintained that Kolb's interpretation of the work of Dewey, Lewin and Piaget, upon whom he based the development of his learning cycle, was selective and did not really represent the facts. Although Kolb talked about the 'Lewinian Model' of impulse, observation, knowledge and judgement, Miettinen maintained that Kolb's research is based on observations of only a small section of Lewin's work described by Lippit (1949).

Miettinen (2000: 68) compared the work of Dewey and Kolb and concluded that Kolb does not take into account Dewey's distinction between habit, 'the great flywheel of society' that enables society to function predictably when faced with recurring challenges, and the habit that tyrannically traps us into behaving in a particular way without thinking of alternatives. The use of habit is very important to our functioning, and Covey (1990: 46) in his book *The Seven Habits of Highly Effective People* states, 'Habits are powerful factors in our lives. Because they are consistent, often unconscious patterns, they constantly, daily, express our character and produce our effectiveness or ineffectiveness.' Habits, because they are often unconscious, tend to be a form of single loop activity rather than a form of double loop learning, both of which are discussed in Chapter 9.

Much of our lives are spent on automatic pilot, eg taking our normal route home after work and then realizing after we arrive that we cannot remember anything other than the work problem we were contemplating. We just do not think consciously, never mind reflect, on many of the actions that we undertake. This is a natural process that prevents our conscious brains becoming overwhelmed with all the things that we need to think about; however, it is not included in the learning cycle. Kolb's learning cycle also does not illustrate the fact that empirical (ie experiential) thinking based on action has limitations:

- It may result in false conclusions.
- It may not help us understand and explain change and new experiences.
- It may cause mental laziness and dogmatic thinking.

Miettinen also suggests that Kolb's experience and reflection occur in isolation and that there is a necessity for the individual to interact with other humans and the environment in order to enhance the reasoning and conclusions drawn. As we will see in Chapter 9, 'Experience, learning and change', the dangers of drawing wrong conclusions are less likely to occur when the individual interacts with others and the environment because the hard edges of life provide a 'reality check' on weaker concepts and hypotheses.

Reynolds' (1997) article, 'Learning styles: a critique', and Holman *et al*'s (1997) article, 'Rethinking Kolb's theory of experiential learning in management education', both argue that although the famous circle has been extremely influential, especially in management education in the United States and the UK, it is rarely seen as problematic. It locates itself in the cognitive psychology tradition, and overlooks or mechanically explains and thus divorces people from the social, historical and cultural aspects of self, thinking and action. Holman *et al* (1997) suggested that the idea of a manager reflecting like a scientist in isolation on events is like an 'intellectual Robinson Crusoe'. They argued that the social interactions of a person were very important to the development of self, thought and learning. Furthermore, they suggested that Kolb's theory was fundamentally cognitivist and had a number of limitations. The main criticism was that the four stages of the cycle – concrete experience, reflective observation, abstract conceptualization and active experimentation – were independent and represented a dualism or dialectic opposites, eg active experimentation and reflective observation.

In addition, Holman *et al* (1997: 145) disagreed with the idea of progressing sequentially through the cycle, and argued: 'Learning can be considered as a process of argumentation in which thinking, reflecting, experiencing and action are different aspects of the same process. It is practical argumentation with oneself and in collaboration with others that actually forms the basis for learning.' They also recognized, without going into detail, that emotion and individual differences play a significant role in the ability to learn. There has also been much scepticism about learning styles inventories based on the learning cycle (Hall and Moseley, 2005).

Another limitation of the learning cycle is that emphasis is placed on an individual's experiences rather than those of a wider group of shared experiences among people. This has been recognized and Baker *et al* (2002) and Desmond and Jowitt (2011) discuss the co-construction and reflection on experiences.

In an article titled 'Corn circles in search of a spaceship?', Taylor (1991: 258) aptly sums up many of the limitations of circular models used in the search for meaning:

> They first began to appear about 25 years ago. Neatly laid-out circles in the pages of training textbooks, journals and Industrial Training Board publications. They quickly came to seize the imagination of a growing band of training professionals. They must have been created by a superior intelligence, being so neat and logical and all. There were of course variations in the patterns observed, but these, it was discovered, were due to differing environmental conditions. Being a pragmatic and opportunist bunch the practitioners, although faintly curious about where they came from, what they actually meant, and who controlled them, were so much more interested in associating themselves with the phenomena so as to establish their own professional credibility and status. The mystery and novelty soon became displaced as attempts were made to elaborate and integrate the phenomenon into the known universe. Within a few short years the 'systematic training model' [or 'training cycle' to some] became the orthodoxy of the training profession.

Circles and other simplistic models do have a significant value, for both the provider and the participant, in terms of accessibility and applicability. Some models, while being more accurate representations of reality, may tend to be underused and sometimes disregarded as a result of their complexity. Kolb's learning cycle can be regarded as a minimalist interpretation of the complex operations of the brain and therefore it is not surprising that this model is somewhat limited in describing the learning process. However, Kolb and Kolb (2009: 309–10) have upgraded the circle model into a learning spiral:

> The experiential learning cycle is actually a learning spiral. When a concrete experience is enriched by reflection, given meaning by thinking, and transformed by action, the new experience created becomes richer, broader, and deeper. Further iterations of the cycle continue the exploration and transfer to experiences in other contexts.

Conclusion

This chapter began with a consideration of the growth of experiential learning and the development of an experiential society. We defined experiential learning as the sense-making process of active engagement between the inner world of the person and the outer world of the environment. In addition, we have seen that there is a considerable dissatisfaction with the nature of traditional formal education and training and that for us to learn more effectively it is desirable for us to learn from direct experience when appropriate. We also examined the influential Kolb's learning cycle and observed that it has a number of limitations. Experiential learning, of which Kolb's learning cycle is a part, has been identified and endorsed throughout history and remains the strongest and most enduring of the learning theories.

Coaching and facilitation, good practice and ethics

> *Good reflective practice takes practitioners beyond mere competence towards a willingness and a desire to subject their own taken-for-granteds and their own activities to serious scrutiny. Competence is not enough.* JOHNSTON AND BADLEY, IN HUNT, 2005: 246

Introduction

This chapter will explore the roles played by a coach or facilitator of experiential learning. The chapter also examines the good and not so good practices involved in coaching or facilitator interventions, including emotional engineering and the use of power, control, and climate and value setting. Much of the latter part of the chapter concentrates on dimensions of ethical behaviour, and we offer case studies and scenarios that surface ethical dilemmas. Finally, a range of codes of practice are compared in order to identify the central themes of these guidelines for professional conduct. In some places the illustrative focus is on management development using the outdoors; however, all the facilitative and ethical themes found in this chapter are relevant to the complex processes of facilitation. Other chapters in the book also offer further guidance to coaching and facilitation.

The notion that people can have powerful learning experiences is of considerable interest to anyone involved in experiential learning. However, discovering the essential ingredients that might make an experience profound and strongly positive for learning is likely to prove rather elusive. Experiences are potentially more powerful when the coaching or facilitation process acknowledges the deep, complex and holistic nature of learning. The consideration of the place and space, the activities, the social and emotional dynamics, sensory stimulation, and the stretching of intelligence capacities with appropriately challenging goals or aspirations are some of the salient ingredients that facilitators have to juggle with. In addition to this chapter, many of these issues are covered in other parts of this book.

A booming business?

Experiential learning emerges in a mixture of disciplines such as traditional education, rehabilitation, coaching, therapy, corporate training and person- nel development, outdoor development and adventure, and recreation-based training and development. All involve experiential learning in different ways, using differing approaches, and so it is unlikely that there is any easy solution to generic, universal standards of competence.

Ulrich and Hinkson (2001) comment that more than £20 billion is spent annually on global corporate leadership development programmes alone and O'Leonard (2012) estimated that US corporate training groups spent $67 billion in 2011. The sums of money involved are very large and inevitably some sectors of the industry have experienced increased criticism. An article by McGrory in *The Times* (London) in 1998 titled, 'That's enough bonding, I resign' commented: 'Big-name companies are estimated to be spending £550 million a year dragooning staff on to activity courses which occupational psychologists claim build team spirit and foster a more harmonious working environment.' Williams (1996) noted that management training and consul- tancy had mushroomed to a spend of over £2 billion a year and that there were over 2,700 firms specializing in it. The numbers are large, and still grow- ing. With such growth come inevitable calls for standards of competence and ethical guidelines. While organizations delivering such programmes increase, so does the variety of locations and methods used. Society is becoming more litigious, governing bodies increasingly embrace competence and standards language, and the insurance industry is more discerning. Consequently insti- tutional governance and inspector–watchdog roles are proliferating.

The deliverers

> Role model. Mentor. Counsellor. Outdoor Educator. Instructor. Friend. By whichever name they are called, Outward Bound Singapore instructors are, undeniably a special breed. Their work is not merely the transfer of skills or knowledge, but, more importantly life values. They challenge participants to see the possibility in impossibilities, to dig deep within themselves for what is seemingly absent, to stretch to greater achievements.
>
> (Outward Bound Singapore brochure, undated)

To find a collective term to describe this role is clearly problematic. The brochure does, however, make clear the significance of competence and good practice for those interacting directly with learners. The term 'trainer' is derived from the Old French trahiner (to drag) from the Latin trahere (to pull). In contrast the word 'facilitator' has a different flavour or feel to it, and comes from the Latin facilitas (easiness). This meaning then is to do with making it easier; to help (Bee and Bee, 1998: 1).

In the United States, the Association for Experiential Education convened a task force of 115 global experiential practitioners and produced a document titled *Definitions, Ethics and Exemplary Practices (DEEP) of Experiential Training and Development (ETD)* (DEEP, 1999). This document set out guidelines of good practice, and contained definitions of trainers and facilitators. A facilitator is an 'individual responsible for managing the learning environment to assist individuals/groups to achieve value from the learning process'. A trainer, however, is said to be 'a practitioner who leads and directs prescribed learning for skill development, towards measurable explicit results' (DEEP, 1999: 18–19).

Boud and Miller (1996a) caution the use of titles; the word 'facilitator', they suggest, comes with much conceptual baggage, having resonance 'with humanistic psychology and work with individualistic concerns' (1996a: 7). They opt for the French term 'animateur', but they are worried about the association with 'organization and acting'. Likewise Allison (2000a: 45) suggests careful use of phraseology, as words portray values. He debates a range of terms and advises equal caution in describing learners as 'kids', 'punters', 'clients', 'youths' or 'participants'. Using the word 'client', he suggests, locates providers in the 'market of consumption'.

Titles can also affect status. The Chartered Institute of Personnel and Development's guide to outdoor training (IPD, 1998) gives guidance on the choice of suitable development providers, and makes reference to two kinds of training staff. They regard tutors as 'those who should have the experience and qualifications in training, development and facilitation' (1998: 5). Instructors, however, 'have experience in outdoor activities – for example, canoeing or climbing – for which they will usually have qualifications from an approved body (but not always – a few activities are not covered by qualifications).' They also suggest that a progression exists from instructor to trainer roles, and comment (1998: 5):

> Tutors will often have got into outdoor training because of their interests in outdoor pursuits, and they may also be competent as instructors in one or two activities, while instructors may have ambitions to become trainers. Even if individuals are competent both as instructors and tutors, however, the distinction between these two roles is important for managing events, dealing with delegates at an appropriate level, and for health and safety reasons.

Experiential provider roles

What then are the key roles of providers of experiential learning? Developing people involves a qualitative change to the way individuals are, bringing out latent potential. The DEEP initiative (DEEP, 1999: 8–10) defines experiential training and development (ETD) as 'a client centred approach to individual, group, and organizational learning, that engages the adult learner, using the elements of action, reflection, transfer, and support'. Experiential learning, they state, 'synthesizes knowledge from practices of experiential learning, adult learning and organizational development', and has a number of key roles:

- **Relationship development** – services that enhance interactions and motivate individuals through short-term events. Examples include energizing, incentive/reward, networking and celebration events. These events are purposeful and incorporate elements of reflection, transfer and support, as distinct from entertainment and recreation events, which do not.

- **Performance enhancement** – training in skills and competencies that result in improvement of personal, team and organizational effectiveness. Examples include communication skills, executive coaching, performance management and conflict resolution.

- **Consultation/intervention** – services addressing the interaction between behaviour (individual, leadership and team) and business setting elements (eg reporting line structures, communication and decision-making processes, incentive/compensation systems). Activities may include analysing misalignments among these pieces, advising on possible growth/change initiatives, and coaching.

In the UK key industrial overview bodies have been set up by the government to establish vocational qualifications and set performance standards. Each sector has a *key purpose statement*. For training this statement is: 'to develop human potential to assist organizations and individuals to achieve their objectives'. This statement has a business focus to it and it is aimed at human resource development specialists, particularly within corporate training departments. This is in contrast to the much broader, life-values approach adopted for example in therapeutic or youth rehabilitation work, where facilitators require a very different set of skills.

Power and control are fundamental to the styles of delivery by learning providers. Arising from his investigations into 'expert telling' versus finding out and experiencing, Carl Rogers (1969), the eminent US psychologist, made controversial statements about teaching, declaring that anything that can be 'taught' is rather inconsequential. His focus was concerned with the intrinsic limits of what teachers can do. He explored the nature of teaching and learning, expressing concern with the ephemeral nature of what he called the 'jug and mug' approach to learning, where the so-called expert pours knowledge into the mugs, the recipients. His interest lay with the nature of 'learnercentred learning', and was concerned that the provider should not always control the agenda. Experiential learning providers regularly face such issues of power, control and intervention, as Table 3.1 highlights.

Bentley suggests that 'Facilitators concentrate on providing the resources and opportunities for learning to take place, rather than "manage and

TABLE 3.1   A dichotomy of power and control

Learner-centred	Provider-centred
Providers work with the natural curiosity and concerns of the learner.	Passive learning is encouraged.
There is a learning contract.	The provider has a rigid syllabus to get through.
Real issues and problems are worked on and used as vehicles for learning.	Trainees learn by memorizing, and use artificial case studies.
Feedback on self-performance is encouraged.	Learning is monitored, examined and assessed by the trainer.
Learners are considered to have a valuable contribution to make.	The trainer is the repository of knowledge.
Learners are trusted to learn for themselves.	The teacher/trainer knows best.
Responsibility for learning is shared with the learners.	Trainees wait for the trainer to lead.
The learning provider offers resources to learn.	Learning is limited to the trainer's knowledge.
Learners continually develop the programme.	The trainer dictates the flow of the programme.
Learners and providers have joint responsibility and power.	The trainer has responsibility and power.
There is a climate of genuine mutual care, concern and understanding.	Trust is low; trainees need constant supervision, and the trainers remain detached.
The focus is on fostering continuous learning, asking questions and the process of learning, and learning is at the pace of the learner.	Knowledge is dispensed in measured chunks decided by the trainer.
Emphasis is on promoting a climate for deeper, more impactful learning that affects life behaviour.	Emphasis on here-and-now acquisition of knowledge and skills to do the job.
There are no teachers, only learners.	The teacher/trainer is, and remains, the expert.

Taken from Colin Beard, 1980, Course materials, Training the Trainer control" learning' (Bee and Bee, 1998: 2). Power and control are explored by Heron in *The Complete Facilitator's Handbook* (1999) and he offers three approaches to facilitation. The first is the hierarchical mode where the trainer is leading from the front and in charge. In this mode trainers provide meaning, interpret events and take responsibility for major decisions. The cooperative mode is where power is shared and the trainer guides the group to be more self-directing and collaborative. The third mode is autonomous, where the facilitator respects the group's independence and autonomy so that people are given the freedom to find their own way.

Intruding complicators or enabling animateurs

Good experiential learning providers can help to change hearts and minds, and life values. Poor experiential providers can be seen as patronizing, and their performance can become an exaggerated ego trip. This is explored by Rae (1995) using a three-dimensional grid of skills, concerns and competence to examine a classification of trainer types. With the grid came a range of titles: professional trainer, humble expert, endearing bumbler, shallow persuader, boring lecturer, directive instructor, oblivious incompetent and arrogant charlatan! Trainers have also been variously described as martyrs, science boffins, chat-show hosts, army officers, actors, magicians and many other names.

Greenaway (2008) describes some approaches to experiential learning as far too structured and didactic. Furthermore, recent research by Williams (2012: 137) suggests participants on solo experiential programmes do not even 'require a facilitator to tell them what they should be learning and that they will identify for themselves the outcomes that are meaningful and important'. In seeking to establish the essence of good practice, however, Allison (2000a) describes six fundamental, defining characteristics of high-quality outdoor learning, arguing that if they are not present then the experience will lack quality. One key ingredient is the authenticity of the facilitator. Similarly, work on excellence in facilitation (Wickes, 2000) suggests that high levels of peak experience can occur more often when providers 'tread lightly'. Wickes offers a map of 21 key ingredients of facilitator excellence including: creating the right climate; getting in – rapport; creating experiences that work; creating engaging, memorable and meaningful experiences; helping people review, articulate and share personal learning; making it easy to disclose and share experiences; maintaining a constructive atmosphere; and creating a powerful, emotional and satisfying experience.

The choice of when or how to intervene or not is at the heart of good practice. To intervene at every step along the way is likely to be counterproductive. Those who facilitate behavioural changes in individuals, groups and organizations can, in their desire to deliver a showcase performance, create pressure that overrides a key principle that 'Animators need to operate in ways that make their own interventions increasingly redundant, thereby avoiding the use of their own power to create dependency and thus exercising control over the learners' (Boud and Miller, 1996b: 16). A gradual reduction in control and intervention over time can help, allowing learners to build on their experiences and develop confidence. Adler (1975) in his work on group psychology refers to the four stages of dependency, counter-dependency, independency and finally interdependency. Learning providers continually debate these fundamental issues; the safety of learners lies not only with the physical nature of the experience, but also in the intellectual, moral and emotional domain.

Dysfunctional learning

Some feel about experiential education the way Hemingway felt about making love: Don't talk about it, you'll only ruin the experience. We know it's good because it feels good, and as G. E. Moore, the philosopher said: good is good, and that's the end of the matter. It can only be defined in terms of itself, it has intrinsic worth so there is no other standard to judge it by, it requires no further justification. The values are 'self-evident.' Let the mountains speak for themselves!

(Nold, in Wichmann, 1995: 113)

This leads us to consider a central question in experiential learning: can the experience speak for itself? Loynes (2000) explores what he calls 'indigenous learning', which he regards as more authentic, 'real' and 'natural', and argues that learning shouldn't be overly interfered with. He notes that experiential learning can only occur when people attach meaning and value to their experience, but regards experiential learning as 'natural' when people do this themselves, or with colleagues participating in the experience. Intervention by others, he argues, especially when there is an element of imposed morality, theory or judgement, can disturb or interrupt the emergent indigenous learning and negate it as experiential learning. This can be accidental or deliberate. Underpinning this important debate about the transactive nature of experience, and the degree to which facilitators intervene, is the extent to which the learning is planned or allowed to emerge (Megginson, 1994), which we explore in Chapter 5.

Loynes (2000) refers to the Hitler Youth Movement and corporate team building as two very diverse and different examples of dysfunctional experiential learning using the outdoors. In a thought-provoking style, he suggests that facilitators should refrain from creating a proving ground for fixed ideas. Experiential learning, he suggests, should be a source of emerging ideas, rather than a place to prove other people's fixed ideas. Loynes notes that, instead of imposing pre-packaged theories or ideas to generate pre-prepared solutions, providers should allow people to build their own theory from their own action. The dualism of intervention and non-intervention is not simplistic. The degree to which providers intervene or deny or fail to provide opportunities for people to tell and share their experience, through their stories, is an important psychological consideration. McLeod (1997: 100) comments that 'very often the existence of a personal "problem" can best be described as a response to silencing, the unwillingness of others to hear the story that in some sense "needs" to be told'. Central to the experiential provision is this notion that individuals and organizations may need support and encouragement in order to tell their story. Neutral intervention is at the heart of a client-centred practice (Rogers and Freiberg, 1969), and encourages people to tell their story.

Intervening

Heron (1990) conducted extensive research into facilitator interventions. He offers a range of interventions, including echoing, selective echoing, open and closed questioning, empathetic divining, checking understanding, paraphrasing, logical marshalling, following, consulting, proposing or leading, bringing in and shutting out. These interpersonal skills form the essence of good facilitation, and similar behaviours were identified by the Huthwaite Group (Rackham and Morgan, 1977) and used in 'behaviour analysis'. They include proposing, building, supporting, disagreeing, defending/attacking, testing understanding, summarizing, seeking information, giving information, bringing in and shutting out. In checking understanding, for example, the facilitation phrase might be 'So can I just check this – what you are saying is...?' This gentle checking intervention encourages and checks the story, rather than redirecting it. Selective echoing involves the facilitator in selecting 'some word or phrase that carries an emotional charge or stands out as significant in its context' (Heron, 1999: 266). This is done in order to give the client space to explore, in any direction, the significance of what has been reflected or echoed back to him or her. Such intervention involves a degree of selective interpretation without leading the story, and helps client focus. Likewise, in therapeutic work, McLeod (1997: 114) refers to similar facilitator interventions:

- **Approval.** Provides emotional support, approval, reassurance or reinforcement. *Accepting or validating the client's story.*
- **Information.** Supplies information in the form of data, facts or resources. It may be related to the therapy process, the therapist's behaviour or therapy arrangements (time, place).
- **Direct guidance.** These are directions or advice that the therapist suggests for the client either for what to do in the session or outside the session. *Structuring the process of storytelling.*
- **Closed question.** Gathers data or specific information. The client responses are limited and specific. *Filling in the story.*
- **Open question.** Probes for or requests clarification or exploration by the client. *From a narrative perspective, open questioning can be used*

to invite the telling of a story or to explore the meaning of elements of a story.

- **Paraphrase.** Mirrors or summarizes what the client has been communicating either verbally or non-verbally. Does not 'go beyond' what the client has said or add a new perspective or understanding to the client's statements or provide any explanation for the client's behaviour. Includes restatement of content, reflection of feelings, non-verbal reference and summary. *Therapists using a narrative approach may wish to communicate to the client that they have 'heard' the story, or may attempt to focus attention on a particular aspect of a story.*

- **Interpretation.** Goes beyond what the client has overtly recognized and provides reasons, alternative meanings or new frameworks for feelings, behaviours or personality. It may establish connections between seemingly isolated statements or events; interpret defences, feelings of resistance, or transference; or indicate themes, patterns or causal relationships in behaviour and personality, or relate present events to past events. *This response includes a wide range of narrative-informed interventions, centred on the general goal of retelling the story in different ways.*

- **Confrontation.** Points out a discrepancy or contradiction but does not provide a reason for such a discrepancy. This discrepancy may be between words and behaviours, between two things a client has said or between the client's and the therapist's perceptions. *In narrative therapy, the client is encouraged to resolve the tension or incongruity between opposing versions of a story.*

- **Self-disclosure.** Shares feelings or personal experiences. *The therapist gives an account of his or her own story, either in terms of relevant episodes from a personal life story, or framed in terms of a therapeutic meta-narrative, or drawn from a myth and other cultural sources.*

High-quality facilitation requires complex intervention skills, and providers should consider the degree to which they are open and transparent in describing their own values around which they operate; otherwise, because of the power they hold, they can have undue influence on other people's beliefs and values. Many forms of intervention exist, including metaphoric interventions, discussed in Chapter 7, and gestalt interventions.

Coaching and facilitating: developing wisdom

The notion of 'powerful learning experiences' has been alluded to by a number of writers over the years: such experiences have often been regarded as associated with so-called 'higher levels' of learning. Of particular interest are: contemporary work on neuro-chemical 'highs' from learning (eg endorphins); high intrinsic motivation, peak experiences, and self-actualization (Maslow, 1968); spiritual intelligence/self (Chopra, 1996); 'moral intelligence' (eg Gardner *et al*, 2001); 'flow' learning experiences (Csikszentmihalyi and Csikszentmihalyi, 1988); creativity, innovation and the centrality of 'playful mind states' (eg 'relaxed alertness') (Neulinger, 1976); 'dramaturgy' (Martin *et al*, 2004); 'existentialism' and 'meaningful experiences' (Rogers, 1969); and 'deep' or 'transformational' learning (eg Marton *et al*, 1993).

Gardner (1993: 291), in his second edition work on multiple intelligence titled *Frames of Mind*, made reference to four higher levels of cognitive operations that went beyond a straightforward notion of 'an intelligence'. These were common sense, originality, metaphoric capacity and wisdom. He also noted that it was the 'sense of self' that placed the greatest strain on his multiple intelligence theory, and that this was a prime candidate for second order ability.

Facilitating high levels of learning requires considerable experience and a degree of wisdom. Egan (2002: 19) refers to wisdom in facilitation: 'Helpers need to be wise, and part of their job is to impart some of their wisdom, however indirectly, to their clients.' He then says that two authors defined wisdom as 'an expertise in the conduct and meaning of life' or 'an expert knowledge system concerning the fundamental pragmatics of life'. Egan offers many characteristics that might usefully inform the practice of facilitation:

- self-knowledge and maturity;
- knowledge of life's obligations and goals;
- an understanding of cultural conditioning;
- the guts to admit mistakes and the sense to learn from them;
- a psychological and a human understanding of others; insight into human interactions;
- the ability to 'see through' situations; the ability to understand the meaning of events;
- tolerance for ambiguity and the ability to work with it;
- being comfortable with messy and ill-structured cases;
- an understanding of the messiness of human beings;
- openness to events that don't fit comfortably into logical or traditional categories;
- the ability to frame a problem so that it is workable; the ability to reframe information;
- avoidance of stereotypes;
- holistic thinking; open mindedness; open-endedness; contextual thinking;
- meta-thinking, or the ability to think about thinking and become aware about being aware;

- the ability to see relationships among diverse factors; the ability to spot flaws in reasoning; intuition, the ability to synthesize;
- the refusal to let experience become a liability through the creation of blind spots;
- the ability to take a long view of the problem;
- the ability to blend seemingly antithetical helping roles – being one who cares and understands while being also the one who challenges and 'frustrates';
- an understanding of the spiritual dimensions of life.

Egan references Ellis, the founder of Rational-Emotional-Behaviour Therapy (REBT), noting that one of the most useful interventions helpers can make is to understand and challenge learners' irrational beliefs within their 'self-talk' or inner dialogue such as:

- Being liked and loved with irrational self-talk that says, '*I must always be loved and approved by significant people in my life.*'
- Being competent, with irrational self-talk that says, '*I must always, in all situations, demonstrate competence, and I must be both talented and competent in some important area of life.*'

Facilitation requires an awareness of other dimensions of irrational self-talk, which include:

- having one's own way;
- being hurt;
- being danger free;
- being problemless;
- being a victim;
- avoiding;
- tyranny of the past;
- passivity.

Coaching for learning and development

> You get the best effort from others not by lighting a fire beneath them, but by building a fire within.
>
> (Bob Nelson)

Coaching, formally or informally, is often the main form of learning and development in many work operations and the CIPD (2012: 5) annual *Learning and Talent Development Report 2012* remarked that, 'in-house development programmes and coaching by line managers [are] still seen to be the most effective practices'. Coaching is a very direct form of support that can result in quick and effective changes of behaviour and some large organizations have brought in whole teams of experienced coaches producing successful results. Coaching skills are applicable in most areas and for this reason coaching guidelines and implementation techniques will be discussed. This section will address:

- The nature and benefits of coaching and mentoring.
- The qualities and roles of a coach.
- The stages of the coaching process.
- Developing trust.
- Gaining commitment to action.
- Giving feedback.

The benefits of coaching

The CIPD (2012) have noted that coaching is a very useful form of development and there are many benefits for the following reasons:

- It provides a regular opportunity for the team leader and advisor to discuss levels of performance.
- It is flexible and can be undertaken when it is needed and around work requirements.
- It is targeted at the needs of the individual.
- It allows targets to be agreed and then monitored.
- It can be part of a regular series of development and can therefore be linked to previous coaching sessions.
- It connects formal classroom training with actual practice.
- It provides much opportunity for two-way communication between the team leader and the advisor.
- It can be carried out in real work situations.
- It can build rapport between the coach and the learner.
- It can be targeted at specific actions and be standalone.

The value of coaching would appear to have a positive impact on employee attrition in contact centres. Significantly, only 29 per cent of centres that provided at least two hours/agent/week of coaching had attrition problems: However, this increased to 48 per cent of contact centres that provided less than two hours coaching/agent/week (ContactBabel, 2005).

Coaching or mentoring?

Both coaching and mentoring in their purer forms are designed to bring about a desired outcome focusing on a joint agreement about behaviour, motivation and commitment. In some forms of coaching, eg high-level sports coaching, high pressure is sometimes applied to the person being coached; however, this is rarely successful in work situations.

There is some confusion about the differences between coaching and mentoring and much of this arises because quite a few of the approaches overlap with each other. The two are described below and then 'coaching' is used as a general term throughout the rest of this chapter.

Coaching

It is believed that the word 'coaching' evolved from the skills required to handle a team of horses attached to a stagecoach. Coaching has been subdivided into four areas: tell, show, suggest, and stimulate (Clutterbuck, 1998). Generally speaking, coaching involves the improvement of performance directed at enhancing specific skills. The coach and learner agree targets and the coach provides direct feedback on behavioural performance over a period of time. A definition is:

> Coaching is the process whereby one individual helps another: to unlock their natural ability; to perform, learn and achieve; to increase awareness of the factors which determine performance; to increase their sense of self-responsibility and ownership of their performance; to self-coach; to identify and remove internal barriers to achievement.
>
> (MacLennan, 1995: 4)

Mentoring

The term mentor originated in Ancient Greece when Odysseus went to fight in the Trojan War and gave responsibility for bringing up his son, Telemachus, to his friend Mentor. Mentoring involves developing and advancing the whole potential of an individual. It is often a long-term relationship where the goals and the process are owned by the learner. The mentor is often a form of resource for the learner and it is the learner who controls the process.

The qualities of a coach

Good coaches should be able to create an environment that is conducive to learning and it is their personal attitudes which allow the interaction to happen successfully. Successful coaches are:

- able to detach themselves;
- accessible;
- credible;
- good communicators;
- good listeners;
- interested and attentive;

- knowledgeable;
- knowledgeable about the organization;
- patient;
- perceptive;
- supportive;
- technical experts.

The roles of the coach

To develop the talents of employees a coach needs to use a variety of approaches and roles but not necessarily all at the same time. A coach should be:

- an advisor;
- a confidant;
- a counsellor;
- a friend;
- a guide;
- a motivator;
- a role model;
- a supporter;
- a teacher.

Stages in the coaching process

There are a number of stages in the coaching process and while they are not firmly fixed it is certainly beneficial for most of them to be utilized. A systematic approach will help ensure that the quality of the coaching is high without imposing an artificially imposed environment.

- *Inform the learner when the coaching session will happen.* Coaching may happen on an ad hoc basis when there is an opportunity, but in most circumstances it is less unsettling if the learner has the chance to prepare themselves in advance.
- *Minimize the potential for anxiety.* If a person is anxious they are more likely to be defensive and construct barriers that hinder true communication with the coach.
- *Break the ice.* It is advisable to begin coaching sessions with a light-hearted discussion that puts the learner at ease and which develops a positive rapport.

- *Invite the learner to comment on their performance first.* Asking the learner to begin the session allows them to take some control and thus reduces possible tension. It also enables discussion of aspects of which the coach may not even be aware.

- *Ask questions.* It is often better to ask questions and guide the learner to assess themselves rather than directly presenting them with evidence of non-conformance. Of course, there may be some individuals who will not openly acknowledge shortfalls in skills or who may even be oblivious to them.

- *Acknowledge strengths.* It is important to acknowledge where people have been doing well because if there is no recognition of positive behaviour it may decline. Furthermore, giving genuine praise, where merited, will enhance confidence and motivation and encourage further learning.

- *Areas for improvement.* From a psychological perspective it is often better to discuss, 'What could be done better?', than 'What went wrong?' Presenting an area as a deficiency is a negative approach and it is better to look optimistically at upward trends in performance. A popular strategy is to begin with, 'What went well?' and then follow this with, 'What could have gone better?'

- *Agree targets.* Arbitrarily imposing targets for a learner often fails to get their commitment and may result in resistance. A more productive approach is to ask what can be achieved and negotiate an objective that is challenging but achievable. Setting a target that is too ambitious may only result in demoralizing the learner if it is not reached. Stretch targets are acceptable, unachievable ones are pointless and undermine the learner and the organization.

- *Support and motivate.* Coaching sessions provide a very good opportunity to develop a closer relationship with the learner and this enables them to be encouraged and motivated.

- *Is there anything else?* Before the coaching session is concluded it is often helpful to ask if there are any other areas that haven't been discussed. By using this invitation other areas of concern may also be addressed.

- *Arrange date and time for next session.* Setting targets is insufficient if there is no particular deadline by which they should be achieved. By arranging a time for the next meeting this gives a focus to the agreements and motivates the learner to implement the actions.

Trust

It should come as no surprise that there is little trust in dysfunctional personal relationships. Similarly, societies or countries with a considerable degree of fraud and criminal activity have less trust, are less productive and therefore less wealthy than those with greater levels of trust. It is evident that mutual trust needs to be encouraged within call centres to ensure that they operate efficiently and create a positive working environment. There also needs to be a high level of trust between the coach and the advisor if the relationship is going to work effectively. This encourages openness, which allows the learner to believe in the benefits of coaching and buy into the whole process.

Committing to action

Changing behaviour is a challenging and difficult thing to achieve with other people and with ourselves. Think of the number of New Year's resolutions that you have made and how many of them have lasted for only a short time. Likewise with our health, we know that it is not wise to smoke or eat or drink too much but changing our behaviour is remarkably difficult.

The reality in many cases is that we know exactly what behaviour is needed but there is something missing to bring it about. Part of this might be willpower and this is where the coach is especially valuable. By including someone else in the process there is an increased responsibility for the learner to live up to the agreed commitments and do what they promised. There is also more incentive to do so when someone else will be checking on the achievements at a later stage. In some circumstances the coach can hold a metaphorical mirror up to the learner and describe some of the work elements that are not being achieved.

Setting targets

There is a large amount of performance data available within contact centres and this can often be used in the process of setting targets and appraising individual accomplishments. When a person achieves a target this does not mean further improvement is unnecessary; instead, strengths should be applauded and built upon to encourage excellence and to model behaviour that inspires co-workers. Where areas are not so strong they should be identified and agreement reached about the best means of improving them. These targets may then be set as goals to be achieved and revisited at the next session. The assumption should not be made that the coaching provided during the current session will be enough; where appropriate ongoing support should be provided. These learning goals should then be practised and enhanced on a regular basis in the workplace.

Challenging targets

Identifying accurate targets is an art form rather than an exact science and it can only be achieved through careful negotiation with the learner. The Yerkes-Dodson Law (1980) explains that when a target is not challenging enough there will be insufficient motivation to do anything about it. Alternatively, if a target is too challenging and is not reached it will undermine the learner's confidence. Not surprisingly, a balance is needed but this often cannot be identified in advance and it is better to ascertain this through discussions and negotiations with the learner.

Fifteen questions to ask the learner

1 How committed are you to achieving these targets?
2 If you were the coach and I were the learner what would you say to me?
3 What do you think your colleagues think about the quality of your work?
4 What types of person do you least like handling?
5 What have you done to develop your skills in handling difficult people?
6 How do you feel when you don't achieve targets?
7 How do you feel when you reach or exceed targets?
8 When you are feeling tired how do you maintain energy levels?
9 What could you do to increase your motivation?
10 How much of your potential are you achieving in your work?
11 How would you solve this situation?
12 What other strategies could you try?
13 Why does this matter to you?
14 What is stopping you doing...?
15 If you could do things differently what would you change?

Giving feedback

Giving honest feedback is not an easy thing to do and some coaches shy away from it, thus defeating the purpose. However, being honest does not mean that the limitations of the learner have to be starkly presented to them in a personally threatening manner. Ideally, the feedback should be invited by the learner, not presented by the coach and it should be done in a manner where the learner does not reject the information. Holding back on giving honest information so as not to cause offence prejudices the chances that the learner's behaviour will improve. The true message should not be so deeply hidden that the learner is unable to recognize it. In order to do this:

- Feedback should be clear and specific.
- It should focus on the behaviour and not on the person.
- It should focus on behaviour that can be improved.

- It should be invited where possible and not thrust at the learner.
- It should be delivered in a timely manner.

The importance of timing

Coaching feedback should be delivered in a timely fashion. If the period of time between the behaviour and the feedback is long then the coachee may not remember what happened or be less inclined to do anything about it. This means that the coach or team leader needs to be up to speed with all the metrics and behaviours of their team. Learners will know which coaches and team leaders are on top of their jobs and those who are not. It is therefore necessary to be up to date and also to set a good example. Providing prompt feedback is a more successful means of behavioural change. This can often be done through listening in to calls and providing guidance and recommendations as soon as the call ends.

Gestalt intervention: an individual coaching example

Gestalt therapy is an experiential form of psychotherapy that emphasizes personal responsibility, social and environmental contexts, a focus on the here and now present moment and self-regulating adjustments. Gestalt coaching focuses on the 'here-and-now' by increasing awareness of the sensory and emotional self, in both the coach and the client, and the resultant connectivity of the inner self and the outer world. Gestalt coaching uses such principles to provide a robust theory and practice of experiential learning and change at an individual, team and organization level. It is applicable in both indoor and outdoor environments, the focus being on the individual and his or her relationship to others. The 'here-and-now' approach to experience allows change to emerge naturally – the paradoxical nature of change – as opposed to planned change, which is traditional in our institutions, and is still largely modelled on a militaristic approach. A key outcome of change that occurs in this way is increased shared meaning between participants in an organization, because change comes through good contact and dialogue. People feel more empowered and start to create and re-create their own environments. Anybody wanting to improve the soul of the organization should take a look at what gestalt has to offer. The following is a case example of using gestalt in coaching.

The individual was a senior executive in a large corporation, and the key issue was building confidence to move on to higher levels of work. Working in a global organization, she was concerned about raising her profile with a large assignment on the international stage. As I listened to her, she spoke with dissatisfaction about previous work she had done, being critical about her own performance. What I heard, though, was a number of key achievements where she had played a significant part. When I pointed this out and gave her some positive feedback, she shrugged my comments off and moved quickly on to something else. This had happened a couple of times already.

In the cycle of experience she was not spending time in resolution and withdrawal, enjoying the satisfaction of her achievements and celebrating her success (and no doubt that of others too). This was retroflection, turning energy in on herself, this time in a critical fashion. There was also a projection – other people were bigger and better than she was (despite her being a very tall person!). The feeling I was experiencing was sadness.

I gave her the feedback on what I observed her doing. I also pointed out that spending time in satisfaction and celebration was very confidence-building. She again shrugged this off and moved on. I stopped her and expressed my then irritation. I told her I felt as if my comments did not matter and I was not valued. This was the same process she went through to undervalue herself and probably others.

At this point she stopped and acknowledged what she was doing. I encouraged her to slow down and breathe for a few seconds. A lot emerged as a result of this. Some of the explanations were complex and interlinked – her role as a woman in this large corporation, personal difficulties balancing her work with the needs of her young son and an element of blaming herself for not doing enough with him. An underlying introject or 'rule' that emerged was around 'getting it all right'. It was very difficult for her to let herself off the hook.

Rather than trying to do anything about the specifics she was now talking about (which in any event would have meant stepping over the boundary), I felt she needed to learn how to stop just doing something and stand there! I encouraged her to spend time in resolution and withdrawal, focusing on her physical sensations more and breathing fully. This was the polarity of her busyness – taking time, relaxing and appreciating what she had achieved. I gave her some techniques to use so she could build a routine of spending more time in this relaxing and satisfying place. This process would give rise to natural change in how she approached things, rather than putting a plan in place for her to be different. (supplied by David Willcock, Liberating Potential)

Life coaching

A life coach can make a difference in helping people to attain potential and to develop personal life goals. Many coaching professionals tell us that business-coaching processes will often branch out to embrace a number of important client life-balance issues. Life goals can of course offer greater vision and focus but they can also present barriers: some people can get overly concerned with a need to get somewhere, and attain the 'ideal future'. A focus on getting somewhere, or knowing something, or getting something is good, but if it means a person develops a tendency to negate present experiences, reducing them as a means to the dream end, then this can result in dissatisfaction with the present, as if the present is somehow an obstacle that gets in the way of the future (Wilson, 2012b). Life experiences are not fully savoured. Life is deferred, put on hold and so much of life can become less rewarding than it might be. Disappointment results on arrival at the goal or destination as it is often not where the journey was supposed to end up. In Chapter 7 we discuss the emotional dynamics of issues such as perfectionism (Mallinger and De Wyze, 1993) in more detail.

In reality the *present* is in essence all we ever have! Eckhart Tolle talks about developing a new state of consciousness, and the development of a detachment to the ruling ego that creates much dysfunction that leads to unhappiness, anger and jealousy (Tolle, 2006). Planning for future experiences while focusing on the joys of *experiencing* the *here and now*, can make for a better balance in life, and a richer life experience. The balance between planned versus emergent learning is explored in more detail in Chapter 5. Here we suggest the learning combination lock model has potential for life coaching and below we offer a set of core life coaching questions connected to life balance, covering our six dimensions of belonging, doing, sensing, feeling, thinking and being.

Seven core life coaching questions based on the learning combination lock model:

1 What are your *important relationships* – with people and places – and with other than the human world? (*belonging dimension*)

2 What do you want to *do more of* in your life? (*doing dimension*)

3 Describe the most pleasurable sensations in your life... eg the smell of bread cooking, the early morning fresh air, etc, they can be very personal too. How often are you aware of these pleasures? (*sensing dimension*)

4 What gives you positive *feelings* in your life...? (*feeling dimension*)

5 What things would you really like to *know more* about? (*knowing dimension*)

6 Who do you want to *be* – who are you now – what do you want people to say about you when you have gone to another world? – He/she was a... person, who.... (your *being dimension*)

(www:colinbeard.co.uk)
and one extra question:

7 What would you consider to be your important Life Gifts?

For example: different intelligences… Do you recognize your abilities: to be word smart (Linguistic intelligence), to be number smart (Logical/mathematical/ scientific intelligence), to be spatially smart (Visual/spatial intelligence), to be sound smart (Musical intelligence), to be body smart (Bodily/physical/ kinaesthetic intelligence), to be people smart (Interpersonal intelligence), to be self smart (Intra-personal intelligence), to be emotionally smart (Emotional intelligence), to be nature smart (Naturalistic intelligence), to be innovative and creative (Creatively smart) and to be life smart (Spiritual, moral and existential intelligence).

Facilitation: setting the climate and conditions

Wickes (2000), in a research paper titled 'The facilitators' stories', discussed aspects of facilitator excellence and peak experience in management develop-ment programmes. The first item on his list is creating a good climate. How do facilitators create a good climate for learning? Heap (1996) addresses the con-ditions under which people learn best and argues that learners are more moti-vated to learn if the events meet their particular needs. He suggests the design principles shown in Table 3.2. Within this context of rules and values settings, Heron refers to six important dimensions of facilitation, as shown in Table 3.3.

Ground rules and values

The learning climate can also be influenced by ground rules and working values. Heron (1999) creates three types of ground rules and, in a section on what he calls culture-setting statements, offers advice to establish a group culture that will enable learning to flourish. *Discipline ground rules* set out the boundaries of behaviours, such as arriving on time and giving full atten-tion when someone is working on issues in the middle of the group. *Deci-sion-mode ground rules* relate to planning and choosing what the group does, how the decision process might change at a later stage and so on. *Growth ground rules* are focused on commending sets of behaviours that will intensify personal learning and awareness, appointing self as the guard-ian, pointing out when someone forgets and so on. They might include lis-tening with discernment not judgement, asking for support from others if needed and offering support if you can. Heron also created six dimensions of facilitation (Table 3.3).

TABLE 3.2   Establishing the right climate for learning

Term	Meaning	Example
Congruence	The presenter should practise what he or she preaches.	If the course is about listening skills, the trainer should demonstrate use of listening skills.
Trust building	Participants will work best when there is a trusting atmosphere.	If participants know how feedback will be handled, they are more likely to be more trusting and open with one another.
Clear purposes	The purpose of each event should be clear.	Participants will know why they are undertaking the event.
Emphasize the positive	The emphasis should be on how to get things right.	Give plenty of positive feedback.
Create ownership	Ideas should come from participants themselves.	The trainer should ideally facilitate this learning process in a non-didactic way.
Whole people	Participants' home and non-work lives affect how people feel and learn.	The trainer should enable participants to share these whole-person concerns in a safe environment.
A complete process	The event should be considered as a whole.	Learners should be able and willing to put the training into practice.
Client-centredness	People find most value in the ideas they discover for themselves.	The task of the trainer is to respond to those needs flexibly and individually.

Example of culture setting and ground rules

Culture setting – a set of values as the basis for being and learning together:

- being cooperative and non-competitive;
- creating a safe, supportive and trusting climate;
- being experientially risk-taking and non-defensive;

TABLE 3.3   The six dimensions of facilitation

The six dimensions of facilitation	Facilitative questions
1. The planning dimension	How will the group meet its objectives by means of an effective programme?
2. The meaning dimension	What meaning will be given to group experiences and actions?
3. The confronting dimension	How will the group's consciousness be raised in order to deal with facilitative issues?
4. The feeling dimension	How will emotive aspects of the group be handled?
5. The structuring dimension	How will the structure and methods be formed?
6. The valuing dimension	How will the integrity of the group be nurtured?

- being vulnerable, and open to areas of inner pain, chaos, confusion and lack of skill;
- being open to our personal presence and power;
- exercising autonomy and the voluntary principle;
- participation in the political life of the workshop;
- adopting a spirit of enquiry without dogmatism and authoritarianism;
- exploring multi-modal, multi-stranded learning;
- having an open, transparent workshop process;
- enjoying ourselves;
- affirming confidentiality.

(adapted from Boud and Miller, 1996a: 78)

Reviewing self-practice

The term 'reflection' is evocative of a number of images: mirrors, tranquil scenes in still waters, thinking idly about past times, and forms of meditation come immediately to mind. In the context of education and training, though, the term is often used specifically to signify an important stage in the learning cycle where a complex and deliberate process of thinking about and interpreting an experience is undertaken in order to arrive at a new understanding of events and our part in them.

(Hunt, 2005: 234)

Much of the theory and practice of learning that we introduce throughout the book applies to both participants and providers. Here we simply explore reflection for the purpose of self-review.

Learning from doing is the basis of good practice for experiential providers, but doing is not the same as learning, and the importance of the reflective process is that it is a deliberate, conscious act. From this we find out more about our own learning and working relationships (Hunt, 2005). Hunt reviews the nature of unspoken, 'tacit knowledge', where practitioners 'just know' even though it cannot be described or written about, and considers the dangers of not defining and bounding practice. In offering practitioners something to reflect on, Hunt asks what responsibility the reflective provider has for encouraging participants to reflect on their own work and/ or learning processes. She quotes Johnston and Bradley (Hunt, 2005: 246):

Reflective practice at its best is neither just a set of operational techniques nor a clearly identifiable group of academic skills, but is rather a critical stance. Good reflective practice takes practitioners beyond mere competence towards a willingness and a desire to subject their own taken for granteds and their own activities to serious scrutiny. Competence is not enough. The reflective practitioner has to become, if not an *agent provocateur*, an educational critic who is willing to pursue self and peer appraisal almost to their limits.

Hunt, while offering an interesting theoretical and historical perspective on reflective practice, also examines her own personal experience on the subject of writing as opposed to merely thinking about practice. She focuses on (2005: 248):

- a particularly positive experience;
- an occasion when her interventions seemed to have made a real difference to someone's learning;
- a negative experience where things seemed to go badly wrong;
- an experience she found hard to handle;
- something trivial but which made her think, 'What's going on here?'

Continuous professional development (CPD) involves a systematic maintenance, improvement and broadening of knowledge, skills and personal qualities necessary for execution of professional and technical duties in professional working life. Self-review is an essential element in day-to-day experiences. Maintaining and developing professional competence and sharing expertise are recommended by Benson (1987) in *Working More Creatively with Groups*. In a chapter called 'Keeping your practice going', Benson advises that such reflection and reviewing requires concentration, persistence and hard work. He acknowledges that there is a client/participant expectation that deliverers are whiter than white, and so sometimes it is important that facilitators are also allowed to feel the pain of growing and failing and learning. Benson advises a system of ongoing recording as essential to developing powers of observation. This would enable facilitators to examine individual and group behaviour and to become reflective practitioners, creating dialogue with ourselves, to clarify thoughts, review practice, express feelings, gain a deeper awareness and thus improve. He also offers some survival procedures, as shown below.

Survival procedures for creative group workers

- Avoid crucifixions – do not try to save, rescue, or work it out for everyone all of the time... avoid being seen as a saviour, guru, or charismatic leader because we crucify our messiahs, shoot our presidents, and forget our pop stars more quickly than you would find comfortable.
- Don't push the river upstream – the more you do the less they do... what is required is the light and sensitive touch... learn to work from where the group is and go with the flow...
- Wait quietly until the mud settles – learn to wait and watch and listen. In this way your awareness is focused on the group and not just on your needs. Do not feel that you must intervene immediately.
- Learn to forgive yourself... make mistakes, and feel inadequate at times... be compassionate with yourself...
- Cultivate goodwill – help to explore self-defeating behaviours. And discover more positive ways of being.
- Make up your own rules – no book can give you the rules or the prescription... each group is different... do not be afraid to improvise... use your imagination... and intuition.
- Do your best and that is that.

(adapted from Benson, 1987: 249–51)

Ethical behaviour

Like every other professional, training professionals work by assessments and value judgements. Training implies certain dealings in which one has to make a choice among various options. A choice, which implies solving a certain problem, implies formulating a value judgement about the available alternatives. Such a choice is generally based upon an ethical decision.

(Bergenhenegouwen, 1996: 26)

Helping people to learn is seen as intrinsically good, a virtuous activity that, until recently, has avoided some of the more serious debates about ethical practice. Good practice and competence come with good judgement born out of experience, and to an extent depend on the maturity of the profession. Ethical practice, however, is seen as different; while underpinning good practice, it is also regarded as being concerned with morality and integrity.

The nature of an ethical decision, as opposed to any other decision, is problematic, and the word 'ethics' actually covers a very broad range. The process of defining ethics is difficult, and dictionary definitions variously portray ethics as involving the science of morals, dealing with a branch of philosophy concerned with human character and conduct, or embracing rules of good behaviour and the principles of professional conduct. The principles of ethical conduct and professional practice move beyond legal compliance or satisfying customer needs. We now scrutinize the deeper, fundamental choices trainers face in everyday practice that are of an ethical nature, and analyse how ethical issues are constructed within a social, political and environmental context, and guided by principles of virtue and moral conduct, all of which change over time.

There is of course an ethical dimension to all that an experiential provider does, and one could therefore reason that all choices have something to do with ethics; it is only in their relative importance that they differ. The choice, for example, of deciding to take a contract or decline it and leave it to someone else, deciding which training methods would be most suitable for a set of clients, or how much or how little preparation needs to be done could involve ethical dimensions. At the most simplistic level, ethics might be considered as 'moral relativism', involving a set of choices between right and wrong behaviour, intentional or unintentional. There may not be a 'right' or a 'wrong' answer, but choice is inexorably linked with morality.

Petrick and Quinn (1997) regard ethics as the study of individual and collective moral awareness, which relate to judgement, character and conduct. In attempting to define ethics these writers embrace personal and institutional issues, fairness, exploitation, morality and right or wrong conduct. They introduce the breadth of the ethical debate that we now analyse in more detail. But first we consider a simple scenario. Read this and then reflect on what you might do.

Practical case study: facing difficult choices – a scenario

This is an account of a management development event that actually happened, with many factors altered to disguise the identities of the people involved.

The incident

On the last evening of a three-day team-building event, following the evening meal, many of the delegates from a creative computer design company stayed up drinking in the bar into the early hours. This culminated in a fire extinguisher being set off at around 5 am, a vacuum cleaner being left switched on outside someone's room, and generally lots of noise and disturbance right through the night.

Many of those involved in these 'high-spirited games' were high-profile individuals in the company, including the CEO, and the most senior instructor representing the outdoor management development company.

The next day

This was the final day of the programme. At breakfast there were two distinct camps: those who thought that the previous evening had been 'a good laugh' (ie those who had participated in the late-night pranks) and those who were extremely upset at the goings-on, owing to the disturbance, the lack of consideration for others and the image that it presented of the organization. Some delegates were sufficiently upset to be all set to abandon the remaining day of the programme and return to work. 'If that's what you call team building, you can forget it,' one person was heard to say. One group of two or three delegates were particularly offended by some of the language used towards them and others the previous night, and felt that 'apologies were in order'.

The intended programme for the final day was as follows:

09.00	Travel to water park (about 45 minutes' drive by minibus)
10.00–12.30	Land-/water-based activity, culminating in giant raft build
12.30–13.45	Final review; formal end of programme
13.45–14.30	Return to hotel; delegates depart

The antics of the previous night had resulted in a 'team' that was now worse off than when the programme had started. The group were just about to leave for the last morning of events. A few people, including the facilitators and the managing director, were left in the hotel breakfast room. If you were one of a number of facilitators hired to work on this event by the outdoor management development company... what would you do to rescue this event?

The answer to the scenario might be, 'It depends.' It depends on whether you hold the view that the outdoor instructors in this scenario were simply contracted to 'help' on the management development programme. The situation might have been avoided by a company policy on alcohol, or adherence to a code of conduct. Were the instructors involved guilty of unprofessional conduct or was it really a corporate managerial issue for their senior staff to deal with? Did the instructors get involved in the drunken party at the request of the director, or is that not significant? Should the instructors involved have courteously bowed out early on that evening? These are some of the many moral decisions about the conduct of the clients and facilitator alike. One text that covers these and other ethical issues presents over 60 dilemmas. They are outlined for discussion in *Outdoor Experiential Leadership: Scenarios Describing Incidents, Dilemmas, & Opportunities* (2006) by Smith and Allison.

Ethical relativism is reflected in the nature of one's personal style of operating. Margerison (1988: 103), for example, refers to four consulting role models: doctor, travel agent, detective and salesperson. Margerison describes the consulting styles in detail, and suggests, 'We all have an approach to giving advice based upon a consulting model. It may not be written down, but it reflects itself in the way in which we consult and give advice.' The four consulting styles provide an indication of mindsets that can occur in the consultation process. The medical analogy is of a doctor approaching the client or organization, looking for *symptoms*, making a *diagnosis* and then *prescribing* the *medicine*. The travel agent approach is question based and more client centred, where customers get what they ask for. The idea that consulting is a form of detective work or investigation generates a consulting style based on finding the *culprit* who committed the *offence*, apportioning *blame* and instigating punitive solutions. Finally, the salesperson sells the organization a pre-designed intervention to address their needs.

Personal and organizational styles and cultural differences may occasionally be difficult to separate from the notion of integrity. Jones (2001) conducted research into ethical practice and interviewed trainers who anonymously admitted to placing bets on consulting and training sales outcomes, and competing with one another to get contracts. As a result they felt they were guilty of unethical practice. They wanted clients to take as many contracts as they could possibly sell in order to win bets. This, they claim, was due to the organizational culture that they worked in, one they found difficult to resist, and their description of events potentially locates them as victims, blaming the organizational vow for this ethical erosion. Personal integrity has a high value placed on it, yet an organizational pressure to perform can result in inexcusable behaviour (see Whyte, 1960) and some organizations have set up confidential phone 'hotlines' for employees to report ethical concerns anonymously.

Block (2000) in *Flawless Consulting* refers to the shadow side of consulting, and argues that the negative reputation of some consultants is more to do with ethics than competence. Part of the problem, Block suggests, is due to promises made and the commercialization of the 'service', which can become too packaged and standardized. Block makes reference to a number of tensions between care and commercialization; of promising magic through re-engineering or the excellence movement; of entertainment rather than learning; of collusion between top management and consultants; of buying fashion trends. He also cautions that all consultants will have stepped over the moral line at one time or another, and that people must not try to solve all the problems in becoming what he calls the 'super-someone'.

A question of balance

Learning providers working with corporate clients encounter conflicting views on how 'workers' should be looked after by 'management', and this can result in a climate within a programme being potentially at odds with the everyday world of the participants. The same issues can arise with any programme provider and client, such as 'youth' and 'youth workers'. Phillips and Fraser (1982) argue that if such programmes encourage people to develop skills that are not supported or valued by the organization, then the scene is set for a battlefield of recriminations.

Money also underpins the climate and operating behaviour. Dybeck (2000) debates the balance of commercialism and altruism, and illustrates his discussion with reference to the history of Brathay, a charitable organization based in the UK Lake District National Park. Dybeck describes how financial pressures during the history of the organization meant that it was difficult to maintain youth development initiatives, an area of work on which Brathay was founded. He argues that the charitable roots of many experiential providers like Brathay influence their operational culture and can create a tension with some aspects of private sector commercialism. Scott, the founder of Brathay, stated in 1967 that 'the idea that... good fortune called for a share of the family wealth to be allocated for charitable purposes has no doubt been the origin of most of the existing charitable trusts' (Dybeck, 2000: 113). There are also fundamental differences between the public sector and the private sector in terms of accountability, to the public or shareholders. These dualities create a wide range of ethical issues, for example:

- client centred and organization centred;
- workers and management;
- needs and wants;
- work and life;
- soft and hard skills;
- commercial and charitable;
- business and environment;
- corporate loyalty versus personal values;
- whistle blowing or keeping quiet.

Many ethical issues simply involve the careful balancing of the needs of those involved. However, ethics can also encompass a broader raft of organizational issues such as health and safety, balancing the needs of individuals as well as the organization and the selection of consultants. Ethical decisions might also involve training practice, confidentiality, sexuality, copyright issues, cultural issues, dishonesty and improper behaviour. Ultimately all providers have to decide what makes sense to them, and in so doing construct their own moral code. Some decisions are more difficult than others, as we shall now explore, and this requires all facilitators to take responsibility to review and learn from past experience.

A different kind of ethical issue arises in youth development programmes, where the 'highs' experienced on outdoor wilderness adventures can be temporary, and later prove debilitating. Euphoric adventures can leave young people vulnerable in the longer term, with subsequent feelings of disappointment, feeling low and feeling let down on return to their home environment (Davis-Berman and Berman, 1999). However, such disillusionment and potential crisis can be avoided by good practice, and Barrett and Greenaway (1995) suggest ways to overcome these negative effects, recommending a four-stage realignment approach to change:

- close-to-home introduction;
- Outward Bound away-from-home experience;
- city-bound – working on preparation for the last stage;
- homeward-bound – for supported transfer of learning.

Tragedies and accidents also generate considerable deliberation on the subject of ethics. On 9 May 1996, five expeditions launched an assault on Everest. Twenty-four hours later one person had already died and 23 other men and women, mainly amateurs and paying clients, were struggling for their lives. In all, eight climbers died that day. Climbing protocol on the crucial turnaround time on the summit attempt was ignored, and three guides, with very high levels of professional practice, lost their lives. Speculation took place over the reason for the tragedy. The media spotlight, the competitive nature of the business, the commercial impact of a successful summit, personal reputation and oxygen deprivation all entered the ethical arena in the debate that followed. The event has been extensively analysed in books and journals (see, for example, Dickinson, 1998; Krakauer, 1997), and it is used as a case study in ethics by Hunt and Wurdinger (1999: 129). They point out that one guide:

> [who] died as a result of his attempting to aid his stricken client rises to an extremely high level of a key moral virtue – courage. Similar acts of courage evidenced themselves throughout this expedition both by guides and by clients. Thus one can see that this case is extremely complex in its mix of virtues and vices. Internal and external goods germane to the practice are interwoven in a manner that defies simple judgement and analysis.

The negative use of personal skills is to be found in all walks of life. Experiential providers occasionally witness individuals who use their newly acquired interpersonal skills, such as assertiveness training, to sustain negative attitudes towards work, confidently yet dishonestly defending their negative 'can't be bothered' behaviours with assertive vigour. Likewise corporate interest in emotional intelligence can be used for dubious reasons, as a form of emotional engineering.

Emotional engineering

Teaching people the 'corporate smile', for example, might be interpreted as emotional engineering, and this raises ethical issues concerning the authenticity of imposed and artificially generated positive moods. Fineman (1997: 13) argues:

> learning is inextricably emotional and of emotions. The traditional cognitive approach to management learning has obscured the presence and role of emotion... we need more explicit frameworks, derived from the literature on emotion, to place emotion as both a product and a process of learning. Special attention is required to the growth of corporate emotion engineering.

Fineman (1997: 18) talks of the management of McDonaldized jobs that 'have been subjected to fine-tuned routines of emotion control and programming', and refers to the work of Hochschild (1983), who writes about the psychological 'work' done and the corporate 'feeling rules', in personally maintaining the corporately desired impressions. The term 'emotional labour' is used. Emotion in this sense is seen as something in the human machine to be controlled and learnt, in a neo-Tayloristic form. Emotion-as-performance is a competency that does not really require an ability to read or express emotion in any depth or variety. Fineman argues, in contrast to Goleman (1996: 18), that the gung-ho view is that 'In an era of tough love it is the emotionally lean who are most likely to survive.' Hopfl and Linstead (1997: 9) are also critical of the scientific analytical approach by Goleman, and they suggest (1997: 5) that 'rationality has led to a relative neglect of emotional issues in organisational life'. Emotions are often dealt with in a functional way so that we 'discount our feelings, deny them to ourselves, project them on to others, rationalize them away or keep them private... treatments of emotions in the workplace concentrate on handling at the surface level what is apparent in conflict, or the encouragement of more open displays of the more positive emotions...' (Hopfl and Linstead, 1997: 8).

The corporate demand for staff training in emotional intelligence creates ethical issues for learners and experiential providers alike. Boud and Miller (1996a) describe a 'stripping down' of emotional intelligence so as to reshape employee attitudes for corporate profit. Fineman (1997: 19) in a similar vein argues that the ability to feel 'shame, embarrassment or guilt' is crucial to making ethical judgements, and that the push for business profits can easily override personal conscience. Fear of being 'caught out' and 'public pressure', he suggests, shape management actions, rather than the conscience of the organization. Reid and Barrington (1999: 142–43) argue that loyalty to the organization should take priority over and above personal beliefs or 'favoured causes'. These suggestions can create tensions and emotional conflict. In having concern for the environment, Greenpeace comment that too often they have to act as the 'active conscience of industrial society' (Rose, 1996).

In exploring ethics we conclude that the subject is essentially about choices that concern practice and conduct. The broad and boundless nature of ethics means that models and guidelines can be appropriate to help providers solve ethical problems.

Ethical models

Priest and Gass (in Barnes, 2000) divide ethical issues into two types: *principle ethics* and *virtue ethics*. Others refer to these respectively as *coded ethics* and *situation ethics* (Scott Peck, 1997). Principle or coded ethical issues are answered by predetermined rules or principles. Many of these are to be found in the codes of good practice we examine in detail next. A well-known example is the Ten Commandments. Decisions become a matter of principle, and as such they can be seen as relatively independent of the specific situation. A facilitator looks to these externally set codes or rules to inform judgement. External agencies often create these socially constructed, *de facto* sets of basic tenets. Virtue or situation ethics on the other hand involve answers that have to be considered in the light of each specific situation or scenario as it occurs. They might, for example, depend on personally held values and beliefs, or be culturally determined. Here the facilitators have to look inside themselves to find the answers.

Choices and judgement are value-laden and so involve axiology and morality, but holding the moral high ground is always risky. Hunt (1995) refers to the internal and external success of the goods and services provided. If the contracting organization believes that a good service has been provided, but the provider knows that corners were cut and that the work was not of a high standard, the external goods were successful but the internal goods were less successful. The facilitator did not have the satisfaction of a job well done. The latter then is one of virtue, where standards of excellence are set internally by each professional facilitator. Hunt (1995: 335) quotes McIntyre as saying 'a virtue is an acquired human quality, the possession and exercise of which tends to enable us to achieve these goals which are internal to practices and the lack of which prevents us from achieving such goals'. Hunt argues that it is not just technical skills and interpersonal skills that make up ethical practice; intellectual virtue and moral virtue also make up ethical practice. Knowing how to perform technically and interpersonally is intellectual virtue, but this has to be guided and propelled towards a proper end by moral virtue.

The ethical subjects operate at three levels, and all stakeholders share some responsibility for setting and maintaining the ground rules, climate and behaviour. The negative consequences of not doing so can incur differing degrees of harm. We create a tier system (see below), similar to a risk management approach.

Ethical subjects – three levels:

1 **meta issues** – societal, trends, contextual, future;
2 **organizational-level issues** – culture, state actions and interventions;
3 **personal issues** – methods and behaviours.

Ethical decision making – three tiers:

1 **most serious** – because they affect large numbers of people, cause greatest harm, are on the verge of illegality;
2 **less serious** – for example, deliberately misleading people;
3 **less harm** – might include unintentional actions that negatively affect people.

Similarly, Kitchener (in Hunt, 1995) offers a model that creates a five-step approach to help facilitators find the answer to ethical questions, suggesting the issue is moved on up through each layer if the answer is not reachable at the previous layer:

1 **intuitive** – gut reaction as to what is right;
2 **option listing** – options, ramifications and outcomes are considered and weighed up;
3 **ethical rules** – written in established codes of conduct;
4 **ethical principles** – autonomy, fidelity, justice, choice, loyalty, respect;
5 **ethical theory** – either a *balancing* approach, taking action that has less harm to clients, with the greatest positive outcomes to the greatest numbers; or a *universality* approach, creating a decision that might be applied to all similar situations.

Thus we see that ethical choices can be made by individuals and underpinned by their own culture, styles of operating, philosophy, concerns and moral values. They are internally set. Next, we explore the nature of externally decided, institutionally set codes of practice.

Codes of practice

Ethics then is the application of moral standards to good practice. For more experienced providers the decision-making process becomes intuitive. Hunt argues that ethics should have a central role in the maturing profession of experiential education and offers two scenarios to illustrate his central debate about the role of virtue between and within professions. One involves a person who is under the control of psychiatric care; the other involves a person who faces a corporate edict. At a basic level both scenarios described by Hunt revolve around client decisions to participate in experiential activities, and the consequent use of coercion and intervention by others. In the first scenario the decision to come down from a high-ropes course appears to involve three people. The participant is a patient at a psychiatric hospital, and he wishes to come down. The instructor, in adopting a principle of 'challenge by choice', agrees to bring the client down, but is asked not to do so by the psychiatrist from the hospital, who informs the instructor that the youth is about to face an important psychological breakthrough. The facilitator is reminded that she is merely the employee of the hospital and is therefore under the supervision of the psychiatrist. Hunt then presents scenario two as a corporate scene where a woman refuses to participate in an activity, claiming that it has nothing to do with management skills. The CEO intervenes and suggests that non-participation will reflect badly on the company. The facilitator decides that the decision to intervene with staff of the company is ultimately the decision of the CEO.

Hunt portrays these scenarios to unravel the deeper and more profound issue of whether practitioners set their own standards that govern their work, and the extent to which they merely act as technicians, providing a service to organizations. The extent to which the experienced practitioner is *permitted* to intervene in this relationship between the organization and its members, or *morally obliged* to do so, is embodied in the notion of 'professional practice'. The relationship hinges on power, consent and respect for the individual, and the extent to which this is dealt with within the profession or left to others who contract the service.

Ethical responsibility might then lie with individuals, organizations or, at a higher level, the profession or the state. What then do professional bodies regard as the basic guidance required for the development of professional codes of good practice?

Professional bodies and the professional codes of practice

The professional bodies regard facilitator responsibility as stretching beyond the boundaries of caring for participants or clients. There are other considerations outlined in numerous codes of conduct for development trainers and facilitators, produced by many associations and institutions, and they have many common ingredients. The globally constituted members of the DEEP initiative explore five main responsibilities, whereas the Institute for Outdoor Learning (formerly the Association for Outdoor Learning) in the UK examines four areas (see Table 3.4). The latter code is detailed in the box below.

TABLE 3.4 Broad categories of responsibility

Global DEEP Initiative	UK Institute for Outdoor Learning
1. Responsibility to self.	1. Professional integrity.
2. Responsibility for professional development and conduct.	2. Professional responsibilities and relationships.
3. Responsibility to clients/customers.	3. Professional standards.
4. Responsibility to profession.	4. Environmental and cultural responsibilities.
5. Global responsibility.	

Institute for Outdoor Learning code of professional conduct

A fundamental principle of membership is an understanding that the conduct of each member can be justified ethically and morally at all times and will bring credit to themselves and the Institute and the outdoor profession.

The purpose of this Code is to set out the standards of behaviour agreed to and upheld by members of the Institute as they cultivate and promote special values and importance of outdoor learning experiences.

1 Professional integrity

- Members should maintain the highest of standards and values. Members should demonstrate fairness, consistency, honesty, tolerance, compassion, truthfulness and discretion during their work out of doors.

- The Institute may be judged by the conduct of its Trustees, Officers and Members. Consequently all members of the Institute should conduct themselves in a befitting manner.

- The logo of the Institute may not be used for personal or commercial purposes.

2 Professional responsibility and relationships

- Members have a duty of care to each participant and should accept their responsibility to protect the dignity, privacy and safety of all those for whom they are responsible. Members should define and respect the boundaries between personal and working life and never misuse a leadership position whatever the age of the client.

- When dealing with other members, agencies, clients, students, sponsors or the general public, members should present themselves as responsible persons and in a manner that inspires confidence and trust.

- Members should manage the activities for which they are responsible with due regard to student, client and staff emotional and physical welfare, complying with all legal requirements and Health and Safety guidelines.

- Members should accept that discrimination on the grounds of race, gender and sexual orientation have no place in outdoor learning and should be challenged if displayed.

- Members should safeguard confidential information relating to participants and use discretion when there is a particular need to share essential information with professional colleagues.

- Where a member delegates any activity or welfare responsibilities they should understand that the ultimate responsibility remains with themselves.

- Members should respect fellow members. Public or private reference to the conduct, integrity or quality of service of another member should be expressed with due care, accepting that there is a clear moral obligation to challenge unprofessional conduct.

3 Professional standards

- Members should work only within the limits of their competence and experience, acknowledging and adhering to commonly accepted, current best practice and standards.

- Members should maintain and develop their personal, professional competence and when possible share their expertise with other members and contribute to the debate on professional matters.

- Members should respect the needs, traditions, practices, special competencies and responsibilities of other institutions, associations, agencies and professions that share a common interest in Outdoor Learning.

4 Environmental and cultural responsibilities

- Members should conserve the natural environment, endorsing the principles of sustainable use and minimum impact.

- Members should be sensitive to the impact of their operation on the local community and cultural setting within which they work and minimize any adverse effect.

- Members should encourage knowledge, understanding and respect for the cultural setting within which they work.

FIGURE 3.1 Environmental issues: people and responses

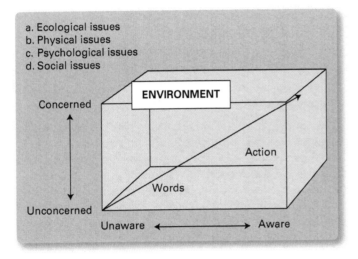

a. Ecological issues
b. Physical issues
c. Psychological issues
d. Social issues

ENVIRONMENT

Concerned

Action

Words

Unconcerned

Unaware ⟵⟶ Aware

Good practice: the environment

Most ethical codes of practice embrace environmental concerns, and the reduction of environmental impact can take place in many ways. Cooper (1998: 90–91) classifies the negative impact we have as ecological (disturbance to wildlife, trampling, etc), physical (damage to property, footpath erosion, etc), psychological (lack of respect for others, when one group or person affects the enjoyment of another) and social (noise, litter, dangerous driving, etc). The position people take towards environmental issues varies considerably (see Figure 3.1). Environmental impact reduction requires the right attitude, a degree of environmental education and understanding and, ultimately, a preparedness to take action. All three are important.

Support for the improvement of the natural environment by experiential providers who use the outdoors might include a whole range of new ideas, utilizing a broader range of instruments of change:

- carrying out experiential activities that contribute to the environment;
- stating environmental support through policy or on letterheads or products;
- encouraging the education and awareness of learners; signing up to and working with voluntary codes or charters of conduct towards the environment;
- reducing waste and dumping by using recycled materials creatively;
- directing tasks and practical action towards a productive end – such as tree planting or restoration;

- making donations to direct practical action groups;
- encouraging governing bodies to support environmental research;
- using annual access agreements or licences to caves, land or water to create fees for environmental repair;
- where possible, purchasing environmentally friendly clothing and outdoor equipment;
- considering carbon debt repayments and other innovative schemes (making courses carbon neutral).

Ironically, a great deal of experiential learning takes place in the natural outdoors, yet few recognize and fully value this free resource. Sadly, corporate environmental awareness training rarely utilizes the powerful attributes of the natural environment as a learning medium, as we discuss in Chapter 4. Environmental awareness training still takes place predominantly in classroom settings, and environmental concern is largely seen to be the domain of engineers, scientists, and health and safety specialists. The innovative use of the natural environment as the location for learning is described in many sections of this book. We hope some of our thinking will offer you new ideas.

Conclusion

It is not possible to create a once-and-for-all set of rules to guide good practice and behaviour, as the subject remains under continuous debate and negotiation from all stakeholders. Acting in a befitting manner, creating high standards and values, demonstrating fairness, consistency, honesty, tolerance, compassion, truthfulness and discretion, all form the underpinning conduct of good providers of experiential learning, whether it be facilitating, coaching, training or educating. We might look elsewhere, to external institutions, for codes of behaviour and guidance, or we might look within ourselves to find the answers.

> If people live with criticism, they learn to condemn. If people live with hostility, they learn to fight. If people live with ridicule, they learn to be shy. If people live with shame, they learn to feel guilt. If people live with tolerance, they learn to be patient. If people live with encouragement, they learn confidence. If people live with praise, they learn to appreciate. If people live with fairness, they learn justice. If people live with security, they learn to have faith. If people live with approval, they learn to like themselves. If people live with acceptance and friendship, he or she learns to find love in the world.

(Anon)

The next six chapters focus on each of the tumblers in the learning combination lock model.

PART TWO
The learning combination lock model

Learning environments: spaces and places (The belonging dimension)

> *The science of designing learning environments is currently remarkably under-developed.* FEILDEN, 2004: X

Introduction

The sense of belonging is affected by the outer world experience: the people around us and the more-than-human world. The social aspects are covered throughout this book and so this chapter will mostly focus on the effect of the more-than-human world, especially the spaces and places where the experience of learning occurs.

Are there optimal places to learn? This important question remains largely unanswered in contemporary literature on learning, yet the place in which we learn, as we shall now show, is very significant to the learning experience. This is a two-way process: the place influences human behaviour and human learning. Interaction occurs with the human (social) world and a more-than-human world (MTHW) (Abram, 1997). In this chapter we explore a diverse range of places or spaces, outdoor and indoor, real or virtual, social or more than human, natural or artificial, private or public, formal and informal that can influence the experience of learning. These are the issues that are the concerns of the first cog in the learning combination lock: the *belonging* dimension.

Often learning programmes focus on activities, with less focus on the needs of space or place. This can reduce learning effectiveness. Indeed there is a saying that if you were a fish the last thing you would discover is the water around you! As we shall now demonstrate, there is a close relationship between learning and working, learning activity design and the learning environment/s in which they take place.

The importance of space for reading, thinking and talking

An approach to reflective learning, referred to as *'Coffee and Papers'* (see Beard, 2010) got its name from learning and development settings in hotel lounges where the learning experience was designed to be comparable to reading the Sunday newspapers, in a relaxed environment, with a relaxed but focused mind state. Essentially it consists of an invitation to individuals to read themed articles and to intentionally relax in an environment that is special for each individual. *Coffee and Papers* typically generates high levels of learner engagement and knowledge generation through the process of individual reading in a retreat simulation, followed by social conversational learning. The experience is designed to develop a specific sensory-cognition, or body–mind state of 'relaxed alertness'. Individuals experience comfort, with a degree of solitude, to enhance concentration and thinking. Coffees, teas, fruit juices, croissants and fruit add to the sensory experience. The quiet solo experience involves individual, internal conversations. After a period of solo reading the group re-assemble and construct collective conversations, critically exploring the range of readings. The acquired collective knowledge can be substantial. One senior manager said of one such session:

> One of the more effective learning community development exercises, in my view, followed the coffee and papers sessions each morning. During these sessions, differing views concerning the same articles were discussed and new insights developed based on individual experience outside the articles. This led to a spin of ideas that spurred more new ideas, and re-shaped some of my initial thoughts of the articles. It appeared that many of the participants shared this experience regarding the coffee and papers sessions.

The articles are themed, such as organizational development (OD) and taken from both scholarly and professional journals: *Harvard Business Review, People Management,* and *Management Learning, Management Education and Development, Training and Development, Industrial and Commercial Training, Sloan Management Review,* and many others. Hardly Sunday morning reading! In the corporate world one chief executive sat in her stockinged feet on a stool in a hotel lounge, surrounded by strawberries coated in chocolate, and coffee and croissants and papers. She said: 'Colin, I am in heaven. I never have the time to read any more. I have lost the power to think or read with any depth these days… I am enjoying this experience so much!' Senior executives admit to the pleasure at effectively being given permission to experience an extended period of *thinking* and *concentrating*. The *place* signifies that *time* for concentration is important and a legitimate extension of work.

The UK National Health Service facilities managers and HRD managers concerned with new workplaces, and the various barriers to change thrown up by organizational culture (see Beard & Price, 2013) might find a coffee and papers approach a pragmatic means of gaining executive buy-in to the strategic possibilities inherent in new workplaces. The *coffee and papers* experience had a profound effect on a whole organization. Staff in the UK's National Health Service (NHS) have responsibilities to sustain professional development through reading of evidence-based clinical practice. Time to read about such clinical practice, however, had largely diminished by the dominance of everyday activities; the *doing* dimension of learning. Concentrated reading and the subsequent collective sharing was not happening for a number of reasons, including that of guilt associated with relaxed reading at work. Reading might not be interpreted as *doing* work. However, the staff of one primary care trust (PCT), having experienced *coffee and papers* on a training programme, put forward what turned out eventually to be a successful proposal brought to senior managers under the workplace umbrella. The proposal, as part of an 'Inspiration Award' scheme in 2009, included some of the following required actions suggested in order to implement this idea:

- Encourage staff to write *reading time* into their objectives.

- Develop a marketing campaign across the PCT showing that it's okay to sit and read clinical material.

- Provide education for managers to help them understand how to enable staff to absorb current evidence.

- Understand the cost of allowing staff time to absorb evidence, but also calculating and understanding the cost, service and other benefits.

- Purchase resources to make reading easier.

The provision of, and the informal legitimization of reflective space within working environments is under explored. The importance of such experiences to the corporate progress is highlighted by Ray Anderson the well-known CEO of the Georgia based, global company Interface Carpets: when he realized he had little understanding of the notion of sustainable development he started reading more widely, and more critically, about his role in it as a business leader in society. His reading changed his views, his business and his life. The company is widely recognized as leading the way globally in business sustainability, winning many international awards. Significantly, the dawning experience for Anderson, often referred to as an epiphany, was initiated through reading with an open yet critical mind.

What we are witnessing is the evolution of new spatial ecologies. The richness is exciting: spaces and places for human functioning are diversifying. Places and spaces are designed for or occupied for various functions or purposes: for meetings, for creativity, for sharing and constructing knowledge, for reading and quiet reflective work, just to name a few. A new city-wide ecology of spaces might also be emerging, as highlighted in the case examples described below.

Space for working and learning — ECHQ & GCHQ

In the knowledge economy learning and working are converging phenomena. Pragmatism guided the redevelopment of a London headquarters of global property consultancy E C Harris. The head office or ECHQ, as it is labelled, was re-designed as a solution to several strategic challenges, notably differentiation and rejuvenation of their surveying practice, intent on projecting itself as 'the built asset consultancy'. Space utilization is their business. The developed design involved some 20 per cent of the available space as a semi-public front of house with clever but discreet security. Their workplace was reconfigured, tiered and layered with some 900 staff accommodated by 545 'work stations'. The project is credited with dramatic increases in profitability, staff satisfaction, and knowledge generation, as well as a significant reduction in space requirement per head and CO_2 emissions.

The three key layers of the workplace were as follows: Layer one created public areas available to anyone including the practice's clients and collaborators. This area was welcome 'public' space, for staff and visitors involving the café/social dynamic as a conversational form. Layer two was available though less formally recognized for 'friends' of ECH to have space to work, online, with a desk. Layer three was a restricted 'staff' hot desk and milieu of varied light office spaces, designed to achieve a richer range of spaces for different conversations, with efficient density without packing, and allowing for 'clusters' of mobile teams. The result was that the traditional desk is no longer the fixed space at which a worker is expected to sit. ECHQ approach for me was significant in that if it were to be replicated in collaboration with other businesses in the City of London, then possibly, for the first time, there would be an ecology of spaces and places providing a network of home and 'away' spaces, for inner and outer conversations that mirror the understanding of the whole person spatial-functional awareness of management learning and knowledge creation in a rapidly changing world (Beard & Price, 2012)

GCHQ is a very different organization, concerned with, for example, anti-terrorism and cyber-space monitoring. The benefits from a significant workplace re-design were significant. Their new circular building looks rather like a football stadium from the air. The outer ring, however, is not seating as in a stadium but a circular area or walkway called The Street. The new building encourages new ways of working, reducing response times, and the outer circular ring of walking space is the modern equivalent of the peripatos. A work-anywhere culture was developed: more open plan areas, greater desk and knowledge sharing, and agile team working.

Indoor learning: the new classroom

Indoor learning environments in schools, colleges, universities and train-ing centres are undergoing a metamorphosis, and change of label, from 'classrooms' to 'learning spaces'. The changing language is a signpost of the transformation. Future learning spaces will provide greater flexibility and mobility of people, knowledge, furniture and other artefacts (see Figure 4.1).

It is said that students spend approximately 20,000 hours in classrooms by the time they graduate (Fraser, 2001). Despite this fact, little is known about designing learning space: the classroom has remained relatively unchanged over the past 100 years! Typically, indoor learning environments have been strongly associated with 'lecture theatres', 'classrooms', and 'textbooks'. The term 'learning space' embraces a somewhat contemporary and broader campus: including e-learning technology and virtual discus-sion groups; distance education; common informal areas such as halls and other social group spaces; informal furnishing such as sofas; outdoor green spaces such as woodlands, lakes and decking; and amphitheatres, atrium- and mall-style spaces. Individually tailored learning is currently in vogue, as is technological change. Experiential learning will increasingly reach out into local communities and the broader learning environment of the future will be considerably different.

Contemporary thinking about learning environments is reflected in a broad definition offered by Indiana University, who define a learning envi-ronment as:

> A physical, intellectual, psychological environment which facilitates learning through connectivity and community.
>
> (http://www.indiana.edu/)

One substantial university research programme on learning environments in the United States notes that:

> Well established research shows that students learn best when they are actively engaged rather than being passive observers... there are three avenues an

institution can promote to foster active student learning. First, certain teaching methodologies, such as problem based learning, promote active student involvement. Second, the classroom furnishings can either enhance or hinder active student learning. Thus, tables and moveable chairs enhance while fixed-row seating hinders active learning. Finally technologies which require student initiative, such as interactive video-discs, promote active learning.

(http://www.-lib.iupui.edu/itt/planlearn/execsumm.html)

Physical issues such as furnishings, air quality and acoustics, lighting and colour clearly impact on learning.

The architectural mantra is that 'form should follow function'. Form has, however, traditionally dictated function: many learning spaces in schools and universities throughout the world are designed by facilities managers. In the UK, a Design Council report, *Kit for Purpose: Design to deliver creative learning* (2005), notes that current learning environments tend to:

- reduce the range of teaching and learning styles possible and affect the interaction between teacher and student;
- undermine the value placed on learning;
- not adapt to individual needs;
- hinder creativity;
- be inefficient, wasting time and effort;
- cost more in the long term.

The pedagogy of space remains underdeveloped. The design of learning spaces in formal education has traditionally been restricted by complex building regulations and procurement procedures. But new designs are now emerging, with a focus on the kinds of spaces required for modern learning activities: group learning, spaces for deep concentration, spaces for being innovative or creative, for being analytical, and spaces for quiet reading (see the 'coffee and papers' exercise earlier in this chapter). Architects use a range of terms for such spaces, such as *den* for team learning, *club* for knowledge interaction, *hive* for individual processing and *cell* for concentrated study.

Becher (1989) uses an 'ecological' approach to workplace design, and refers to the need to observe the movements of people or tribes and their creation of territoriality. This notion of 'territoriality' highlights power and politics and ownership in the use of learning spaces. Ideally, experiential learning might enable learners to be architects of their own space, with opportunities being provided to continually reshape and redesign psychological and physical space, as individuals and/or in collaboration with others.

Both indoor and outdoor learning spaces, whether real or virtual, are usually constructed spaces rather than 'natural', thus presenting opportunities to rethink and reconfigure space for learning. The ubiquitous garden shed, or its equivalent, has significance for individuals as a place of inventive learning. Research by Golding (2005) in Australia highlights gender issues in the use of learning spaces by rural communities. From a diverse sample of men in rural towns, around 95 per cent prefer to learn in practical situations, hands on, and outside wherever possible. For many rural Australian men with limited formal literacies, appropriate space may take the form of a fire shed or outside at an agricultural field day or demonstration. The existing literature on the effectiveness of situated learning supports such research observations (eg Lave and Wenger, 1991). People prefer to learn in situated contexts: often in practical situations akin to where they work or feel 'at home'. Ongoing research has also been conducted since the 1980s on a neighbourhood 'house'-type model that is attractive to women but not necessarily to men.

The outdoor elements of the learning 'campus' are increasingly important to the student choice of university, affecting the quality of the learning experience. Such spaces might include timber decking, amphitheatres and artificial lakes; these informal spaces are increasingly being used for more formal learning, with learning spilling out of the classroom into such spaces. Innovative relaxation 'lecture theatres' with seat hammocks slung from roof beams are to be found in Turku Polytechnic in Finland and such examples serve to illustrate how the learning environment can be specifically designed so as to enhance certain mood or mind states, such as relaxed alertness, a concept we explore later in the book.

Learning spaces also have micro-climates consisting of tiles, ceilings, walls, floors, desks, books, computers and many other objects, all of which can be used in creative ways to enhance the learner experience. The floor is ideal to create models and concepts with large groups of people, using masking tape, large pieces of coloured card and other training aids. The walls are places to create 'graffiti walls' using decorating lining paper, so that people might contribute thoughts or reactions to events through drawing or scribbling words or phrases. Walls can also be used to place and move stick-it labels, or to project colours or images to influence mood. It is likely that futuristic classrooms will have walls that become large functional working spaces, made of glass in the form of a touch screen that can be written on. In this way, handwritten material and electronic text, pictures, diagrams and other images can be interchangeable and moved by hand (rather than with a mouse), in a similar way to the functions found in interactive whiteboards. This is good news for the kinaesthetic learner who prefers not to sit behind a desk for long periods. Technological developments increasingly influence the design and use of learning space, with interactive whiteboards and large plasma screens emerging in classrooms, enabling the capture of 'live' intellectual property.

FIGURE 4.1 Twelve school design principles based on brain-based learning research (from Lackey and Fielding, 1998)

Twelve school design principles

1 Rich, stimulating environments – colour, texture, 'teaching architecture', displays created by students (not teacher) so students have connection and ownership of the product.

2 Places for group learning – breakout spaces, alcoves, table groupings to facilitate social learning and stimulate the social brain; turning breakout spaces into living rooms for conversation.

3 Linking indoor and outdoor places – movement, engaging the motor cortex linked to the cerebral cortex for oxygenation.

4 Corridors and public places containing symbols of the school community's larger purpose to provide coherency and meaning that increases motivation (warning: go beyond slogans).

5 Safe places – reduce threat, especially in urban settings.

6 Variety of places – provide a variety of places of different shapes, colour, light, nooks and crannies.

7 Changing displays – changing the environment, interacting with the environment stimulates brain development. Provide display areas that allow for stage set type constructions to further push the envelope with regard to environmental change.

8 Have all the resources available – provide educational, physical and the variety of settings in close proximity to encourage rapid development of ideas generated in a learning episode. This is an argument for wet areas/ science, computer-rich workspaces all integrated and not segregated. Multiple functions and cross-fertilization of ideas are the primary goal.

9 Flexibility – a common principle in the past continues to be relevant. Many dimensions of flexibility of place are reflected in other principles.

10 Active/passive places – students need places for reflection and retreat away from others for interpersonal intelligence as well as places for active engagement for interpersonal intelligence.

11 Personalized space – the concept of home base needs to be emphasized more than the metal locker or the desk; this speaks to the principle of uniqueness; the need to allow learners to express their self-identity, personalize their special places and places to express territorial behaviours.

12 The community-at-large as the optimal learning environment – need to find ways to fully utilize all urban and natural environments as the primary learning setting, the school as the fortress of learning needs to be challenged and conceptualized more as a resource-rich learning centre that supplements life-long learning. Technology, distance learning, community and business partnerships, home-based learning, all need to be explored as alternative organizational structures for educational institutions of the present and future.

(from Lackey and Fielding, 1998)

Educational designers such as Australian Truna Turner (2005), in examining the epistemologies of immersive video gaming, suggest that design principles of gaming offer potential for new forms of educational literacy within an interface of the virtual learning environment. Such video games engross players in complex and challenging activities and signpost potential future design for virtual experiential learning. E-learning is undergoing dramatic changes, becoming more experiential, and a new term *e²-learning environments* has emerged (electronic-experiential learning) (Beard, Wilson and McCarter, 2006).

But US research suggests that there are concerns about space within educational learning environments, as public spaces are diversifying while private spaces are declining:

> given the need for solitude, it is ironic that what most universities do is to create an environment in which students are rarely alone. Intent on forming a campus community, campus architecture creates communal spaces: classrooms, student living quarters, outdoor quads, dining halls, recreation centres, and now even libraries are places to be designed to be with others. Where, then, do they go to be alone... Where is the private space?
>
> (Behuniak, 2005: 11)

Paradoxically, contemporary educational thinking requires greater student reflection on personal and professional development within formal education. Reflection usually requires access to private thinking space, something which is well known by the outdoor learning profession.

Outdoor learning

Outdoor learning environments are also undergoing a transformation: outdoor locations for learning are much more than an outdoor classroom, or a vast recreational playground, or a battlefield of unpredictable wilderness elements. Outdoor environments have a long history of providing very special spaces for individuals to learn, in a profound way, about themselves and their social interaction with others, as we shall discuss throughout this book. There is clearly more to the outdoor learning environment than merely a utility location; it is an integral component of the learning experience. There is much to learn from the use of the outdoors for learning, especially in terms of working with nature and the seasons and the elements. The learning process is transactive, with learners interacting with other learners, with facilitators, and with place and space. However, a long-established question exists within the outdoor learning community concerning the extent to which facilitators should intervene when the learning space itself has a profound influence on the learner: the outdoor professionals ask '*to what extent can the mountains* (metaphor for place) *speak for themselves?*' Merely 'being' in nature can be a powerful experiential intervention in itself, and this theme is central to contemporary developments in therapy, including, for example, nature therapy, adventure therapy and horticultural therapy.

The 'outdoors' conjures up words such as 'natural', 'earth' and the 'environment', all of which are used interchangeably in the literature. Yet the extent to which the outdoor environment is contrived or natural is also worthy of further exploration. The natural surroundings of mountains, lakes and 'fresh air' energize and revitalize people, and beckon them back to their primitive roots. Consalvo (1995: 2) introduced her book of ready-made games for trainers with the following comment, which illustrates the immense sensory richness of the natural environment. Let the imagination flow and recall the sensations:

> Blue sky, red sunsets, white puffy clouds, green fields speckled with flowers, pine covered paths, moonlit meadows, crickets chirping, birds singing, snow crunching under foot, the smell of the spring thaw, summer sweetness, autumn decay, a salty breeze, burning leaves, the squish of mud, the sting of hot sand and the cold of snow are just a few among the plethora of sensory images we experience while outdoors. These sensations often tap emotionally and spiritually uplifting memories.

This quotation conjures up so many essential facets of the experience, which some providers cherish while others take for granted. The outdoor environment is essential to creating pleasurable sensations and positive moods. The environment gives us natural ecstasy, and there are many elements or ingredients that can be used to increase sensitivity to learning:

- the changing seasons;
- wet, humid and dry;
- differences in day and night;
- unpredictability of the elements;
- dramatic landscapes;
- natural art;
- remoteness;
- heat and cold;
- ebb and flow of tides;
- natural rhythms of life;
- topography;
- flora and fauna;
- spiritual awareness;
- wild sounds.

These natural elements can be further divided into their sub-components. 'Remoteness', for example, could include solitude, space, quietness and mental 'sorting-out time'. A cave is a good place to sit alone and listen to our inner voices as we experience total darkness, solitude or sensory deprivation for a short period. It is also a place to develop communication skills for phone and videoconference work; talking in the dark with other colleagues provides no visual clues.

Disappearing boundaries: indoor–outdoor, natural–artificial

Indoor and outdoor places have much in common; they both have the word 'door' in them! The opening of doors, metaphorically speaking, presents people with new opportunities; to go through the door in order to arrive somewhere else. When we use the term 'outdoor learning' we tend to think of a place, outside of the house, the space where the learning can occur; it is the so-called natural environment in which many experiential activities are conducted. The provision of experiential programmes is predominantly concentrated in two types of setting or environment: indoors, in rooms, and outdoors, usually but not exclusively in places of scenic beauty. The two differ greatly, but the boundaries blur as the outdoors meets the indoors and vice versa. Opportunities exist for experiential providers to diversify the use of the outdoor and indoor milieu, too.

The outdoors can be brought indoors through simulation, when people create the outdoors through fantasy. Saunders (1988) describes a number of examples of indoor 'simulation gaming' under the umbrella of experiential learning. He includes an example of a game called Island Escape, where participants are stuck on a volcanic island that is about to explode, and comments that 'whilst this is a fantasy game, participants rapidly introduce themselves to other people, and reveal their backgrounds, interests and skills' (1988: 136). Saunders argues that simulation gaming combines the features of games (rules, players, competition, cooperation) with those of simulation (incorporation of critical features of reality). He suggests that it can be used most effectively for encouraging communication, and as a diagnostic and prognostic instrument. 'Diagnostics' involves detective work to identify issues for people to work on, with case studies that replicate the essential features of a real-life situation, while the 'prognosis' involves predicting future performances of people. The simulation takes place indoors, in a classroom or hotel for example, and uses a fantasy island for participants to escape from.

Other common examples are the well-known team decision-making exercises such as the NASA Moon Game and Desert Survival. There are now a whole range of resources using outdoor 'scenarios' for use indoors: stranded on an island, stuck in the jungle or marooned at sea, for example. One brochure describes how trainers can enhance realism with a set of

20 slides that will make participants glad they are warm and dry. Greenaway (1999) offers an interesting, insightful view of the terms outdoors and indoors. On his website, he refers to 'indoor–outdoor management development'. Greenaway describes this indoor gaming as being in direct contrast to the outdoors, where metaphorical associations with work are provided by mountains becoming cashpoints, canoes becoming taxis and ropes becoming telephone cables. These interesting trends demonstrate how indoor trainers liven up sessions by bringing in the excitement of the 'simulated outdoors', while some outdoor trainers concern themselves with metaphoric links to the indoor world of work, ensuring transfer and justifying the use of outdoor management development. Greenaway goes on to look further at the similarities, not the differences, noting that the outdoors and the indoors have much in common:

- **Powerful images.** Both real and simulated outdoors evoke powerful images.

- **Neutral settings.** Real and simulated outdoors provide a neutral setting where participants will be equally disadvantaged.

- **Back to basics.** Without sophisticated technology to assist or blame, the demands and issues tend to be simple, basic and inescapable. Excuses and pretensions tend not to survive for long in 'survival' situations (whether real or imagined).

- **Novice learners.** The novelty of an outdoor scenario (real or simulated) instantly places managers in the role of the learner. This willingness to appear before peers as a 'learner' seems more likely in an outdoor setting than in a setting that more obviously resembles work and in which a manager is already supposed to be reasonably competent.

- **Span of relevance.** To bridge the gap between outdoor and work settings generally requires a wider span of relevance than bridging the gap between two work settings. Practice in making connections across wide gaps increases the range of experiences that managers can bring to bear on any one problem.

- **Depth of learning.** Where learners do succeed in making connections between two very different settings, they tend to be at more profound levels. It is important to distinguish here between the relatively superficial connections that are designed into exercises, and the more profound connections made by individual managers when flashes of insight jump across the gap between 'outdoors' and 'work'.

- **Versatility.** Managers can more readily test, discover and demonstrate their potential and versatility (an important asset for managers facing change) in settings or simulations that are most different from their everyday work.

- **Enhanced realism.** Both approaches claim to make the training experience more realistic, but what could be further from reality than imagining that a neatly trimmed lawn is an alligator swamp or that a mountain top is a cashpoint (both outdoor training exercises), or imagining that an air-conditioned training room is a jungle or an Arctic wilderness (both indoor training exercises)? These would all be triumphs of the imagination over reality! What is surely meant by 'realism' in these contexts is more intense involvement – whatever the balance of fact and fiction, and however similar or different to work the experience may be.

In the latter point Greenaway explores the nature of reality and its relationship to the degree of engagement or involvement of the participants, a subject explored at length in our Chapter 5. Scores of outdoor locations define and enhance experiential learning. The parameters of the term 'outdoors' are not limited to land-based activities. Some providers use sailing vessels to provide experiential learning. It is both outdoor and indoor learning. Figure 4.2 describes such an experiential training programme in Oman that uses tall ships.

Outdoor experiential development can of course take place on boats, outdoors or indoors, in the air, on water, in underground caves or on land. But all these locations can be still further divided. Land can include habitats or terrain such as jungle, forests, desert or mountains. Figure 4.3 illustrates a range of environments, and it is clear that the experience can be enhanced if there is an understanding of the opportunities that the places and spaces offer for learning.

Reaching out: learning in city space

The urban environment is attracting more interest from experiential providers for a number of reasons. The city environment can be closer to home for many people, and it is rich in social and cultural learning opportunities. Sometimes referred to as the 'concrete jungle', it can be exhilarating and exciting. Proudman (1999) suggests that there is a need to 're-mystify' the urban environment. The traditional powerful wilderness 'solo' as a meditative experience might also take place in an urban cathedral. It can also be frightening and intimidating, and can be seen in a negative light. Our own international outdoor management development work in places such as Kenya and Beirut has highlighted to us the real and very different risks associated with venturing outdoors to work in a city environment, as opposed to the comfort of the hotel or National Park. High levels of anxiety about venturing out into the city were expressed by many African and Arab participants on one development programme. That urban safety management should be taken seriously and offered as 'challenge by choice', addressed in Chapter 3, is an important rule.

Urban outdoor programmes can provide development opportunities that are similar to wilderness programmes. The recognition of the value of urban

FIGURE 4.2 Experiential learning through the tall ship experience

The tall ship experience

Shabab Oman is the Tall Ship of Oman, which is the only Arab country to use sail training as an experiential learning platform. The ship, a 52-metre barquentine, was purchased second hand in 1977 and had previously been the Captain Scott. She was built in Buckie, Scotland, by Herd and MacKenzie and commanded by Victor Clarke, who also skippered the Gordonstoun School vessel the *Prince Louis* and therefore has a lineage with the principles of Outward Bound and Kurt Hahn.

Shabab Oman commenced sail training in Oman in 1978, providing adventure training in groups of 24 from the armed forces of Oman. She has continued, steadfast in this role, for 27 years and to date some 600 trainees have passed through the ship. The basic concept is to provide sail and adventurous training, using the medium of the sea to develop personal skills, leadership potential and to foster teamwork. This in turn recalls Oman's long seafaring traditions and instils a link with history while pitting participants against the present-day challenges of the sea to deliver a powerful learning experience.

The Experiential Training Concept: Trainees embark for a period of three weeks when the ship is operating on the coast of Oman and for up to four months when the ship deploys abroad. The trainee group consists of a mix of all branches of the armed forces, police and occasionally civilians. The group works and lives together within the confines of a sailing ship and they learn basic elements of seamanship and navigation while developing life skills of team working, problem solving and leadership. The idea of using the sea as a levelling medium from which to launch an experiential learning programme is not new and yet it possesses the potential to reveal quickly a person's inner strengths and weaknesses. The sea provides an ever-changing and challenging environment, which pits a person against an unrelenting, unforgiving and formidable opponent. Trainees develop self-confidence through the successful completion of previously inconceivable tasks, working at height and in atrocious weather conditions, which infuse an enduring sense of achievement and often greatly enhanced self-esteem.

The sea can provide some of the most difficult environmental living and working conditions known, and facing these challenges can result in a powerful emotional and spiritual experience: from a towering sensation of euphoria to possible moments of despair. Although these actual sensations may be short lived, they carry a powerful memory capacity and one which is likely to remain for a lifetime. The resultant experience can be a personal watershed and deliver life-changing properties. Sail training in the Middle East with young members of Oman's armed forces has proved to be a highly successful enterprise and one which continues to provide a valuable Outward Bound learning experience, in the mould of Kurt Hahn's principles.

By Chris Biggins, Commander, *Shabab Oman*

FIGURE 4.3　The environmental grid

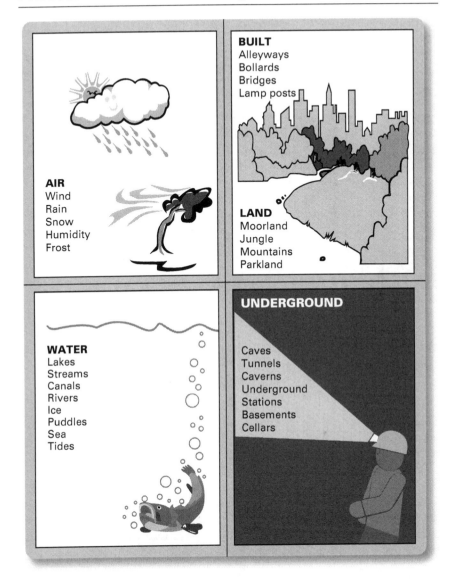

socio-ecology underpinned the development of the 'urban wildlife movement', emerging originally in the UK from the heart of Birmingham in 1979. There is a fantasy connection here too, as J R R Tolkien's *The Lord of the Rings* was based on wet woodland, known locally as Moseley Bog, and it was the protection of this site that became the inspirational force that mobilized the early pioneers of the urban wildlife movement. Urban wildlife projects can make ideal activities for people to undertake as the activities for experiential learning, a subject that we explore later in this chapter. Urban parks, woodlands and waterways can serve as places for adventure experiences. The urban canal system offers opportunities to journey on land and water, and the physical environment of buildings and walls provides ideal abseil and climbing opportunities. In the United States, the term 'buildering' has been coined to describe this activity (Proudman, 1999: 331). The urban environment includes bollards, kerbs, lamp posts, pavements, trees, gutters and benches for innovative use in experiential programmes. Urban spoil heaps can provide for scrambling and biking. In the UK, one outdoor activity centre has benefited from funding from the Lottery and built a 'rock park'. The first of its kind in the UK, it consists of huge boulders lined by bridges, allowing climbers to cross from one to the next in continuous sequences. This leads us to consider the nature of artificially constructed learning environments, and where the boundaries of 'real' environments and 'artificial' environments interface, a subject of much debate. Many so-called natural landscapes are indeed created by human activity.

Artificially created learning spaces

an exceptional creation – a corner of the world that is immensely old, full of surprises, lovingly and sometimes miraculously well maintained, and nearly always pleasing to look at. It is one of the busiest, most picked over, most meticulously groomed, most conspicuously used, most sumptuously and relentlessly improved landscapes on the planet.

(Bryson, 2000: 1–2)

The landscape in most countries is not particularly 'natural'; indeed 'naturalness' is very much a contentious term (Beard, 2003). While most landscapes are artificially created by human intervention, we are now witnessing new forms of artificial environments being created in cities for the purposes of adventure learning and play, and they often emerge in areas of industrial dereliction. In the UK, in Sheffield, many artificial recreational sites have developed in an ad hoc cluster, and have transformed urban decay and dereliction. It is here that Europe's largest dry-ski resort can be found, with ski-slopes, snowboarding facilities, toboggan rides and ski water-jumps, and they have all been built on old spoil heaps. Nearby, converted out of semi-derelict buildings, 'The Foundry' was a first for Britain in that it was the start of a new breed of fully commercial indoor climbing walls, attracting 60,000 people at its peak in 1996. It was host to the first European indoor climbing championships. But it was young students who turned their undergraduate dissertation ideas into a reality, and created 'The Foundry' climbing centre.

Located nearby, a skateboarding and rollerblading building called 'The House' was created by unemployed young teenagers by transforming an old abandoned warehouse. They were initially just enthusiasts, wanting somewhere to stunt-play and have fun, and they seized upon an opportunity to rent a derelict warehouse. These young people now operate a successful business, providing skateboarding and rollerblading for many other young people. Their experience of 'business' is exciting and natural for them, and it has grown from their own indigenous experience and sense of adventure. They simply shifted from play to entrepreneurial activity, following their natural instincts. This illustrates experiential learning at its best. Their business brings with it a whole subculture of clothing, music and language, and 'The House' appears to be a replacement of the 'youth club' for some of their customers.

Attarian (1999: 345) defines an artificial environment as a 'man made structure, device, or environment that simulates a natural setting, which can be used specifically for teaching or participating in outdoor activities'. Such structures can take many forms. A climbing 'wall' can be located on the outside or inside of a building, or in an alleyway at home within an urban or in a rural environment. Artificial white-water rafting courses are now being used for firefighter rescue training of crash victims located in rivers, and complex aircraft flight simulators have long been used for pilot training. In the United States in Arizona in 1970, the first major artificial surfing environment called the 'Big Surf' was created on an island lagoon.

The use of artificial spaces for experiential learning is of greater significance than has hitherto been realized. The urban environment lends itself to urban community initiatives, with inner-city schools and other urban groups, and it is the environment where many of the 'at-risk' youth are growing up. Working with urban projects can provide opportunities for youth development and management development alike. It is also in the urban environment that many young people are using initiative, in a very entrepreneurial way, turning their experience of urban play into business ventures: experiential learning at its best?

In 1994 a company called Rockface in Birmingham in the UK created a much broader leisure experiential environment, again from a derelict warehouse in the city. While the climbing walls form the foundation of the centre experience, there are also bars and restaurants. The centre offers a range of experiences for different visitor groups, including programmes for people with disabilities, training for executives, children's activities, and family fun and adventure. The climbing walls are adorned with a range of artefacts, such as artificial drainpipes and toilets, which amuses many of the teenagers. The walls and ceilings house abseiling platforms, rope bridges, a Jacob's ladder, a tower game and an artificial cave. The cave has been created using wooden panels to form a box structure around the rear of the climbing walls. Painted black to create almost total darkness, the caves also house climbing holds, chimney breasts, ramps and circular tunnels of various dimensions, and the routes change levels using trapdoors in the floors or ceiling. In darkness people experience many sensations, some 'natural' and some artificially stimulated. Masses of thin ropes dangle down from the ceiling in places on to people's backs, and some floor areas are crunchy natural gravel. Small bells tinkle to give delicate sounds, which the designers have built in especially for people with various levels of sensory disability. The site is continually evolving and it is difficult to classify it as a teaching classroom, a recreational site, a fun-fair or a leisure centre. It is this multiple perception that underlies its unique success as a place to experience.

Quite by chance, some cities are developing their 'adventure zones', replacing old industries and the world of production and traditional 'work' with rejuvenating businesses involved in the world of leisure, tourism, training, coaching, play, learning and adventure:

places of work	to	places of adventure, coaching, leisure and learning;
workers	to	business owners and managers;
mines/mechanical production	to	places for recreation and play;
derelict	to	regenerative in nature;
environmentally damaging	to	reducing recreational pressure on the natural;
old industries	to	new ones.

In time some will become institutionalized, moving from:

inventive fun	to	recreation;
recognized recreation	to	competitive sports;
sports	to	Olympic sports.

Pedagogy and personal development

Amid the urban factories and surrounding streets young people create their own challenges and rewrite the rules of education. They learn through play, fun and recreation. Although the overt goal might be the challenge of new stunts, pedagogy and personal development clearly underpin such experiences. Ironically, these skills often become institutionalized as 'qualifications' as governing bodies embrace the skill repertoire. Qualifications exist for sailing, swimming and gymnastics and are already well established, but new skills are emerging for skateboarding, stunt-biking and indoor climbing. The young climbers' Spider Club in the UK developed its own star ratings for young climbers, enabling them to progress systematically through stages of learning. This development grading was partly in recognition of the unsuitability of the adult international route classification system based on the 'degree of difficulty' (Arran, 1998). The young climbers start at a grade associated with recreational fun climbing, but opportunities are provided for the development of more serious competitive climbing if children want to.

Experiential learning: urban climbing and young people

The initial development of Levels of Climbing for young people: Spider Club awards – The Foundry, Sheffield, UK.

Five indoor levels of competence – leading to two outdoor levels:

- **White Spider**. I can climb to the top of the basic vertical wall; I can belay using a stitch plate under close supervision; I can tie a figure-of-eight knot with help; etc.

- **Yellow**. I can safely put on a safety harness; I can describe the differences between top roping, leading, bouldering, traversing and soloing; etc.

- **Orange**. I can tie a bowline knot with a fisherman's knot as a stopper; I can belay a lead climber with close supervision; etc.

- **Green**. I know how to tie off a stitch plate; I can tie a clove hitch knot; etc.

- **Blue**. I can 'down-climb' a route of grade 15 on any Foundry walls; I can traverse both sides of the corridor using only features for feet, and red/blue handholds; etc.

- **Purple Outdoor Spider**. I can climb a top-roped grade severe on limestone; I can climb a top-roped grade severe on gritstone; etc.

- **Gold Outdoor Spider**. I can demonstrate how to protect a climb by placing cramming devices, wires and hexes as running belays; I can name and describe the characteristics of three types of rock; etc.

(Arran, 1998)

These urban adventure sites allow for competitions with carefully simulated routes being designed for coaching, training and development programmes. But the young climbers are also forming a new breed; some have not tasted so-called 'real' natural outdoor climbing at all. Artificial climbing walls are now used by 82 per cent of UK climbers, 42 per cent of them on a weekly basis.

Technological advancements have given rise to artificial ice walls that have the consistency of toffee and so return to their original shape ready for the next climber. All these artificial environments offer the advantage that they can easily be manipulated or altered.

Reconfiguration of the learning environment creates a new set of challenges, and new climbs or skate stunts are being sought by many young people as they search for their own adventure learning on the doorstep, after school and particularly in the winter months. Surface technology and route design are key to this thriving new business area of simulated indoor activity-based learning and play, and there are clear technical, social, environmental and commercial advantages. These sites also create new opportunities for providers of experiential learning, for corporate training or youth development programmes.

If nature is experienced as uncontrollable or inaccessible then the natural environment is likely to be increasingly copied, manipulated, simulated, altered, merged or upgraded with human-made components. Such manufactured environments suit many commercial outdoor ventures and such developments might provide opportunities for the design of new learning environments. The simple list below of outdoor activities illustrates the diversity and complexity of the term '*artificial*'. The term artificial can refer to:

- *a device* (such as a bolt, gadget, or equipment);
- *an activity* (canyoning, coasteering, roller-blading, indoor climbing);
- *the elements* (artificial snow, artificial lights, simulated wind, simulated waterfalls);
- *structure/location* (a climbing 'wall', rollerblade, rafting or slalom 'courses'); or
- *whole environments* ('resorts', adventure 'zones', adventure 'islands').

The advantages of simulated recreation environments

- Social:
  - can take part regularly; high levels of accessibility, by walking or public transport; for the urban and rural population;
  - potential for greater social interaction: crowds, spectators, cafés, clothing, music, youth culture, etc;
  - reduced trespass, eg mountain bikes on footpaths;
  - reduced conflict with other users: public on streets, as in skateboarding, and in National Parks, as in mountain biking;
  - located off the streets.

- Commercial:
  - potential to increase the number of participants and beginners;
  - all-season participation possible;
  - suitability for experienced and beginners;
  - creates a new market of participants;

- suited to experiential development programmes for managers, youth, children, etc;
- equipment and clothing sale/provision at location;
- café/bar and tourism functions;
- time and space zoning.

● **Environmental:**
- controlled environment: 'conditions';
- less susceptibility to the unpredictable elements of the natural environment;
- less travel: people and equipment;
- potentially less environmental impact;
- less direct physical environmental damage;
- less pollution; – less ecological damage;
- less environmental unpredictability;
- less risk.

● **Technical:**
- mimic the 'best bits': features and obstacles;
- local natural environment may not contain the necessary features in one place;
- a valuable training resource;
- creating new champions, in sport and recreation;
- added safety for training of pilots, schoolchildren/youth, managers, firefighters etc;
- artificial lighting provides winter opportunities in the UK:
- floodlit;
- controllable conditions;
- can create unique/unnatural challenges: totally new and not found in natural conditions – beyond the natural.

Significantly, these artificial environments also offer locations for the four-step approach that is discussed in Chapter 3. Barrett and Greenaway (1995) offer ways to overcome the negative effects of youth returning from significant wilderness experiences. Urban locations can offer entry and exit stages for residential wilderness programmes shown in Figure 4.4. The urban location provides a step in the process for people to realign themselves, and so avoid the negative shock and consequence of a sudden dramatic return to start-point environments.

FIGURE 4.4 The four-stage support wave

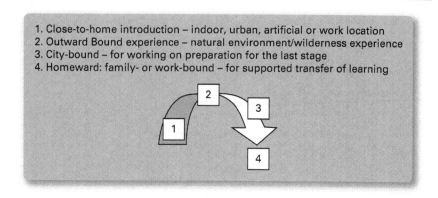

1. Close-to-home introduction – indoor, urban, artificial or work location
2. Outward Bound experience – natural environment/wilderness experience
3. City-bound – for working on preparation for the last stage
4. Homeward: family- or work-bound – for supported transfer of learning

Empathetic strategies and the outdoor therapeutic 'effect'

Concern about the overusage of the wilderness by an ever-growing population escaping to the outdoors seeking a 'fresh air fix' has been expressed by Ogilvie (1993) and Cooper (1998). Ogilvie suggests that this degradation is now on a scale such that lip service to environmental issues is no longer enough, and that the traditional attitude of outdoor users to use the environment as a playground or testing place for the self can place them in the uncaring category. Ogilvie embraces this notion in his adapted version of John Adair's action-centred leadership model involving the *team*, the *individual* and the *task*. Ogilvie adds a fourth dimension, the *earth*, arguing that now it would make sense to construct this model with a fourth circle (see Figure 4.5). Likewise Mortlock (1984) warns against professional insensitivity towards the environment and suggests that there should be an awareness of, respect for and love of *self*, balanced against an awareness of, respect for and love of others, balanced against an awareness of, respect for and love of the *environment*.

With the pressure to provide learners with novelty (Irvine and Wilson, 1994), some providers feel that adrenalin-raising activities or confrontational-type experiences will excite and motivate people (see, for example, Vanreusel, 1995). The requirement of challenge and risk can also create adversarial, aggressive approaches to the natural world, where some elements of nature are seen as providing a powerful negative force to be overcome.

The use of the outdoors as an educational 'resource' has a long history in Western culture. Charlton (1992) notes that there have been many protagonists of the view that there is not a single social ill or physical problem that would not respond to a course of treatment in the outdoors. Charlton also notes a prevalent dichotomy of approaches towards the outdoors, using

FIGURE 4.5 The team, the task, the individual and... the environment

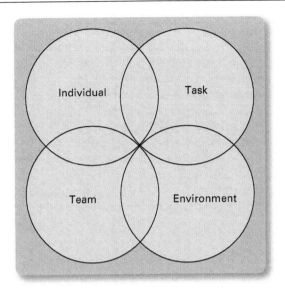

terms such as 'combative' (conquering) towards the natural elements, or 'empathetic' (affinity). The historical perspective of the outdoors as a therapeutic environment is reflected upon by Charlton, who comments that in the scouting movement, it was long ago regarded that exposure to wilderness was a suggested cure for everything from flat-footedness to 'bad citizenship'!

The environment has long been regarded as an important place for healing, repair and personal development. Miles (1995) offers a US view on wilderness as a healing place, a place for programmes helping people 'at risk', renowned for its rehabilitating power, for recuperation, for developing management skills, for personal spiritual well-being and for youth work. Significant epistemological and ontological challenges face such research. 'Biophilia', for example, concerns the environmental effects on people such as the post-operative patient recovery rates when subjected to stimulation in the natural environment; the results are promising. The person–environment relationship is of course a two-way process, and the subtle impact of the natural environment on our health is now receiving more attention. Research that was carried out long ago by Ulrich (1974) set out to measure the attractive and aversive human physiological responses to natural phenomena. It suggests that combative strategies may operate against natural stimuli that are produced when we are in natural outdoor environments. Some early research was carried out on post-operative patients in hospital and early indications were that patients who overlooked natural green space had shorter post-operative stays and fewer post-surgery complications, and required less medication and analgesics.

More recently, Kellert (1993) suggests that spending time in green space has many positive physiological responses such as reduced heart rate, reduced blood pressure, and increased cognitive functioning, performance and creativity. These responses are said to come from a number of stimuli such as colours, textures, natural smells, decreased noise pollution or more interesting sounds, such as running water, and exposure to the elements (wind, rain, heat, cold, etc). Doctors now advise 'countryside walks' as an alternative option to drug or medicine prescriptions.

The natural environment is a place for learning about self-healing, although many people remain sceptical about the claims made, doubting the power the natural environment has. The sceptics rely on others to prove it to them, yet the overwhelming evidence suggests that it is the very spiritual and emotional nature of the outdoor environment that underpins the reason for its power; perhaps it cannot be measured. This leads us towards a realization that indeed there might be something very, very magical 'out there'. The truth about nature and the nature of truth are elusively intertwined.

Outdoor environments: therapeutic experiential learning

Although healing and nature, and learning and change, are closely related, the role of the outdoors in the healing process is little understood. This is due partly to the dominant old paradigms of psychology and psychotherapy: Freud is said to have actively steered therapy away from the world of nature, thus driving a wedge between psychology and nature (Burns, 1998). However, with the emergence of family therapy there was a move away from the introspective analysis on the couch. Burns describes the early embryonic work of Milton Erickson, who often assigned clients tasks involving interactions with nature, thus replicating traditional healing practices of the past. This use of tasks in nature is of interest in experiential learning.

'*Adventure therapy*' and '*nature therapy*' are emerging outdoor initiatives that warrant closer examination in order to illustrate this point:

Adventure therapy is said to be an active, experiential approach to group (and family) psychotherapy or counselling:

- Utilizing an **activity base** (cooperative group games, ropes courses, outdoor pursuits or wilderness expeditions).
- Employing real and/or perceived (physical or psychological) **risk** (distress/eustress) as a clinically significant agent to try to bring about desired change.
- Making **meaning**(s) (through insights that are **expressed** verbally, non-verbally, or unconsciously that lead to behavioural change) from both verbal and non-verbal introductions prior to (eg frontloadings) and discussions following (eg debriefings) the activity experience.

- Punctuating isomorphic connection(s) (how the structure of the activity matches the **resolution of the problem**) that significantly contribute to the transfer of lessons learned into change behaviour (Gillis and Thomsen, 1996).

(http://fdsa.gcsu.edu:6060/Igillis/AT/front.htm)

In this definition the healing process of nature is largely unacknowledged: nature is omitted and perceived as utilitarian, as a functional backdrop in adventure therapy. Conversely, *nature therapy* or *ecotherapy* presents a more integrative role for nature in the therapeutic process. *Ecotherapy*, for example, is said to be a healing process that seeks to enlarge and enhance people's body and mind–spirit perception through a greater connection to the wilderness; it deepens the sense of connectedness with nature, and helps overcome other forms of alienation in people's lives. Nature therapy can embrace a healing role for specific plants and animals: working with injured orphaned birds, for example, can result in a healing effect on young people facing a similar predicament. (See www.naturetherapy.com.)

Therapeutic applications seek to improve healthy behaviours and reduce unhealthy behaviours, and to develop mental and physical well-being. The plethora of emerging disciplines of nature therapy, ecotherapy, conservation therapy, adventure therapy and horticultural therapy all have much in common in that the environment, to a significant extent, acts as the therapist: professionals involved in such therapeutic work grapple with this and other issues which lie at the boundary of learning and therapy. Gilsdorf's enquiry (2003) into the professional identity of providers of these experience-based therapies notes that the field is relatively young, with more questions than answers. He attempts to shed light on the link between learning and therapy with reference to the work of Bateson (1981, in Gilsdorf, 2003) (see also Chapter 2), who refers to a number of levels of learning. Learning level 1 focuses on content learning, Learning 2 is the learning of strategies, structures of thinking and habits, and is clearly linked with personality traits. Gilsdorf suggests that Learning 3 goes further:

in that it is basically concerned with the reassessment of established strategies, structures of thinking and habits. In other words learning 3 describes much of the process which, when explicitly put into a certain professional context, is called therapy. Education, at least in its institutional forms, has narrowed the scope of learning almost exclusively to teaching content and is also focusing heavily on cognitive learning, neglecting emotional as well as psychomotor aspects. Experiential and adventure education has mostly countered this tendency. Cultivating and increasing the therapeutic potential within adventure, instead of **delegating it to the domain of therapy**, could thus be an important step in the process of the establishment of a truly different learning culture.

(p 59, emphasis added)

One leading UK charity concerned with substance misuse challenges individuals to build self-esteem, self-confidence and motivation through the power of activity in wildlife-rich environments (Hall, 2004). The catalytic triangle used by the programme is that of nature, activity and relationships. One person describes how the programme of dry-stone walling in the National Parks changed his life, and how he went on to become a self-employed landscape designer as a result of the programme. The question of the role of the activity such as dry-stone walling and the healing power of the natural surrounding environment in the therapeutic process becomes interesting. Abbot (1987: 148) suggests that the activity should:

- require a group effort for their success, and therefore encourage interpersonal cooperation and trust among the group;
- consist of adventurous activities which involve some degree of risk;
- be physically demanding and therefore require or induce some physical fitness;
- be conducted in a natural environment;
- generate a sense of achievement, usually as a result of the individual's own efforts.

The role of the environment is explored in detail by Burns (1998), who suggests that there is some consensus among environmental psychologists that we are hard-wired with powerful adaptive mechanisms as part of our psychological and biological make-up and that these are triggered by natural stimuli. The environment, particularly the outdoor natural environment, has much more to offer than just a 'location' for the delivery of experiential learning. The environment is an integral and powerful part of experience. This is significant in terms of the design and delivery of experiential programmes. A skill that is increasingly required of learning providers is the ability to provide a range of environmental experiences and, where necessary, to manipulate, in a positive and beneficial way, many of the environmental ingredients that make up a powerful learning experience.

Sustainable learning environments

Some organizations fail to respect the fact that they make direct profit out of the natural environment, regarding nature as a free resource. Encouraging people not to take the environment for granted, to take positive action and give something back to the environment can be promoted in so many different ways, and such behaviour can help to avoid environmental alienation and exploitation. Despite the fact that the earth is the bank upon which we draw all our cheques, the economic value of the environment is underestimated. The environment has an important role in any enterprise. The environment provides a place to deposit waste, the arena for recreation and adventure, and the places to venture on holidays. If we harvest too many natural resources then the environment becomes degraded, and education, leisure and recreation are all adversely affected. But there are clearly difficulties associated with merely applying monetary values to nature.

Caring for and valuing the natural environment is more than just the design of low-impact activities. For many businesses going 'green', being empathetic towards the environment or being 'environmentally friendly' can unfortunately be perceived as a trade-off between profit and corporate citizenship. As a result, some organizations remain distanced from sustainable development, a process that meets the needs of the present generation without compromising the needs of future generations to meet their own needs (WCED, in Beard, 1997). Some outdoor educational institutions regard themselves as environmentally friendly and divest themselves of responsibility through their teaching of environmental education. Ultimately a preparedness for some form of environmental action is required other than 'education' in order to repair the environment: someone has to plant the trees and repair the erosion caused by footpaths. The four main impacts are:

- **physical impact** – of the structures, buildings, and damage to walls, property, damaging fires;
- **social impact** – on local community such as noise at night, drunkenness, litter...;
- **psychological impact** – when one group spoils the experience of another...;
- **ecological impacts** – disturbance to wildlife, collecting eggs, trampling on nests, having a picnic on a shingle seashore where terns nest.

We encourage many experiential learning providers to buy environmentally friendly equipment and clothing, and so support market trends in this direction. We also encourage facilitators to increase the levels of environmental awareness in clients by generally acknowledging the beauty of the environment they are working in, and by making their own personal contribution. This can be done in many different ways, for example procurement processes, such as the purchase of recyclable flooring, washable flipchart paper, pens and pencils made from recycled plastic vending machine cups, or by those using the outdoors for learning by rebuilding dry-stone walls, by planting trees or by funding others to do the practical work. We can also make our activities carbon neutral, reduce energy consumption and resource depletion. We discuss more of these issues in the chapter on facilitation and codes of practice with regard to the environment.

For people working in the outdoors we now offer an optional, slightly amended model below (see Figure 4.6). It might be interpreted as more balanced, as it consists of three inner world and three outer world dimensions of learning. Thus if we include the senses there are seven dimensions of learning in total, and in this model we deliberately separate the social (human) world experience from the more-than-human world (MTHW) experience and in doing so we emphasize the neglected complexity of the more-than-human world, including the so-called 'natural' world, the 'artificial' and material world. Both the human and more-than-human world experiences are of course part of the belonging dimension of learning.

FIGURE 4.6 A seven-dimensional model that embraces the more-than-human world

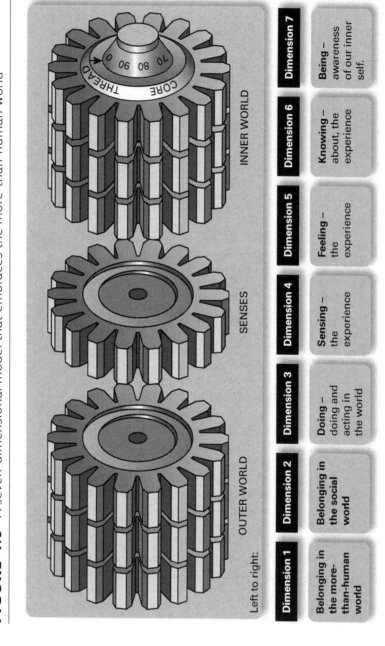

Conclusion

The chapter has highlighted the theory and practice of learning space, presenting a diverse range of case studies: from tall ships to sheds, caves, climbing walls and urban dereliction. We have explored a diverse range of environments for learning, and taken a closer look at the emerging pedagogy of space. We considered how *signpost terminology* points us to the future, with contemporary defining parameters of 'learning environments' identifying a wave of global transformation. This signifies a break away, metaphorically and physically, from the restricted nature of the traditional classroom.

Multidisciplinary specialists are at last interacting: designers and managers are talking to learning specialists and significantly to the learners themselves. Much has been learnt from the outdoor learning community, and there exists a constant shift and blurring of boundaries of indoor–outdoor and natural–artificial. Artificial nature is growing and moving indoors. We believe that good learning environments will increasingly provide areas that maximize the flexibility and mobility of people, the mobility of information and the mobile nature of the very spaces and places we inhabit in order to learn and work.

Learning environments continue their journey of transformation. The 'classroom' boundaries are blurring, reaching out into communities. Technology is taking indoor learning out into the streets and beyond. The future is exciting but the global campus of experiential learning must be environmentally sustainable.

Experiential learning activities (The doing dimension)

> *Many people mistake activity – the doing of things – with experiential education. Maxine Greene reminds us that experiential education is really an internal process by which people can 'wake up' and construct a coherent world for one's quest for freedom and transformation by integrating a variety of perspectives and vantage points.*

LAURIE S. FRANK, 2011: 64

Introduction

Experiential learning has a long history, although it might well have suffered misinterpretations along the way! One ancient (AD 551–179) but well-known Chinese Confucian philosophy is the saying '*I hear I forget, I see I remember, I do I understand*'. This aphorism laid the early foundations, the lineage, for subsequent Western interpretations concerning experiential learning. If we are simply told, then we forget, if we watch, we might remember, but if we do the real thing this is the best way to learn. Or is it?

In the late 1960s this Chinese aphorism gave rise to the 'Tell Show Do' instructional techniques model by Edgar Dale (1969). But what do we mean by 'do', and what is meant by the 'real' thing? Aphorisms do not offer detail – a Confucian saying is open to interpretation within the language of the 'Chinese way'. If it is translated at face value it can so easily lose its original Eastern depth of meaning. 'Doing' is perhaps better interpreted as 'practice': in this sense engaging the whole person. Let us offer a slightly more exacting translation of the saying for you to ponder on. I want you to at least imagine a Confucian philosopher saying it in a Chinese 'way':

To hear something is better than not to hear it,
To say something is better than just to hear it,
To know something is better than just to say it,
To practice something is better than just to know it...

(reproduced from Beard, 2010)

To practice is to experience it, to feel it, to sense it, to understand it and to *immerse* oneself in doing it regularly, for the self. The experiential learner is always part of a rich milieu of shifting experiences, both social and more-than-human; he or she also enriches it with his or her personal contribution (Boud and Walker, 1990). This reciprocity, this continuing complex and meaningful interaction with the world, both human and more-than-human, is of central concern to our understanding of the term *experience*. Doing something by being physically active has been wrongly regarded as a central principle for experiential learning. Doing something clearly might involve more than physical activity. Doing something surely involves sensing, and thinking, and feeling. Some people say they are practical minded and that they don't like theory. They say they like to be active, and get hands-on, yet Kurt Lewin (1951) suggests that there is nothing so practical as a good theory!

Too much doing can lead into the activity trap. Uncritical doing, without thinking can be risky. At the European Experiential Educators (EEE) conference in Greece in 2012 many delegates informally discussed the idea that less 'doing' might indeed result in more learning! Too much 'doing' can be limiting. Experiential thinkers such as the Norwegian Fridtjof Nansen suggest that if we take to, or do adventure, it should be in order to see the 'land beyond', explore what is hidden, and to respond to the call of the unknown including the *nature life* or the friluftsliv. Others like Maxine Greene take a similar view about what we purposefully do in life, but from a slightly different perspective. She suggests we learn to *wake up*, and in the act of doing things consider what might be and what is not yet. Her ideas are rooted in the concept of *freedom*, and perspective change, a theme that is found in other great thinkers such as Mezirow. Similar views are adopted by Friere in his exploration of oppression, and Rogers in his exploration of freedom from a therapeutic perspective (see Smith and Knapp, 2011). 'Doing' in experiential learning terms is much more than just a physical activity: action linked to *purpose* and *will* present more life options.

Many educators, therapists, adventure programmers and corporate learning and development specialists have developed specific types of experiential learning within their practice. Issues such as how we plan for experiences, or discover them, the sequencing and timing of learning experiences, the way any experience is discovered or introduced, its degree of perceived relevance and reality, and the combination of people, places, materials, rules and restrictions all present a potentiality infinite and rich experiential milieu.

FIGURE 5.1 An interpretation of Edgar Dale's Cone of Experience

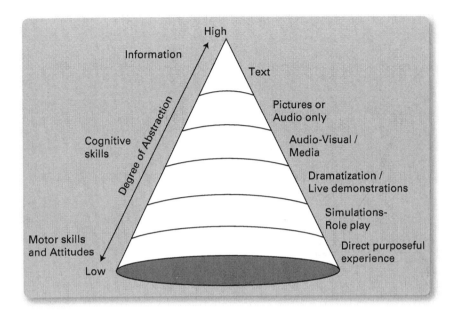

In this chapter we introduce these important fundamentals, and in doing so create a typology of activities along with the rationale or theory in use. This chapter will offer some innovative and pragmatic examples found within current experiential practice in order to demonstrate the application of the typology. The subject of the experiential of 'doing' things is the subject of the second cog of the learning combination lock.

The changing milieu

> Experience is created in the transaction between the learner and the milieu in which he or she operates – it is relational. An event can influence the learner, but only if the learner is predisposed to being influenced. Similarly, the learner can create a fruitful experience from a limited event, but only if there is something with which they can work.
>
> (Boud *et al*, 1993: 11)

There are many methods available for facilitators to use in order to help people to learn through experience. In experiential learning the fundamental 'method' is the provision of the experience. This is illustrated in Dale's Cone of Experience (1969), shown in Figure 5.1. He argues that learners retain more information when 'doing' purposeful experiences, as opposed to 'hearing' or just 'reading' about the experience.

Adventure learning

In outdoor and adventure learning, outdoor pursuits such as canoeing, climbing, camping and raft building have traditionally been the experiential 'activity' for learning. Rodwell (1994: 133) describes traditional outdoor approaches that use recreational or adventure activities thus: 'Outdoor training usually requires the trainee to perform a series of tasks which incorporate outdoor pursuits such as... climbing, abseiling, caving, orienteering, canoeing, sailing... and they usually involve training for management skills, team-working skills, personal development and physical challenge.' Badger *et al* (1997) confirm this relatively high level of outdoor pursuit activities in their research into outdoor activities being used in management development programmes and noted that, in their sample of 100 firms, respondents said that they had participated in the following activities:

Rock climbing 79

Orienteering 47

Sailing 16

Canoeing 37

Camping 31

Rafting 16

Caving 16

Others 74

The last figure is the interesting one and it represents the tip of the iceberg of change in the design of learning activities used in outdoor programmes. The 74 per cent of 'other' forms of activity represents a very diverse array of experiences. One company brochure, Black Mountain (1996), demonstrates this movement away from traditional management development activities:

> This shift towards a wider spectrum of delivery techniques has attracted a dedicated professional team that can design and deliver indoor seminars, outdoor exercises, desktop simulations, experiential games, video projects or motivational events. Over the past five years we have moved away from the use of outdoor pursuits in response to our clients' needs which have become more focused and sophisticated. As people become more exposed to development techniques more effective and high impact solutions are required.

Outdoor learning is moving away from an overemphasis on old paradigms, where the outdoor pursuits of 'canoeing, climbing and caving' are used to teach 'teamwork, communication and leadership'! The level of sophistication of provision parallels the deeper understanding of experiential learning. Provision now gives greater consideration to pre-activity interaction, review and transfer, and follow-up activities, and learners' needs are identified more carefully. Learning can be enhanced through the design of learning activities that embrace the milieu of adventure, fun, leisure and recreation.

Planned or unplanned experiences?

The extent to which both experiential providers and learners plan to learn from experience, or whether it just happens, is an important consideration. For many people life's journey, and the learning from it, is not at all planned. Life simply emerges and unfolds. Others are more proactive and plan many of their more meaningful life journeys. Significantly, the extent to which people learn from any journey or experience depends on many factors.

Educational psychologists define learning as a change in the individual caused by 'experience'. However, 20 years of experience in a job, for example, does not directly equate to 20 years of learning. How people create and manage their 'experience' is crucial to the process of learning. In order to help people to get the most from experience it is necessary to unleash curiosity so that people actively seek learning, so that they can plan to unveil something that was previously hidden. It is equally important that learners can respond to unanticipated and unplanned experiences as they occur. Megginson (1994) examines why people take different approaches to self-directed learning. He refers to these two basic approaches as planned and emergent learning, and created a grid, reproduced in Figure 5.2, to represent four types of learner. He researched these four different learner types, and classified people as those who have high or low pre-planning for experience, and those who are high or low in emergent, responsive learning strategies. Megginson noted that there are two fundamental challenges that face those who help others to learn. Some people, he suggests, do not take responsibility for the direction of their own learning and some people do not learn from the experiences they have. Planned learners take this responsibility for the direction of their learning, whilst emergent learners respond to and learn from experience. Adventurers are thus high on emergent learning and low on pre-planned learning strategies, whereas the sage is high on both. Warriors are low on emergent strategies, and so Megginson recommends activities to hold them in awareness of immediate experience. For adventurers he offers a set of goal-setting activities. The sages, he suggests, can find their own development directions. Sleepers can find any planned or emergent changes daunting and so techniques such as the use of written reflective logbooks can enhance emergent learning. The use of learning plans for the coming year or month or from a future project can develop proactive learning strategies. Gestalt verbal awareness sensitizing can help, such as the use of stream of conscious thought talking. Here each statement is preceded with 'I am aware of...', eg 'I am aware of my feelings of anxiety at the moment.' This can be used during an experiential event when people can express the experience they are having in their terms, and thus first acknowledge and then develop their learning from their experience. This can help access the rich reservoir of thoughts, feelings and impulses about an experience that might otherwise lie dormant. Facilitation strategies

FIGURE 5.2 Planned and emergent learning

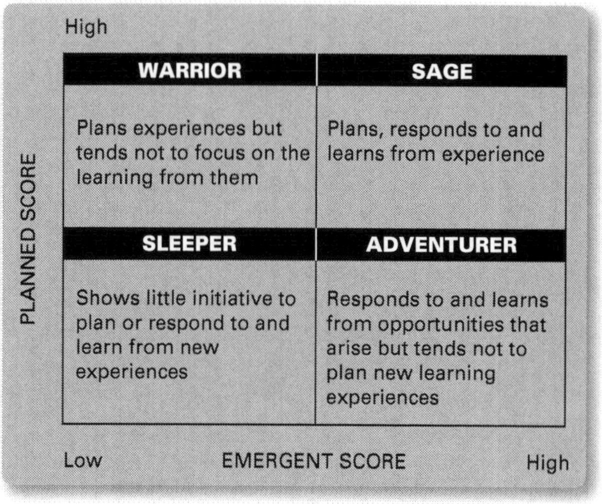

require an understanding of sleepers, warriors, adventurers and sages; then different training methods can be applied so as to maximize their emergent and planned learning.

Dramaturgy

The concept of planned and unplanned learning can be further explored in dramaturgy, which recognizes that learning design and learning outcomes can be both anticipated and unanticipated. Martin *et al* (2004) offer a holistic and creative approach to programme design and a large section of their book on outdoor experiential learning is devoted to very creative courses and games, game logistics and game descriptions. The authors draw on pioneering work by the Czechs and Slovaks on experiential dramaturgy:

> Dramaturgy means 'the art of theatrical production' the main task of which is to examine the links between the world and the stage. The 'dramatist' chooses themes from society and a place that reflects these themes. Pieces of work and music are then chosen to reflect these themes.
>
> (Martin *et al*, 2004: 15)

There are five stages involved in developing dramaturgy:

1 Development of the main course theme.

2 Development of the scenario (first part).

3 The practical dramaturgy (activity/game creation and selection).

4 The completion of the scenario.

5 The dramaturgy on the course.

The authors then refer to the work of Holec (1994, in Martin *et al*, 2004: 17) in order to explain dramaturgy in more detail:

> This term, known rather from the sphere of theatre, film and TV, became one of the most often used in recent years. Dramaturgy is a method of selection and time order of the activities with the aim to reach the maximal pedagogical effect. It integrates, within itself, the questions (and also answers) concerning the participants on the course (their age, mental and physical maturity...), time and space. The key thing for all dramaturgy considerations is to determine and realize the pedagogical, educational, recreational and other aims, which the course wants to reach.

In dramaturgy the programme is flexible and very holistic, and there are often continuous, reflective changes to the content as facilitators constantly re-examine the goals or objectives. The activities are often rewritten and the programme reshaped (sometimes on a regular basis at nightly meetings) to match the learner's needs. Here unanticipated learning is experienced and is central to the design.

Martin *et al* describe in detail 30 games under four sections: creative, social, physical and psychological (reflective/emotional). Such a classification is useful and our own experiential learning master classes help facilitators create a folder of activities under such headings in order to carry out a detailed analysis of the essential ingredients.

Innovation, activities, resources and objects – a simple experiential typology

The purposive nature of learning means that in some programmes it is very necessary to determine the 'wants' of the learner, ie what the learner perceives to be his or her need; and the 'needs' of the learner, ie what the facilitator perceives the learner needs. The combination of the determined needs and wants can then be expressed in terms of learning outcomes. This requires in addition an understanding of the culture of the people and the organization, the resources available and practical considerations, such as whether the programme can be residential. In each experience the choice of combination of these variables is the underpinning precept of the educative process that is experiential learning.

Restaurants offer a diverse menu for take-away meals, offering a great deal of choice. Up to 150 options adorn such menus; this is only possible because common to many options are a few central ingredients. Likewise in experiential development programmes there are often common activities, but the outward manifestation of the experience is different. Determining, for example, issues of theme, place, objects, activities and rules is a function

FIGURE 5.3 The learning gaps: altering time and place to increase learning

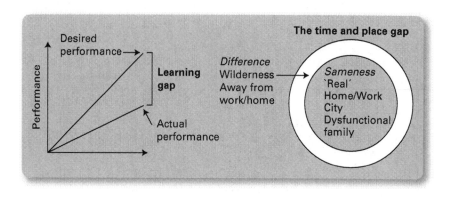

of the milieu necessary to create the learning outcomes. For example, an organization whose internal culture is competitive may require competition to be reflected in the learning experience. In contrast, an organization that operates by consensus may find a competitive milieu a counter-productive experience. However, exposure to experiences outside the cultural norm of the organization may be a catalyst to stimulate creativity and innovation. It is a question of effectively determining what outcomes are required for the individuals, groups or organization, while recognizing that the learning is a continuous, long journey.

The need for learning often reflects a gap, or imbalance, in skills, knowledge or attitudes, and the learner is helped, to varying degrees, to move from his or her current way of operating to a preferred way of operating through the learning experience, as shown in Figure 5.3. The journey away from the norm of 'sameness' often helps people to see this gap more clearly. Sometimes, however, there is also a need for 'metaphorical space' to escape, to 'sense' release and feel free.

Journeying over periods of time and through physical and metaphorical space is an important component of any learning. The journey from where the learner is to where the learner needs to be is fundamental to the experiential process. Knowing the needs can determine the focus and end point. Knowing the participants can determine the start point, distance to be travelled, and the number of steps necessary to achieve the destination. Lifelong learning means that the end point of the learning journey is, however, little more than a staging post that, once achieved, enables learners to embrace a new set of challenges. A journey might venture into another place, away from the everyday environment, so as to gain a different view or perspective. Creating the right medium or milieu for a learning journey is thus a function of a number of considerations. To assist the planning of creative experiential learning programmes we offer a typology, shown below.

A basic experiential learning programme typology

- Set a **target**, goal or objective, where goals create an underlying 'state of mind'.
- Create a sense of a **journey or destination** – physical movement and exercise; people, information and objects are moved from A to B.
- Allow participants to **exercise many forms of intelligence**.
- Create and sequence a **theme** of **social, mental, psychological and physical activities** – mind, spirit and body.
- Adjust the **elements of reality**.
- Stimulate the **senses**.
- Use **construction or deconstruction in activity design**: a physical object, eg bike, wall or raft or a non-physical item, eg a clue, phrase or poem.
- Design social **collaborative or competitive strategies**.
- Create **combative and/or empathetic** approaches to the environment.
- **Create restrictions**:
  - obstacles;
  - sensory blocking, eg blindfolds;
  - rules;
  - procedures.
- Provide elements of real or perceived challenge or risk.
- Set time constraints.
- Allow people to deal with change, risk, success and failure – stretching personal boundaries.
- Design sorting and/or organization skills – a mass of data, information to sort or activities to do or consider.
- Include functional skills such as surveying, juggling, map reading, knot tying, etc.
- Design quiet time for reflection – physical or mental space.
- Allow the story of the experience to be told.

(adapted from Beard, 1998)

Adventurous journeys

Underpinning all of these ingredients is the learner journey, and a physical journey or activity can be an isomorphic representation of a wider life journey. The physical journey can be orienteering, a short walk in the hotel grounds or distance travelled in kayaks. 'Outward Bound' is a nautical term referring to the outward journey of a ship: Outward Bound schools had a strong focus on sea expeditions. This is partly because Kurt Hahn collaborated with a businessman in shipping, Lawrence Holt, in his early days to develop his ideas and schools.

Many outdoor and indoor experiential programmes design into the experience a journey and movement, often involving the building or construction of things: physical objects, such as canisters or bikes; and non-physical objects, such as theories, poems or art. Physical exercise on such a journey impacts on learners' energy–tension balance, as physical exercise is known to be one of the most powerful positive regulators of mood, a subject we examine in Chapter 7. Rules and restrictions, whether real or perceived, can impede or speed progress. Likewise problem solving can include collaboration or competition. Many things can influence a learning experience.

Adventure, whether indoor or outdoor, requires an element of real or perceived risk to which the participant is exposed through their engagement in an activity. This risk can be physical, emotional, intellectual or material. 'Adventure' embraces many facets of people's lives and it forms the basis of the experiential milieu. The dictionary suggests that adventure is a 'remarkable incident', 'an enterprise or commercial speculation', 'an exciting experience' or 'the spirit of enterprise', and an adventurer is 'one who engages in hazardous enterprise'. 'To be an adventure an experience must have an element of uncertainty about it. Either the outcome should be unknown or the setting unfamiliar' (Priest and Ballie, 1995: 307). The 'venture' part of the word adventure implies the element of travel, with or without a purpose. The many dictionary definitions of the term 'expedition' are that of *a journey with a definite purpose*. In expeditions there is also a target or goal, and a time constraint.

A plethora of activities are currently offered in locations around the world offering adventurous travel as experiential learning. Eco-adventure travel is an area that has increased rapidly over the past decade to become one of the leading areas of income for the tourism industry today (Swarbrooke *et al*, 2003). Greenforce, Frontier and Earthwatch are three such organizations that offer an unusual and new combination of learning journeys that I have termed *edventure*. These organizations construct a new form of multi-learning experience for young people, containing a subtle mix of educative features for self-development: adventure, travel, environmental or community development work and skills in scientific wildlife monitoring. These organizations are usually charities recruiting paying volunteers to support wildlife projects around the world. Coral Cay is a not-for-profit organization at the cutting edge of eco-tourism that recruits volunteers to gather information about some of the world's most endangered coral reefs and rainforests around the world. Volunteers are trained in a range of skills including scuba diving, coral-fish identification and survey techniques. What is particularly interesting is that research by Nolan (2004) highlights the 'learning' element as a key motivational driver for people joining as volunteers, but some such experiential projects remain almost exclusively for those who have, or are able to raise, the necessary funds.

Greenforce was inspired by the commitments made at the Earth Summit in Rio in 1992 to identify and protect the biodiversity of the planet. One brochure is titled 'Work on the wild side! Conservation expeditions'. Volunteers are offered an 'experience of a lifetime'. These and many other practical environmental organizations grew out of the great demand for an educational 'experience'. Frontier is a non-profit organization promoted by the Society for Environmental Exploration, and has the following in its 2000 brochure:

> Taking part in a *Frontier* expedition is a once-in-a-lifetime experience... Future employers will be impressed with your achievements both in getting there and in succeeding in your project. Many former volunteers have used their expeditions as the basis for project and dissertation work for Bachelor's Degrees and Master's Degrees. Frontier is also a 'Sponsoring Establishment' for Research Degrees through the Open University, the ONLY volunteer conservation organization to have achieved the status of a field university. If you want a career in conservation and overseas development work, *Frontier* is the only option. With all volunteers eligible for a level 3 BTEC qualification in Tropical Habitat Conservation just on the strength of ten weeks of training and work on a *Frontier* expedition, becoming a volunteer gives you a chance to kick start a career in this highly competitive field. A recent survey found that 62 per cent of ex-*Frontier* volunteers have achieved such careers thanks to their experience with *Frontier*.

Operation Raleigh selects young people to take on major expeditions around the world, and they too offer such projects in the international dimension of their development programmes:

> Challenges in the outdoors, and involvement in community or environmental projects, are well established as a successful means of developing staff. Combining these with intensive international work in remote areas, Raleigh creates a framework within which learning can be transferred to the workplace. Working and living with people from different backgrounds for an extended period helps equip employees for today's fast-changing and demanding business environment. Working in real time, generating solutions to real problems, the experience proves sustainable and effective at developing the following qualities: team-working, leadership, interpersonal skills, confidence, motivation and assertiveness, initiative, flexibility and resilience, adaptability, maturity, awareness of self and others.

Expeditions

Wilderness programmes in the United States and Australia use expeditions that last as long as 100 days, and these are often times to reappraise life. They often result in powerful life-impacting learning and, as such, expeditions are still used by many organizations to offer development opportunities for young people in growth, self-development and active citizenship. In the United States there are Family Expedition Programs to assist dysfunctional families coping, for example, with at-risk youth. The expedition thus becomes the opportunity to construct a microcosm of the family life journey so that it can be reappraised and re-navigated in real life. Other forms of adventurous journeys are also used for youth and adult development programmes. In 1978 Operation Drake was launched in the UK. With the success of Operation Drake, Operation Raleigh followed in its footsteps in 1984. Its aim was to develop leadership potential in young people through their experience of the expeditions. Operation Raleigh, renamed Raleigh International, sends 'venturers' between the ages of 17 and 25 years on a 10-week expedition. Expeditions are being increasingly used in many other ways, from management development to adventure tourism. The UK Institute of Management suggest that:

> There is growing evidence that expeditions are gaining an emerging prominence and profile within the realms of human resource development (HRD). Arising from this evidence is a suggestion that expeditions contribute to personal growth or development of desirable capabilities that are relevant to work contexts...

> (Surtees, 1998: 25–26)

Advertising for expeditions is increasingly found in management journals. More adults are engaging in such life-enhancing journeys; even virtual expeditions can now be found on websites! Surtees (1998) completed an interesting comparison with our learning activity typology and found that expeditions have remarkably similar ingredients. Allison (2000b), in his research on post-expedition adjustment, discusses some of the possible themes emerging from an extensive empirical study of young people returning from an expedition, and addresses the need to re-examine epistemological and ontological perspectives used for research into experiential learning. His study focuses on the now widely recognized phenomenon of post-expedition readjustment into everyday life, and Allison argues that this can be seen in a positive light (rather than being likened to a form of posttraumatic stress disorder). Allison suggests that the loss of expedition friends, community and the expedition environment might simply indicate the adjustment pains of positive personal growth brought about by such powerful experiential learning. Among the personal growth themes emerging were:

- increased tolerance and patience;
- increased awareness and appreciation of more basic things in life;
- a change in environmental values, eg recognizing how people use their cars to travel very short journeys that are easy to walk;
- an understanding of the intensity and nature of the new friendships and the comparison of those with friendships at home;
- better relationships with siblings;

- a greater sense of personal and spiritual perspectives on life;
- a sense of service and giving;
- a change of self-concept.

(adapted from Allison, 2000b: 71–77)

Allison was able to draw out these themes that relate to the individual sense of being, where young people clearly see the world in a very different light when they return home following this powerful experiential learning event.

Journeys can take the form of smaller detailed micro-hikes over a few metres of the floor of a forest or the circumference of a tree! Journeys can involve an orienteering exercise, or they can involve simply getting objects or people from A to B. They can be metaphorical, in thought only, and mind journeys form the basis of guided fantasy work in therapy, a subject that we also cover in later chapters:

> A typical guided fantasy would engage the client in envisioning himself or herself as undertaking a hazardous journey, overcoming obstacles, meeting a wise person, and returning with a gift or message. In such a scenario, the therapist intentionally engages the client in constructing a 'self-as-hero-on-journey-of-liberation' story, as a means of empowering the client and helping him or her to celebrate his or her own powers and capabilities.

(McLeod, 1997: 81)

Planning the journey and the learning from it is one of the key skills of the experiential provider, and it is of immense significance to the learner.

Sequencing learning activities

Another key consideration in the 17-point typology is the sequence of activities. Primer activities often include ice-breakers and acquaintance exercises to reduce inhibitions or to create trust, empathy and teamwork (see, for example, Schoel *et al*, 1988). Experiential activities also develop skill, knowledge or awareness, and often start with specific narrow skills and then move on to aggregate or 'broad' skills such as teamwork, communication, time management, emotional intelligence or leadership. This use of narrow 'activities' has to be examined in the light of their function. Broader and more complex activities provide depth to the experiential learning process, as is seen from the framework in Figure 5.4. Adapting the model of Dainty and Lucas (1992), this simple framework can be created both to classify outdoor and indoor experiential learning programmes and to show the sequencing of activities from play to intense self-development over the period of a programme.

Narrow skills such as listening or questioning can be focused on first. These might be built on later, as they are a subset of skills for teamwork or communication, which are very broad skills. Narrow skills can also be less developmental and more functional, for example knot tying, map reading or

FIGURE 5.4 The experiential wave

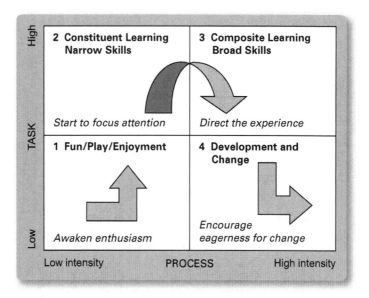

juggling skills, and they may be included to build up to complex functional skills for a journey such as orienteering.

By combining Cornell's flow learning (1989) with a model by Dainty and Lucas (1992) we have created the following four-stage sequence or activity wave:

1 Awaken participant enthusiasm with ice-breakers and energizers.

2 Start to focus attention with medium-sized activities and narrow skills.

3 Direct the personal experience with larger, broader skills.

4 Share participant enthusiasm using regular reviewing activities.

Mind and body

So far in this chapter we have been discussing physical activity predominantly in the outdoors. It is important to remember that experiential learning involves a linking of the mind and body. In this section we now consider some aspects of addressing adventures of the mind. We discuss the mind–body links in more detail in Chapter 6 about the senses, and in Chapter 8 on knowing and intelligence.

In athletics, computing and city finance, it is the young who dominate: they are fast off the blocks. But other professions, such as wine tasters, judges and prime ministers, seem to be dominated by older people. Why is this?

When people are young they have the advantage of speed of mind and body, yet as they get older they retain a distinct advantage, and it is called 'experience'. Both young and old have different advantages. The brain shrinks with old age (Robertson, 1999) and it is crucial to keep the brain fit. The brain is a very powerful machine, requiring 'attentive' rather than passive stimulation. Brains need stimulation and it is crucial for the shaping and remoulding of the electrode 'muscles' of the mind (Robertson, 1999). Some outdoor experiential programmes do not engage the brain sufficiently and the mind–body balance is a consideration, as is the affective–cognitive balance. Books on brain-teasers for trainers are now available as off-the-shelf learning activities.

The left side of the brain works on logical, linear processing and is also concerned with language, reading, writing and analysis. The right side of the brain is concerned with intuition, parallel processing, images and metaphors, patterns and visual recognition. Left-brain stimulation can be created by designing appropriate elements of problem solving into the development activities, and, significantly, examples of daily mind stretchers are to be found in nearly all daily newspapers.

Challenging the mind: mental olympics – cognitive, mathematical–logical examples

1   Challenging cognitive exercises can be added to other exercises, eg the coded game: 12 M (months) in a Y (year)
   365 D in a Y
   4 W on a C and so on...

   Or more complex:

2   Explain the reason for the distribution of the following letters above and below the line: A.........EF...HI...

   ...BCD......G......
   (For solution see base of box) *Or:*

3   This urban exercise utilizes three street bollards in the city centre, labelled as a, b and c. Tyres are numbered 1, 2, 3, 4 and 5. They are placed one on top of the other in order with 1 at the top of the pile at bollard a. The tyres must be relocated on to bollard c in the same order but the following rules apply:–
   Only one tyre may be carried at any one time and must be placed in a pile before any other tyre can be picked up.

   – A smaller number must always be placed on top of a larger number.

Some people might need to be started off, ie 1 to c, 2 to b, 1 to b, 3 to c, etc.

This session can be used with time limits with certain allocated members carrying the tyres, whilst coordinators, who can be restrained in any way by rules or restrictions, tell the carriers what to do. An example is that the coordinators might be some distance away and operate their instructions by walkie-talkie, or in a coded language. Printed T-shirts with numbers, symbols or letters are ideal for many of these exercises. T-shirts can have + or ÷ or × printed on the backs for people to complete calculations.

Or:

4   Build mathematical challenges into other activities, eg physical, recreational or navigational activities. The 'bike it' exercise (see Beard, 2010) involves constructing or assembling a bike – exercising the many forms of intelligence. Here participants are provided with a set of accounts, and activities to carry out for money, including the solving of cryptic clues, mathematical problems, theoretical models to create, journeys to undertake, team skills to decide, jobs to divide – all to build a bike, through earning money to buy the parts, or expertise. But the frame and the handlebars are hidden in the city or the wilderness of the National Park, and clever problem solving will find them – but that requires brainpower.

(Solution = straight and round letters!)

Rules and obstacles

In Chapter 3 we discuss the good practice of climate and ground rule setting. These are important functions and require careful consideration. Many other simple rules, obstacles or procedures can also influence the degree of adventure, challenge or difficulty of any experiential activity. These rules and obstacles can also allow greater flexibility in a programme design so that the experience can be altered and levels of challenge can be reduced or increased. Time constraints, for example, might mean that items such as bike parts can only be purchased during specific times. Two-way radios can be used on certain frequencies; battery life can be measured or curtailed. Solar panels can be used to charge batteries or equipment so that people can only carry out some tasks when the sun is shining. Items can be placed in the way of routes and the journey might only be allowed at night or through certain territory. Instructions can be given on a tape recording through earplugs so that only one person can hear them at any one time. Communication might be restricted to coded whistles or translated into another language.

Obstacles can include sensory deprivation or sensory adjustment, and might include blindfolds, earplugs, glasses to improve or remove vision, nose pegs or gloves to remove feeling or to create clumsiness. Tarpaulins can be used to separate teams and they might be allowed to pass items only through a narrow aperture. Sorting and organization skills are also important: a mass of data, a mass of information to sort and make sense of, or activities to decide who does what and when. Why? Because knowledge is one thing; organized knowledge is a million things! The range of combinations within the milieu increases the level of challenge. While the milieu is endless, it does need a degree of focus, structure and reason.

The following rules and restrictions apply!

1 The time limit to complete the activities is just 220 minutes.

2 Each activity can be completed only once and will earn you money.

3 Each activity requires you to estimate your projected earnings and to submit it to the facilitator before commencing.

4 Physical activities will be paid in dollars; mental tasks will be paid in Euros.

5 The four teams will have radio contact for 10 minutes only during each half-hour.

6 One team member must be blindfolded at all times. One person must wear gloves at all times. For blindfold and glove wearing, rotation of the wearers is allowed.

7 A sum of 10 dollars will be paid for each digital picture of the team 'completing' an activity.

8 An up-to-date set of accounts must be ready for inspection at any time.

9 Teams A and B will submit a mind-map plan of their proposals to the facilitators before commencing.

10 Teams C and D will not be required to produce a plan.

Constructing and deconstructing

Construction and deconstruction is a core concept in learning. It can be applied to physical objects, from bikes to rafts to dry-stone walls and bridges, and has been an essential component of many outdoor experiential programmes. Other options include the construction of something that is non-physical, such as a diagram or theoretical construct. This can be done using cards and masking tape. Plastic kits like giant Lego blocks are off-the-shelf devices used to create artificial 'tasks' and sold on many training websites: they can easily be assembled and disassembled. The plastic kits do not create real tasks – their reality is metaphoric. 'Ready-made kit' used to take the form of traditional planks and drums, used in raft building in outdoor teamwork development, but these are increasingly being replaced by a plethora of new manufactured artefacts. Everything from tank driving to juggling is being used by some providers in the search for novel forms of learning activities, as the increasingly sophisticated and discerning audience may get bored if they have 'done it before'. Irvine and Wilson (1994) challenge some of the mystique about some outdoor experiential events, and argue that 'novelty' might form the basis of such a rationale. They also quote Long and Galagan who suggest that the outdoors is where educational and organizational norms do not exist for people to hide behind.

The core experiences can also be deconstructed: rafts and planks and drums type experiences involve building something, getting wet, testing and then racing the product in a competitive sense. These experiences can then be re-engineered into alternative projects. The advantage is that the client can be given choices, and alternatives: corporate buy-in and involvement can be increased.

Telling the story – using physical objects

In experiential learning a range of inanimate and 'unreal' objects are used for people to project thoughts and feelings on to. Assagioli (1980) developed the idea of psychosynthesis, which partly uses a whole range of imaginative techniques so that people can project their inner thoughts and emotions on to images or symbols. This can enable, allowing expression of issues that lie deeper in their inner self, including emotional issues. Projection onto objects appears to remove some of the embarrassment that occurs in traditional face-to-face talking; deeper forays into the 'personal' become possible. For example, discussions or reviews can use 'natural stones', selected by participants to enable them to talk about themselves, say, in terms of why they chose that stone. By talking about the colour of the stone, its shape and size, personal meanings and values can be vocalized, and feelings and values can be *projected* on to the stone. People also talk about their *inner* self as being different: the stone only represents what people see on the outside. It is much harder to talk about these things candidly in person to person, or person to group. The position of the stones in relation to the others can also be significant in terms of the way groups or teams see themselves. Group difficulties can be broached more easily. In the case of natural stones, the objects become the metaphor to transfer meaning.

Russian dolls can be used to symbolize people, power and position of other people. Playing cards can be used: diamonds represent hard *facts*, hearts explore *feelings*, spades dig deeper – *findings*, and clubs explore possible *futures* (Greenaway, 1996). One technique devised to control either excessive dominance or shyness by young people in a group is called 'having the bottle to speak'. It has a double meaning. It involves using a plastic bottle, and people wanting to speak must wait for an opportunity to take it from someone else. If a person with the bottle has finished, he or she holds it out for others to take it, and as a sign of friendship people help to create discussion by sharing the talking and taking and holding the bottle. For some it is hard to *have the bottle to try it*. The technique can also be used to ensure silence to those not holding the object and the technique can illustrate fairness and balance of talk time.

Learning activities: exploring reality

> Hanging by a single rope 80 feet from the ground, controlled by a colleague whose previous knowledge of ropes was tying his shoelaces, could not under any circumstances be described as a game.
>
> (Butcher, 1991: 28)

In order to help people learn from experience, learning providers use a combination of activities and draw on drama, sculpting, role-play, art, stories and metaphors. They encourage learners to express thoughts and ideas about their experience. However, the degree to which these activities are perceived as 'real' or 'relevant' can have a significant effect on the learning experience. We have previously described a range of learning activities and offered a simple typology. We now consider these learning activities in terms of dimensions of 'reality', exploring how 'reality manipulation' can offer opportunities to unlock learning potential. While levels of reality can be reduced or increased to influence learning, making the right choices requires a clear understanding of the processes involved. In this section we offer a range of examples of 'real' and 'simulated' activities, and give guidance on the raising and lowering of reality in experiential learning. We now focus on a deeper understanding of the second cog in the learning combination lock.

What is a real experience?

Item four in the learning typology was 'adjust elements of reality'. What is this term *reality*, and how might providers work with it for the benefit of learners? Harwood (2005: 224), in her work on storytelling as an organizational development tool in the healthcare sector, refers to Bohm, an eminent physicist, who created the notion of 'presented' reality and 'represented' reality:

> Presented reality is viewed by Bohm as the classical Newtonian physical universe comprised of 'objects' or 'things' that are observable through the five senses, and about which there is common consensus, for example the price of a loaf of bread or how many part-time workers there are in the organization. In contrast, 'represented reality' then ascribes meanings to presented reality, for example 'that supermarket charges too much for its bread' or 'part-time workers tend to be women'. These realities are not 'in' the data itself but are interpretations of what the data means, and thus open to alternative readings.

In higher education the degree of subject *relevance* is an important consideration for students and pedagogic research into affective motivational states reports that a significant number of students, when asked to comment on what lecturers might do more of or less of in lectures, called for an increase in the degree of 'relevance' and 'reality' of the material they present (Beard, 2005). Outdoor learning providers claim high levels of reality in their programmes, and Krouwel and Goodwill (1994, p 220) argue that reality is the key advantage to using the natural outdoors for learning as 'reality is perhaps the greatest asset of all in management development programmes that use the outdoors. There is no artificiality in the exercises outdoors; the problems are real, the issues are dynamic, the constraints are felt. There is no need to act – it is the real world.' This implies that the learning activities are very 'real activities' as opposed to artificial 'games'. We argue that such a concept of 'real' requires greater scrutiny.

Martin *et al* (2004: 58) argue that dramaturgy games are: '"life as if" or "a draft for life". Games create a model world, allowing people to enter various life situations that are otherwise not accessed by them, to experiment with various situations or roles and to explore their reactions to their new situation.'

The games are said to connect with normality as the emotions, processes and interactions during the game are 'real'. Likewise, Price says that in outdoor development work, 'It is important that it be totally real because then you get real emotions, real fear, high anxiety, high or low morale, real aggression and real learning' (Price, cited in Bank, 1994: 10). Butcher (1991: 26) stresses the need to reproduce the work environment during company training sessions, to make learning more 'realistic': 'It is essential that training programmes have included in their designs, components that reproduce these problems, in a more tangible and realistic form than has been employed by many training consultants in the past.'

Holman *et al* (1997) consider this 'vague and indeterminate nature of reality' that results in the meanings of experiences being contested. In our view, understanding the impact of construction, deconstruction and orchestration of all the elements of 'reality' is a key requisite for experiential learning.

High levels of reality do not always present the best option for learning. What does Butcher actually mean when he refers to 'tangible and realistic'? Reality appears to have many different interpretations for different people. 'Real' might equate to the 'workplace-like' space, the degree of 'relevance' of the activity, or the extent to which the outdoors is seen as a real place. In the previous chapter we explored how the notion of a journey might involve venturing away from the routines of the real home or real community environments in order to learn. Reality might refer to real tasks or activities, to the real people involved (eg negotiators), the real skills developed, the real objects used, the real learning outcomes or the real place in which the learning is undertaken. The notion of 'reality' is a much more complex phenomenon than is often realized, and, as we shall now argue, it requires greater exploration in terms of its impact on learners.

Butcher, an ex-army training officer, avoids a deeper exploration of 'reality' in suggesting that 'hanging by a single rope 80 feet from the ground, controlled by a colleague whose previous knowledge of ropes was tying his shoelaces, could not under any circumstances be described as a game' (1991: 28). Reality, in this situation, is not located with the activities, but rather in the form of real emotions that can emerge from such a situation, and which can heavily influence learning (we investigate emotions in Chapter 7). Perhaps Butcher views reality through the influence of his background in the armed services, where trainers 'use experience based training to prepare people for the discomfort, depersonalization, and emotional strain encountered in combat' (Walter and Marks, 1981: 3). These combative styles from the armed forces often intentionally use 'in-your-face' techniques that push and prod as a form of 'distressed learning' designed to increase anxiety levels and so stimulate learning (Yerkes and Dodson, 1980). Distressed learning works for some people but such methods can be rather crude, creating a superficial confrontation of emotions such as fear and trepidation, thus teaching people to tame, combat and suppress their fear as if in preparation for real warfare. Rightly, this interpretation of reality and of experiential learning is not a panacea for all learning.

If learners cannot experience the 'real thing' they can of course experience something that is perceived as real, in a physical sense or an emotional sense. Learning environments can also be seen as unreal, bearing no resemblance to the learner's customary environment. The military use a combative approach to the outdoor environment and it was the military that first used artificial climbing blocks for training. This manipulation of facets of the learning environment might suggest that the space for learning is simply another element to be artificially choreographed as a 'bag of tricks'. Space for learning, as we explore in detail in Chapter 4, is an important consideration. Steve Van Matre (1978, 1979) helps children to understand how photosynthesis occurs by getting them inside a leaf-shaped tent, with ping-pong balls, where the children pretend to manufacture sugars. And at a higher education level learning can spill out of the classroom into the wider community, as seen in the case study below on law clinics.

Case study: law clinics: using high reality strategies in experiential learning

Law clinics have their roots in the United States, where Law is normally a postgraduate course. They remain a widespread method of legal teaching, often having the dual purpose of meeting the massive unmet need for legal advice in a jurisdiction without a comprehensive legal aid system, as well as maximizing the student learning to make up for the general lack of a later work-based stage of learning.

There has been a substantial growth in law clinics in many countries – including Australia, South America and South Africa – but in the United Kingdom they remain uncommon. Clinics may take a number of different forms – including placement-based (or extern-ship) clinics; clinics which offer a pure representation service (such as the Free Representation Unit in London);

and full casework and representation models (such as Northumbria University's Student Law Office) which are effectively full in-house law centres.

The Northumbria Student Law Office is a compulsory element in the undergraduate law degree, with about 130 undergraduate students working for a full year under the supervision of 15 practitioner members of staff. In any given year the programme will take on 500–600 clients, with problems ranging from employment to divorce, from consumer disputes to top-level criminal appeals, and from housing cases to human rights applications.

Case Study 1

'A' was convicted of involvement in armed robbery and given a substantial prison sentence. He contacted the Student Law Office and over a period of four years various groups of students worked on his case, identifying potential grounds of appeal against the conviction. The students then helped 'A' with his application to the Criminal Cases Review Commission, who referred the matter back to the Court of Appeal. The students then briefed a leading Queen's Counsel to represent 'A' at the appeal, and they helped to prepare the case for its hearing. The conviction was overturned as being unsafe, and further groups of students then helped 'A' with his application for compensation for his wrongful conviction. Running such long-running cases is obviously a major challenge, but the case provided a number of generations of students with valuable learning in analysing the criminal law – and in rectifying a serious miscarriage of justice.

Case Study 2

N's mother died in a nursing home after some months of severe neglect. There was a substantial delay while the prosecuting agencies decided whether to bring criminal proceedings against the owners of the home. When they decided not to prosecute, N decided he wished to sue the home on behalf of his deceased mother. However, to do this the executors of the will would have to bring the action. They did not wish to do so as they had only agreed to act as executors as a favour to the family. The students helped N to draft the documents to the High Court to replace the executors, and they briefed a supervisor in the Law Office to represent the client at court as they lacked the right to appear in court at that level. With this case the students not only learnt a huge amount about an area of law that they had only studied in brief, they also had the opportunity to draft documents for the High Court, to advise and assist their client and to brief counsel and attend court.

In management training Kirk (1986: 87) suggests that there are three main dimensions of reality to consider: participant reality, theoretical reality and resource reality. Participant reality involves the extent to which the design and content of the learning event relates to the learners and their jobs, organizational environments, personal abilities and expectations.

Theoretical reality is the extent to which the content of the learning event relates to the existing body of knowledge concerning the nature of management and management learning. The nature of reality lies in questioning the theoretical models or concepts that are being applied and whether these are 'real' or 'true'. Resource reality is the extent and cost of resources that go into staging and running the learning events and whether the expenditure can be justified. If learners do not relate their 'experience' on a programme to their experience in real life, then the experience is likely to be criticized as having little relevance and this can affect the transfer of learning. Binstead and Stuart (1979) focus on three other dimensions of reality and offer reasoning and guidance for adjusting the degree of reality. They elaborate on the reality of the process of learning, the reality of the tasks that people complete and the reality of the environment in which people are learning.

High levels of reality do not always result in more significant learning. Although it is hard to tap into past, present and potential future experiences of learners so as to create high perceived reality, high-reality strategies can:

- integrate learning and work role activities;
- take the learning event to the job;
- bring the job to the learning event (tutor-led);
- bring the job to the learning event (participant-led);
- provide a range of alternative activities within the learning event;
- change the work situation to match the learning event.

(Binstead and Stuart, 1979)

There are situations where lowering reality permits a different kind of learning. Low reality may be appropriate, for example, when more radical alternatives need to be considered, so that new horizons can be opened up. We can use fantasy to reduce inhibitions, and role-play to allow a feeling to be expressed or to create a feeling that 'This is not really me; I am just playing a part.' This kind of learning involves moving out of the reality of self in order to see something different. High-reality events would appear to be inappropriate and often dysfunctional when: 1) there is a need for growth- rather than maintenance-orientated learning, eg to allow a learner to consider radical alternative behaviour, ideas, etc; or 2) there is sufficient threat invoked in high-reality situations for it to be a barrier to learning.

Managers building and sailing a raft might experience a low reality in terms of environment (they don't usually work outside) and of task (they don't usually build and sail rafts). There is high reality in terms of process (they do use teamwork, communication skills, etc in their work – but then, who doesn't?). The process skills practised on a mountain do not always get 'transferred' back to everyday behaviours. High transfer techniques might allow the learner to progress slowly to high reality as in the negotiating case study below.

A practical case study: altering reality

Negotiating public access to the UK countryside: skills development

The early part of the course uses 'narrow skills' practice. Negotiating is a 'broad skill', involving many narrow skills such as listening, questioning, diplomacy and so on. On this course we thus deconstructed 'negotiating' into its many narrow sub-skills such as influencing, persuasion, listening, tactics, entry, developing rapport, closing and so on. The latter part of the course then used broad skills practice, but with varying levels of reality or simulation. The exercises were as follows:

From: LOW CONTENT REALITY

Exercise A: Redecorating the office

The material was taken from a standard loose-leaf package on negotiating. It is a paper exercise. There is no incentive. It concerns a contract price to decorate an office suite. Content reality is low. The written case material on decorating contains a review sheet that looks at the forces in use in negotiating and the approaches that can be used by the two sides. People are asked to identify opening gambits and write their answers on paper.

Exercise B: Driving a bargain

A written exercise about cars – people are told that this is a warm-up for a real car exercise when people can pit their wits against real negotiators! This adds to the incentive to concentrate on all exercises. Here the content reality is again low – the people involved do not negotiate car prices in their jobs.

Exercise C: Buying a new car

Real cars are used. Real logbooks are used. Real car prices are offered. Car book prices are available. Cars can be inspected and faults found, both inside and outside, as they are located in the car park. The keys are made available. One is an uncleaned four-wheel drive and the other is a nicely valeted VW Polo. The brief informs people, 'You have moved to the National Park and need a four-wheel drive for bad weather and to tow your new caravan.' False money is used but a prize is offered. The people that the participants negotiate with are real trained negotiators and they are located in an office where the deals will take place. Final agreements are written in sealed envelopes so that the winners can be decided later. Content reality is again low; process reality is high.

To: HIGH CONTENT REALITY

Exercise D: Negotiating access to UK land on behalf of the public

Here we use high content reality and high process reality. Real negotiators are again present. Real information is provided – facts and figures on sheep headage payments, ranger support offered, wall damage payments and litter arrangements. Participants are real access officers or public rights of way officers. They are observed on video by the rest of the group. The incentive is to try to do a good job in front of their peers, to try to put all the skills and knowledge acquired on the course into practice, and they try to meet their own pre-set prices and subsidy targets decided in their negotiating plans. They argue their case with real negotiators and are debriefed afterwards. The video is then replayed with self- and peer assessment taking place.

(Beard, 2005)

Fantasy

Fantasy is a form of psychic play, suspending reality. It is not just for children and the technique is frequently used to frame the mental state. In *101 of the Best Corporate Team-building Activities We Know!*, Priest and Rohnke (2000: 5) offer fantasy as one type of 'framing' the way an experiential activity is introduced. They make reference to the popular 'fantasy or fairy tale introductions that include such items as spiders, sharks, alligators, poison peanut butter, radioactive yoghurt, nitroglycerine, TNT, corrosive acid, floods and forest fires'. One UK company offers many innovative theatrical-based training techniques, including *animating ideas* where people can 'Extend the boundaries of experience and realize your dreams and themes, through your own fantastic animated creations. You select the style, develop the characters, devise the stories and provide the voices... Hours of endeavour. Seconds of footage. Years of satisfaction' (Experience Creative Development, 2000).

Fantasy 'kits' for use in training offer many set scenarios: stranded on an island, capsizing on a lake or being stuck in a jungle. Brochures suggest that reality can be enhanced 'with a set of 20 slides that will make your participants glad they are warm and dry'. Participants are even given 'I survived the rainforest badges' after completion of the programme! Learning activities deliberately move from fantasy to reality. In *The Handbook of Management Games*, Elgood (1984), although not entirely satisfied with the term 'game' because its use may detract from the seriousness of purpose, discusses the nature and value of games, simulations and exercises. Elgood (1984: 8) identified four criteria that a game should satisfy:

1 It has a sufficiently clear framework to ensure that it is recognizably the same exercise whenever it is used.

2 It confronts the players with a changing situation, the changes being wholly or in part a consequence of their own actions.

3 It allows the identification beforehand (if desired) of some criterion by which it can be won or lost.

4 It requires for its operation a certain level of documentation, physical material, computation or administrative/behavioural skill.

Three models of games were identified by Elgood. The first are *definitive models* in which there is a clear answer and desired result to the game. This reflects the creator's view of the world in which, if certain behaviour occurs, there will be a specific result. The second type of game involves *probabilistic models*. This type of game is not as rigid and predictable, and allows for individual behaviour. It helps to create awareness of alternatives and the fact that people are prone to misunderstand what are thought to be common concepts, eg workers negotiating a wage structure with managers. The third type of game is concerned with *individual models*. These involve exploring and comparing the individual solutions to the game in a non-judgemental way that recognizes the value of differences. Elgood (1984: 12–13) categorized games as follows:

- games based on a definitive model:
  - traditional model-based games;
  - puzzles;
  - in-basket exercises;
  - mazes;
  - programmed simulations;
  - enquiry studies;
  - encounter games;
  - adult role-playing games;

- games based on a probabilistic model:
  - structured experiences;
  - organization games;
  - organizational simulations;
  - practical simulations;

- games based on individual models:
  - in-basket exercises;
  - exploratory games.

Fantasy can create a sense of atmosphere, excitement and adventure, involving suspending disbelief, and the use of magic and mystery. Some adventures tend to be completely set in a fantasy world, or they might involve moving from the real world to the fantasy world and back again. This often requires some form of trigger between the fantasy world and the real world; for example, in *The Lion, the Witch and the Wardrobe* (Lewis, 1980), people walk into the wardrobe and into the land of Narnia. A secret code might be hidden in a cave, and there might be a 'quest'. Many of the characters in children's fantasy go through rites of passage, with helpers 'guiding them' into maturity: they learn to believe in themselves, and their lives are enriched from the experience of the quest.

Guided fantasy is a journey of the mind involving images with a deep symbolic meaning. Fantasy and guided imagery can be used to develop more awareness of thoughts and emotions, leading to the creation of greater self-awareness and personal growth. Relaxation techniques also use guided fantasy to take people on a mind journey to favourite places and imaginary environments that lower the heart rate and stimulate positive feelings. *The Temple of Silence* (Ferrucci, 1982) can be adapted: set in an imaginary world, and a story we tell concerns a journey up a cold, snowy mountain, where we arrived at a cave. Sitting by a fire in the cave is a wise old man – the sage. We had opened the door of the training room to let in some fresh air and as we lay on the floor in the dark the wind got up and it started to snow heavily and the snow actually came into the room! The atmosphere was beginning to change as the reality blurred with our fantasies: two participants from Outward Bound Singapore had never seen snow before! Workshop participants were later asked to go out into the surrounding fields and woods and find somewhere to be alone with their thoughts, somewhere they could not be seen and where they could not see anyone else. This was to let their imagination develop even further.

Play and reality

Play, as observed in a variety of mammals, would appear to indicate that play serves to *rehearse and exercise skills* in a safe environment. This can be seen in kittens playing together, stalking and pouncing. Recognition of the value of play is not a recent phenomenon. Games have been played for thousands of years and there is clear evidence from the Egyptians of 'acrobatics, gymnastic games, tug-of-war, hoop and kicking games, ball and stick games, juggling, knife throwing, club throwing, wrestling, swimming, guessing games, games of chance, and board games' (Booth and Moss, 1994: 5). Plato (1953) advised that any builder must first play at building. It is clear from general observation how successful children are with learning where play forms a key role. By the time they are three children have learnt to walk, speak, handle a variety of objects, control their limbs and bodily functions, and operate in social environments. They learn in a 'natural' way and, it would appear, often carry out an activity just for fun; more importantly, they appear to enjoy themselves. It is normally non-threatening and usually conducted in a safe environment for themselves and for other children. Significantly, 'their involvement with the learning process is total. There is no separation between learning, play, work, and leisure. Life is all of these at once and its process is spontaneous' (Heap, 1993: 16).

Play also offers a powerful mind state for adult learning. Adults may require permission to play because attention is focused on 'ought to be' doing or 'could be' doing: worries and concerns, regrets and mistakes, about things in the future and of the past, can present inner barriers, preventing the states needed for learning (Carlson, 1998; Mallinger and De Wyze, 1993). Mallinger and De Wyze (1993: 171) comment that:

> A workaholic parent may be physically present but non-existent as a nurturing parent... Each stage of [child] development lasts for only a very brief time, and once completed, will never be repeated. Miss out on enough such experiences, and you will end up with only a pale, vitiated sense of ever having had children.

In contrast, children experience play as just 'being', naturally living 'the moment', the 'here and now'. Piaget (1927), who studied his own three children and other children, identified three types of play:

- **sensorimotor play** – involves the practice of behaviours and exploratory learning often seen in young infants;
- **pretend or symbolic play** – found in children from two to six years;
- **games with rules** – played from the ages of six or seven years upwards.

Children often seem to enjoy free play with materials such as sand, paints, water and clay. They frequently become totally absorbed in this creative process and the materials provide an opportunity for learning about the nature of materials, conservation of material, spatial, textural and other dimensions.

In the years 1890–1920, $100 million was used to build playgrounds in the United States (Cohen, 1987). These playgrounds were formed in order to minimize delinquency and improve morals and health. The first adventure playground was built in Copenhagen in 1943, and its director Bertelson stated, 'There can be no doubt that in the case of so called difficult children, free play presents a solution to their problem' (Cohen, 1987: 32). This initiative led to the establishment of the International Playground Association, with Bertelson defining an adventure playground 'as a place where children are free to do many things that they cannot do elsewhere in our crowded urban society' (Cohen, 1987: 32). The assault courses that are used by adults in management training exercises are a sophisticated form of playground.

Unfortunately, not all children play. The economist John Stuart Mill was not allowed to play by his father, who wanted his son educated from birth. Similarly, Froebel, born in Thuringia, Germany in 1782, had an unhappy childhood and, influenced by the writings of Rousseau, developed a kindergarten (garden of children) where children could, like flowers, 'blossom'. This was a reaction to the drilling methods used in schools, and in the kindergarten children were allowed to play and were encouraged by adults. Also, play in children is not always undertaken in a light-hearted and pretend manner, as can be seen in Golding's *Lord of the Flies*. Play has the potential to have a negative influence.

So how do we experience play as adults? It is difficult to draw boundaries that clearly define play from other forms of activity, and Smith *et al* (1986) described how it is also difficult to categorize the various types of play. However, they identified five main characteristics of play:

- **intrinsic motivation** – the child plays for the sake of play and not for other external reasons;
- **positive effect** – the child enjoys and finds satisfaction in the play;
- **non-literal** – play is pretend and is not taken seriously;
- **means/ends** – the child is more focused on the process and behaviour rather than the actual outcome;
- **flexibility** – there can be a variation in the context or form of behaviour.

Play for adults includes not just sporting activities and board games at Christmas but, according to Cohen (1987: 15), psychological games in which he included 'encounter groups, growth movements, self-help groups of some sorts, following the guru, self therapies, and all kinds of ego-fests. Obviously, many people take these activities very seriously and some need help. But for many people, going to groups has become a form of "deep" play.' Furthermore, the playing of games would appear to be an activity that is conducted by children of all ages. Berne's (1973) *Games People Play* proposes that we all possess within us the ability to play the role of parent, adult and child in our interactions with others.

What is all too apparent in this discussion about games is that they are an essential learning process for young people to develop the skills necessary to survive in later life. Games develop cognitive, affective and behavioural skills that can be used in both personal and work lives. For adults, involving oneself with certain types of play activity, with the exception of formalized games, is often frowned upon. It is assumed that as adults we are mature and have passed through the stage of playing games.

Suspending reality: drama and role-playing

Generally, there is felt to be a very sharp distinction between learning and amusing oneself. The first may be useful, but only the second is pleasant.

(Brecht, quoted in Willett, 1977, p. 72)

The quotation above creates a cynical juxtaposition of amusement and learning: Pollock (2000) coins the term 'infotainment', reporting that 'companies are turning to music, storytelling, visual art and even comedy in order to develop their people, engender creativity in the work-place and enhance the corporate image'.

We now explore role-*play*. Drama is defined as: 'The enactment of real and imagined events through roles and situations. Drama enables both individuals and groups to explore, shape and symbolically represent ideas and feelings and their consequences. Drama stimulates and shapes aesthetic development and enjoyment through valuing both affective and cognitive responses to the world' (Curriculum Corporation, 1994: 16, in Attard, 2001).

Role-playing techniques have been roughly classified as:

- performed or imagined (passive or active) (Hamilton, 1976, in Attard, 2001);
- scripted or improvised (Hamilton, 1976, in Attard, 2001);
- involving one individual or many;
- participants required to play themselves or somebody else;
- participants required to play themselves under a familiar or unfamiliar set of circumstances;
- stooges may or may not be used in role-plays – and sometimes are used as *agent provocateurs*;
- subject may be pre-briefed and deceived, or pre-briefed and not deceived, or not pre-briefed at all;
- scenario inductions can involve one-line prompts or several;
- participants may be constrained into a highly structured-response format or, alternatively, be given a free-response format.

(adapted from Yardley-Matwiejczuk, 1999: 36)

The list provides innovative facilitation ideas. Role-play can facilitate problem solving and enable people to enhance awareness and understanding. It can have a degree of spontaneity. However:

> In reports of such role-play activities there is an overwhelming assumption that we all know what we are talking about when we mention role-play. Occasionally hints emerge, about aspects of induction or technique, that suggest the authors might know a thing or two about good practice, but these are rarely articulated fully or made explicit. Moreover, there is no evidence of a critical stance towards the question of whether role-play is being appropriately or inappropriately utilized.

(Yardley-Matwiejczuk, 1999: 34)

Playwrights from Sophocles to Brecht have used their 'plays' to teach, and convey facts and political attitudes to their audiences, but variations from the traditional play now exist. The term 'spectactors' is used to describe a technique that involves people moving from observation as 'watchers' to being involved as 'actors'. *Invisible theatre*, for example, might involve two people walking into a shop where they start to argue about something. The real people eventually take sides and then join in! But there are ethical issues here that we examined in Chapter 3.

Drama is potentially attractive to many adult learners as many people watch plays, films or soap operas and become affected by the experience. There is a distinction between using dramatic techniques as a teaching method and teaching theatre. Theatre is an art form that focuses on a product: a play or production for an audience. Drama used in experiential learning is more informal and focuses on the process of dramatic enactment for the sake of the learner, not an audience. This teaching technique is referred to as 'creative dramatics' in order to distinguish it from theatre arts. Classroom drama is not learning about drama, but learning through drama. Drama's goals are based in pedagogical, developmental and learning theory as much as or more than being arts-based. Significantly, the focus is on the growth and development of the learner rather than the entertainment or stimulation of the observer.

By means of dramatic activities students use and examine their present knowledge in order to induce new knowledge. Bolton (1985) argues that while school learning is an accruing of facts, drama can help students reframe their knowledge into new perspectives. Therefore, this teaching technique places the learner at the centre of the programme design and encourages reflection and the development of greater understanding of self and others. Facilitators, too, can utilize the reflective dimension of drama in training programmes. This will help participants to make a personal commitment to training and develop greater knowledge about themselves and others and their role in the workplace. Drama works on the theory of raising a dilemma. A facilitator stops the action, and the learners offer possible methods of resolving the situation. The actors play out the various suggestions in context, and debate can follow concerning the outcomes.

According to van Ments (1994), the idea of role-play, in its simplest form, is that of asking people to imagine that they are either themselves or another person in a particular situation. Learners are asked to behave exactly as they feel that the other person would and, as a result, they and/or the rest of the class will learn something about the person and/or situation. Role-play then is a form of imaginization and communication that can be used for different purposes. Different types of role-play demand different approaches – the way in which the role-play is introduced, the description of roles, the facilitation and the post-play analysis will vary according to the type of role-play that is being used. It can be used, for example, to describe or demonstrate events, to practise skills, to give feedback or to sensitize people to reflect upon events.

Case studies: circus and radio

OLS Unique Solutions is a small business based in the UK, and prides itself on its creative approach to finding training solutions for the commercial sector.

Case study 1

OLS was asked to help energize and motivate an HR department after they had been through a major organizational change. The client requested that the end result could only be achieved through team cooperation and, secondly, that there needed to be scope to see colleagues 'in a new light'. OLS designed a workshop where the delegates had 48 hours to devise, rehearse, resource and perform a circus show lasting 45 minutes for an audience of 300 schoolchildren. Specific skills varied from erecting the big top and learning clowning performance and trapeze to top-quality sound production. After the workshop, the HR manager described the event as 'the most effective team build I've ever been involved in'.

Case study 2

OLS was involved in a key strategy meeting for a national public service provider. The senior team was facing a major piece of strategy development work that required a positive mindset to ensure success. OLS set the team the challenge of producing a professional-quality 30-minute radio play. This involved designing, scripting, recording and the post-production of the piece. The initial reaction of the team was of disbelief, as they did not feel they could accomplish such a task in the time-frame. However, by the end of the day, all the individuals were amazed and felt enormous pride at what they were able to achieve. As a result of this new-found confidence, the business meeting the following day was highly positive and effective. On completion of any delivery, the evaluation phase focuses on the outcomes. Feedback is vital.

The case studies explain why many leading-edge outdoor experiential providers like Brathay in the UK possess drama studios and art labs as well as kayaks and climbing equipment.

Metaphors and storytelling

There is a traditional saying, in 'metaphorical speak', which is, 'Let the mountain (the experience) speak for itself.' There is a school of thought, however, that the experience, in the form of stories, needs to be told.

The *story* is one of the basic tools invented by human beings for the purpose of gaining understanding. Indeed stories solidify our memories, and everyone looks for opportunities to tell their stories in one way or another (Schank, 1992). Collison and Mackenzie (1999) assert that there have been great societies that have not used the wheel, but none that have not used stories to generate ideas, morality and values. The earliest stories were probably chants or songs and contained epics, myths, parables, fables, fairy tales and folk tales:

Asked to name the most powerful communication tools, few business people would be likely to list storytelling amongst them. That, however, may be changing, as organizations are re-awakening to the potential of one of the oldest forms known to man of passing on knowledge. In the UK, the organizations ranging from large retailing firms to government agencies are finding that working with story is a highly effective way to facilitate internal and external communication, develop teams and leadership skills, and to engage the attention of clients and customers.

(Collison and Mackenzie, 1999: 38)

Parkin (1998), in *Tales for Trainers*, describes the use of stories and metaphors to facilitate learning. She refers to the use of sets of cards that ask people to describe themselves as birthday presents or cartoon characters, or smells, or drinks. People might respond, she illustrates, by saying they are teddy bears because they are soft and cuddly, or that they are like water because it is pure, it flows and it supports life. In personal development, facilitators can create fantasy metaphors, and Parkin describes how the inexpressible can be explored by speaking in a non-prosaic language. The tale of the 'ugly duckling', for example, is a classic story relating to self-esteem. Parkin offers examples of stories aimed at personal development, business development and a wider world context. They can help people to 'analyse and maybe change their views about themselves and their levels of self-esteem' (Parkin, 1998: 18).

Storytelling and conversation analysis have also been used extensively in social science research and in conference work where management development issues and concerns need to be brought to the forefront (Gold, 1996; Gabriel, 1998; Samra-Fredericks, 1998). The core of all psychotherapy is also based on storytelling, as clients tell and retell their stories as individual life-story or personal narrative. McLeod (1997: back cover) argues that 'all therapies are, therefore, narrative therapies, and that the counselling experience can be understood in terms of telling and re-telling stories. If the story is not heard, then the therapist and the client are deprived of the most effective and mutually involving mode of discourse open to them.'

The *survival note* is an example of the use of story to help surface and explore organizational culture. Teams are asked to agree and write a basic survival story of the key things that a replacement team would need to know about working in the organization. They are asked to focus on and describe to the newcomers the key to maintaining their existing 'way of doing things' to minimize the impact on existing customers or clients. Facilitators can also use stories to lessen participant anxiety, by creating stories that contain elements of self-disclosure, as seen below.

A short self-disclosure story

Learning from mistakes: interviews – an unfortunate incident on a Scilly island

The Scillies are known as the Fortunate Islands. Colin Beard tells a true short story of one unfortunate experience on the way to this island for an interview. He caught the wrong train, got off the train, tried to get a taxi to catch up with the right train – an intercity express – but... no money, he went to the bank, oh no... queues, eventually in the taxi he was back on track, arrival at the heliport... oh no... he was booked on the helicopter the previous day... strange but he thought it was today! It was the wrong day for the interview... what a silly mistake... he met the local vicar waiting in the queue... he was supposed to be on the interview panel! Was delayed by fog the previous day... he invited Colin to stay... then more fog and delays, arrived eventually on the Scillies... oh no... they gave the job to someone else the previous day...! Back home to lots of 'How did you get on?'

A note left by father-in-law (the moral of the story): 'S/he who never makes a mistake never makes anything!'

Below is a second specific case study on the use of images and stories, through the use of cartoons.

Case study: adjusting reality – art and images

The use of cartoon images as a reflective tool embraces a mixture of art, humour and storytelling and, as Janni of the Royal Academy of Arts comments, 'arts-based learning is all about using different parts of your brain' (in Pollock, 2000: 19–23). Artists can be employed to create such images. Back in the early 80s Colin Beard used an artist to assist in a training programme for Shell executives in their prestigious Lensbury Club on the Thames. The delegates were people who were close to retirement, and to help them to move into semi-retirement they were asked to work with a Shell initiative, designed to help environmental projects. It was called the Shell Better Britain Campaign. Coming to terms with some of the difficulties of facing retirement, as well as working with environmentalists and environmental charities, was difficult for the people concerned. The culture of the organizations that they were likely to meet was probably going to be very different from their own. In their new role as officers for the Shell Better Britain Campaign, their job was to help advise groups and offer grants. By the end of each day the artist had many of their fears and concerns sketched on to huge sheets of paper in the form of cartoon images. It was cathartic to smile and laugh together at the images of Shell executives in Batman capes, abseiling down the Shell HQ in London, armed with rucksacks of information on the environment! Bulges of cheques filled the side pockets, and some were falling out, slowly floating down to the ground. The drawings also showed Inland

Revenue letters about their tax, pensions, expenses and other issues hanging out of their back pockets, reflecting some of the other more personal concerns!

The cartoons were great fun and they helped in the 'seeing' and 'airing' of difficult subjects. The funny, depersonalized neutrality is a strength in cartoon work. The 80s were the time when adult comics boomed (Mallia, 1997: 93), and our inspiration to use this medium came from more established superhero characters like Bob Kane's Batman in Gotham City and from *Peanuts*, created by the great Charles Schulz.

Management development and cartoons

Comics or newspapers can present cartoon strips to convey important messages in both adult work and youth work. We have also used stereotypical cartoon images to explore issues. One is of a woman sitting knitting on the sofa and a man reading the paper and ignoring comments from his wife, 'It's not what you say, it's what you don't say... and the way you don't say it!' Messages lie within the humour, in the script or image, and the events and actions, as well as in the physical characters of the people portrayed. An interesting account of the use of comic strips we came across, by Mallia (1997), refers to pioneering experiments with an ongoing soap-opera-style comic to aid the development of total quality management programmes (Kaizen) in a Maltese microelectronics industry. Comics, Mallia suggests, are capable of inducing interest in young and old alike, and yet have the potential to be a powerful reflective tool. One of the earliest definitions of this genre is by Waugh, who suggested in 1947 that a comic is a form that must include these following elements: 'A narrative told by way of a sequence of pictures, a continuing cast of characters from one sequence to the next, and the inclusion of dialogue and/or text within the pictures' (Mallia, 1997: 96).

Here then we see the close link between cartoons and the art of storytelling and journeying. Parkin (1998: 3) comments that storytellers would typically be travellers or minstrels, passing on important information from town to town:

> Storytelling was seen as a vocation requiring many skills, such as powerful communication, appropriate use of language, insight, sensitivity and accuracy, and in order to do the job well, the storytellers had to develop their own minds in ways that other people at that time did not. They had to develop their memory and visualization skills, and using these skills, be able to trigger memorable pictures in the minds of their listeners, for it was in this way that the information would be best understood and remembered.

Parkin suggests that the ingredients for a good story are characters, a good plot, some sort of conflict and a resolution! Experiential providers might also consider becoming adept at storytelling, as 'scenarios' often form the backcloth to experiential activities. Consalvo (1995) suggests that scenarios that are fantasy or patently artificial require the internal consistency of a 'good story' to facilitate the suspension of disbelief, 'buy-in' and active engagement of the trainees. Harrison is quoted in Mallia (1997) as saying that 'the cartoon is a drawing which (a) simplifies, and/or (b) exaggerates'. Some cartoons, however, are intrinsically complex.

Comics, Mallia suggests, are next in line for acceptance within the world of experiential learning and, as a unique form of entertainment, 'comic strips have become a social phenomenon. Their ability to capture contemporary economic and social events with remarkable accuracy and finesse means they are preferred areas of study for... educationalists, who, at one time were apt to moralize about comic strips, [and] now use them as a teaching aid' (Schetter, 1992: 35). Mallia suggests that the use of comics for instructional purposes is infinite. For example, he suggests that they can be used to act as ice-breakers at strategic points in the lessons, or to create interest in a subject being discussed. They can aesthetically elevate traditional instructional text, inspire emulation, generate tools for a new channel of communication for the learners and project an atmosphere of informality.

In a cognitive capacity, comics can:

- communicate information;
- simplify instructions;
- be used to illustrate a point being made;
- be a tool in linguistic instruction;
- stimulate discussions;
- be a source of visual culture;
- be a mnemonic tool of cognitive retention.

(Mallia, 1997: 103)

Cartoons can be used to explore the outcome of learning, to compare different perspectives of the same event, to reflect upon emotions, or tell something about the people involved. There is a tendency to think cartoons are concerned with jokes and that humour must pervade. Humour might, however, provide clues to underlying issues or feelings. Cartoons can allow difficult issues to surface in a non-threatening way. Stories can be created using speech bubbles or thought bubbles and captions (see Figures 5.5 and 5.6) and unfinished statements or speech prompts can also be used to lead the storylines in a certain direction: useful in the development of reflection or review.

If cartoons are to be drawn then warm-up exercises are needed and hints and tips can be provided on facial expression and movement. The sequence of pictures and speech bubbles go from left to right, ie whoever speaks first should be on the left of the picture, and it is necessary to start drawing any sequence from front to back, ie first draw whatever is nearest to you.

FIGURE 5.5 Simple line drawing practice and reflection bubbles

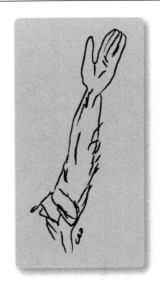

Using photographic images and computer software

Digital camera images can be used for cartoons or newspapers. These images can be simply brought together and reduced into a cartoon strip by importing them into presentation or drawing packages (such as MS PowerPoint). Speech and thought bubbles can be inserted and filled in by learners (see Figure 5.6). Learners can select and sequence images. Similarly, instamatic cameras can be used to record images, and the photos can be sequenced (and rearranged) on a flip chart, allowing captions and speech bubbles to be added by hand on to the flip chart paper.

Cartoons and comic strips offer powerful reflective tools. Combining art, dialogue, situations and outcomes, they can tell the story succinctly and humorously. Cartoons capture the essence of what is going on; rather than attempting to be an exact record, cartoons can help us dig deeper emotionally. *Cartoon cards* are available for trainers to purchase (see Terrell, 2000). Each has statements and images about characteristics of people in teams. Another technique is *photo snapshots*, a photo-in-the-mind method that can be used through pretending the learner is a camera, creating snapshot images in his or her mind between blindfolded periods. This can be used to create flashbacks of, for example, special events or moments, or to revisit special places through imagination. They can be described to others by the 'camera' person.

FIGURE 5.6 Reflective tools – digital camera images and speech and thought bubbles

Reflections on reality – reading and writing

Finally we consider the use of reading and writing as a powerful reflective tool in experiential learning, as 'biographical' work. Writing techniques are recognized and valued as important in facilitating experiential learning, and there are many techniques and formats that can be used. One technique is *lifelines*, a method involving people using rope or string to create a sequence of waves representing highs and lows in life. A knot is tied along the line to delineate the point in life where people are now and so reflective thoughts and discussion can then focus on 'What next?' A second technique, *Life Stages*, involves writing about events in life as if they were chapters of a book. McLeod (1997: 62) describes psychodynamic narrative and structured life story interviews, where he begins by asking people to think about their life as if it were an unfinished book, with chapters representing major parts of a person's life. It is suggested that there should be between three and eight chapters, and each chapter requires a name and an overall content description. The links between each chapter are also discussed in his work. Other techniques might include:

- **writing lists and mind maps** – clusters of ideas on the topic;
- **guided imagery** – involves free writing stimulated by an image such as 'being on a journey';

- **stepping stones** – reviewing formative life experiences from the vantage point of the present;
- **the daily log** – to record the day's events;
- **the period log** – to record a current period in the writer's life;
- **dialogue** – creating a dialogue with a person, event or object from the writer's life;
- **altered point of view** – writing about oneself in the third person, or about someone else in the first person.

(from Lukinsky, 1990, in McLeod, 1997: 77)

Another technique is writing one's own obituary, or that of a colleague through the process of interviewing. *Critical incident techniques*, *good practice audits* and *journal keeping* are all explored by Hunt (1999) in an excellent chapter on reflective practice.

Reading is something that many development trainers might incorporate more in programmes. Reading clearly provides opportunities for adventures in the mind, although it is perhaps seen as an academic thing to do, associated with school, university or college. We provide details of a reading experiment in Chapter 4. In the experiment we create a relaxed ambience and use a 'coffee and newspaper' approach to reading, exploring and encouraging indigenous thinking and modelling without any pressure. Tony Buzan (2000), in his book on speed reading, refers to Vanda North, who is ranked as one of the world's fastest readers. After speed reading training, she realized that 'For 21 years she could have been reading twice the amount, with better comprehension, or she could have read exactly the same amount and had nearly a year extra to be with friends, to travel, to explore and to have even more fun!' This is a good investment strategy under anyone's terms.

Rafts and planks... or real projects?

Many experiential learning providers are now working closely with the National Parks officials, NGOs and other organizations to use real environmental or community projects for experiential events (Beard, 1996). Such programmes, while being more empathetic to the environment, can have a real purpose and a productive end, rather than simple pack-away simulation activities that await a rebuild by the next client. More significantly, real projects may have a positive motivational impact on learning, affecting the way participants engage in the learning experience. Corporate facilitators report high levels of motivational energy towards projects that are 'perceived' as doing *good work* of a charitable nature: they have altruistic appeal. This phenomenon requires more research, but this connecting with community and earth appears to have high value and is increasingly important in holistic experiential learning.

Popular community projects include the building of playgrounds for children, and delivering hospital radio programmes or theatre performances. The options are indeed endless and with creativity the benefits can be considerable to all parties concerned. Charities such as the Royal Society for the Protection of Birds (RSPB) and the National Trust in the UK offer 'team challenges' in their brochures, and have specialist staff to help to coordinate such projects. These tasks are suitable for learning activities. This also has management development benefits in terms of social accountability, social auditing and the notion of business as a positive social force.

Doing and reviewing

Learning can of course be enhanced, or diminished, with reviewing. Whether it is called reflection, debrief or reviewing there are similarities in that they all have a potential role in supporting learning.

How active reviewing supports learning and change

Active and creative approaches to reviewing create good opportunities for reflection, communication, learning and development because they can readily:

- engage and develop a wide range of learning style preferences;

- connect the worlds of thinking, talking and doing;

- produce holistic, dynamic and focused learning;

- access intuitive and tacit knowledge;

- enrich the experience of learning from experience;

- enable some testing of ideas within the learning process;

- increase the range of strategies for the effective transfer of learning.

Whenever people get stuck in rituals and clichés encountered in verbal modes of review, introducing active and creative modes can help to free up the process: the opportunity to think and communicate in *pictures* or *patterns* or through *mime, movement* or *drama* or through *verse* or *music* provides alternative modes that help people get *unstuck*. Participants discover new ways of thinking, new ways of expressing themselves and new ways of understanding and explaining things. It is true that new angles can be discovered through astute questioning in all-talk reviews, but new angles can often be more readily produced by changing the ways in which people create, tell and compare their stories about their experiences. For example:

- **For sharing an experience**: the storyteller (learner) reflects on their experience by making a storyline showing their ups and downs. The storyline becomes a visual aid that allows the audience a glimpse of the big picture before hearing the detail of the ups and downs.

- **For talking about group dynamics**: the storyteller arranges and rearranges objects into patterns showing how roles, relationships, and group performance have been changing.

- **For examining critical moments**: the storyteller recreates critical moments through action replay. Typically, participants replay themselves. New information emerges when the replay is paused and people are interviewed about what they were doing, feeling and thinking at the time. This re-staging of key moments tends to bring out greater honesty and understanding.

- **For exploring future scenarios**: the storyteller walks through a large map of past journeys and new possibilities, tries different choices, explores new routes and discovers various consequences.

It is difficult to achieve this quality of reflection when following the more passive traditions of private reflection or group discussion. Fruitful private reflection requires a high level of mental discipline that includes sustained curiosity, accurate recall, high self-awareness, the ability to see other perspectives and plenty of imagination. More perspectives are clearly available in group discussions, but when people sit in the same chair all the time, it can look and feel as if everyone is stuck in the same place – both physically and mentally. Whether reflecting alone or in groups, active and creative methods increase engagement and movement and sustain the dynamics from which change is more likely to arise.

Successful transfer of learning will also be more likely if the review process has been engaging and holistic. Not only is such learning more reliable, it is also more aligned, more integrated and more ready-to-use.

Provided by Roger Greenaway, an international specialist in Reviewing Skills Training.

http://reviewing.co.uk

Conclusion

Mumford (1991: 31) suggests that 'if we provide individuals with a greater capacity to learn from the widest possible variety of opportunities, we are empowering that individual to be in greater command of his or her destiny'.

Experiencing rich learning opportunities is the essence of experiential learning, and this chapter has outlined the basic ingredients used in the design process. This 17-point typology acts as a general guide to the learning activity design process, and serves to highlight the importance of design skills in experiential learning. Together with the learning combination lock model this typology is useful to create a development needs analysis for clients.

In this chapter we examined the creative use of activity sequencing, planned and unplanned learning, and the use of journeys, large and small, from life journeys and expeditions to orienteering and micro-hikes. Sensory blocking, fantasy and play, the provision of rules and obstacles, problem solving, and the use of objects for a variety of purposes were all briefly explored so as to set the scene for detailed work in later chapters. This milieu provides a multiplicity of innovative ideas to select from so as to enrich the learning experience; however, good practice and a sound theoretical understanding must always underpin the choices made.

Also in this chapter we investigated in some detail the effect of altering the nature of perceived or actual 'realness', and how it influences the experience of learning. The use of activities that include training kits, traditional outdoor recreation, circus, radio production, cartoons, theatre, drama, art, storytelling and writing all received attention. We clarified the many facets of 'reality' and we explored how altering these facets provides opportunities to unlock more learning potential.

Training is sometimes conducted as part of staff 'away' days. Being away from the daily working environments can result in the everyday cultural norms and expectations being shed. Away removes some work distractions and the sense of play can reduce inhibition, suspend reality, increase enjoyment and stimulate relaxed alertness. Different perspectives surface, status and egos can fade into the background. However, as we have shown, much will depend on the quality and care with design and delivery; but no matter how thorough the planning, important outcomes can derive from unexpected experiences.

Sensory experience and sensory intelligence (SI)
(The sensing dimension)

The perfume of a loved one inhaled by one of our 23,000 daily breaths is scanned by 10 million olfactory receptors capable of detecting approximately 10,000 different odours.

BURNS, 1998, NATURE GUIDED THERAPY, P 55

Introduction

This chapter highlights the importance of our senses, sensory awareness and our sensory intelligence in the experience of learning. The human senses receive a great deal of information about the outside world. The human inner world also generates considerable sensory data both from the body surface, and also from sensors inside the body. The senses therefore play a key role in connecting these inner and outer worlds.

It is the sensory experience – what we see, hear, smell, touch and so forth – that, in simple terms, results in observations, followed by varied reactions. Sensory awareness is an underestimated phenomenon: sensory data coming in influences our thinking, feeling and judging, therefore it might be said that *sensory intelligence* (SI) is potentially more significant than emotional intelligence (EQ). SI might be considered to be a more advanced self-awareness state. But of course these components elements of an experience are not divided or sequenced in such a simplistic way.

Amplification and habituation

Sensory awareness can enrich the human life experience. We can of course learn to amplify sensory experiences that bring more positive feelings: fresh baked bread, the morning air, crisp snow, the buzzing bees in the warm sun, fresh coffee. The downside is that these experiences can habituate, if experienced too often! Sensory intelligence (SI) and sensory awareness can similarly enhance learning. Whether it be the spoken word, handling an object, or watching the demonstration of a particular skill, the senses are the means of contact and communication with the outer world: between people and the non-human or more-than-human world. This basic fact that we communicate through our human senses can be so easily forgotten by trainers and facilitators. Equally important is the realization that we need to regularly experience changes in sensory stimulation to avoid habituation, or sensory dulling through overuse of one sense mode. This is why whole person experiential learning strategies recognize the important role of the human senses, a role that should not be underestimated.

The senses, six, seven, or as many as twenty or more, are central to the way we receive, perceive and experience and judge the human and the more-than-human world. Although sound, smell, sight, touch and taste are five commonly quoted senses there are many others: interoceptors sense blood pressure and oxygen content, while others monitor temperature and pain. Mechano-receptors aid balance and speed, acting in a way like a human GPS system, tracking and interpreting time and spatial form. This human GPS monitoring system, as we will show in this chapter, is extremely important in experiential learning; bodily and kinaesthetic spatial awareness is a fundamental component of *sensory intelligence*. Indeed the body as a whole plays an important role in the human understanding of very 'complex' things, particularly as the mind has a tendency to categorize and classify. Also significant in terms of the human sensory capacity is the notion of gut feeling or intuition, transcendental or 'out of body' experiences, and 'sublime' and 'spiritual' feelings: these are 'sensed'.

How many senses?

1 Visual

2 Auditory: inner outer dialogue/voices

3 Kinaesthetic/bodily/touch – muscles and other parts of the body send signals

4 Smell – Chemo receptors

5 Taste – Chemo receptors

6 Sixth sense?

7 Temperature receptors

8 Pain receptors

9 Others.

These can be further divided: eg number 3 above, Kinaesthetic experiences, consist of:

- Interoceptors: detect internal bodily reactions – blood pressure, heart rate, hunger, mood, arousal, etc.

- Tactile: touch primarily through skin.

- Vestibular sense: balance, gravity and acceleration.

- Proprioceptors: processing balance and body position through muscles, ligaments and joints.

The human senses: untapped potential?

The following highlights the great potential for using the senses to enhance learning from experience, by allowing subconscious knowledge to be accessed and developed:

Sight: the rods in the eye detect colours in shades of grey and they can sense shape and movement. We have about 120 million rods. Amazingly, our eyes react in emergency situations and we can see much better: we see details we normally cannot see!

Smell: The nose, at its best, can tell the difference between 4,000–10,000 smells.

Touch: People who are blind use their fingertips to read Braille by feeling the patterns of raised dots on their paper, as there are about 100 touch receptors in each of the fingertips.

Hearing: The auditory nerve carries messages from 25,000 receptors in your ear to your brain.

Taste: 10,000 taste buds inside our mouths; even on the roofs of our mouths.

These facts highlight the potential for sensory experiences to increase human capacity/functioning.

External and internal signals, received through our sense receptors, are said to act as raw material for learning 'experiences' to be 'constructed', through the process of perception (Gross, 2001). The human experience is, of course, much greater than the sum of the individual bits of sensory data. Perception or processing moves the experience beyond sensation, and involves the memory bank of experiences, and higher processing levels, including the subconscious. Consider the following quotation by Peter Jarvis:

All of our experiences of our life-world begin with bodily sensations which occur at the intersection of the person and the lifeworld. These sensations initially have no meaning for us as this is the beginning of the learning process... Thereafter we transform these sensations into the language of our brains and minds and learn to make them meaningful to ourselves – this is the first stage in human learning.

(From Peter Jarvis (1999), writing on adult education...)

The importance of this sensorial world to experiential learning appears, at least in this account, as not particularly significant. Jarvis suggests that the senses initially have 'no meaning', until they are 'processed' and 'transformed'. Now consider a contrary view, presented by Robert Kull in his book about his year in Patagonia, called *Solitude: Seeking Wisdom in Extremes*. Kull lived in remote Patagonia so as to study the experience of solitude for a PhD:

In conceptualising, organising, and thinking about these sensory impressions, the immediacy of experience can easily be lost. It requires patience and practice to soften this habitual activity by over and over letting go of thought and analysis to simply stay with the swirl of sound just as it is without trying to do anything with it.

(Kull, 2008: 279)

Here we see that Robert Kull suggests a contrary position; that the act of processing raw sense data, essentially thinking about it, can spoil the complex 'immediacy' of the experience. Similarly Sheets-Johnstone (2009: 380) describes such events as 'Instances in which we are at a loss for words, so stunned by something we cannot speak': partly due to the inadequacy of speech when it comes to describing movement or emotionally laden events that move us. This subject will be of concern to the experiential coach, educator or facilitator and so in this chapter we explore this core issue, concerning processed versus raw sense appreciation, particularly in connection with their role in experiential learning. The chapter also offers guiding thoughts for facilitation on a range of sensory dynamics: the notion of sensory intelligence, sensory arousal, sensory reduction, sensory stepping, sensory overload, solitude and silence. The chapter will also consider how the written and spoken language has a negative side effect that is not well known, namely its role in distancing us humans from nature, and the beauty of the more-than-human world.

So what is sensory intelligence?

Sensory intelligence is the degree to which we develop our ability to be aware of, and work with our own sensory states. It is also about how we learn to read our sensorial pleasures and displeasures, to work with both positive and negative sensory experiences, within ourselves, and within others to develop individual, community and organizational creative energy and collaborative effort so as to improve life and planet balance (Beard, 2012). The regular commuter going to work often looks bored and tired of the journey. Sat next to the commuter is a visitor to the town or city. The tourist is excited by the experience, and the pleasurable sensory stimulation makes them alert for more. Why is there this difference when the stimuli are potentially the same? Can the stimulation awareness button be reset? These are fundamental questions that affect the processes of learning.

Sensory intelligence involves developing our awareness, and to practise:

1 being aware of our SENSORIAL relationship with the world, particularly the immediacy of the here and now and its impact on the self;

2 tuning into, working with and managing immediate SENSORY EXPERIENCES, particularly pleasurable ones that have zero cost;

3 reconnecting our senses with the positive and negative, natural and spiritual elements of the self, through guided sensorial experiences, particularly in uplifting social and/or outdoor natural environments;

4 developing an ability to motivate the self through life-enriching, SENSORY EXPERIENCES;

5 developing an ability to recognize and tune into the SENSORY NEEDS AND EXPERIENCES of others;

6 working with SENSORIAL EXPERIENCES typically found within our important relationships.

(Beard, 2013, audio book)

Let's give some simple examples to guide practice.

Re-awakening the senses of a whole community:

People had to walk to their jobs, and to whatever shops were still open. We began encountering each other on the streets, 'in person' instead of by telephone. In the absence of automobiles, and their loud engines, the rhythms of crickets and birdsong became clearly audible. Flocks were migrating south for the winter, and many of us found ourselves simply listening with new and childlike curiosity, to the ripples of song in the still-standing trees and the fields. And at night the sky was studded with stars! Many children, their eyes no longer blocked by the glare of house lights and street lamps, saw the Milky Way for the first time, and were astonished. For those few days and nights our town became a community aware of its place... The breakdown of our technologies had forced us to return to our senses, and hence to the natural landscape in which those senses are so profoundly embedded. We suddenly found ourselves inhabiting a sensuous world that had been waiting, for years, at the very fringe of our awareness, an intimate terrain...

(Abram, 1997: 62)

The quotation above, from *The Spell of the Sensuous* by the philosopher David Abram, describes the effect of an experience that triggered a sensory re-awakening in a local population. Following the impact of this hurricane on their town people experienced the world around them very differently.

Sensory awareness returned to them. Ordinarily for many people everyday experiences incorporate an avalanche of stimuli, arising from the sounds and sights of cars, from televisions and street lights, and added to by other consumptive data, all appealing to our senses through advertising media. This sensory world continually attempts to sell us goods, images, services and formulated experiences. This can easily create a human world that becomes sensorially dulled, a world that has blocked out many pleasurable naturally occurring sensory phenomena. Technology in this story clearly added to the estrangement.

However, technology can also work in conjunction with the bodily experience: the continuing development of gesture-based technologies (GBT) for example, where fingers, hands and arms are now used to manipulate information – eg in the iPod, iPad and iWall – heralds a potential return to the use of the bodily movement to aid mental processing (Beard and Price, 2012). When we present statistics or graphs these forms can often seem unintelligible to non scientists, yet new and very creative research (Gwilt *et al*, 2012; Gwilt, 2013) aims to translate such traditional complex scientific data into sensual physical objects, where contours, texture and colour of the physical form allow the data to be sensorially read or interrogated. This is a very different way of experiencing scientific data! Ironically the distancing of the human from the more sensorial world was even more profound as a result of the evolution of the human written and spoken language.

Language and the human sensorial experience

Language is sensorial, emanating from the body: complex sounds use the air of our breath, whereas written language takes the form of a kinetic dance across the page. It is what makes us uniquely human. Language can surprisingly have both a positive and a negative effect on the experience of learning, particularly in relation to how language shapes our experience of the sensuous outer world. Good communication involves language that appeals to the senses: a study of Shakespeare reveals a language that powerfully communicates to the eyes, ears and to our human feelings: to 'gaze an eagle blind', to 'hear the lowest sound', and so 'gross in taste' (Knight, 2002: 83). Language, particularly in this poetic form, generates rich sensory pictures for a world created inside our heads. Yet language is also problematic: language is spoken one word at a time, and the written language is read one page at a time, line by line. Thus both the written and spoken word are essentially linear in format, which can limit human understanding of complex, multi-dimensional, interrelated issues. Sheets-Johnstone (2009) in a chapter titled 'On the challenge of languaging experience' notes how the brain and body essentially work with our three-dimensional world: up/down, right/left and front/back.

Facilitator briefing

The briefing involved about 20 of the 40 staff involved in a very complex activity. The meeting was about the delivery of The Great Langkawi Race for 90 very senior and talented clients at the Westin, Langkawi Island, Malaysia in late 2012. The delivery had to go to plan. A lot was at stake, and a very professional delivery was expected by the client HR department. What they required was perfectionism: nothing must go wrong and safety must not be compromised. For the water activity alone the local fire brigade from 'Fire and Rescue' were to be on standby on a jet ski, and two instructors were to be in kayaks, with several staff on the beach.

In a small hotel nearby the senior and experienced facilitator stood up and spoke. She carefully explained: *There are 90 senior clients involved. There are three groups of 30 with three sub group teams in each. There are three major activities: 1) Fast and Furious; 2) Slow and Steady; and 3) Hybrid. Within these there are many smaller activities. Each group will have 30 people doing each of the major activities. Each group will select 10 people to allocate to each of the three major activities.* More detail followed. *This group will be based at* [...]. I looked around. There were facial expressions that suggested to me that more than a few people were not getting this. It was hot and they were tired. Written briefings of this complex experience had taken me several readings to sort it all out in my head when I received it over the internet some weeks before, back in the UK.

One of the activity facilitators in the audience who was not so afraid to speak said: *Let me get this straight, so there are*...? Following yet more verbal detail there were more puzzled faces. However, the facilitator then got up and took hold of a whiteboard pen. She drew the three teams in boxes along the top axis of the board and colour coded them: the blue team, the green team and the red team. Below these she then drew big boxes down the left side axis: 'Fast and Furious', then 'Slow and Steady', then 'Hybrid'. She had created a three by three grid. Then the number 10 was written each grid space... it all became clear. The group frowns disappeared. A new visual spatial form had clarified things alongside the verbal brief. The insufficiency of the linear nature of speech had been overcome.

(Colin Beard, Langkawi, November 2012)

Sheets-Johnstone (2009) and others (Lakoff and Johnson, 1999; Gallagher, 2005) also note that the period before written and spoken language is often referred to as *pre-linguistic*. Gestures, noises and facial expressions would have naturally played an important role, although *pre-linguistic* implies a language vacuum, as if no language existed. These authors reject such an idea, and instead they suggest that language might have evolved from a basic sound-gesture phenomenon, very much linked to the sensual more-than-human surrounding world. This sound-gesture sensorial evolutionary precursor to the spoken and written word might be better acknowledged if the term '*post-kinetic*' phenomenon were used (Sheets-Johnstone, 2009: 5). Humans continue to furnish everyday language with these bodily-spatial metaphors in order to aid mental processing. For example, we say: to *support* our case, to use *step by step* logic, to *grasp* a concept, and to feel a bit *down* every now and then. *Further*more, we study *Higher* or *Further* Education (see for example the work of Lakoff and Johnson, 1999). Our mental reasoning is thus underpinned by a rich language of spatial bodily metaphors; clearly learning is not a purely cognitive process, as somehow disembodied as tradition has largely held.

The body and the brain are also connected to the senses. The work of Nina Bull in the 1950s is particularly illuminating in this respect and it is described in Sheets-Johnstone (2009). Nina Bull hypnotized people into one of six emotional states and they would later describe these emotional states in neuromuscular or bodily terms. In later experiments participants were read a selected description from one of their own reports and they were then locked into that emotional state by hypnosis, and told they would not experience other emotional states until they were unlocked. When asked to get into another emotional state they reported how they were unable to access these new feelings or emotional states because they were stuck in the previous specific postural or bodily attitude: 'I feel light – (so) I can't feel depression' (Bull, 1951: 84, 85, in Sheets-Johnstone, 2009: 200). The locked body muscular posture had prevented access to the new feelings: the body–mind synergy couldn't function.

Reasoning and learning also arises from the integration and interaction of our brains with our bodies as an *embodied* experience, and this occurs within a particular environment, as *embedded*. The connected relationship of the brain, body and environment should not be underestimated in experiential learning. It is illustrated in practice by the 'Walk the Talk' pedagogy described later in this chapter.

The separation of the human from the more-than-human sensorial world is linked to the evolution of language. In very simplistic terms the shift occurred from early sounds anchored in the onomatopoeic, a long word relating to speech rooted for example in the sounds of the natural world (a name or word mimicking the sound of a particular bird, for example). Such sounds were aided by bodily gestures also. This language was further developed by the use of pictographic and ideagraphic language (picture based and idea based). This use of the sounds developed into more complex form with the use of the rebus. The rebus used words that have natural meaning on their own to create a new word with no root natural meaning, such as *bee* and *leaf* to create a new word *belief*. Ultimately this gave birth to the sounds and shapes of the simpler aleph-beth, or early alphabet which once linked the spoken and written word with the sensorial earth: the letter Q, for example, was a pictorial representation of a monkey with a tail in the original Hebrew *aleph bet*, which predates the English alphabet. The work of David Abram (1997) skilfully shows how the sensorial more-than-human world has thus been intercepted and distanced by the development of the alphabet, and the written language. However, pictographic languages such as Chinese still retain their original connectivity with the earth. What appear to the Western eye as complex Chinese symbols are relatively simple if the original pictorial form is understood: the word for 'rest', for example, has pen strokes or lines which are derived from a picture of a person sitting under a tree. Gestures were and still are also important for language: it is said, for example, that the Italian dictionary has a supplement of important gestures. The inadequacy of human language, and its sensorial distancing effect, is illustrated in recent research in remote Patagonia by Robert Kull (2008). His frustration with the inability of the written English language as he struggles to make notes for his PhD about *solitude* is expressed with a stark honesty:

> I drop the notebook and feel myself sink more deeply into the world. All desire to write disappears. What has happened to my flow of language? I fall mute before such wonder and beauty. I try to describe the delicate shades and patterns of shifting colour as wind swirls water around immovable rock, but my images feel dull and trite. There is no dance between word and world. What I see and feel begs a sensuous tango, but my words march static and stiff in lines across the page.

> (2008: 184)

It appears the mountains certainly do speak for themselves! The traditional Outward Bound approach to facilitation in the 1940s may have been more significant than hitherto recognized (see the following Box).

Six generations of facilitation techniques

1940s Let the Experience (Mountain) Speak for itself.

1950s Speak on behalf of the Experience

1960s Debrief the Experience

1970s Frontload the Experience

1980s Isomorphically frame the Experience

1990s Indirectly Frontload the Experience

Taken from Priest, Simon, Gass, Michael and Fitzpatrick, Karen (1999) Training corporate managers to facilitate: The next generation of facilitating experiential methodologies. *The Journal of Experiential Education*, June (22), 1, p50, ProQuest Education Journals.

Written and spoken words fell silent: the sensorial experience, in its raw state, spoke instead very directly and personally to Robert Kull. Processing such experiences onto paper became almost impossible for him. Mental processing and subsequent attempts to capture the experience in writing failed. Kull notes that:

> Coming into Wilderness Solitude is like studying where everyone speaks a language you have forgotten so long ago now it seems completely foreign. You know you have something important to learn, but you don't understand. I take time to keep listening and listening. I hear the voices of nature and try to translate what I hear into conceptual thought language so I will know I understand in my mind. But the language of nature cannot be translated into human concepts. It is deeper and different. I realise I have heard and understood when my heart softens and opens to love and peace and beauty around and within me.
>
> (Kull, 2008: 279)

Kull avoids a glorification of his special solo adventure: his writing does not become the stuff of gendered heroics. His deep, quasi-meditative experiences are often preceded by a significant sensory awareness: of his breathing, and of the awareness of simple objects or sounds around him. This is often referred to as a *mindless* state (see for example Tolle, 2006), where little or no mental processing occurs. The experience just is; it is raw and unprocessed, it possesses a magic quality. Related notions include spiritual intelligence, centring and presence, and these are covered in more depth later and also in the chapter on knowing. Meditative experiences take us beyond our three-dimensional world mentioned earlier. In listening to our breathing we also access the fourth bodily inside/outside dimension, – and possibly even the fifth life and death dimension?

> At rest or in meditative experiences, insides are commonly present only in the form of breath and the silence that rings in our ears. All is quiet. But it is also warm and alive.
>
> (Sheets-Johnstone, 2009: 373)

Interpreting and misinterpreting words

Natural and *wilderness* are also difficult words to characterize or interpret: language can be clumsy and inadequate at times. Many words in everyday use that have been taken for granted as understood increasingly come under critical examination, particularly in academic journals, through deconstruction narratives. Let us give an example of what we mean. The creation of an urban-wilderness opposite or duality is seen by some as being particularly unhelpful. For some writers this duality is typical of dominant Western narratives. It is in this vein that Willis (2011: 95) cautions the use of the language word *wilderness*, as being somehow special and elite, or superior, and usually as somehow *sublime*. In an American context, with reference to the work of Cronon (1995), Willis offers a critical interpretation of this word *wilderness*. She cites the US national parks as a 'gendered privilege', preserved so that the nation's men could retreat there and forge themselves anew. Recent work (Norris, 2011) also challenges the basis of many outdoor education practices, suggesting they have been uncritically adopted, as experiences originally derived from indigenous peoples. These include the solo, vision quest and other phenomena associated with rites of passage. These deconstructionist narratives are critical, enlightening, opening up new vistas, questioning the taken-for-granted. Yet this genre of adversarial academic writing, where key words in use have to undergo a meaning deconstruction test in the quest for a milieu of alternative interpretations, can potentially be unhelpful, as Jay Griffiths suggests:

> Literacy is an epistemology of the built world, physically, in libraries in towns, but metaphorically too, the constructed artifice of our written culture, book-bound, which encourages our philosophies and values to move even farther away from nature – to say nothing of the constructs of deconstructionism and postdeconstructionism.

(Griffiths, 2006: 19)

This quotation from Griffiths (2006) comes from her book called *Wild: An Elemental Journey*. Here she offers an alternative to the term wilderness.

Going 'Away': outdoor sensory awakening experiences

It is with these critiques in mind that we want to consider the importance of the sensory experience in nature and wilderness. Outward Bound has long embraced a particular form of sensory awareness, through the form of the 'solo', where people venture into wilderness alone, for several days, finding space to ponder about life and self, and be at one with nature. Kurt Hahn's educational vision insisted that true learning required periods of silence and solitude as well as directed activity. These and other core ideas served as the driving force behind the establishment of many prominent institutions of the time such as The Duke of Edinburgh Scheme, United World Colleges and Outward Bound.

Interestingly, the majority of outdoor development providers in the UK are clustered in the places that are designated as Areas of Outstanding Natural Beauty or National Parks. It is said that the Lake District National Park in the UK contains the largest cluster of development training organizations in the world. Within this vast range of special outdoor environments, rich sensations connected with the more-than-human world are experienced that can take learning into the realm of an exciting adventure. Outward Bound Singapore (OBS) is located on the beautiful island of Pulau Ubin, sometimes referred to as the Adventure Island. The location was specially selected for outdoor development activities that use the local rainforests, mangrove swamps, a quarry and the surrounding seas and offshore islands. Outward Bound Singapore also has a swimming pool in the tropical jungle, and a gymnasium and many climbing walls and towers. The climate in Singapore is humid and warm, and some 'classrooms' for learning are covered but not completely walled, and a cool breeze replaces air conditioning. These rooms are neither indoor nor outdoor: words give rise to definitional and descriptive dilemmas. *Indoor* and *outdoor* and *rooms* are difficult to clearly define.

Sensory acuity can be heightened when the everyday sensory overload is reduced or eliminated. When total darkness and silence exist inside a cave the conditions are ideal. Sight is redundant, so other sensations become enhanced. We listen out for any noise and it is accentuated by the acoustic echo, we smell the damp air and feel the creeping cold. We learn about the intricacies of communication in a cave where visual cues are eliminated. This can have interesting results, including enhanced listening behaviours. Other experiences might reduce or enhance visual communication: blindfolds are often used in outdoor education (see, for example, Priest and Rohnke, 2000; Martin *et al*, 2004; Neuman, 2004). Gloves can be used to reduce tactile sensations of the fingers. Bare feet sensorially increases the body connection with the earth. Contrasting sensations provide a change in stimulation.

Sensory experiences can raise awareness of our flow with, or against the natural rhythms and energy levels of the body in relation to our human and more-than-human surroundings. In outdoor learning common divergent sensory stimulations include, for example, light and dark, noise and silence, shelter and exposure, calm and energized, food satiation and hunger, loneliness and gregariousness, solitude and crowdedness, hot and cold air, wet and dry clothing. The combinations are endless, and on a grander scale, fire, water, earth, mountains and rivers are just some of the many sensory features of the natural or urban environment that can be used to influence learning, a subject we cover in Chapter 5. Chris Reed (1999) refers to the five basic elements in the outdoor environment: earth, air, fire, water and spirit and suggests that they are symbolically important. Fire, he suggests, is a symbol of action and creativity, and of destruction and new life. Fire can send people into simple, meditative, reflective states simply by being watched. Water can symbolize feelings, emotion and dark undercurrents. Air symbolizes ideas and intellectual pursuits but also insubstantial dreaming and lofty idealism. The fifth element, spirit, pervaded all that Reed's group did over a weekend but he noted that 'the ether is invisible, insubstantial but ubiquitous'. Higgins (1996, 1997) refers to other elements by adding weather, shelter, food, darkness and silence.

Our human senses often remain in tune with the natural rhythms in the environment. Sensory channels can be pre-sensitized prior to an experiential activity or event. Such sensitizing is a vital part of our ability to create a good experiential learning climate that enables the doors of our mind, body or spirit to be opened up. Tuning-in with learners to sensory experiences can be supported using *continuous stream talking* (inside the head talking or vocalized/spoken to the outside) generating responses to immediate sensations and feelings: 'right now I sense the...'

Silence is powerful in helping to raise sensory awareness, as is meditation. Rainforests offer extremes of sensory stimulation: numerous animals continuously send out signals, such as warning signals of an encroaching predator. Animals can sense a storm coming well before the rains, and much earlier than humans. Humans learn to *read* natural signs in this way. Our senses can be alerted to read other changes: in light, humidity, wind, colour and shadows. Experiential learning is as much about observing and reflecting as it is about *doing*: the outdoors is a good place to sharpen observational and sensing skills.

The Norwegians have an important concept they call *friluftsliv*, or feeling at home with nature (Barnes, 2000). Native American people, and their beliefs about nature, are discussed in an article called 'Spirit of the Earth' (Peard, 1999), which offers an analysis of a speech by a Native American chief, and in doing so offers two extreme perspectives on nature taken by Western civilization and by Native Americans. The dichotomy, although over simplistic, is presented thus:

Native American	Western civilization
at home in nature	fear
belonging	ownership
community	individualism
spiritual	capital
sustainable	exploitation
freedom	domination

Mohawk (1996) describes how Western fairy tales paint pictures of nature as foreboding and dark. 'Natural' places are where Hansel and Gretel got lost, and where Sleeping Beauty was surrounded by thorn bushes and immense forests. Natural places possessed 'wild' animals and 'savage' people, and both had to be tamed. The psychological origins of such negative mindsets are not only rooted in ancient folklore: they are found in contemporary law, negative corporate environmental policy (to reduce the impact of…), and environmental taxation (to pay environmental taxes, to suffer penalties) (Beard, 2000).

In 'Fire in the sky', Walker (1999) explores the three dimensions of 'self, others and nature', as used by Colin Mortlock. He proposes some activities that he suggests can improve participants' interconnectedness to the earth and to awaken the human senses:

- self-introductions (respect for diversity of individual stories, how you got there);
- sitting on the ground or natural materials (simple contact with the earth);
- sitting to talk in circles not lines (cyclic nature of life processes and natural things);
- being inactive and alone (quietening down, going inwards, inviting nature in);

- walking differently from in the city (eg slowly, silently, blindfolded – unfamiliarity);
- walking barefoot (direct contact with dewy grass, rock, wood, earth, leaves);
- walking in unfamiliar places (gorges, undergrowth, logs, snow);
- leading, giving help (risking, reaching out, human care and contact);
- being led, receiving help (expecting understanding human care and contact);
- focusing on natural rhythms (tide, wind, sunset/rise, stars, moonrise/set, night sky);
- focusing where possible on wood fire (natural processes, history of life, universe);
- telling, inventing and listening to stories, legends of the earth (images of other ways of life);
- sleeping on the ground, if possible outside (expanding awareness, dreaming);
- sitting silently observing together (sharing different perceptions of the world).

(Walker, 1999)

Experiential learning in the natural outdoors can also provide ways of reframing our thinking about the natural environment, by altering our inner scripts, changing the 'metaphors', 'images' and 'labels'. Using the natural environment for corporate environmental awareness training could be a powerful awakening, yet ironically environmental training rarely uses the environment as a teaching medium! (see Beard, 2000).

The senses in higher education teaching

Susan Behuniak (2005), US professor of political science, in developing a 'pedagogy of solitude', is exploring how digital sounds and technological devices (iPods, computers, e-mails, televisions) can threaten the very silence and space needed for contemplation. Behuniak argues that in the fast-food-like stream of contemporary education, the incursion of these portable technologies into private space appears to create environments in which the learners cannot hear themselves think! Behuniak refers to the research by David Strayer, a professor of psychology, who argues that when aural flooding occurs the eyes will go to a place or thing but that place or thing will not actually be seen or registered. Tuning in and out of sense registration is an important concept to consider in the experience of learning.

In contrast, a substantial range of contemporary techniques exist for stimulating the senses: PowerPoint presentations, interactive whiteboards, video clips, sound bites, blindfolds, masks, drums, whistles, coloured cards, special effects lighting. Yet language can inhibit in other ways. If a lecture experience is dominated by excessive periods of unskilled oration, poor artificial light, stale air, and the immobilizing effects of rows of uncomfortable seats, the senses become dulled. The experience is deprived of the beauty and richness of learning because of the limited sensory experience. The same might be said for textbooks and researchers have recorded paradigm shifts from all-text-based design to visual language representation, thus building a dynamic relationship between text and graphics using multi-graphical representation. Graphical interpretations become a vehicle for useful communication that harbours the potential to convey concepts in various ways. The relationship between textual and visual representations in the design of multifaceted graphics can be enterprisingly and influentially integrated, with technology developing a new generation of texts that offer a new form of 'visual language' (Lin, 2005).

Neuro-linguistic programming (NLP) acknowledges the clear link between thinking, language and behaviour. The three words explain the notion: neuro is thinking, linguistic is language and programming refers to behaviour/actions. NLP research reveals that we think in patterns. Think of hot chocolate and it might be that we smell it, see it, or feel its warmth on a cold morning. These represent the dominant three thinking patterns of pictures, sounds and feelings and gives rise to what is termed VAK analysis (referring to visual, auditory and kinaesthetic representational or 'rep' systems), often used by facilitators and trainers. The way we use mental maps relates to sensory perception, and research shows that people tend to concentrate on one or two senses. People find it easier to remember things when associated with sensory recall, and NLP practitioners call these 'accessing cues', involving eye movements and speech categories. Examples include 'I see what you mean', 'I hear what you say'. These cues offer insight into the sensory associations and the preferred thinking mode of learners, helping facilitators to read the learner and modify communication to be in tune with learners and not just the sender.

Higher education lectures increasingly use PowerPoint presentations: but they can so easily dull the senses. Such presentations can be made more stimulating using a variety of sensory techniques. In the business and the environment lecture the lecturer might tell students about the possibility of making a lot of things from recycled plastic (auditory dimension). This can be stepped up a sensory level by also holding up a fleece made of recycled bottles, and a carpet made out of corn (visual dimension). Samples might be passed around so that students can feel (tactile dimension) the softness of the plastic fleece. This sensory stepping has the tendency to gradually raise levels of interest and engagement. Video clips can be added, to emerge out of one of the photographs on screen: an internationally renowned speaker, Ray Anderson, with a powerful presence, speaking to the US senate about greening business and sustainability. Traditional lectures can be transformed from a predominantly oratory experience to a multimedia (multi-sensory) experience offering a richer experience in order to help a broader range of learners to engage and understand.

However, there are potential problems associated with the increased stimulation by the use of technologies. A counter argument is that although technology enables us to influence people's senses, with ultraviolet light, strobes, the internet, computer presentations, iPods, large screen images and quadraphonic sounds, the overusage of multi-media can also create sensory flooding or sensory overload. Increasingly it might be that there is little or no space for thinking!

A single medium, rather than 'multi-media', can result in stimuli focus. An example of this in an educational setting is the use of 'digital learning objects': small bites of animation, audio recordings, assessment items, movie clips, still images and diagrams. With these 'learning objects' the educational content is broken down into constituent components, and these 'free standing' components typically focus on a single educational objective or concept. Tutors are able to select learning objects on an individual basis and construct teaching materials from them as required. In the UK the learning networks of the Higher Education Academy are building cooperative banks of such learning objects for exchange.

Using our different senses for learning: walk the talk

1. Embodied learning in practice: walking and talking the learning

HE postgraduate students researching the history of the development of the environmental movement are given a 300-year database of important dates and other key information. This document has been developed over many years by previous professional environmental staff and in recent times by university students. This embraces the notion of 'inheritance' – whereby the materials developed by participants are passed on and further developed by the next generation of participants. Different groups of people research different issues starting with these inherited materials; environmental law, the voluntary sector, government departments and reports, and other significant events. The sheer volume of information and the sense of not knowing can be overwhelming, giving rise to anxiety. Over the weeks the whole group initially produce basic fact-sheets and folders (or Wikipedia) on voluntary sector organizations, laws and other issues. These materials are also passed on to the next cohorts.

After several weeks of seminars, research sessions and discussion groups, a large integrative spatial map is constructed showing the history of UK environmentalism, either on the floor or a large table using a base template of laminated coloured cards given to each specialist research group: blue for laws such as the National Parks Act, yellow for NGOs, grey for quangos such as the Countryside Agency or Natural England, orange for key events in history such as the War or the Mass Trespass. Colour coding can be a powerful learning tool or trigger. In addition, they use numerous other blank cards that they furnish with dates and other information. All the essential kit is presented to the students in a plastic video case.

The map, created by the students, reveals the extent of their knowledge of the subject and when finished students walk-the-talk (talk through the history while actually walking the time lines) right up to the present day. The students defend their case orally (viva) as they move physically through time offering a milieu of critical narratives depending on their perspective and context. There are no 'right' answers. In addition, the walking and gesturing means that a kind of 'kinetic melody' is composed, as the embodiment of the journeyed narratives supports the learning. This walking and talking kinaesthetically aids learning, and reinforces the complexity of the scenarios, creating a kinaesthetic imprint, as understanding is tested in a visual-oral way. The experience thus consists of individual and group research, as they construct the historical map, and offer oral defence and further explanation.

The same process can be used for literature reviewing, or the examination of business products (see Beard, 2010). Texts are spread out in a large space and debated and discussed as people move around them – the spatial reorganization and debate is key. Students explore similarities and differences, creating multiple interpretations.

(For a full account see Beard, 2010)

Sensory stimulation in learning and therapy

The only book titled *Sensory Intelligence* has been produced by Annemarie Lombard from South Africa (2007). The text is based on her experiences as a therapist and her work explores the impact of people experiencing positive and negative effects resulting from their differing sensory thresholds.

Purpose built, multi-sensory spaces have been created for therapeutic work with children and adults with special needs. Using primary sensory stimulation and relaxation techniques, carers and patients share the sensory 'experience' together (see www.snoezelen or www.spacekraft). This sensory therapy is designed to allow individuals time, space and opportunity to enjoy the sensory components of the environment at their own pace and free from the demands of other thinking activities. The sensory environment provides pleasant sounds and music, light displays, appealing aromas, and contrasting textures to stimulate the senses and improve the quality of life for persons with a variety of learning difficulties and physical problems. Pinkney (1999) states that the aims of this sensory therapy are:

- to provide a stimulating environment to heighten awareness;
- to provide an interesting atmosphere to encourage participants to explore their environment;

- to provide an environment offering security, allowing participants mental and physical relaxation;
- to provide an unrestrained atmosphere where participants feel able to enjoy themselves;
- to stimulate the senses in order to create a sensory picture;
- to stimulate the sensory building blocks that make up perception.

This list appears to offer a useful set of underlying conditions for any experiential learning activity! The company SpaceKraft manufactures white and black rooms:

> The white room uses light and sound and is accompanied with white furniture and walls to create an environment that can help relax, calm and stimulate individuals. This therapeutic environment has a proven record with clients with various difficulties from profound and multiple to moderate needs. Mainstream schools are now recognising the value of such a resource. Imagine the White Room as a blank canvas where a colourful palette of lights are projected to give a stunning world of colour and imagery. Relaxing music gently plays in the background whilst the Vibro Acoustic Seat resonates deep bass sounds through the body. All these combine to provide a powerful sensory experience and valuable tool for carers and teachers. The Black Room... black helps with particular visual problems; brightly coloured items against a black surface are easier to identify because the black doesn't reflect the light... UV paints, shapes, bubbles and fabrics along with UV fun tubs are very popular... Ultra violet is also used extensively along with UV reactive equipment. Imagine the Black Room as a darkened theatre where occasionally a glowing hand held object appears as if by magic.
>
> (www.spacekraft.co.uk. Visited 21 June 2005)

Sensory stimulation, emotions and mood

Colours change our emotions: warmer colours have faster impulse or wavelength frequency. Room colours alter moods and can be adjusted using projection: coloured glass or plastic, or coloured light bulbs or overhead transparencies or electronic software. Red stimulates blood and is good for activity areas. Violet is good for sleep, calms the body and balances the mind. Blue lowers blood pressure and reduces stress, whereas green balances the body and is a spirit colour. Negative ions are known to produce good moods and these negative ion concentrations are found after rainstorms and around bodies of circulating water such as waterfalls, seashores and rivers. They may even be associated with shower water. Positive ion concentrations produce bad moods and are associated with smog or warm, dry winds (Thayer, 1996). Watching fire, listening to the flowing water and noticing the silence are powerful experiences. Breathing the clean morning air, savouring and appreciating basic shelter and food, and experiencing darkness are less common everyday experiences for increasing numbers of people.

For stressed people these can be very welcome experiences. However, they must be treated like the volume control when listening to your favourite music: too loud and the stimulus can be painful, too low and it has little impact. The ideal stimulus solutions for learning lie somewhere in between, and they can vary according to our needs and moods.

Nature-guided therapy

Rehabilitative strategies, using sensory stimulation, also occur in 'Nature-Guided Therapy'. Burns (1998) explores the evolutionary connectedness of people and place and offers sensory stimulation as a central approach for therapeutic interventions. Significantly, he quotes the work of historian Roszak who lays responsibility for psyche–environment detachment in psychological theory and practice squarely at the feet of Freud, who, he says, actively steered therapy away from the outer world of nature: 'As much as any other Positivist philosopher of his day, Freud toiled under the influence of one of the most commonplace images in our language: the spatial metaphor that locates the psyche "within" and the real world "outside"' (cited in Burns, 1998: 4).

In bringing nature back into the work of therapy, Burns uses a sensate focusing process involving nine stages:

1 Define the problem that needs addressing.

2 Define the desired outcome.

3 Assess whether ecotherapy is appropriate.

4 Formulate the therapeutic programme.

5 Select a relevant sense modality.

6 Create a sensate focusing task.

7 Commit the client to the task.

8 Explore the post-task experience and learnings.

9 Teach ongoing sensate focusing tasks.

A case study: the exploration of self

Visual manipulation: using masks for self-development

Masks can serve as useful metaphors, particularly during times of change. Masks can assist in getting into the hidden and unknown (Johari Window, Luft, 1961). Masks can help to unlock ideas that normally remain hidden in the subconscious, and can provide a vehicle for the expression of these

new insights (Johnstone, 1981). Creating masks can accelerate learning in a number of ways. Masks can:

- deepen our understanding of ourselves as we surface and explore our unconscious or unacknowledged assumptions, which have been taken for granted (Schein, 1992);

- focus on the uniqueness of each individual's situation; this is not a simple puzzle with a right answer but a complex issue with a range of possible solutions (Revans, 1982);

- use metaphor to assist us to identify (or clarify) our sense of self, our strengths and our 'over-strengths';

- access the creative side of our brain, which uses images, shape, colour and takes a holistic view;

- take us beyond aesthetics and art – we are not creating pleasing objects that are gentle to the eye but are identifying strong statements that help us to explore within and express ourselves more fully;

- provide the opportunity to work with others, gain feedback and support and have fun;

- offer a hands-on, kinaesthetic activity.

Example: Using masks in coaching and mentoring

Making masks engages the right creative side of the brain, using metaphor, symbolism and thinking holistically, using imagery. For many mentees, accelerating their learning through using both sides of their brain simultaneously is an unfamiliar and challenging process. Their typical work demands much of the left logical side of their brain, which engages in linear processes and language. Working in a kinaesthetic way can stimulate creativity, leading to unexpected insights and 'ah-ah' moments. These may not emerge through more usual mentoring processes that rely on only visual or auditory communication. Masks can be part of a process of expressing how you perceive yourself (Goffman, 1971). They can also provide an opportunity for gaining feedback on how you are perceived by others. This kinaesthetic process, involving feedback from others, can also help to unlock aspects of our subconscious mind. This technique can be used as a reflective tool to explore where one is, and also as a visionary tool for expressing how one wants to be, either in our career, or our whole life plan. Such processes form the core of coaching and mentoring practice. As mentors, we also need to constantly reflect on our practice and strive for self-development. Masks can also be valuable tools in our development: as mentors we should consider our shadow side or over-strengths. Do you recognize any of the following images in your mentoring practice?

- Mr Fix-it (always looking to deliver solutions);

- a mirror (merely reflecting back our mentee's concerns);

- a waiter (offering a menu of choices);

- a crow (pecking at certain issues);

- a wise old owl (dispensing wisdom).

In experimenting with processes such as mask making on ourselves, we will gain greater insight not only into our own professional practice but also into the processes we might suggest or employ with our mentees.
Written by Vivien Whitaker and Toby Rhodes.
(For a fuller account see Beard, 2010)

Inner sensory work: presence and anchoring

In order to develop deeper sensing, the traditional view of reality, as perceived through our everyday stimuli of the senses, is best suspended. This facilitates entry into forms of unconscious learning. How can we do this? Senge *et al* (2005: 88) refer to three stages that can support deeper 'knowing': sensing (observe, observe, observe), presence (retreat and reflect and allow inner knowledge to emerge) and realizing (acting with natural 'flow'). Presence requires sensing from a deeper source, sensing the subtlety of the experience. This, they say, can result in a heightened awareness and a panoramic sense of knowing (Senge *et al*, 2005: 89). It is at this point we see the delineating boundaries of the combination lock model disappear: in reality there are no boundaries between the senses, no boundaries between the mind, body and spirit, no boundaries between the inner world and the outer world, between self and others (including other fellow species). In Chapter 8 you can read a number of life experiences that illustrate and explain these phenomena and are found in the sections on naturalistic and spiritual intelligence.

Gardner (1993), in his work on multiple intelligence, makes reference to higher-level cognitive operations that go beyond 'an intelligence'. The '*sense of self*' placed the greatest strain on his multiple intelligence or MI theory, and this was a prime candidate for higher or second order ability. Intuition, presence, anchoring, flow experiences, peak experiences, and other similar phenomena all involve the engagement of higher mind states, and such states all appear to involve, to a varying degree, the engagement of the subconscious mind.

Sensory anchoring is a technique used to enter the subconscious mind, and involves a process of developing and holding on to the right mind state through conscious choice. An 'anchor' is a sensory stimulus such as an image, a piece of music, a perfume, or a smell that triggers a certain response in us, such as the ability to access certain mind states, to access certain feeling states, replace unwanted feeling states, or to experience an event or day in a different way. Anchoring develops an ability to tap into inner potential.

In a similar vein the principles of accelerated learning also suggest that people learn faster when the mind–body–cell balance is in good condition. A mind state known as the *memletic state* concerns the balance of: environment-nature (natural rhythms, living things, sense of 'being'), physical (health and fitness, sleep and body rhythms), mental (relaxation, meditation, energy, calm, attention, concentration, sensing, intuitive), and the cellular (food, oxygen, water, toxins). Sensory work at this level is remarkably hard to describe and define but Gladwell (2005: 182), in his book titled *Blink*, offers an exciting array of everyday experiences and research experiments that describe unconscious phenomena of the mind. They are examples of how we *think without thinking*. He offers the example of expert food tasters who have developed a very specific sensory vocabulary, allowing them to describe precisely their reactions to specific foods. The following example from his book highlights the great potential for developing all of our senses to enhance learning from experience, by allowing subconscious knowledge to be accessed and developed:

> Mayonnaise, for example, is supposed to be evaluated along six dimensions of appearance (colour, colour intensity, chroma, shine, lumpiness, and bubbles), ten dimensions of texture (adhesiveness to lips, firmness, denseness, and so on), and fourteen dimensions of flavour, split among three subgroups – aromatics (eggy, mustardy, and so forth); basic tastes (salty, sour, and sweet); and chemical-feeling factors (burn, pungent, astringent). Each of these factors, in turn, is evaluated on a 15-point scale.

Conclusion

The senses significantly affect the learning experience and there is a need for more research into the role of the senses in learning. While the senses act as information conduits, perception plays an important role in the complex interpretation of incoming sensory data. In this chapter we have offered a number of examples where the senses can be used to enhance or reduce the experience of learning. The chapter has explored a range of indoor and outdoor activities that awaken the senses, as well as ideas for sensory enhancement and reduction, sensory flooding and solitude, the use of masks, and the applications of sensory work to higher mind states, learning difficulties, and therapy. We have also explored sensory intelligence, the difficulties of the human language, the development of visual language.

A number of other chapters in this book also contain information on sensory stimulation and deprivation. The practical technique of developing a relaxed alertness as a mind state for study, for example, is covered in Chapter 7, as is the use of music or smell or other forms of mood-altering methods. Sensory reduction can also be used to create challenging obstacles, and these are discussed in sections on learning activities. Our senses also provide us with a mass of information that in turn can trigger certain emotional responses, and it is these emotional responses to experience that are the subject of the next chapter.

Experience and emotions
(The feeling dimension)

> *Emotions and feelings are the key pointers both to possibilities for, and barriers to, learning.*
> **MILLER AND BOUD, 1996: 10**

Introduction

Historically, the expression of emotion has been associated with weakness and irrationality, and frowned upon in many institutions, yet emotions are inextricably linked to learning and development. Boud, Cohen and Walker (1993: 14) emphasized this perspective noting that 'Of all the features that we have mentioned, emotions and feelings are the ones which are most neglected in our society: there is almost a taboo about them intruding into our education institutions, particularly at higher levels.' John Dewey wrestled with the nature of 'experience' and 'experiential learning', and he expressed concern that the emphasis on the intellectual or cognitive side of people alienated them from their immediate environment, and thus from their emotional, affective self (Crosby, 1995). At the heart of this concern lies the question: 'To what degree is learning an emotional experience as much as it is an intellectual one?'

Life's emotional roller coaster can be difficult to navigate at times. Emotions are crucial to a stimulating and satisfying life, but people do not necessarily experience the right emotional waves at the right time, or place, size or frequency. Emotional aptitude can help access and surface unconscious feelings, to control negative thoughts and anger, and to reduce conflict. This can facilitate more understanding of feelings and emotions, allowing progress towards more productive behaviours that positively enhance learning and life: increased calm, the ability to challenge a belief set, or the development of increased sensitivity to self and others. Few people find sufficient time to step back into calm periods to reflect upon life and its ups and downs, and to learn from what has gone before. Emotional intelligence (EQ), it is said, can contribute to an improved life: through improved communication, increased team morale at work, more collaborative working, less energy waste on politicking and game play, thus reducing poor attitude or indifference. Understanding and managing emotional intelligence might represent a good investment.

Eckhart Tolle (2006) suggests that emotions are the body's reaction to the mind, or a reflection of the mind in the body. Emotions arise at the place where mind and body meet: bodily emotions will give a truthful reflection of the mind. This helps to make clear links with our holistic model. In the previous chapter we made reference to the groundbreaking work of Nina Bull who used hypnosis to explore body–emotion connectivity, showing that 'postural attitude' is vital to the ability to feel emotions.

Becoming aware of and understanding emotions, and the shifting emotional dynamics of learners is a difficult but necessary skill for coaching or facilitating. Many emotions are perceived in simple terms as either positive or negative, but this can be unhelpful as negative emotions can take people out of their comfort zone and lead into deep transformational experiences, as we shall mention in the chapter 9. In this chapter, we focus on these roots of human emotions, how we can discover feelings and needs, and develop practical approaches to create space for people to consider their emotional response to an experience. We also explore some of the emotional underpinnings to experiential learning, and examine some of the sub-components of emotions; for example, learning states, humour, fear, pain, identity and anxiety. We take a brief look at a range of new and old ideas that enhance positive change in people, such as mind fitness, imagination, sculpturing, rewiring, mapping, sensory awareness, emotional catharsis and release, the use of rituals, and spiritual feelings and sacred places. In the six-dimensional experiential learning model this is the foremost dimension of the internal state.

Fast thinking

The emotional response to incoming sensory data is subject to long-established neuronal connections in the brain. When people see, hear, smell or feel something, the sensory information is doubled up. One set of information is speedily sent along a short circuit to the amygdala of the brain, through split-second responses. This is *fast thinking*, system 1. The other set of information is logically analysed and reflected upon elsewhere, sent down by the slower route to the area known as the neocortex. This is system 2, or *slow thinking*. If a stimulus has been linked to danger in the past, then the region of the brain called the amygdala will spring into action. This amygdala is in fact the storehouse for emotional memories, and so is a major source of instant reactions and gut feelings, which are hard to ignore (Robertson, 1999). This quick response is mostly for survival, helping people to avoid anything from snakebites or bumping into people to car crashes. However, some fast responses are not always up to date and can be inappropriate in the fluid social world we humans now inhabit (Goleman, 1996). The sight of a dentist or the words 'merger' or 'corporate change' can instil fear and panic in some people, giving a strong irrational reaction in them. Rewiring or reprogramming some of these instant emotional responses to overcome negative feelings and create more positive feelings is a challenge many experiential providers face when providing appropriate training and development. We believe all facilitation requires a sound understanding of emotional intelligence.

Another way to understand these issues is to consider that there are essentially three brains in the human. The old brain is found at the base area where the spinal cord ends. It is reptilian-like, managing the automatic functions such as heartbeat, breathing, and temperature regulation. This we will call the *functioning brain*. The middle brain is higher up and responsible for engaging fast emotional reactions, and this we will call the *feeling brain*. The new brain is advanced and particularly developed in humans, consisting of cerebral frontal lobes that do more complex, slower processing. This part is divided into left and right hemispheres. This we will call the *thinking brain*. Nobel Prize winner in economics Daniel Kahneman has written a book called *Thinking Fast and Slow* (2011); by fast he is referring to the feeling brain, and he also calls it System 1 thinking. By thinking slow he is referring to the work of the *thinking brain*. His book examines some of the myths associated with the supposed primacy of these slow and fast thinking functions. One of the book's main themes is the author's description of how little control we actually have over our own System 1 responses and the degree to which our subconscious intuition, and human biases, affect System 1 choices. Much of our life operates on System 1 autopilot. One of the best pieces of advice he gives is to act calm and kind regardless of how you feel.

The rational–emotional debate continues to attract attention from many disciplines; it has a protracted and contentious history. Over two and a half thousand years ago fundamental modifications of teaching occurred when the old 'reciting' of the Sophists was transformed to embrace a broader 'teaching of the soul' by the use of questioning by Socrates (Crosby, 1995). For Plato, however, emotions were inappropriate territory, as irrational urges that needed controlling, and for Kant emotions were regarded as an illness! Jay Griffiths in 2006 (p 6), commenting on her school experience, remarks that 'emotions came only disinfected. The furies of grief and joy were somehow considered unhygienic, passion a nasty germ.'

Research work on emotions in higher education confirms the significance of emotions in student engagement in learning in higher education (Beard, 2005). The research data shows that students experience a very real emotional journey: one that affects their whole being, containing many significant events that influence their disposition to learn. The roller-coaster experience of 'flourishing or distress' states has adaptive tendencies operating to 'balance' the extremes of energy and tension, acceptance and rejection, pleasantness and unpleasantness, success and failure, solidarity and rejection. These emotions are undoubtedly private and personal but they are also strongly and inextricably linked to the social. Many emotional scenarios appear to contribute to the establishment and maintenance of student identity, and are grounded in significant social relationships. These social bonds with peers, family and lecturers create differentiation, an inherent sense of belonging, and they appear to be influential in the construction and development of self-esteem. Yet students find few spaces to challenge and express their feelings about their learning experience, and Mortiboys (2002: 7) comments that it would be disturbing if universities were emotion-free zones, but noted that 'curiously, so much of the culture in higher education implies that they are'. These deliberations continue to inform the extent to which thinking and feeling are connected.

Communicating with feeling

Marshall Rosenburg (2003), who studied and worked with Carl Rogers, suggests we can improve relationships and create more harmony if we learn to separate observing from judging by using non-violent communication (NVC). To align our lives with our core values he recommends we apply a four-stage model: first *observing* (without evaluating), secondly understanding how we *feel* in relation to what we observe, thirdly to understand the deeper underlying *needs, values and desires* that underlie our and others feelings, and finally the ability to make *requests* that might enrich our lives. At the core of this work is the fact that the human mind naturally classifies and analyses, and in doing so we so easily fall into the trap of giving bad or good judging 'labels' when we observe the behaviour of others. This in turn so easily leads to unproductive and/or destructive communication and interaction. Rosenburg suggests we learn to observe without moralistic judging, and to get to the heart of our feelings about others or self through understanding our unmet needs and the unmet needs of others.

Compassionate communication and compassion-focused therapy

Powerful theory and practice systems for education in the emotions

Love and compassion are necessities, not luxuries. Without them, humanity cannot survive.

(H H Dalai Lama XIV)

There exist today, a fairly broad array of curricula and approaches for education in the area of emotional mastery. However, I will present here what I consider to

be two complementary and uniquely powerful, research-based theory
and practice systems for both understanding and teaching emotional
awareness and mastery – Compassionate/Non-Violent Communication (CC),
developed by Marshall Rosenberg, and Compassion-Focused Therapy (CFT),
developed by Paul Gilbert. As will be summarized below, through both CC and
CFT, we learn to apply a concept that is key to learning emotional balance: that
our thoughts underlie our emotions, and that we can learn to transform 'thought
habits', and thereby increase our emotional resilience. With CC and CFT then,
we learn to transform from blame and judgement thinking (a key contributor to
most difficult emotional states), toward understanding and compassion, which
are actually some of our deepest needs as human beings. We then become
more able to access and express our higher (and happier, as CFT research
shows) selves.

According to Rosenberg, our learned language of blame and judgement can
lead to unconstructive and often damaging emotional states. Below is a
simplified summary:

- Self Judgement Thinking Leads To... Anxiety, Shame and Depression.

- Other-Judgement Thinking Leads To... Fear and Anger.

The practice of the CC process, with time, facilitates an internal shift – as we
learn to translate learned (anger-inducing) blame and 'should' thinking to
increased self-awareness, through looking at our underlying feelings and
needs. We thus move from a sense of alienation (from ourselves and others), to
a greater understanding and connectedness, through four main steps/
processes:

- Learning to think and speak based on direct observations, versus biased
  evaluations.

- Acknowledging and taking responsibility for our feelings, by realizing that
  outer circumstances are just the trigger for our feelings; the cause is our
  blame-based thinking, and our attempt to fill needs is at the root. This leads
  to deeper self-understanding, and we are able to move from passive or
  aggressive communication, to honest, assertive self-expression.

- Building an awareness of our (and others') underlying universal human
  needs (such as for well-being, connection/compassion and meaning).
  This creates true self-empowerment – by building an awareness of our
  underlying needs, as well as constructive thinking to help realize them.

- Learning to make requests versus demands.

Through the CC process then, we learn to look and listen within. The CC
'needs-consciousness' facilitates an ever-growing process toward a more
honest self-understanding: we become deeply self-connected, which
Rosenberg says is perhaps the greatest use of NVC, and which then allows us

to more compassionately connect with others. In the process, we build a sense of shared humanity and acceptance, with a realization that all human behaviour is an attempt to meet needs.

Both CFT and CC provide uniquely effective processes for working with one of the most challenging emotions of all – anger. Rosenberg uses the term 'anger transformation', for the process (described above) through which we learn to translate our blame thinking, to awareness of underlying feelings and unmet needs. The critical link between blame thinking and anger is well-documented by social psychologist Timothy Wilson, who reveals that blame thinking is significantly higher than average in parents who are physically abusive, and that interventions designed to teach new belief systems are effective in decreasing abusive behaviour.

CFT's founder Paul Gilbert, has developed a three-pronged model of 'Emotional- Regulation Systems', which not only has powerful applications in emotional education work, but also highlights the benefits of CC (and CFT) practice. This meaningful, applicable, and research-based therapeutic model, is summarized below:

● The 'Threat System'– associated with anger and fear (or 'fight or flight') states.

● 'The Drive and Resource-Acquisition System' – associated with pursuits and 'wanting'.

● The 'Soothing and Safeness System' – associated with kindness, connection and 'non-wanting'.

CFT brain research has highlighted the power of this approach related to emotional resilience: among its core findings is that teaching people to shift from judgemental and unconstructive self-talk, to more compassionate, self-soothing internal dialogue, reduces depression and anxiety and increases happiness ratings. As Russel Kolts (a CFT practitioner) describes, teaching and practicing compassion (for ourselves and others) develops the pre-frontal cortex associated with the 'Soothing and Safeness System' (where we are happiest), and at the same time weakens the amygdala area, associated with the Threat System. So CC and CFT both serve as an antidote to fear-based thinking; both systems help us dwell increasingly in the 'Soothing and Safeness System'. It should be noted that 'Mindful Self-Compassion Training' is a CFT-related approach, with similar practices (in an educational context), but was beyond the scope of this illustrative piece.

It is worth pointing out that the skills taught through CC and CFT systems incorporate the core areas of emotional intelligence, as defined by Daniel Goleman, primarily: self-awareness, emotional regulation (self-soothing), and interpersonal skills, such as compassion and assertive communication. It should also be noted that a key (proven) aspect in the effectiveness of both CC and CFT is mindfulness – *the ability (and commitment) to detach from our emotions through self-awareness.* As for educational applications, CC-based educational approaches include a broad array of exercises, centred on practicing mindfulness in the four key areas of: observations, feelings-awareness, needs consciousness and requesting versus demanding. An example is the anger transformation process briefly mentioned above; another type of exercise that is foundational to CC work is empathetic listening practice. Two core CFT training approaches are compassionate imagery (toward self and others), and compassionate self-talk and self-coaching practice.

Based on deeply meaningful (research-based) theories and practices then, CC and CFT processes can provide a powerful foundation for educational work in the area of emotional mastery. CC and CFT theory and work can help us contribute toward, in the words of the late educator Paulo Freire, 'the creation of a world in which it is easier to love' – where we are better able to understand and connect compassionately with ourselves and one another.

Diana Kubilos, MPH; dkubilos@yahoo.com

Trainer, Facilitator and Program Developer, Malaysia.

Emotion and experiential learning

Crosby (1995: 11) suggests that 'we find ourselves in continual transaction with the physical, psychological, mental, spiritual world, and philosophy should be a systematic investigation into the nature of this experience'. It is frequently the case with traditional education and training that emphasis is placed upon cognitive and intellectual considerations. In order for any experience to be interpreted as positive, learners require a number of constructive attributes, including confidence in their abilities and self-esteem in order to recognize the validity of their own views and those of others. Other attributes include support from others whom we work with and bounce ideas off, and trust to generate confidence in the validity of the views of others and be able to incorporate them with our own where necessary. It would therefore appear that, for learning to occur and an opportunity for learning not to be rejected, there has to be an attitudinal disposition towards the event.

In essence, the affective domain can be seen to provide the underlying foundation for all learning. Postle (1993: 34), in support of this perspective, quotes Heron as saying: 'Valid knowledge – knowledge that is well grounded – depends upon its emergence out of openness to feeling.' He continues by drawing on the work of Langer: 'the entire psychological field, including conception, responsible action, rationality and knowledge is a vast and branching development of feeling'.

Here it is important to explore briefly the notion of emotional intelligence (EQ) particularly given that more holistic approaches to human understanding are adopted in experiential learning. Emotional intelligence is defined by Bagshaw (2000) as 'the ability to use your understanding of emotions, in yourself and others, to deal effectively with people and problems in a way which reduces anger and hostility, develops collaborative effort, enhances life balance and produces creative energy.' The notion of emotional intelligence as 'EQ' was popularized by Goleman (1996) by building on the ideas of social intelligence as developed by Howard Gardner and others in the development of multiple intelligence (MI theory). Goleman argued that having a high EQ was a different way of being smart, and his focus was on the emotional competence required to be a star performer. Some authors, such as Woodruffe (2001: 26), are more sceptical about such claims, arguing that it is not new territory. Woodruffe refers to emotional intelligence, in an article titled 'Promotional intelligence', as simply a new brand name for a set of long-established competencies. Woodruffe quotes one company making great claims that emotional intelligence can 'identify and develop better internal leaders, maximize productivity, create more effective teams, improve the selection process, reduce turnover, boost sales, improve organizational culture and morale, stimulate creativity and cooperation, and outperform the competition'. If only success in business were that easy to achieve.

Goleman also based much of his thinking on research by Salovey, who classified emotional intelligence into five main categories: 'handling one's emotions, managing emotions, motivating oneself, recognizing emotions in others, handling relationships' (Goleman, 1996: 46). To be able to understand this as an emotional basis to learning is of primary significance to experiential providers, who are increasingly called on to understand, manage and contain the emotional climate of their learners or clients. Fineman (1997) lists the work of many influential writers on the subject of the debilitating nature that anxiety, fear and stress have in interfering with learning, but notes that emotions are seen as 'unwanted' and 'undesirable' in the rational, logical workplace. The rules of emotional expression are corporately defined and there can be significant differences, as between individuals' privately held feelings and the emotion they display at work. These are some of the emotional issues addressed in high-ropes courses. The 'leap of faith' involves climbing to the top of a telegraph pole, releasing one handhold then another and standing upright, and then building up courage to leap towards a trapeze. Inability to reach the trapeze results in the safety harness kicking in; grabbing the trapeze results in an emotional high. Success, however, is about sensing and handling the fear and later transferring the learning to other life situations; these are key learning outcomes.

Managers learn to survive, learn how to avoid blame, learn how to operate in their organization and learn when to be deferential. These, according to Salaman and Butler (1990), are emotional behaviours that can help to avoid the painful experience of being singled out or blamed, and because we need allies. It is suggested that such fear-based management strategies in the workplace are likely to be ineffective and undesirable (Applebaum *et al*, 1998). Also emerging is popular literature on the negative aspects of fear-based parenting, citing evidence that young people, in these climates, are likely to self-destruct (Gray, 1999). Fineman (1997: 21) also comments that, in virtual working, networking and teleworking, 'managers will need to learn new ways of defining and expressing their feelings, status and identities, while developing alternative approaches to managing others' emotional lives under these working conditions'.

We experience an array of emotions, although researchers continue to debate which emotions might be of a primary nature. Goleman (1996) reports primary candidates as anger, fear, shame, sadness, enjoyment, surprise, love and disgust. Some primary emotions, such as fear, have an important impact on learning. Moods can be regarded as a subset of emotions, but they are said to be different from emotion in that:

> We can think of mood as a background of feeling that persists over time.
> Usually our moods are subtle, but sometimes they can be intense and
> overwhelm us. Moods are not the same as emotions, but they do have a great
> deal in common with them. Moods are sometimes defined as less intense and
> longer lasting than emotions, although this lower intensity isn't true in the
> case of serious depression. Unlike most emotions, moods don't seem to have
> an identifiable cause. That is, there usually isn't an obvious cause-and-effect
> relationship between our moods and events. This isn't true of emotions.
>
> (Thayer, 1996: 5)

Thayer regards the central dimensions of mood as a balance of energy and tension, and he says that mood indicates a greater tendency to do certain things. A person often says 'I am in the mood to…'. The experiential provider is expected to manage the mood and emotional climate of learners to varying degrees, but it is this energy–tension balance that is of significance, as a reduction in tension, for example, can increase energy levels. Moods are also heavily influenced by rhythms, and chronobiologists call these 'endogenous' biological rhythms, as they are governed by our internal biological clock. This internal clock becomes more apparent to us when we fly across time zones and the disrupted internal clock then makes us feel less alert or more energized in time with the old time zone, a phenomenon known as jet lag.

Thayer notes that energy levels rise to their highest levels in the first third of the day, around noon. They then drop in the mid- to late afternoon, reach a sub-peak in the early evening and decline until sleep, thus creating the rhythmical wave of daily energy. Larger waves are created by seasonal variations such as the reduction of light in winter, and these too are of significance to mood. Moods are also influenced by exercise, food, drink and fresh air, and the daily energy wave underpins many of the basic strategies for the active management of moods. 'Positive, optimistic thoughts accompany positive moods: in other words moods and thoughts are congruent'

(Thayer, 1996: 35). Thayer discusses state dependency, a phenomenon whereby, if we learn something in a particular mood state, we remember it better when we are in that same mood state, and Thayer, using a banking metaphor, suggests that there are separate mood memory banks for particular positive and negative moods.

The power of the emotional state

Morris (1969: 158) suggests that the object of any struggle is to experience 'optimum stimulation':

> when a man is reaching retirement age he often dreams of sitting quietly in the sun. By relaxing and 'taking it easy' he hopes to stretch out an enjoyable old age. If he manages to fulfil his 'sun-sit' dream, one thing is certain; he will not lengthen his life, he will shorten it. The reason is simple – he will give up the Stimulus Struggle.

Although this 'struggle' for balance in life, for optimum experience, is largely an emotional one, it can take on many dimensions. Megginson (1994), now a retired HRD professor, writes down ten goals each year. These are goals that he wants to achieve to create balance in four main areas of his life: his mind, his body, his emotions and his spirit. To ensure a consistent focus each day he sets specific 'SPICE' goals: spiritual, physical, intellectual, career and *emotional*: these help him either to stay on course or to change direction. Adler (2000: 6) in offering a 'Life Content Model' suggests that:

> 'Being' is the ultimate goal type. To be 'happy', 'content', or 'fulfilled' is as near as we get to understanding human desire… Quite simply doing, knowing and getting is with a view to being happy rather than sad. Some people, however, are 'being' people even on a day-to-day basis. They experience the 'now' rather than putting off being to some future time, which may never be. They take time to stop and smell the roses.

Deferment is a common way that reduces the value of life experience. The 'being' is always delayed until later: 'When I get this, then I will…'. This presents a basic underlying life tension, an emotional imbalance of 'being' versus 'getting'. The phenomenon of 'being' emerges in many forms in the literature on experiential learning, psychology, adventure and sport. Yaffey (1993: 10) describes this emotional phenomenon of 'pure perception, uncontaminated thought and freedom to Be' as the key ingredients in the state of mind known as 'peak experience', a term originally coined by Maslow (1971).

We now examine more closely the nature of 'being', and we look at experiential opportunities that can create stimulation for optimum learning (see Figures 7.1 and 7.2).

FIGURE 7.1 Catching waves and finding calm

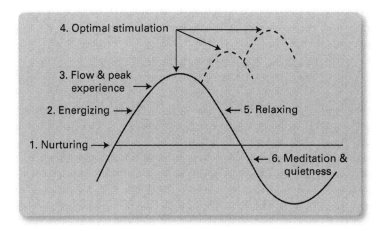

Emotional waves

The idea that life experience is a continuous stimulus struggle was a topic examined in *New Scientist* in an article called 'Thrill or chill' (Schueller, 2000), with photographs of white-water rafting, surfing, paragliding and other extreme sports. The article describes how some people will do anything for high levels of stimulation, to get an adrenalin rush, while others prefer the quiet life. People can of course get an adrenalin surge without jumping off a building or hang-gliding. Farley, a former president of the American Psychological Association, described how those who push the frontiers of the mind rather than the body could get an adrenalin rush through other means. He said, 'Einstein was way beyond the handrails. He was literally creating his own vision of the Universe. What sustained his mental life was the "thrill of it"' (Schueller, 2000: 23). Significantly, this adrenalin rush can also come during mentally demanding learning. As with any adventure, the pleasure comes once you have landed safely and the relaxing opiates called endorphins gush through the body; the natural ecstasy is produced from the learning, creating strong positive emotions. Experiencing a high can be exhilarating, a form of peak experience, and it can come in many guises. But providing learners with repeated high-energy activity may produce low returns for the learners if their optimal stimulation levels are exceeded (see Figures 7.1 and 7.2). High-energy seeking can also be overplayed. The troughs shown in Figure 7.1 represent emotional relaxation – calm waters, the lulls between the waves, the time to smell the flowers – and they are as important as the high-energy waves. Balancing the energy and the emotional waves is significant to the experiential provider's role.

Experiencing emotional calm

Finding emotional calm is essential sorting time. It is also time just to 'be', and involves stepping back and finding mental and physical space to think. A practical exercise in experiencing calm is given later in this Chapter; it is an example of getting inner calm and stimulating the senses. Experience has to be reflected upon so as to make sense of it, by making connections to other experiences. So-called 'mindless' activities appear to have a clear function in that they allow the everyday sensory bombardment to cease for a while, allowing the mind to sort things out and take stock:

> The same sort of spontaneous sorting through of existing information occurs during certain mindless, rhythmic physical activities like jogging, swimming laps or mowing the lawn; or during habitual routines that no longer need the conscious brain's full attention, such as showering or commuting on the same route each day. Just as it does during sleep, this spontaneous process of reflection allows one to momentarily suspend the intense flow of new information to the brain. This enhances the processing of existing information, thereby preparing the person to handle the demands of the rapidly changing environment.
>
> (Daudelin, 1996: 39)

Daudelin (1996) offers some fascinating thinking on the process of reflection, and refers to the work of J Allen Hobson, professor of psychiatry at Harvard. Hobson's book, simply called *Sleep*, explains how sleep reduces the level of incoming sensory data and allows for the reorganization and storage of information already in the brain, thus better preparing people to handle the demands of the working day. This same sorting and filing also occurs during waking time, through activities that appear to be of a mindless nature. This is often what is happening in some adventure programmes when people plod the mountains or drift over water in Canadian canoes. Other activities include meditation, prayer or journal writing. Similarly, the garden shed or greenhouse is a place for people to potter, find space to be alone or to plan the day; there are classic everyday thinking alone times. We have already mentioned that the Outward Bound solo involves people being alone in wilderness. Voluntary castaways left alone on islands have provided unique television footage of personal interactions and relationships. Significantly, such programmes often contain interviews of people describing their unique and special place to be alone, whether it be a hilltop, a rock outcrop, a sandy beach or an old barn. They are personal places to think and sort things out, and the provision of this space is essential in experiential programmes.

Meditative experiences, for example, can generate more intense states of mind:

> There are many words for the extreme forms of joy. In the Buddhist tradition, it is called bliss and is considered to be a natural state arising from non-attachment and compassion. Meditation is a way of attaining it. When a person is no longer bound by his desires or emotional needs, then life can be

experienced as bliss. Many other religious practices bring about ecstasy, literally standing outside oneself. In ecstasy we transcend time and space.

(Wilkes, 1999: 256–57)

It is useful to explore these emotional states prior to, during and after experiential activities (for example, see the practical case study on flow learning through relaxed alertness later in this chapter). Fox (1999) offers three ingredients at the top of a list of 32 recommendations to experiential providers to encourage spiritual experiences: 1) allow time for relaxation; 2) allow time for solitude and personal reflection time; 3) allow time to explore and interrelate with nature alone.

By combining the 'adventure waves' of Mortlock (1984) with the flow learning of Cornell (1989) and the work of Dainty and Lucas (1992) we can create a six-stage emotional wave (see Figure 7.2):

1 **Create conditions for pre-contemplation** – reading, thinking, imagining.

2 **Awaken participant enthusiasm** – ice-breakers and energizers.

3 **Start to focus attention and concentration** – medium-sized activities, narrow skills.

4 **Direct and challenge the personal experience** – larger, broader skills.

5 **Share participant enthusiasm** – using reviewing activities.

6 **Encourage quiet personal reflection.**

Energy waves are implicit in many other development models, such as the four stages of nurturing, energizing, peak activity and relaxing developed by Randall and Southgate (1980) and the gestalt cycle (see Figure 7.3). A six-stage programme developed by Porter (1999) can also represent a wave of change, and consists of entry, pre-contemplation, preparation, action, maintenance and relapse or integrated change. Throughout this book we focus on numerous 'waves' that form the holistic learning experience. Ice-breakers stimulate the first wave, and energizers add stimulation to subsequent waves. Pre-sensitizing exercises can increase the awareness of sensory systems and hence the experience itself, prior to a wave. The pacing of energy waves, and the sequencing of physical or mental activity is equally important; rising waves can be full of adrenalin, whilst the subsiding wave can induce endorphins and cause calm and relaxation, important to reflection time. Too many waves of any one kind may result in habituation and reduced responsiveness and so monitoring energy levels is important.

Heron (1999: 233) refers to the ability of facilitator pace to influence energy and mood levels: speech modes *clock time* and *charismatic time*, are two such examples. Clock time is 'verbally dense, fast, loaded with information, somewhat urgent and in a subtle way over-tense'. Speech in charismatic time is warm and slow, and tends to contain pauses and silent moments. The voice mode here is deeper, has clear, rhythmic inflections and sounds almost poetic. Clock speech waves are staccato in form, whereas charismatic speech

FIGURE 7.2 Learning waves

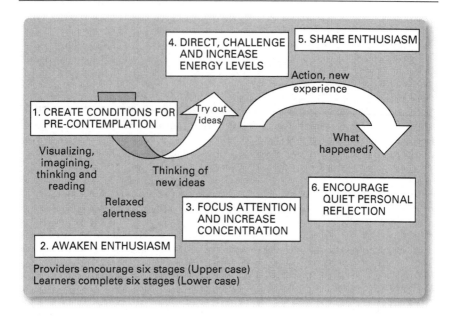

FIGURE 7.3 The gestalt wave

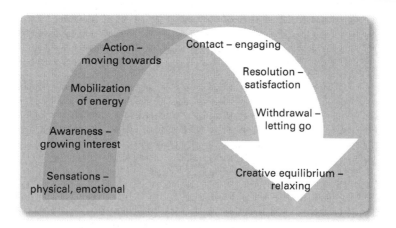

waves are gentle and rolling. The voice is a powerful tool that can be used to create a range of effects.

Flow learning

'Flow experience' is considered by Macaloon and Csikszentmihalyi (Boniface, 2000: 66) and it is suggested that activities 'must be finely calibrated to a person's skills – including his physical, intellectual, emotional and social abilities'. The idea of matching activities to these four criteria within learners is clearly an important skill for learning providers in the design of enhanced learning. Getting people to focus and concentrate on a specific task, or to focus on an object in an almost meditative way, reduces or removes many other external stimuli, and removes attention from self-centred emotional needs; it is the basis of a powerfully positive experiential state of mind. It is a state of mind that leaves behind boredom and worry. In much of the literature relating to this subject, reference is made to these and other special and spiritual environments in the emotional, intellectual, phys-iological or physical sense. In literature on adventure, for example, Miles and Priest (1990) say that personal transcendence is also experienced when risk is courted and met, when we invite adventure into our lives.

Boniface (2000) offers an excellent analysis of these and other positive experiences, and refers to the work of Csikszentmihalyi, who suggests that people who are deemed 'beginners' do not experience the much-sought-after socio-psychological condition of flow, because beginners find the activity demanding, and conscious thought and/or anxiety are present in high levels: a form of conscious incompetence. In order to attain flow states, certain levels of experience, skill and conditioning appropriate to the level of chal-lenge must first be attained, moving through levels of conscious (deliberate/clumsy) competence to unconscious (automatic/without thought) compe-tence (Strangaard, 1981).

Opportunities for flow experience lie somewhere between tasks that are too simple and those that are too challenging. The relationship between perceived risk, level of challenge and personal competence thus appears to be a central factor in the flow state experience. Such powerful experiences have also been referred to as 'peak experience' or 'peak performance'. These terms are used interchangeably, but there are some essential differences. Wil-kes (1999) suggests that a flow state is a form of extreme joy: it is character-ized by extreme concentration, a loss of self-consciousness and an altered perception of the passage of time. Athletes and artists experience it; indeed, she suggests that all activities that are perceived as highly meaningful can yield flow states. In competitive swimming some people are able to swim fast in a focused state yet see their own hands in slow motion flowing along the glistening water, and enjoy the experience with an almost out-of-body sensation. Jazz musicians, comedians, and teams report achieving these flow states (Hopfl and Linstead, 1997). In intense creative artwork some people almost enter the picture and lose track of time. Csikszentmihalyi made spe-cific reference to artists, and concluded that painters must want to paint, and that it was the students who were able to savour the emotional 'sheer joy of it' who went on to succeed as serious painters (Goleman, 1996: 107).

Flow or 'optimal experience' can be broken down to its constitutive parts. Csikszentmihalyi identifies them as 'conditions of flow':

- challenging activity requiring skills;
- clear goals and immediate feedback;

- merging of action and awareness;
- concentration on the task at hand;
- the paradox of control;
- loss of self-consciousness;
- the experience is autotelic.

To create these characteristics in learners would be ideal, as peak performance is associated with superior functioning, often described in athletes as having an underlying state of clear mental focus, combined with a highly energized state, relaxed yet adrenalin-ready, and in control and confident. Wilkes (1999: 250) argues about the design of programmes: 'we cannot make flow and joy happen, but we can provide the interior situations where they are most likely'. In chapter 4 there is a very simple yet natural and practical example of how to encourage a form of relaxed alertness through reading, develop a playful approach to intellect and create powerful productive learning. Deep reading and deep thinking can be powerful parts of an experiential programme, and can give rise to original, indigenous learning.

Experience, learning and 'identity'

All learning is grounded in prior experience. The past consists of banked emotional 'experiences', and these can both drive forward and restrict new learning from experience. Elements of change represent the unknown, and can cause concern about the future: the comfort zone becomes over-stretched. Why is it, however, that some people adapt to challenging experiences sometimes whereas at other times it is difficult? Risk can be high or perceived as high, but it is usually fear that underpins the deeper feelings of worry and concern. These fears become strong barriers for some; for others it is a powerful drive presenting an adventure. Martin, Franc and Zounkova (2004: 82) offer extensive coverage of psychological and emotional safety in outdoor learning, and they explore facilitator and participant psychological risk. What is suggested is that clear strategies are needed to predict problems, to reduce the intensity of activities when required, and to develop sensitivity to culturally mixed groups. The concept of 'challenge by choice' is often a foundation principle in outdoor learning, and the authors suggest that facilitators avoid pushing people to open up. It is also suggested that psychologically oriented activities are not presented one after another.

Fear is in essence the body's reaction to the mind, more particularly the egoic mind. The fragile ego is frequently under threat. Fear, often in a subconscious way, involves the identification with the mind projection to a threat of a future or past event, resulting in tension, worry and anxiety. The mind often seems to compulsively seek to avoid or escape from the immediate experience of the now, of the present moment. Yet being present in the moment shifts the self into a state of no worry or anxiety (Tolle, 2006).

The need to attain the future, trying to get somewhere else as if the present is an obstacle, can result in a poor life experience as the present is in essence all we ever have. Elsewhere we refer to this as a deferring life habit as people focus on getting something, knowing something or having something that will give supposed meaning to life. This can so easily negate the immediate life experience.

Postle (1993: 34) addresses barriers on a more personal level:

> as I see it, we often cling, with the intensity of addiction, to the comfort that comes from staying with our preferred mode and keeping away from the other modes. I remain convinced that this is usually because at some point in our history, one or another – or all – of the four modes of learning may have become debilitated or ruined. If this debilitation or damage was severe, whether locally or generally, then staying with the preferred mode may also successfully defend us against the feelings associated with that early hurt. If so, then our interest in action, or dreaming up futures, or caring, or arguing, whichever most keeps quiet our painful history, can indeed come to have the intensity of addiction.

Attributing an experience with a positive or negative emotional interpretation may influence the degree and type of learning. Postle (1993: 37) describes three kinds of learning that inhibit us:

- **omitted learning** – lack of love in an upbringing, which results in a person being unable to receive or give love;
- **distorted learning** – can occur when a person is told that he or she is hopeless, not talented, etc;
- **distressed learning** – learning that occurs with distress in the form of forced learning and compliance.

These are significant issues to learning providers. Negative learning experiences significantly influence our outlook on life, how we interact with others and with our experiences, and even the extent to which we are prepared to venture into new learning experiences. Postle (1993: 38) emphasized the vast importance of previous experiences in the shaping or avoiding of future experiences:

> Distorted, omitted and distressed learning have vast power. They can drive people into the most bizarre forms of 'I have to' or 'I can't' behaviour. They compel us to devise and install incredible personal and social behaviour rules with the purpose of supposedly keeping us safely in our familiar 'comfort zone'. We may then go too often to the same parts of life's landscape and rarely or never to other districts.

Negative emotions and feelings can inhibit present and future learning. This may lead to the conclusion that a negative experience will also lead to negative interpretations about the experience. This need not be the case, and many of life's most powerful learning opportunities occur as a result of painful experience. People hate work when there is too much to do, and often dream of not having to work at all. Yet people fear being unemployed and celebrate finding employment. More significantly, what we do at work is often a significant element of the description of our identity, 'what we do for a living'. This point is also illustrated by Parr (2000). In her book on education and identity, she describes her research with mature women returning to education and how, on the face of it, their reason for entering education later in life is the wish to gain the qualifications they did not gain at the 'conventional age'. Digging below the surface, however, she uncovers more complex reasons. She declares that the reason to return to education was:

> as much about identity as it was about paper qualifications. It could have been described as a 'life-raft' for some students – as one of them said 'it's saved my sanity'. What emerged very clearly from what they said, was the desire to redefine at least part of their identity, to see themselves in a different way and exert a degree of control over some aspects of their lives.
>
> (Parr, 2000: 1)

Parr goes on to describe how, when people are questioned about their education and learning, superficial responses can be misleading. Many women, when a trusting climate was developed, talked readily of trauma in their lives. Some questioned the way in which they had been defined by others, and talked of the social pressures on women to conform to a particular identity. Some told of psychological, physical or sexual abuse, overbearing parents, alcoholism or the death of a child or other family member. For many there was an inner drive that steered their return to education, and it was associated with power and control, confidence building, independence, self-image or a desire to prove their ability. Despite the fact that a number of women had experienced their early school educational experience as largely negative, many saw their return to (adult) education as positive and therapeutic, as a form of cathartic leisure activity, by doing something for themselves for enjoyment. This presents an interesting juxtaposition of leisure and learning. Perceiving their learning as a 'leisure experience' and paying to learn made it more enjoyable and increased their motivation.

Practical ways to access feelings

> The razor blades are in a safe place (but I can't help noticing that length of rope in the garage!!!!)... I will phone you soon for some quality psychotherapy.
>
> Regards.
>
> (from a Master's-level student letter to her tutor)

In this section we further explore humour, metaphors, trilogies and storytelling as tools to access and influence the emotional connection to learning. We offer additional ways to work with emotions in experiential learning, including techniques to surface feelings and challenge emotions.

Sensing, surfacing and expressing both positive and negative feelings require skill and care. Difficult feelings do not go away by being denied or censored: to deny feelings is to deny learning. Good practice allows the richness of the emotions of learning to be expressed in a way that maximizes understanding of learning processes. To access deep emotions in learning can be difficult, as there is associated risk. Emotions are often perceived as dangerous, unknown territory.

The emotional climate – mood setting and relaxed alertness

Learning is more effective if people are in the right frame of mind. In the last chapter we explored the psychological state known as 'relaxed alertness' as an optimum inner state for learning. Such a mind state requires the development of a certain ambience and mood, with the associated stimulation of certain senses. New tools continually enter the marketplace that are designed to stimulate senses and affect mood, and these include 'relaxation glasses' and 'mind-lab' audiotapes. Adverts exist for 'progressive accelerated learning', using state-of-the-art sound technology to create and encourage particular types of brainwave patterns. These apparently enable people to experience a focused state of consciousness and, because the brain gives messages to the body, sounds and light pulses can influence the physical condition. Music and stories, for example, can generate special moods or mind states: police advice to pubs is to play music from children's programmes to reduce aggression on the streets at closing time. Music affects the rate of breathing, blood pressure, pulse rate and muscle activity, and specific types of music can be played to correspond to brainwave activity. Music wavelength can correspond to welcoming, or the raising of energy levels, reflective mood induction or preparation for departure. Pulses of flashing light and sound vibrations are known to influence brainwaves and therefore mental and emotional states. Many writers comment on the power of music in facilitation and, in particular, in the importance of setting the atmosphere or learning climate (Benson, 1987; Robertson, 1999; Heron, 1999). Four main types of brainwave can be stimulated: alpha waves indicate alert relaxation, when the brain is open to new information and thought processes are clear and calm; beta waves are present in the state when we are most able to use critical faculties, solve problems and make decisions; theta waves are slower still and support creative thinking; delta waves indicate deep sleep.

Olfactory sensations are also important (Wilson, 1997: 282):

- Orange improves communication.
- Basil and lemon increase mental clarity.
- Pine is refreshing and inspirational.
- Ylang-ylang relieves anger.
- Bergamot is calming, and found in Earl Grey tea.

Many smells are now available as canned products, and they allow for experimentation with sensory stimulation to influence the mood and ambience.

A practical exercise: experiencing calm

Use before sorting time or solo time:

- Make yourself comfortable: find your own place to lie or sit relaxed with your hands down by your side or clasped on your lap.

- Read these instructions once and then proceed.

- Concentrate on the enlarged circle below.

- First take three minutes to listen to your own breathing.

- Now concentrate on the exact middle of this circle O; use only your peripheral vision, and slowly stimulate your senses:

  – see three objects around you;

  – hear three sounds;

  – smell three things;

  – feel three things.

(You might have a slight feeling of an out-of-body experience.)

Robertson (1999: 240) describes how volunteers were easily tipped from sadness to elation by simple techniques. He describes some simple experiments he conducted, such as how simply pulling eyebrows upwards for a few seconds can change people's mood. Moment by moment the brain is changed by experience: by what people think, see, hear or remember. By using a variety of relaxation exercises and brain gymnastics, Robertson suggests that people can make their experience more effective.

Overcoming fear

Emotions influence everyday behaviour, and they can have a distorting effect on learning. Johnson (1996: 185) describes in detail a case study where he changed powerful, fear-based blockages in a person in a maximum security prison, a rich context in which to explore ideas about working with experience on such emotional issues. Johnson reports that he 'tapped into his emotions… unblocked an emotional dam, unfroze his major emotional plumbing and facilitated his renaissance'. Some of the basic issues addressed in this and the previous chapter are that anger and aggression are often based on fear, and that trust is a strong antidote to fear. Fear is one of the strongest primary emotions, which can be both conducive to improved learning and toxic to learning. Fear is the result of powerful emotional circuitry embedded in the brain resulting in a conditioned response. Mallinger and De Wyze (1993) describe these fears as being present in many people and they describe people who pride themselves on being reliable, hard-working and self-disciplined; they are indeed regarded as perfectionists. Their offices and homes are neat and organized, and they are always in control. They are successful and financially secure. The downside is that although they may be confident and poised on the outside, they may be hurting inside, for their standards are so high that they constantly set themselves up for disappointment, and such perfection may prevent them from enjoying life and even forming relationships. Being too much in control can result in being out of control. Such fears need managing so as to create balance. Learners with signs of being 'too perfect' might have:

- a fear of making errors;
- a fear of making the wrong decision or choice;
- a strong devotion to work;
- a need for order and a firm routine;
- emotional guardedness;
- a tendency to be stubborn or oppositional;
- a heightened sensitivity to being pressured or controlled by others;
- a need to know and follow the rules;
- an inclination to worry, ruminate or doubt;
- a need to be above criticism – moral, professional or personal;
- a chronic inner pressure to use every minute productively.

(adapted from Mallinger and De Wyze, 1993)

The research that produced Mallinger and De Wyze's book, *Too Perfect*, was initially conducted on neurosis, but many of the doctors professionally associated with the authors commented that the findings were close to many of their own behaviours. The book describes how being overly in control can get completely out of control, encouraging people to look at their own mental scars produced as a result of fear. The suppression of fear, a fear of the truth, of how it actually is, is a reason for much misguided behaviour, especially managerial actions at work when there is reluctance to be honest, with other people and one's self. People often fail to see that there is something fundamentally wrong. Harvard professor Chris Argyris describes how

FIGURE 7.4 The communication iceberg

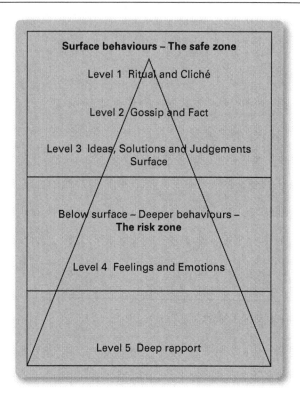

this phenomenon affects communication at work. His article, 'Good communication that blocks learning' (1994: 77), says:

> What I have observed is that the methods these executives use to tackle relatively simple problems actually prevents them from getting the kind of deep information, insightful behavior, and productive change they need to cope with the much more complex problem of organizational renewal... and they do not surface the kinds of deep and potentially threatening or embarrassing information that can motivate learning and produce real change.

The communication blockage can be further illustrated by reference to the communication model in Figure 7.4. People are experts at rituals and cliché, gossip, fact, solutions and judgements at work. It is the 'functional communication' of work, for some managers. The communication triangle has significance for experiential learning providers, in reviewing and reflection skills. If learners are not in touch with their own fears, emotions and feelings, then a priority need is to help them to access the right levels of inner communication through deeper levels of rapport, to move beyond the superficial haze of rituals and cliché, facts and solutions.

Argyris (1994) argues that logical, robust, solutions-focused behaviour is not always appropriate and that in the name of positive thinking managers often suppress what everyone needs to say or hear. In a self-protective haze of defence, single loop responses provide single loop solutions. The fix-it hat is donned and the same old fix gets the same old responses. Trusting others to make mistakes is part of the process of letting people learn, yet managers when coached to let go of being in control describe feelings similar to having had addictive cigarettes taken away. There is a sense of redundancy in not being able to fix.

> It is not difficult for people to identify with the notion that work life is 'emotional'. Fear, worry, contempt, envy, anger, infatuation, loneliness, pride, joy, guilt, tedium and so forth are embedded in working experiences – to a greater or lesser degree. The extent to which they are overtly expressed, or publicly admitted, depends on the nature of the individual and the openness of the organization's culture. Emotions can be seen to shape, and be shaped by, myriad work actions, such as decision-making, training, selling, persuading, hiring. Learning – creating, retaining and reproducing new knowledge or behaviour – can be regarded as implicit or explicit to these activities.
>
> (Fineman, 1997: 13–14)

Learners do tend to talk more easily about any emotional elements of experience in the past tense rather than the 'here and now' but experiential providers can encourage learners to speak about their experience in the 'here and now', in continuous dialogue. Sometimes a range of questions, such as 'How are you feeling right now?' when a person is on a high-ropes course, can be the simple trigger required to surface the inner feelings. Similarly the question, 'Has anyone else had these feelings?', can encourage other members of the group to become aware of and express their feelings. Observation of body language by providers, especially facial expressions, and carefully and gently feeding back what is seen can also be a trigger for learners to express feelings.

Mapping and accessing emotions

Experiential learning providers use techniques to help participants map out fears. By revisiting past experiences some of the unwanted circuitry in the brain can be rewired. 'Fear maps' can be created – and then rewritten. Asking people when they have been sad, bad or glad in their life can be a very productive start to this process. Recent research in Higher Education used emotional maps to highlight the roller coaster of felt emotions, and the importance of identity and relationships over the student year (Beard, 2005). Maps can also be used to help people see where they have been or want to go to. Take the London Underground map. The real rail lines do not travel in straight lines as the map would have us believe, but if the map showed reality it would be far harder to use.

In a critique of Kolb's theory of experiential learning, Holman, Pavlica and Thorpe (1997) argue that this learning theory is placed within the cognitive psychological tradition and tries to explain social, historical and cultural phenomena in a very mechanical way. However, far from 'functioning systematically and mechanically, a person's inner life reflects interpersonal transactions, for example conversations and dialogues. In this way, thinking, even when alone, always remains quasi-social' (1997: 140). What they are saying is that people talk to themselves; we all have our inner dialogue. Before a difficult or undesirable event this inner talk can be destructive or positive. Thinking and reflecting through the inner talk is a quasi-social phenomenon, because we have inner conversations with ourselves through these other inner people. We refer to this in *The Inner Game of Tennis* by Gallwey (1986) in the final chapter. Wilkes (1999) in *Intelligent Emotion* has a chapter devoted to 'The people who live within us', and recommends that people train and develop their own inner family. She suggests that 'our culture encourages us to think of ourselves as one person and no more' (1999: 39).

Psychologists have called the main personality the ego, which is Latin for 'I'. It is usually the leader of the family but if it becomes too dominant all the rest of the family are silenced! Using positive affirming language can overcome some self-destruct language of this inner family of the self, as sometimes just one inner person takes control of the others. However, there are ways to take back control. One voice inside the mind is the critic, talking all day long, and seemingly setting many of the rules by which we live. Challenging these rules can be very useful: these rules create many negative and destructive thoughts. Characteristic 'critic conversation' is 'I must never make mistakes', 'I must never look foolish'.

These same rules underpin everyday fears. They have a powerful effect on people, and experiential learning providers can encourage people to re-examine them: underlying these rules is the fear of losing control. Many people do not change behaviours due to fear of what might happen. Fear of losing control or fear of finding something out that cannot be faced, about self or others, can give rise to hesitation and apprehension. The inner voice says it is safer to do it the way we have always done it, resulting in compelling passion to control oneself and others. The Johari Window (Figure 7.5) is useful in exploring these issues. The Johari Window is used regularly by experiential providers to examine how people approach others. It was created by Joseph Luft, a psychologist, and Harry Ingram, a psychiatrist (hence the origin of the name – the Joe and Harry window!). The window shows four panes. The top left-hand window, for example, contains the aspects of self that are known to self and are evident to others. The façade covers aspects that are known to self but hidden from others.

Control brings more apparent safety, comfort and security, in a world surrounded by machines and computers that control the environment. Getting away from mobile phones, satellite systems and predictable, regulated environments might explain why some people stretch themselves by seeking rescue-free wilderness. High-ropes courses are now commonly used in many countries to demonstrate a range of basic emotional responses to challenges. These techniques focus on the emotional base to learning. One development centre we visited had pictures on all the walls showing exciting images that

FIGURE 7.5   The Johari Window

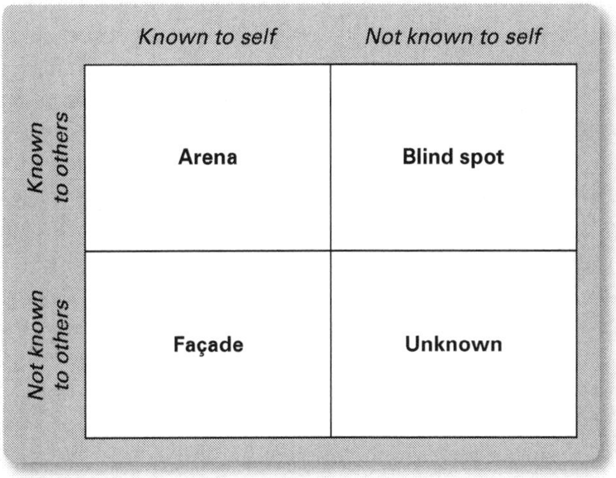

	Known to self	Not known to self
Known to others	Arena	Blind spot
Not known to others	Façade	Unknown

represented many of the basic emotions in life, such as fear and challenge. One image of a sailing boat had a caption that said that a boat was safe when it was in the harbour but that was not what it was designed for.

Learning providers can also help people to address fear with less dramatic methods, asking people to spring-clean the inner rules that sit in their unconscious mind with three steps. Learners can rewrite their own rules and realize that it is OK and human to make mistakes. Learners can learn to value themselves warts and all, loosening the grip of perfectionism:

1 The rule (the left-hand column):

I must never show my nerves in public.

2 Which really means (the right-hand column):

I couldn't stand the embarrassment if people saw me looking flushed and nervous.

3 So we revise the rule:

I prefer not to show my nervous feelings in public... but if I do people will understand. Importantly it would not be the end of the world. Most people feel nervous about these things at one time or another. I might not like it but I can cope with it.

Using trilogies in emotional work

Benson (1987: 203) makes reference to the *I Ching* (Book of Changes) and suggests that the clever experiential group worker should 'use allegories, figures, wondrous speech or other hidden, round about ways, to convey meaning and resolve difficult situations'. Popular, well-known trilogies are also used to help to resolve difficult emotions.

They help people to get in touch with the unconscious inner environment, helping them to read and interpret what is happening, especially cause-and-effect thinking, and so enable them to move towards positive change and transformation. Breaking down the mind processes into simple steps and grasping what is generating external actions and behaviours can be a powerful experiential event for people. Frank (in McLeod, 1997: 25) notes that 'it can be demonstrated that in all human societies people experience "problems in living" that are dealt with through a combination of listening, re-framing, catharsis, interpretation and behaviour change'. Many writers have recommended a variety of basic steps for iterative change, which are commonly used in development training. They have a gestalt feel to them in that the steps help concentrate on the 'here and now' of feelings and so paradoxically result in change.

Calmly speaking the inner feelings is a vital step. Anger as an expression of emotion is all right, but the direction in which anger is sent is more significant: how it is sent and to whom it is sent are key concerns. In dealing with our anger and other emotions we see the usefulness of these trilogies. Anger is actually designed to protect people from a perceived threat, and so they cannot be angry unless they are also afraid. Fear then can induce anger but, when people want to try alternatives, an anger management relaxation technique can be used, as shown in trilogy two. What is so interesting is that there are many such trilogies and they are all so similar. Assertiveness, negotiating, giving and receiving feedback, and criticism training all have common roots in three-step trilogies (see trilogy four). Significantly, all of these trilogies, according to Wilkes (1999), are based on trilogy six, which is the basic trilogy.

Altering the mind: six trilogies for change

Trilogy one: the emotional intelligence

1 **Red light.** Stop; calm down; think.

2 **Amber light.** Say the problem and how you feel.

3 **Green light.** Go ahead and try your best plan.

(Goleman, 1996)

Trilogy two: the self-anger control trilogy

1 First, say **stop**; I don't like this.

2 Second, take a **deep breath**; during exhalation, relax face, mouth, jaw, etc; take a deep breath in; during exhalation, relax hands, shoulders, arms.

3 Lastly, continue with a **slower, more controlled pace**, trying new, less angry behaviours.

(Lamplugh, 1991)

Trilogy three: the calming trilogy for use on others

1 **Calming** the person. Focus on calming his or her emotions, not logic.

2 **Reaching.** 'Uh huh, I see…' (nodding). 'We can sort this out by…' All of this is to develop gradually a less emotional base to the talking, with open-ended questions.

3 **Controlling.** Break the issues down into their basic components and move towards solutions.

(Lamplugh, 1991)

Trilogy four: used in assertiveness, feedback and negotiating

1 **Listen** to what is being said and show that you understand – don't deny, defend or justify.

2 **Focus** on the issues and facts, and seek clarification.

3 **Move** towards a solution and agreement on the solution.

(Fritchie, 1988)

Trilogy five: to dispute the internal voice of defeat – the critic

1 **Thought stopping.** As soon as you hear it, say 'Stop it' to yourself.

2 **Challenging accuracy.** For example, 'Would I really like myself if I were so perfect?'

3 **Making the negative purposeful.** Replace 'I cannot do it' with 'This is a real challenge for me.'

(Wilkes, 1999)

Trilogy six: the basic trilogy map

1 **Revise** the past.

2 **Revitalize** the present.

3 **Redirect** the future.

(Wilkes, 1999)

Using humour and other positive emotions

People can also release excess emotions such as anxiety through relaxation and fun, and the function of ice-breakers and energizers is to do just that. We often ask new university postgraduate students if they think it is possible to have intense experiences that create a state of ecstasy while studying! We are of course referring to flow experience, but they still laugh. However, endorphins are generated by certain physical and mental activities. A sense of humour can be a powerful influence on learning, and studying can become a form of play.

Humour can be a way of facing, making light of and communicating to others the stress that is being experienced. Cognitive and affective learning are not separately lived phenomena.

One reason for being interested in the role of humour, as an emotion in learning, was that we wanted to encourage students to 'let go' of their obsession with grades, and instead to access and gain a greater understanding of the underlying emotions and feelings that influenced their ability to learn. We wanted them consciously to experience flow, take more risks, make learning more fulfilling and let the grades take care of themselves. Some people can connect to their feelings through humour. Real student–lecturer correspondence on distance learning programmes is shown in the four examples below.

Humour in learning

1   'This presentation is a vast improvement on your first assignment, from which my optic nerves are still recovering,' said my tutor on reading my attempt as a student at using a draft standard dot-matrix printout.

    'Positively my last fling! You asked for "lots of comments" – and I have surpassed myself, and I am now off to immerse myself in an extremely large gin and tonic. Not to drown my sorrows but merely to recuperate,' said my tutor on reading the last edition of my 'draft' dissertation!

2   Some student humour during the stressful last leg in the period of doing a dissertation: 'Would it be better to lump the data together? What do you think? Does it make sense? (Sounds like a song!) The razor blades are in a safe place (but I can't help noticing that length of rope in the garage!!!!)… I will phone you soon for some quality psychotherapy. Regards.

    'PS Someone told me you can buy these [dissertations] on the World Wide Web?' (extracts from a letter to me as a tutor from a Senior Training and Development Officer at a major UK hospital studying for a Master's degree)

3 'Well, it's now 12.30 in the morning and I think I should go to bed. This has been a useful exercise for me, even if tedious for you. I look forward to any pearls of wisdom you may wish to cast in my direction.
'Goodnight!'
(Senior Training Manager, London Underground)

4 'Dear Colin, I have added to my draft in the past two weeks but still feel frustrated by a lack of real headway, combined with a growing feeling that I'm not really sure what I'm doing!!'
(Training Manager, Magistrates' Courts)

(Beard and McPherson, 1999)

When people look up to the sky, put on a happy face and smile, it can make them feel good (Robertson, 1999: 241). People can be encouraged to experience sad feelings by slouching with their shoulders low, with head bowed and eyes looking down at the floor. Holding the eyebrows up high for a minute can make people feel more positive. Adopting positive physical postures does work and, for example, it is worth doing before dealing with difficult issues.

Accessing emotions through popular metaphors

Metaphors present a powerful tool to access and explore feelings:

A single word can possess multiple meanings; yet as the common saying goes, one picture can be worth a thousand words. And if one picture can be worth a thousand words, then one experience can be worth a thousand pictures. And if an experience can be worth a thousand pictures, then one metaphor can be worth a thousand experiences. But in the end, a metaphor only possesses value when:

- it is able to interpret the experience
- in a manner that provides a picture
- that produces words
- that have meaning
- for that particular person.

(Gass, 1995)

Metaphors can be used to help people to understand that which might otherwise remain misunderstood or unobserved. Visual–spatial intelligence, for example, can be stimulated by metaphoric interpretations, by developing the ability to learn directly through images and thinking intuitively without the use of verbal language. Heron (1999: 102) suggests that in facilitation, theoretical inputs can be enriched by interweaving them with a variety of imaginal inputs. He offers seven examples:

- **metaphor** – the imaginative use of myth, metaphor, allegory, fable and story to convey meaning;
- **instance** – describing an illustrative incident, or dramatic case study, from real life;
- **resonance** – recounting associations and memories evoked by what is going on, in order to find meaning through resonance with the form of the other situation, which may be from some quite different field;
- **presentation** – presenting non-verbal analogies in the form of graphics, paintings, music, mime or movement;
- **dramaturgy** – combining metaphor with presentation in a creative piece of theatre;
- **demonstration** – showing in your own behaviour, both verbal and non-verbal, what it is you mean; modelling a skill in action, positively showing it well done, and negatively showing how it can degenerate;
- **caricature** – giving feedback to someone by mimicking his or her behaviour and caricaturing, in a kind way, the salient features to which you wish to draw attention.

The imaginative use of myth, metaphor, allegory, fable and story to convey meaning is the focus of this next section. In the 1960s and 1970s environmental campaigners helped people to 'see' concerns about the earth, using titles like *Silent Spring*, *The Population Bomb* and *Only One Earth*. In 1993 a popular book about communication between men and women hit the headlines. It was called *Men are from Mars – Women are from Venus* (Gray, 1993). On the back of this book the promotional piece said:

> Once upon a time Martians and Venusians met, fell in love, and had happy relationships together because they respected and accepted their differences. Then they came to Earth and amnesia set in: they forgot they were from different planets. Using this metaphor to illustrate the commonly occurring conflicts between men and women, Dr. John Gray explains how these differences can come between the sexes and prohibit mutually fulfilling loving relationships.

A metaphor can provide another way of reflecting and focusing on a particular experience, so allowing us to gain new insights. A metaphor is a figure of speech that transfers meaning. The word itself is derived from the Greek *meta* (trans) and *pherein* (to carry). According to Parkin (1998), a metaphor is a comparison, a parallel between two, sometimes seemingly unrelated, terms. Metaphors tend to be used to help people to 'see' or 'connect' in their minds, to and from real or imagined inner and outer worlds. Providers of experiential learning often consider the activities as being more of a medium for learning, a means to an end, and see the value in the process of learning rather than in the nature of the activities per se. The activities employed are important though, as, in theory, they often serve as metaphors in themselves and so strengthen the potential connection between the programme and the workplace (Gass, 1992; Gass and Priest, 1998), ie metaphor is the analysis of experience.

Morgan (1997a) in his book about organizations offers a unique and original mechanism to help us to see, understand and manage organizations. He does it through a series of different metaphors. However, he also offers a word of caution and suggests that insightful learning through the use of seductive metaphors has its limitations: 'Any given metaphor can be incredibly persuasive, but it can also be blinding and block our ability to gain an overall view' (1997a: 347). In other words, metaphors can create ways of seeing and ways of not seeing. Using many different metaphors can thus help us to overcome the limitations of others. Morgan offers 'Bibliographic notes' towards the end of the book, and explains in some detail the historical use of metaphors. He describes how Aristotle suggested that the metaphor was midway between the unintelligible and the commonplace. In a similar vein Black (1979) developed an 'interaction theory' of metaphor and suggests that metaphorical statements have a primary subject and a secondary subject, and that the metaphor works by projecting the characteristics or implications of the secondary subject on to the primary subject, with effectiveness due to the degree of resonance between the two.

Feelings about work are so often expressed in metaphorical terms: 'I am just a small cog in a big machine'; 'I'm in a new team creating a work of art!' Picture-based metaphors help with a way of seeing, thought-based metaphors illustrate a way of thinking, sound metaphors guide a way of hearing, emotional metaphors access a way of feeling and activity metaphors can illustrate a way of doing things. Parkin (1998: 10) in her book on storytelling explains the use of several ingredients in a personal metaphor, using a common saying, 'My head is as heavy as lead', where:

- The **topic** is head.
- The **vehicle** is lead.
- The **ground** is the feeling of heaviness.
- The **tension** is dissimilarity between the two domains, ie lead is metal and the other is head or flesh.

In therapeutic work metaphors help people to surface unconscious thoughts and feelings. The metaphors connect the conscious mind with the unconscious mind. 'Trust' and 'fear' in participants might, for example, equal loss and exposure. In dealing with addictions, trauma or abuse, much of people's sense of existence or personality is beyond their awareness, and the therapist helps to apply the metaphor based on a client's behaviour (Stouffer, 1999). The client creates this self-metaphor with the help and guidance of the therapist, to help access his or her sense of being.

Corporate metaphors are likely to be very different. Metaphors can be used, for example, as concept-forming in a corporate event designed to connect an experiential activity to workplace production issues. High-rope challenges can represent the challenges of real life. Cliffs can represent the challenges of a giant project or that daunting change in life an individual might have to face. Finding good metaphors that enable us to see things differently requires skilled experiential providers. Benson (1987: 204) suggests that instead of coming at problems from rational deliberation and logic, which can lead to protectionism and defence, metaphors can be more intuitive and spontaneous:

> Every method, exercise, or technique then as I use it, is a metaphor: a way of shifting perception and creating meaning. I am not interested in any medium or technique as an end in itself but as a means of engaging people and providing a context for work, which is directly related to the members' level of ability and willingness to act. From this perspective the value of any technique lies not in its skill or knowledge base but in what it points to, its ability to act as a signpost, open up dialogue, and encapsulate meaning.

A metaphor can also be introduced through storytelling, or through cartoon images. These can be powerful ways to reinforce learning from experience, in both the unconscious and conscious. Cartoons, art, drama, models and conceptual frameworks are all enabling media that allow us to readjust our perceptual field, our ways of seeing and understanding the world. They can be powerful cathartic tools, simplifying and reducing complexity on the one hand, but also making emotional issues easier to grasp and comprehend. Many of these techniques were discussed in Chapter 5, where we explored the adjustment of experiential reality. In this chapter we explored the possibility of accessing, in a metaphoric sense, the 'inner family' of people within our minds. This requires careful listening and the construction of metaphors of the person, or 'self-metaphors'.

In the global Outward Bound movement there has long been a debate about letting the experience speak for itself. Rustie Baillie, back in the 1960s, then a course director at Colorado Outward Bound in the United States, first coined the phrase, 'Let the mountains speak for themselves' (Bacon, 1987; James, 2000). Later Outward Bound included the 'Metaphoric Model' to raise awareness of the metaphoric nature of the activities (Hovelynck, 2000). Gass (1995) in his *Book of Metaphors* offers a clear and concise approach to the use of metaphors in adventure programmes, where the matter of letting the experience speak for itself is located alongside many other techniques. He examines the pragmatic use of metaphors in development work, building on his background in therapy, and argues that metaphoric transfer of learning takes place when parallels exist between two learning environments. A metaphor is an idea, object, process, environment, task or description that is used in place of another different idea, object, process, environment, task or description to help people to see or make a connection to reality. If the connection is through an idea, object, process, environment, task or description that is actually identical, and 'real', then the connection is said to be isomorphic (see Gass and Priest, 1998 for a description of examples). The classification offered by Gass is fashioned from the work of Bacon and Kimball in 1989 (in Gass, 1995). Gass created different facilitation techniques, based on six generations of facilitation skills that have evolved over time. In order to demonstrate the purpose and function of the six techniques, Gass uses the internationally well-known outdoor exercise called the Spider's Web. The Spider's Web is an exercise that uses a descriptive metaphor, and involves people trying to get through but not touch a mass of cord usually tied between two trees to create the spider's web. We have rearranged the six examples so that techniques that can be used prior to the event are presented first. Thus:

- *Prior to the activity* taking place the facilitator would ask questions that focus the learning that might occur. The facilitator **directly frontloads** the experience.
- *Prior to the activity* the facilitator would set the scene or context of the activity so as to relate it to the specific learning, eg to the work conditions of participants such as the problems of loading in a warehouse environment, or to the reception desk team, etc. The facilitator **frames** the experience.
- *Prior to the activity* the facilitator might deliberately but indirectly make reference to fictitious events to try to prevent certain behaviours occurring, eg 'We had a group last week that did this and failed because everyone put their "fix-it hats" on and moved straight into solutions mode, preventing discussion from...' The facilitator can **indirectly frontload** the experience.

As we remarked earlier, experiential learning programmes move from *introduction* to *action*, to *reflection* and *transfer*. These four stages all offer opportunities for various interventions and non-intervention, but choosing not to intervene can be powerful, requiring trust in the process, letting the experience or event speak for itself. There are other options to consider after the event:

- *After the activity* the facilitator might not make any insightful comment about the experience. The **experience speaks for itself**.
- *After the activity* the facilitator might provide the group with feedback about their general behaviour after the experience, such as what they did well, what they might need to work on, what they learnt, etc. The **facilitator speaks for the experience**.
- *After the activity* the facilitator would use questions to foster a group discussion about the above. The **facilitator debriefs the experience**.

Frontloading, framing and other techniques can be developed much further. Providers can include appropriate famous film clips, video footage of previous groups, TV soap extracts or cartoon images to send powerful messages. They often work well with young people. These media can reinforce key points, especially if they are seen as coming from other known or respected sources. Such media can be potent when the medium and message speaks for itself, thus providing excellent techniques that remove the scepticism associated with the facilitator who provides instant expert solutions. In contrast to letting the experience speak for itself, or speaking on behalf of the experience, some researchers such as Greenaway (1993) suggest that learners can be facilitators of their own ideas, and self-facilitation is very much a learner-centred approach.

Conclusion

Learning is enhanced when people discover things for themselves, through their own emotional engagement. This requires a commitment to discovery of 'self', with a preparedness for experimentation and a review of personal values, and visions. Although experience is all around people every day, many people do not make the most of experiential opportunities, and it is often the emotional state that prevents maximum return on experience. Emotional intelligence underpins learning as a basic building block. Yet many experiential learning providers, educators and trainers cannot give full attention to emotional issues for many reasons, despite emotional competency being at the core of success in learning. Signposts often point to emotional underpinnings, and experiential learning providers might usefully read the underlying feelings that might restrict or enhance learning and change.

All experience, all adventures are essentially an emotional experience; they are experienced in the mind. In this chapter we have offered ideas as to the role and function of emotion in experiential learning. We offered insight into ways of reading the signs and working with emotions as part of the experience, and we examined ways of accessing the roots of emotion in experiential learning. We also examine other aspects of emotion work in chapter 8, 'Experience, knowing and intelligence'. This chapter explored more ways to access the feelings and emotions dimensions of learning, representing the fourth tumbler of the learning combination lock model. The chapter explored the states of relaxed alertness and the energy–tension balance, as well as mood-influencing techniques, including stimulating scents and body language adjustment. Identity, fear of failure, pride and success, and perfection were seen to play important roles in experiential learning. Accessing techniques included the use of 'mapping' to gain entry to the deeper levels of dialogue of the 'inner voices'. Rewriting our inner rules using trilogies, humour and metaphors were all investigated as means to access emotions.

Experience, knowing and intelligence
(The knowing dimension)

> *At school he struggled with foreign languages and teachers were exasperated by his ponderous way of thinking for a long time before answering questions, and even more by quietly talking to himself under his breath. The boy seemed happiest on his own... The teacher had said that the school would be a better place if he weren't in it... So what was different about Albert Einstein – what enabled him to turn from a difficult boy into a world-famous genius?* **WINSTON, 2003: 311–12**

Introduction

The above question was posed by Lord Winston in a book called *The Human Mind*. At the core of this comment is the interesting subject of thinking slowly. Einstein was clearly a slow but deep thinker, and even from an early age it took time for him to do his careful processing. How do we know, how do we think and what is intelligence? These are important issues to understand in learning from experience. Here we build on issues such as thinking too little, or too much, thinking in patterns, and thinking with emotion, and with the body, making clear links with other dimensions of the learning combination lock model. We explore multiple intelligence (MI) theory and offer ideas for working with these dimensions of intelligence, including a more detailed look at some of the neglected forms of intelligence namely creative, spiritual, naturalistic and emotional intelligence. The chapter concludes then with a very brief consideration of the experience of higher mind states including wisdom.

Human learning: is it really all in the mind?

Theorizing about how humans learn has been subject to continuous reassessment over many years. The sense of incomplete understanding about human learning continues to plague prevailing dominant thinking on the subject. This has led to an unremitting quest for more 'complete' ideas about how we humans learn. Here we introduce a quick and simplistic history that can be remembered in the form of a code: BCHSE. Figure 8.1 below illustrates this simple historical sketch.

FIGURE 8.1 BCHSE: a very simple history of human learning (adapted from Beard and Price, 2012)

Time Period		1900–1940s	1950s	1960s	1970s	1980s	1990s	2000
HUMAN LEARNING THEORIES	B	Behavioural (Ethology, Animal focus)						
		C	Cognitive (Computational brain)					
				H	Humanist (Empathy nurturing)			
					S	Social Construction of knowledge (Social interaction)		
							E	Rich Ecological (Complexity)

Let's explore this in a little more detail to help with an understanding of the past and present ideas about human learning. The following introduces some basic terminology about human learning.

By the early 20th century *behaviourism* (B) emerged as a dominant view, linked to, and associated with, a Western approach and operant *conditioning* (Pavlov, 1927; Skinner, 1974). This was a period with an animalistic focus, where much study was based on stimulating animals to see what the response would be. Conditioned learning was discovered through classic experiments. This approach gradually shifted to *cognitivist* theories (C), which began to surface in the late 1950s. The cognitive focus saw the 'human' as unique, intelligent and rational, and so computational brain processing involving thinking, remembering, analysing and seeking ways to explain and make sense of the world was suggested. Major contributors included Lewin (1951) and Gagne (1974), but perhaps the most well-known was Bloom (1956), who developed a spatial hierarchy of cognition (higher/lower forms of knowing). Hierarchical models can be seen as problematic, particularly as some writers relegate experiential learning as a basic *lower* level of *practical* learning (see for example Young, 2008). By the late 1960s *humanist* theories (H) were emphasizing personal agency and the fulfilment of potential. Perhaps the most well-known proponent was Carl Rogers (1969) whose seminal text, *Freedom to Learn*, expressed a liberating metaphor. For Rogers, feelings, warmth, acceptance and the nurturing of people were central to learning: individuals, if treated in the right way, had it within themselves to work towards solutions to problems. These ideas were instrumental in the development of learner-centred methods. But cultural and social context became increasingly recognized as important (eg Vygotsky, 1978) giving rise to a range of *social constructivist* (S) theories, with learning seen as active, and contextualized. Learners were seen not only as constructing knowledge for themselves, as individuals, but also through social interaction.

Although social constructivist theories remain influential they are now positioned among a milieu of views about human learning, and this multi-disciplinary interpretation we are calling the new *ecological* view (E). It is rich thinking, not dissimilar to the understanding of the ecology of a rainforest. It is seemingly messy. We will only give a brief sketch of this complexity as illustrated in: the role of hidden desires and fears, as in psychoanalytic theories (Britzman, 1998); the questioning of the outdated notion of single intelligence (Gardner, 1983); advances in brain science (neuroscience) leading to a reassessment of old views about our biology controlling us (known as 'biological determinism') (Damasio, 1995); and, particularly significant to our discussions here about a wider recognition of the role of the body in language and mental processing (embodiment) (Lakoff and Johnson, 1999; Sheets-Johnstone, 2009). The senses are also very important to learning (see Abram, 1997), and bodily gestures are also significant to mental processing (Gallagher, 2005). The emotions (Illeris, 2002) are also strongly linked to mental processing. Such diverse works illustrate the ongoing search for more integrative and comprehensive explorations of human learning within and across disciplines (Dillon, 2007), where the connective relationship between mind, body and field can be further explored.

Although far from presenting a complete picture, this historical sketch charts a simple trajectory from ethology to ecology. Knowledge about human learning shifts from animalistic simplicity, rooted in predictability and control experiments such as conditioning, toward complex, ecological interpretations across disciplines (see Sterling, 2003). However, note that the shading in the figure above continues across the chart: new ideas do not negate old ideas, they often add to a richer understanding of human learning. Cognitivist and social constructivist views remain dominant and continue to attract many followers. It is the ecological interpretation that aligns with our multi-disciplinary, holistic modelling, however. Ecological theorists Davis and Sumara (1997: 112) outline this new rich complexity by suggesting that all the contributing factors in any learning situation are 'intricately, ecologically, and complexly related. Both the cognizing agent (*us as humans*) and everything with which it is associated are in constant flux, each adapting to the other in the same way that the environment evolves simultaneously with the species that inhabit it' (italics added).

Thinking with the body and thinking with feeling

Here are two more key terms. The study of how we can know the world is called *epistemology*, and it is linked to the study of 'being' in the world, known as *ontology*. While *knowing* is the focus of this chapter, *being* is the subject of our next chapter, representing the last dimension or cog in the model: they are of course connected as our being influences our way of knowing the world around us and our knowing influences our way of being in the world.

We have suggested elsewhere that knowing involves more than just mental processing. Knowing also involves bodily knowing (this view is known as *embodied cognition*). For now we will simply call this *thinking with the body*. Bodily knowing is also covered in the sensing chapter. Knowing is strongly linked to our environmental surroundings also (this view of knowing is known as *embedded cognition*). A simple way to understand the way the brain works is to work with a slightly more complex idea beyond the 'three brains' we put forward in chaper 7. Imagine now four operational zones as follows. The old brain at the top of the spinal column is reptilian-like, managing the automatic functions such heartbeat, breathing, and temperature regulation. This we will call the *functioning brain*. The middle brain higher up is responsible for the *sensing brain* and engaging fast emotional reactions to the sensing, and this we will call the *feeling brain*. The new brain is advanced and particularly developed in humans, consisting of cerebral frontal lobes that do more complex, slower processing. This part is divided into left and right hemispheres and reference is often made to left-brain and right-brain dominant people. This big frontal part we will call the *thinking brain*. Thus we have the functioning brain, the sensing brain, the feeling brain and the thinking brain. Nobel Prize winner in economics Daniel Kahneman has written a book called *Thinking Fast and Slow* (2011) and by fast he is referring to the feeling brain as feeling tags are sent rapidly to the brain for fast survival decision making. He also calls this System 1 thinking. By *thinking slow* he is referring to the work of the *thinking brain*: here slower more rational processing takes place. His book examines some of the myths associated with the supposed benefits of slow rational thinking or fast feeling-thinking. One of the main themes of the book is just how little control we actually have over our own System 1 feeling-thinking responses, and the degree to which the subconscious mind including our human biases also affects fast thinking. Much of our life operates on System 1 autopilot.

The organizing mind: patterns and creative thinking

A key characteristic of the human mind is that it has a tendency to organize, sequence, differentiate, classify and to generally explore and find patterns of relational connectivity. Every living being tends to categorize (Lakoff and Johnson, 1999): this is important in understanding how the embodied mind works in learning experiences. Lakoff and Johnson give a simple explanation by way of the fact that the eye has a hundred million light sensing cells but there are only about a million fibres leading to the brain, therefore the clustering of information is necessary. This necessary reducing down of information involves data clustering, underpinning why we tend to categorize. It occurs because so many neural connections of the brain cluster information in this way. Such categorization continually occurs in everyday life, in both conscious and subconscious ways: we first observe things in the world then classify them as bad or good, right or wrong, as scary or friendly, as simple or complex, beautiful or ugly.

Complex things are usually complex because they are difficult to 'see'. The bits of the problem tend to have a complicated spatial–relational connectedness. Furthermore a difficulty is that while our human spoken language is an astonishing development, it is also problematic in that when it is spoken it is limited to one word at a time and therefore linear in format. Spoken language thus struggles to describe complicated things, however the bodily GPS system helps overcome such language limitations (see the chapter on sensory intelligence). Spatial metaphors are found, for example, deeply embedded in our everyday speech; the brain often sees things in this spatial way. In order to add richness our linear spoken and written language is enhanced with spatial–bodily metaphors that aid the brain in thinking and processing: *step by step* logic, to *support* an argument, to *grasp* an idea, how time *flies*, to feel *on top of the world*, *lifelong* and *lifewide* of learning.

Let's explore this a bit further in terms of more practical implications for experiential learning. We now give some examples of how the human tendency to categorize can help learning. We will illustrate these ideas by reference to the development of creative, critical and conceptual thinking. We will return again to the subject of Creative Intelligence (CQ) later in this chapter.

The Market Place is a learning experience described in detail in the *Experiential Learning Toolkit* by Beard (2010), along with many other practical experiences. A detailed account of this experience with a focus on the role of pattern detection for creative thinking is also given in Beard and Goode (2013). Both accounts describe how 40 or so commercial products, all having some element of both creative and sustainable environmental design built into them, are emptied out on a large table for participants on an experiential creative thinking programme to initiate the process of organizing, and pattern detection. Participants are encouraged to make sense of what they see by touching and describing in the first instance: people will naturally tend to organize and categorize later as 'higher' levels of thinking beyond description.

A set of products might initially be selected and used by the tutor to illustratively explain and show basic patterns or developmental trends. Continuous discussion, ie the social creation of knowledge, is encouraged concerning the descriptive nature of product and then some of the observable innovative trends. The shift from messy 'practice' to conceptual higher levels of thinking using pattern detection flows well if the categorization process is understood and enhanced. The initial process would involve description followed by a dividing of the products into clusters or categories for convenience: domestic products (toothbrushes, razors, washing-up brushes, nail brushes, etc), technological products (solar panels that charge phones and laptops), and artistic products (earrings made from waste bottle tops/ necklaces made from old magazines). There are of course no hard and fast boundaries. Within these categories participants then move objects on the tables and try to make further sense of what they see using laminated black arrows: these tend to really enhance the thinking processes. Participants move, sort and order the products in any particular way so that they can illustrate any trends or patterns. Other prompt cards are used to facilitate spatial relational pattern detection. Kinaesthetic and sensory experiences along with group discussion and interaction embed the learning (touching, handling, testing out, winding up radios, powering mobile phones, iPods and laptops from a solar panel, feeling soft clothing fabrics made from plastic bottles). Mobility is an essential principle in this learning experience: mobility of people, information and objects.

Supporting critical, conceptual and creative thinking: using laminated prompt cards to facilitate pattern detection

- **First level** describing. **Descriptor** cards: eg WIND UP RADIO.

- **Second level** laminated flow/arrows: highlighting relational **flows**.

- **Third level basic** conceptual analysis cards: eg BUSINESS TO WASTE. BUSINESS TO BUSINESS. PRODUCT DIVERSITY. MATERIAL FLOWS.

- **Fourth level higher** conceptual **analysis** cards: eg DE-MATERIALIZATION (minute yet powerful torch developed as a result of LED bulbs/swipe cards not keys. Less material).

If Higher Education is concerned with 'higher level' thinking skills, is this the same as intelligence? Let us consider this important question. Another significant question concerns how we can work with concepts of intelligence to help people learn.

What is intelligence?

In a book titled *Psychology: The science of mind and behaviour*, Gross (2001: 589) comments on the difficult subject of intelligence by saying that 'perhaps nowhere else in psychology does so much… research and theory attempt to define the concept under investigation'. Old and outmoded views on intelligence considered a potential link between brain size and intelligence, and ideas existed that people with prominent eyes had good memories! (Gardner, 1993: 12). In 2005 the *Times Higher Education Supplement* in the UK carried a front page story titled 'IQ claim will fuel gender row', reporting a paper in the *British Journal of Psychology* where two prominent psychologists argue that men have larger brains than women, apparently making them capable of tasks of higher complexity!

Intelligence testing was first commissioned by the French government, who wished to test and classify persons of lower intelligence for special needs education. These early tests measured children's verbal, memory and mathematical skills and were devised by Alfred Binet, and it is from these that modern psychometric testing instruments grew. Testing is concerned with measuring individual differences in intellect or abilities, and Gross rightly notes that in one form or another, controversial quantitative testing of intelligence has impinged on the lives of most people. While intelligence might be interpreted as that which only tests measure, it is clear that our understanding of intelligence has played a central role in the development of the theory and practice of teaching and learning. Much contemporary thinking about intelligence has advanced due to neuroscience research on brain disorders and brain scanning.

Within higher education intellectual ability is construed as a cognitive benchmark, and wrongly thought to be the same as 'intelligence'. In education intelligence has been strongly linked to cognitive skills such as problem solving, reasoning, critical analysis, judgement, initiative and comprehension. Contemporary academic experiential approaches to assessment, however, are now applying many different measurements, (see fair Assessment, p. 233)

The standard intelligent quotient (IQ) tests have often excluded many of the contextual or experiential sub-theories, including the world outside school or vocational work, which requires many kinds of abilities. Some tests offer a broad assessment: one contemporary online service offered a broad-spectrum IQ test, and scored for the following abilities: arithmetic, spatial skill, logical, spelling, short-term memory, rote utilization, algebraic, general knowledge, visual apprehension, geometrics, vocabulary, intuition, and computational speed. Rather interesting was the inclusion of intuition, which was defined as an ability to develop answers without consciously dealing with the problem at hand. Terms such as 'out of the blue' or 'it just struck me' were said to be associated with intuition. Some scientists believe that intuition is an innate ability to sense what is going on, that this is partly due to the presence of vast archives of experience and that 'intuition is not some paranormal ability to see the future, but a technique of learning what to look for in a given environment, and of doing so without the conscious brain getting in the way' (Winston, 2003: 349). It is intriguing that at times the so-called higher 'thinking' brain is not required for fast execution of certain activities. The subconscious should not be underestimated: it appears it can operate at very high levels.

MASTERY

Evaluation – judge, evaluate, support, comfort, avoid, select, recognize, criticize.
synthesis – summarize, argue, relate, précis, organize, generalize, conclude.
analysis – select, compare, differentiate, contrast, break down.
application – predict, select, assess, find, show, use, construct, compute.
comprehension – identify, illustrate, represent, formulate, explain, contrast.
knowledge – write, state, recall, recognize, select, reproduce, measure.

Drawn from Bass, B S (1956) *Taxonomy of Education: The Classification of Educational Goals*, Longman, London.

STAGE 4

Domain understanding. Higher view.
Learning to learn. Master the learning
process as well as subject 'content'.
Reflection. Research skills.
MASTERY

STAGE 3

Validity. Complexity. Judgement.
Show strengths & weakness. Reasoning.
Arguments. Create opposites – Dichotomies.
Schools of thinking.
CONCEPTS/MODELS.
WAYS OF SEEING

STAGE 2

Analyse. Cluster. Reshape.
Develop arguments. Overlay.
ORGANISE. MOVE. CONSTRUCT. MAP OUT.

STAGE 1

Read. Take notes. Think & reflect.
Ideas. References. Sourcing.
COLLATE. DESCRIBE. DEFINE

Drawn from a multi-media CD ROM 'Mastering University', available from Gower Publications, 2005, and produced by Colin Beard

1. Gathering information and utilizing resources
2. Developing flexibility in form and style
3. Asking high-quality questions
4. Weighing evidence before drawing conclusions
5. Utilizing metaphors and models
6. Conceptualizing strategies (mind mapping, pros and cons lists, outlines etc)
7. Dealing productively with ambiguity, differences and novelty
8. Creating possibilities and probabilities (brainstorming, formulas, surveys, cause and effect)
9. Debate and discussion skills
10. Identifying mistakes, discrepancies, and illogic
11. Examining alternative approaches (shifting frame of reference, thinking out of the box etc)
12. Hypothesis testing strategies
13. Developing objectivity
14. Generalization and pattern detection (identifying and organizing information, translating information, cross-over applications)
15. Sequencing events

Drawn from Jensen, E (2000) *Brain-based Learning: The New Science of Teaching and Training*

The many forms of intelligence

A qualitative, biological view of intelligence, of particular significance to experiential learning, is that intelligence is an adaptation to the environment in which we live. Such a qualitative view is reflected in the early work of Piaget in the 1950s who regarded intelligence as 'essentially a system of living and acting operations, i.e. a state of balance or equilibrium achieved by the person when he is able to deal adequately with the data before him. But it is not a static state, it is dynamic in that it continually adapts itself to new environmental stimuli' (quoted in Gross, 2001: 590).

New insights about intelligence continue to emerge, creating greater breadth and depth to this complex subject. Harvard professor of cognition and education Howard Gardner published many books and articles on neuropsychology and cognitive development before focusing on his seventh book in 1983, *Frames of Mind: The theory of multiple intelligences (MI)*. It was this book in particular that placed his research at the centre of educational theory. Gardner proposes a qualitative view of 'an intelligence' as the psychobiological ability to solve problems, or to fashion products that are valued within one or more cultural settings. He also states quite clearly that 'there is not, and there can never be, a single irrefutable and universally accepted list of human intelligences' (1993: 59). MI theory is based on three fundamental principles (Gross, 2001):

- Intelligence is *not* a single unitary thing, but a collection of multiple intelligences.
- Each intelligence is *independent* of all others.
- The intelligences *interact* otherwise nothing could be achieved.

It would appear that people have differing intelligence profiles and, significantly, there are few limits to the development of these intelligences. Gardner describes a number of categories of intelligence in detail and although he eventually settled on eight, he acknowledges that there may be more. Indeed Gardner created some 20 different varieties of intelligence at one stage in his research. Gardner narrowed these down to seven intelligences then added another, naturalistic intelligence. There are numerous reasons why the concept of multiple intelligence has taken hold in education:

> among these are that the theory validates educators' everyday experience: students think and learn in many different ways. It also provides educators with a conceptual framework for organizing and reflecting on the curriculum, assessment and pedagogical practices. In turn, this reflection has led many educators to develop new approaches that might better suit the needs of the range of learners in the classroom.
>
> (Gardner, in Palmer, 2001: 276)

Gardner also comments on so-called higher-level cognitive operations that go beyond a straightforward notion of 'an intelligence' and remarked that it was the 'sense of self' that placed the greatest strain on his multiple

Several areas of intelligence which form our fifth tumbler

1 **mathematical–logical** – the ability to organize thoughts sequentially and logically;

2 **verbal–linguistic** – the ability to understand and express ideas through language;

3 **bodily–kinaesthetic** – the gaining of knowledge through feedback from physical activity;

4 **musical** – sensitivity to tone, pitch and rhythm, and the ability to reproduce them;

5 **visual–spatial** – the ability to learn directly through images and to think intuitively without the use of language;

6 **interpersonal** – the ability to notice and make discriminations regarding the moods, temperaments, motivations and intentions of others;

7 **intra-personal** – the ability to access one's own feelings;

8 **naturalistic** – the ability to understand and be in tune with one's relationship with the natural environment;

9 **creative** intelligence – the ability to be creative and innovative;

10 **spiritual** intelligence – interconnectedness with the inner and outer world and the ability to sense the higher-self;

11 **moral** intelligence – the ability to act for the wider benefit of society, to have good principles and values.

intelligence or MI theory. The sense of self, he suggests, is a prime candidate for higher or second order ability.

Gardner, Csikszentmihalyi (who developed the concept of flow experience) and Damon embarked on the 'Good Work Project' in 1994 to identify how individuals at the cutting edge of their professions can produce work that is both exemplary and also contributes to the good of our wider society. Their work continues into the new millennium and they continue to grapple with broader societal issues, analogous in some ways to the articulation of and commitment to active citizenship by educators such as John Dewey one hundred years earlier. Dewey was concerned with both morality and spirituality in education, as was Kurt Hahn, the founder of the Outward Bound philosophy who emphasized the four pillars of *service, craftmanship, physical fitness* and *self-discipline*.

Learning experiences should allow people to reveal, explore and develop their own particular life gifts, which might include: an ability to be word smart (Linguistic intelligence), to be number smart (Logical/mathematical/ scientific intelligence), to be spatially smart (Visual/spatial intelligence), to be sound smart (Musical intelligence), to be body smart (Bodily/physical/ kinaesthetic intelligence), to be people smart (Interpersonal intelligence), to be self smart (Intra-personal intelligence), to be emotionally smart (Emotional intelligence), to be nature smart (Naturalistic intelligence), to be innovative and creative (Creatively smart) and to be life smart (Spiritual, moral and existential intelligence).

The following Box offers a detailed practical example of an assessment technique in higher education that provides a rich, experiential way to assess a broad notion of intelligence.

Fair assessment

This undergraduate module was designed to develop students' understanding of nutrition in health and disease with a focus on epidemiology and the role and impact of nutrition in health and disease, including intervention and prevention strategies. The specific assessment criteria were as follows:

● the ability to discuss appropriately the role of epidemiology in nutritional science;

● the ability to evaluate accurately specific issues of nutrition in health and disease;

● critical appraisal of nutritional research;

● the ability to prepare and design an effective nutritional intervention strategy to promote the health of a specific group;

● appropriate selection of ICT in the analysis and presentation of information;

● effective communication using established conventions in scientific reporting.

And the creative way to assess this work through an experiential technique was that:

1 Students will be required to present and submit a **business plan** (20%) for their **nutrition fair stall** to the panel in practical 2. Each student will be allocated an 8-minute slot to deliver (10%) their business plan. Students will be asked to deliver no more than 5 PowerPoint slides outlining their proposals. These slides should be comparable to their formal business plan. Each student will then be questioned by the panel regarding their proposal.

2 Students will be required to **prepare and run a stall** (20%) at the Applied Nutrition Fair. This fair will be held in the main hall on floor 6 and will be **open to other students, visitors, University staff and other academics**. All stalls

are expected to be of a professional standard. Students should consider the following when designing and running their stalls:

- All information should be correct! You will be advising the public.
- All stalls should be appropriately presented and professionally run.
- Students are advised to provide a variety of materials for the public.
- Each student will be allocated one table on which to hold their stalls.
- All students must create and sign a risk assessment in order to be allowed to take part in the event. These risk assessments should be countersigned by a member of the module teaching team prior to the event.
- All students must adhere to appropriate health and safety regulations and risk management strategies.
- The teaching team will be marking the stalls using the attached mark sheet (15%).
- Academic and technical guests will be asked to award each stall a mark out of 5 for 'impact and professionalism'. These marks will be averaged in order to give a final mark (5%).

(Provided by Jenny Williams, Sheffield Hallam University, UK)

Neglected forms of intelligence

A central principle for us that underlies experiential learning is the integration of mind and matter (including the body and environment) and theory and practice. Rather than separating mind and body, emotion and reason, rational and intuitive, people and nature, there is now a growing recognition of the ecological, holistic fusion of these traditional dualities. For this reason we now explore some of the more integrative dimensions of intelligence that remain controversial and marginalized in the traditional literature about human learning. These are: 1) sensory intelligence; 2) emotional intelligence; 3) spiritual intelligence; 4) naturalistic intelligence; and 5) creative intelligence. In these areas thinking remains embryonic, with a developing language emerging that creates new space for the exploration and expression of these aspects and ideas about human learning. Naturalistic intelligence and spiritual intelligence are less neglected by outdoor learning practitioners.

Sensory intelligence – SI

Sensory intelligence (SI) has been covered in Chapter 6 in great detail and we argue that SI might indeed be more important than EQ. Although we do not cover the subject in detail here we do highlight some of the basic links of SI to thinking, remembering and forgetting. In Chapter 6 we also looked at the problems of thinking too much, a subject also covered in Chapter 9, the *Being* dimension of learning, where we discuss the advantages of being able to just 'be' in the here and now.

The role of the senses arises in many ways in experiential learning. In a review of the activities and learning that took place on a training programme with senior trainers in a health care organization all was going well until the review got to lunch on the first day. 'What did we do after lunch?' someone said. But no one could remember. There was a long silence. Everyone was thinking hard. Then someone got up and said: 'I remember we were sat over here, sitting in a circle.' Then almost in unison, everyone remembered the activity, the memory was released, triggered by the sensorial moving bodily (physically) or imagining so in the mind (mentally) to the very space that the activity took place in. This can also happen when memory is triggered by other sensory associations. While working with Outward Bound Singapore we happened to find a yellow circle outside painted on a concrete outdoor training area. We used it to demonstrate the combination lock model. The yellow circle on this programme became the senses with the inside of the circle representing the inner world of the learner, whilst outside the circle represented the outer world. Coloured plastic hoops were placed on the ground to represent the other key dimensions of learning within and outside the yellow sensory interface. These colours, of the main circle and smaller hoops, became very significant to our memories over the next few days of the experiential programme. Yellow became the constant collective group code for the senses every time any sensory issues cropped up; this was of course a simple form of conditioning (code B) in that yellow highlighter pens were regularly held up to highlight emerging sensory issues. This memory trigger was linked to the yellow-lined model outside. This became a type of *sensory learning signature* (after Lindstrom, 2005). Likewise other senses trigger memories, which can enhance and support learning. This is particularly the case with simple icons (eg fast forward arrows), bodily movement, memorable stories, and smells. The senses are also recognized as having a memory *association* role in the development of corporate brands: Intel for example is a classic iconic sound. Martin Lindstrom has researched the phenomena of *sensory signatures* in commercial products and produced a book called *Brand Sense* (Lindstrom, 2005).

Emotional intelligence – EQ

In Chapter 7 we explored in detail the role that emotions play in learning, offering many practical ideas about working with emotions. Here we briefly explore emotions in terms of their specific role in thinking and in relation to whole person notions of experiential learning. Emotions are the bodies reaction to the mind, and emotions are played out in the theatre of the body, particularly in neuromuscular acts: fear and the tightening of the jaw; anger and the clenching of the fists; relaxation and lightness of the body when joyful; the expansion of the chest in triumph (Sheets-Johnstone,

2009). Movement and emotion go hand in hand: we are moved by emotion. This highlights the artificial nature of the cogs in the model; the separated boundaries of the model do not exist in reality.

There has been a rise in interest in the notion of emotional intelligence, or EQ as it has become known. Its popularization was brought about by Daniel Goleman with his best-selling book *Emotional Intelligence* (1996). Goleman drew on the work of Salovey and Mayer in 1990 and created a classification of emotional intelligence as five major domains: knowing one's emotions, managing emotions, motivating oneself, recognizing emotions in others, and handling relationships. These contemporary defining parameters of 'emotional intelligence' thus stress the importance of being able to manage both the 'inner world' (of self) and 'outer world' (of interactions with others, and the environment). The emerging language of intelligence in learning thus considers the complex 'whole-person', and acknowledges the milieu of social interactions and social relationships, recognizing perception, feelings, arousal states, expressive gestures/postures, moods and emotional cues. Our definition of emotional intelligence (EQ) that we offered in an earlier chapter is: 'the ability to understand the emotions in a given learning environment, in yourself (inner world) and others (outer world), to use this understanding to deal effectively with yourself and others, in a way which improves personal and professional development, reduces anger and hostility, generates collaborative effort, enhances life balance and produces creative energy.'

This elevated status of emotions as a measure or quotient of intelligence is rooted in the work of Howard Gardner (1983) on social intelligence. His work is acknowledged as playing a historical role in broadening and redefining intelligence, producing a shift away from the monolithic 'intelligence quotient' (IQ). Gardner influenced educational thinking by highlighting the complex multiple nature of intelligence, and in particular the notion of inter- and intra-personal aspects within social intelligence which currently underpins thinking on emotional intelligence (EQ). Prior to Goleman's publication it was Salovey and Mayer (1990) who, drawing on psychological and cultural literature, proposed what is said to be the 'first formal definition of emotional intelligence' (Feldman Barrett and Salovey, 2002: xiii).

Emotions have been pitched as contradictory to rational thinking and a protracted and contentious history exists as to the role of emotions in learning. The oppositional relationship is said to be located within the Western Cartesian dualism (Damasio, 1996), being 'traced from Plato to Descartes, and from Kant to the Logical Positivists' (Barbalet, 1998:30). For Plato emotions were inappropriate territory, as irrational urges that needed controlling, and for Kant emotions were regarded as an illness! Mortiboys, in *The Emotionally Intelligent Lecturer* (2002), has many interesting experiential activities for learning but he specifically notes that it would be disturbing if universities were emotion-free zones; yet 'curiously, so much of the culture in higher education implies that they are' (p 7). Mortiboys references many educational commentators who over many years have regarded the emotions as 'inappropriate territory'. Interestingly, emotions and emotional safety have always been a core concern of the outdoor learning community, and a significant literature base exists on the subject.

At the heart of concern over 'appropriateness' lies the question we address here: to what degree is learning an emotional activity as much as it is an intellectual one? The role of emotions in learning generates considerable moral and political debate and Boler (1999) in *Feeling Power: Emotions and education* offers a feminist critique of the politics of emotions in learning; she suggests that emotion is a notoriously difficult subject to define and that students find few spaces to express, resist, and challenge. She (1999: 109) remarks that in Higher Education and scholarship, 'to address emotions is risky business' as it opens up a debate about public and private spaces. Emotional dimensions of the learning experience are often denied. Boler explores the taboos of emotions in education, and considers its roots in social control through the 'mental hygiene movement' centred on emotional engineering (girls were taught patience, self-denial, silence, love). Her work is particularly critical of the measurement and intelligence testing movement, and of the self-help, consumer approach to 'emotional intelligence' by Goleman (1996) as a recipe for 'success'.

Boler suggests casting the gaze away from the term emotions; that we call it something else. Our view is that this something else begins to surface as part of the learning space, a new form of 'pedagogical space', where the experience of a physical, psychological and social space permits the development of language, and activities, that explore, express and accept emotions and feelings of self and others. This is an area we also explore in the chapter on learning environments. In contrast, Furedi (2004) is strongly critical of the link between therapy and emotions. Furedi argues that the current 'therapy culture' generates a psychology of 'vulnerability' and warns that this imposes a new conformity through the management of people's emotions. Furedi argues that 'self esteem advocates argue that it is not intellectual abilities, but how you feel that really matters' (p 160): thus 'the promotion of emotional intelligence is symptomatic of a climate of intellectual pessimism' (p 161).

Identifying and classifying emotions is problematic. Biologist Charles Darwin identified a comprehensive range of 30 emotions, which he classified into several categories, and argued that they essentially represented adaptation and survival mechanisms. More recent attempts to categorize complex emotions can also be found: proposals for 'master', 'basic', 'primary' (sadness, happiness, fear, anger, joy) or 'secondary emotions' (subtle variations of primary emotions such as euphoria, ecstasy, melancholy and wistfulness) as found in the work of Damasio (1996) and others. Plutchik (1980), however, concluded that there are endless possibilities of 'emotional classes', which can be determined to some extent by the socio-cultural context or situation. 'Master emotions' such as shame frequently appear in the literature, as in recent work by Frijda and Mesquita (1994) and the shame–pride dichotomy of Kitayama and Markus (1994).

These emotions of pride and shame are said to be related to success and failure in learning and these in turn all play a key role in establishment and maintenance of identity, with the associated sense of belonging, differentiation and self-esteem (Scheff, 1997). A number of sociologists argue that the disposition to learn is grounded in social relationships, and in the construction of identity and self-esteem, and that these occur within the context of success/pride and failure/shame (eg Barbalet, 1998 and Scheff, 1997). Ingleton (1999) remarks that:

> by theorizing emotion as being formed in social relationships and significant in the development and maintenance of identity, its role in learning is constructed at a much deeper level. As such, emotion is seen to be constitutive of the activity of learning… Emotions shape learning and teaching experiences for both teachers and students, and the recognition of their significance merits further consideration in both learning theory and pedagogical practice.
>
> (p 9)

Spiritual intelligence – SQ

In a chapter called 'The forgetting and remembering of the air', Abram (1997) beautifully describes the great significance of the air to past generations. He notes, for example, that the term 'psyche' is derived from an ancient Greek word that signified not only the 'soul' or 'mind', but also a 'breath' or a 'gust of wind'. The air is wind, breath, spirit and language; and the Latin *spiritus* means breath.

> The Navajo identification of awareness with the air – their intuition that the psyche is not an immaterial power that resides inside us, but is rather the invisible yet thoroughly palpable medium in which we (along with the trees, the squirrels, and the clouds) are immersed – must seem at first bizarre… to persons of European ancestry.
>
> (Abram, 1997: 237)

Returning to an earlier definition of intelligence as an adaptation to the environment in which we live, others, in contrast suggest that 'detachment' from our immediate environment and its sensory buzz can enable access to superior creative powers. Stewart (in Walter and Marks, 1981) notes that people discover their deepest self and reveal their greatest creative powers at times when the psychic processes are most free from immediate involvement with the environment and most under the control of inner balancing. This often requires *not thinking too much*. This is what we learn to do in the meditative state. Fox (1999: 455–57) in 'Enhancing spiritual experience in adventure programs' describes many emotions and feelings associated with spiritual experiences in the outdoors, offers an analysis of anecdotal accounts of spirituality, and clusters the accounts under the following headings:

- spirituality as a fundamental aspect of human nature;
- spirituality as a sense of mystery;
- spirituality as a sense of awe and wonderment;

- spirituality as a belief in the connectedness or sense of oneness towards people, self and all things;
- spirituality as aesthetic beauty;
- spirituality as transcendent;
- spirituality as peak experience;
- spirituality as creating a sense of inner peace, oneness and strength;
- wilderness as a spiritual attraction.

Maslow developed a hierarchy of needs and described the base layers as need for food, for shelter, for physical health, for family, for education, for social integration and for intellectual, social and material accomplishments. But it is only when these needs are met that people reach their ultimate stage of human development: a positive state of self-actualization and the realization of one's potential. In this state people pour out playfulness, creativity, joyousness, a sense of purpose, with a mission to help others and with great tolerance, and these are accomplished in an environment of love and compassion. Maslow was perhaps describing a form of spiritual intelligence?

Stringer and McAvoy (1995) in *The Theory of Experiential Education* comment that the following attributes of spirituality were reported by participants of a wilderness experience:

Awareness	Human interconnectedness
Attunement	Inner feelings
Connection or relation to a greater	Inner or self-knowledge
power/deity	Sense of wholeness, oneness,
Inner strength	peace and/or
Values	tranquillity
Shared or common spirit	Intangibility

These lists offer a striking resemblance to the ingredients of wisdom and there is clearly much common ground. A practical example of experiential trainers explicitly using spirituality is found in the following Box.

Using spiritual intelligence

The Findhorn Foundation is an organization that was started in 1962 in a caravan park in Scotland. Currently this successful organization seeks to demonstrate the links between the spiritual, social, economic and environmental aspects of life. Cooperation and co-creation with nature are major aspects of the Foundation's work, and they declare that they are 'at the heart of the UK's largest international community based on spiritual values'.

The Earth Centre in Doncaster in the UK was, from its inception, said to be the world's first environmental theme park. The Findhorn Foundation sent their staff to help in the training of the newly appointed workforce. Indeed The Earth Centre later won a national tourism award as a result of the help that visitors received from on-site staff, who came largely from the ranks of unemployed ex-miners. The staff's special training lasted six weeks, by which time they had to be ready to launch the centre. Some were unable to read or write very well. Most knew little about the environment and most had few if any educational qualifications. What is significant about the training of the local people, however, is that the first stage of the three-part programme was specially designed by the trainers of the Findhorn Foundation. They developed the group, working first with feelings and needs, and nurturing their sense of belonging. Using many of the spiritual principles offered by Deepak Chopra (see the following Box), they examined and explored the important spiritual values associated with this mining community and their 'special place', a place that, like themselves, was undergoing a new and significant transformation. The local environment was shifting from being a coal-mining area to an internationally known green 'theme park'. The men and women were a close community, and hardship had beset them at the time of the closure of the coal mine. Their experiences in the dying last days of industry had been negative, and there was a sense of mistrust.

The people all sat, arms folded, looking in disbelief at the strange trainers from Scotland when they first arrived. There was strong initial resistance, mixed with a strange fascination. Eventually this fascination got the better of the local people; they succumbed to the charm of their experience, and many ended their training by participating in quite challenging events. Many created and read out their own poetry. Many unexpectedly shed tears with other local people as they unearthed some of their deeper feelings about their community and their sense of loss. Their emotional bedrock was not only exposed at times but was strengthened in their resolve to prepare for the next phase of their environmental training. Whilst the local people might have been seen as having low levels of formal education for their role as environmental guides, they eventually proved to be highly capable and well trained. The prestigious tourism award given to them derived largely from the spiritual experiential base that formed a central part of their training.

(Hartmann and Beard, 2000)

Recognizing spiritual intelligence

The emotions associated with spiritual experiences are often difficult to describe. This is illustrated by two very interesting stories in Greg Child's book about mountain explorers, *Mixed Emotions* (1993). The stories focus on the spirit world, death, superstition and unexplainable phenomena. One story is about Roger Marshall on the treacherous mountain, Kanchenjunga.

He was stumbling down the mountainside with his strength slipping away. He was perilously close to falling down precipitous slopes when he heard a Japanese voice; he moved towards the voice, found a rope left by a previous Japanese expedition and descended to safety. But there were no Japanese people present on the slopes that day. Science leads us to seek rational, logical explanations for this: a physiological phenomenon, oxygen deprivation or distorted perceptions maybe? But science and myth are said by some to be one and the same, says Davies (1997) in his remarkable book exploring the botanical findings of important medicinal and hallucinogenic plants; *One River: Sciences, adventure and hallucogens in the Amazon Basin*. Spiritual intelligence locates itself in a person's 'life energy', and Chopra (1996) offers seven active spiritual steps and their appropriate law.

Seven spiritual laws

1 Experience higher, spiritual self; list unique talents and three ways of expressing them; ask daily, how may I help serve humanity? *Law of dharma*

2 Experience silence; commune with nature; practise non-judgement. *Law of pure potentiality*

3 Offer a gift for everyone; receive gifts from life; wish everyone happiness, joy and laughter. *Law of giving*

4 Witness choices in the moment; ask, will it bring fulfilment and happiness to me and others?; ask heart for spontaneous right action. *Law of karma*

5 Accept people and situations as they are; take responsibility for my situation without blame; defencelessness – no need to convince or persuade. *Law of least effort*

6 Make a list of desires and release the list to the universe; remain established in self-referral. *Law of intention and desire*

7 Allow self and others to be as they are; factor uncertainty into my experience; step into the field of all possibilities. *Law of detachment*

(Chopra, 1996)

Naturalistic intelligence – NQ

Feeling a deep sense of closeness to nature and having a fascination with all things natural is part of this intelligence.

I have it in myself. Early in my life I wanted to work with the Royal Society for the Protection of Birds (RSPB). As a boy I had had many special experiences in nature, sometimes feeling 'alone' in its strict sense, but also for me, connected with and close to the species around me. After graduating as a zoologist, I lived in the Amazon rainforests in the 1970s and the experience deeply changed my life. Twenty years later I became lost in a large tract of Malaysian rainforest. While this was potentially a very frightening experience, it became indescribably powerful. A strong sense of connection again emerged: the monkeys were watching me. I sat to observe the beetles and ants going about their everyday business. I was immersed in the intense sounds of cicadas and frogs. It was a beautiful experience that created a very extraordinary sense of 'self' for me.

Later in life two more profound experiences occurred. I lived in a small wooden hut in the mountains in Wales protecting birds for the RSPB, and I lived alone with nature. I knew the birds and their calls. I knew the plants and their Latin names. A few years later I worked again with the RSPB, in an estuary with my own boat and outboard motor. I remember well the night when the full moon spring tides created real danger for the birds. I went out in the semi-darkness of the night in my boat in strong winds and fast-flowing tides, rescuing baby chicks that had been separated from their nests and parents. There were many chicks washed into the tidal waters. Drowning and scared, they were pulled out into the boat and I took them back to dry land. Again I was out there all 'alone', surrounded by natural beauty and driven by some existential force, concerned for my fellow species.

Colin Beard

Words alone cannot do justice to these kinds of experiences. Words are very problematic anyway. *Nature* and *naturalness* are considered contested terms. We are not going to cover these contested issues about words in detail here although we cover some of these issues in the chapter on sensing. For further reading about these contested terms such as *natural* and *wilderness* see for example Jay Griffiths (2006) *Wild: an elemental journey*, and William Cronen (1996) *Uncommon Ground*.

Cooper (1998), an outdoor education specialist, refers to special experiences of spirituality in the natural environment and suggests that such experiences result in a connectedness to the earth, and a heightened sense of being alive. They are located within what are called existential or transcendental phenomena. These experiences, he suggests, can be very powerful and spiritual for some people, and may present a turning point in life. Cooper goes on to recall the experience of a Professor Knowles who, when leading a night-time kayaking session, had an experience which changed his life. He was out with a group of 15-year-old kids from the city as they set off into the night under a myriad of stars. They were then faced with an amazing sight of thousands of glow-worms:

> They were breathtaking. Each tiny glow came from a single phosphorescent light-emitting creature. Suspended like delicate jewels, the larvae of the fungus gnat had emerged to feed, their diffused glow reflecting on the faces of the exuberant students... we listened intently to the night and to each other. I was silent, allowing nature to speak... many students marvelled at the power of beauty and the place's serenity... In my mind, and in the minds of several students, a sacred place was established. It was the site of a special event, a place, if you will, at which individuals united with the powers of nature.
>
> (Cooper, 1998: 65)

Knowles returned to the same lake later with other groups but the experience wasn't the same. Leaders cannot predict such events, but they can set the scene, pre-sensitize people and make use of opportunities as they arise – if they themselves are sensitized to such things. Few people actually experience real darkness or a dawn chorus of birds awakening in the forests. Few people experience the strange silence when surfing waves. At the heart of naturalistic intelligence is an understanding of the human *reciprocity* with the more-than-human world. Abram discusses how for many indigenous, oral cultures a feeling of being truly alone when moving through nature, no matter how desolate or remote, is an alien concept. In order to understand this notion of *reciprocity*, try touching the fingers of another human. What is remarkable is that it not only allows you to feel the fingers of the other, but the sensuous feeling of your own fingers becomes possible. This is so with the surrounding more-than-human world. Sensing, and feeling at one with nature is part of this naturalistic intelligence. More and more people are attempting to make sense of such experiences in their lives. Peter Senge and his co-writers (Senge *et al*, 2005: 63) beautifully describe a wildlife encounter of a colleague. He experienced a sense of oneness, a dismantling of the animal–human boundary:

> As I began to meditate, I looked to my left and saw two huge whales spouting water simultaneously. Then the whales put on the most unbelievable show... My heart was pounding, and I sat there in awe... Then directly in front of me, about a hundred yards out, a lone whale gave me four spouts. Silence. A minute afterwards, off to my left, a whale rolled over four times. And then there was nothing... I felt as if I was bleeding from an open wound. I felt my heart was completely open and had merged with those of the whales. There was no separation between us. I remained in that open state of intense compassion for a long time, feeling as if I were on holy ground, as if I were in a great cathedral. I knew that I would never be the same again.

Sensing and spiritual intelligence

Much of this heightened sense of awareness is a learning experience of a higher order: it is learning beyond the simplicity of the experiential learning cycle. It is more than doing and reflecting. It is deeper. Mind and world are not separate. But often the associated sadness is due to the realization of our separation with nature. Senge and his colleagues refer to a three-stage sequence of sensing, presencing and realizing as part of a powerful experiencing process associated with the transformation of self and organizations:

- *Sensing* requires people to observe, observe, observe and to become at one with the world.

- *Presencing* requires one to retreat and reflect and to allow inner knowledge to emerge.

- *Realizing* is to create a new reality and to act swiftly with a natural flow.

Of interest here is the fact that many mystifying descriptions of moral, spiritual and naturalistic intelligence overlap so strongly. The development of such deep intelligence appears central to authentic change.

The creative intelligence – CQ

The concept of a creative quotient (CQ) is similarly perplexing and scientists have for some time tried to find out why some people experience inspiration and innovation so easily whilst others struggle. Intellect is not suggested as the critical ingredient of creative intelligence. The exact nature of creativity and innovation remains elusive. Interestingly, children seem much more adept at being creative, yet many adults appear to lose this ability more readily.

In the late 1940s Guildford, a psychologist, developed a model of human intellect and founded the idea of convergent and divergent thinking that formed the basis of contemporary research on creativity. IQ tests have primarily focused on convergent thinking but creative people seem able to free themselves from these thought patterns. Characteristics of divergent thinkers include ideas fluency, variety and flexibility, originality, elaboration, problem sensitivity and redefinition. Guildford failed to find a measure for CQ, as indeed have all subsequent attempts by researchers.

Henry (1991) suggests that there are five schools of thought on creativity: grace, accident, association, cognition and personality.

Other writers in the same book examine creativity in terms of metaphors (Morgan, 1997a), problem solving, lateral and vertical thinking (Edward de Bono, 1991), intuition (Agor, 1991) and higher sense of 'self' (Ray and Myers, 1986). To be creative often means disturbing the status quo, and as a result innovators are said to be difficult to manage (Kirton, 1976; Belbin, 1981; Sinetar, 1992; Pinchot, 1997; Amabile, 1993). Innovators are said to be easily bored yet often regard their work as a form of play, and Henry (1991) and other writers support the notion that creativity arises through a playfulness of mind. Martin, Franc and Zounkova (2004) in *Outdoor and Experiential Learning* offer many interesting practical ideas on creative play, arguing that such mind states are encouraged in dramaturgy (which we explore in Chapter 5).

Kraft, in the *Scientific American* journal *Mind* (2005), builds on work of Nobel Peace Prize winner Roger Sperry, who researched left and right brain functions, and suggests that there are four steps to a creative mind: wonderment, motivation, intellectual courage and relaxation. Modern society, he noted, discriminates against the right hemisphere, yet it is responsible for divergent thinking, holistic and intuitive thinking, processing images, melodies, complex patterns such as face recognition, and being responsible for spatial organization of the body. Kraft notes that underlying creative ability is 'curiosity, love of experimentation, playfulness, risk taking, mental flexibility, metaphorical thinking, aesthetics – all these qualities play a central role' (p 20).

It is a long-held belief that play enhances the development of creativity. Neulinger (1974) produced a Paradigm of Leisure categorizing mind states that produce leisure and non-leisure conditions. 'Pure leisure' and 'pure job' are presented at polar extremes of a continuum. The variations are 'leisure-work' and 'leisure-job'. This mind-state concept underpins products of The British Trust for Conservation Volunteers: it sells work-as-leisure conservation 'working holidays'; the landowner pays for the work to be done, as do the holidaymakers: the work contributes to environmental improvement, and is paid for twice and sold as leisure! (Beard, 1996).

Creative people often experience their work as a calling or dedicated vocation: 'Creative people are happy with solitude, and they are less in need of discipline or order. Their dominant need may be to use their brains on complex problems, and this often overshadows their dependency on the approval or opinions of others' (Sinetar, 1992: 113).

Likewise Osborn (1963) argues that a major block to creativity is the tendency for others to evaluate ideas prematurely, and that it is useful to separate idea generation from idea evaluation. Others suggest that managers habitually damage creativity by finding reasons not to use a new idea, because 'people believe that they will appear smarter to their bosses if they are more critical – and it often works. In many organizations, it is professionally rewarding to react critically to new ideas' (Amabile, 83).

Mind state certainly appears to be an important influence in learning to be creative. Falconar (2000: 48) describes these states in *Creative Intelligence and Self Liberation* as:

1 *Detachment*, in which there is a feeling of being cut off, as though the view of the problem was from far away.

2 *Involvement*, so that you became like a spring, feeling the body twisting as the spring tensioned.

3 *Deferment*, avoiding a premature solution, which would probably become a poor one.

4 *Meditation*, reverie and free thinking, in which the mind was allowed to run free.

5 An *indescribable feeling* in which the solution appeared to be on its own.

Falconar notes the sense of joy present in creative people, and says it is an emotion to be cultivated. Creative people, he says, are very aware of this and use it, and he refers to Eysenck's book *Genius*, which alluded to similar mind states. Likewise Maslow also wrote about such mind states in *Motivation and Personality*:

> The feeling of being simultaneously more powerful and also more helpless than one had ever been before, the feeling of great ecstasy and wonder and awe, the loss of placing in time and space with, finally, the conviction that something extremely important had happened, so that the subject is to some extent transformed and strengthened even in his daily life by such experiences.
>
> (Falconar, 2000: 53)

Creativity is concerned with doing things differently. In *Psychology for Trainers*, Hardingham (1998) examines the concept of reframing by using material from the work of Bandler and Grinder (1990) on neuro-linguistic programming (NLP), who offered the following:

An old Chinese Taoist story describes a farmer in a poor country village. He was considered very well-to-do because he owned a horse that he used for ploughing, for riding around, and for carrying things. One day his horse ran away. All his neighbours exclaimed how terrible this was, but the farmer simply said, 'Maybe'.

A few days later the horse returned and brought two wild horses with it. The neighbours all rejoiced at his good fortune, but the farmer just said, 'Maybe'.

The next day the farmer's son tried to ride one of the wild horses; the horse threw him and broke the boy's leg. The neighbours all offered their sympathy for his misfortune, but the farmer again said, 'Maybe'.

The next week conscription officers came to the village to take young men for the army. They rejected the farmer's son because of his broken leg. When the neighbours told him how lucky he was, the farmer replied, 'Maybe'.

Reframing inner scripts can generate significant mind states for creative thought. 'The meaning that any event has depends upon the "frame" in which we perceive it. When we change the frame we change the meaning. When the meaning changes the response changes also. The more reframing we do the more choices we have' (Hardingham, 1998: 116).

Falconar (2000) suggests that Eastern meditative mind states help creativity and he suggests two different ways of thinking. The verbal way, he remarks is uncreative, while the other, consisting of visual images, feelings and intuition, constitutes creative thought. This polemic interpretation is however problematic: verbal expressive creativity is clearly a powerful medium for generating self-expression and creativity, as highlighted in the case study below. One might argue that without such verbal creativity we would not have 'fiction, theatre, and movie scripts, poetry, spoken work, slam poetry, etc' (Trules, 2005). Trules (2005), author of the case study below suggests that while there are many forms that creativity can take, the term is socially and culturally relative: all human beings are capable of being self-expressive and creative (painter, writer, potter, plumber, teacher, or simply a human being living life). It is, he suggests, not just the province of Einsteins (introvert) and Picassos and Dalis (extroverted).

If, then, state of mind is significant for creative work, this has clear implications for the learning environment. People also utilize numerous techniques to create mind states, such as the use of rituals, like showering and getting smartly dressed, using strong caffeine, alcohol or other drugs, and by the denial of sleep or food.

Developing creativity and self-expression using storytelling and solo performance

Professor Eric Trules

I believe that uncovering the personal story within and finding one's own 'personal voice' is an empowering and freeing art form. This kind of self-expression connects human beings across cultures. I am an artist-educator who wants to take this storytelling, film and theatre monologue work around the world, changing it one story at a time.

In 1985, I began directing, then writing and performing solo performance monologues. Two of them were shown at the Edinburgh Fringe Festival. I have taught 'Solo Performance' at the University of Southern California since 1994. From 1991 to 1998, I wrote, produced, and directed an autobiographical 'personal voice' feature-length documentary film, 'The Poet and the Con', about my complicated relationship with my uncle, a career criminal and a confessed murderer. This kind of 'personal voice' filmmaking is the filmic equivalent to 'solo performance' in the theatre.

Later, as part of my Fulbright Scholar work for the University of Malaysia Sabah on the island of Borneo, I taught 'Solo Performance' to Chinese, Muslim, and Malay college-age students – in English and in their native language. I had to find new techniques to teach storytelling because many of my students didn't speak English as their primary language. But with the help of one talented Chinese-Malay student, we found a way to communicate – and to discover the stories that lay hidden within each student. It took time. And trust. And an intuitive process of osmosis for the students to understand what I was looking for, what made a good story for an audience. After working with them for weeks orally, I finally had the students write their stories in Bahasa, their native language. I had them e-mail me the stories. Then I had them translated to English. I worked on them dramaturgically (the craft of developing and rewriting work in the theatre), and I had them re-translated to Bahasa. We went back and forth many times to get the stories as clear and effective as possible. Then we rehearsed for many more weeks. The same kind of language barriers and problems happened all over again. But again, the few who spoke English well helped me and the others who didn't speak English well. And at the end of the term, all the students performed their pieces in front of a full audience; all except one, in Bahasa. The audience cheered.

Original stories are honest, revealing, emotional, heart-warming, hilarious, and effective for a theatre audience. The stories were about sex, love, parents, childhood, ethnicity, death, fear, self-image, friendship, so many more intimate and personal subjects. Stories for a multicultural tapestry of performers: white, black, Latino, Asian, Indian, all the colours of the rainbow that find themselves at the challenging and confusing time of adolescence and young adulthood. College-age stories – by real kids, real people, who are becoming, and are, real writers and artists. In the real, poetic, fractured, eloquent, and profane language that they speak.

I can't say how many times students have told me that this kind of transformational self-discovery and intimate, personal writing work was the most powerful, memorable, and important work they had done during their entire college careers. We all have stories within us. Secrets. Stories that we are too ashamed or embarrassed to bring to light. Who would want to hear these stories? Your horrible relationship with your mother or father? Your tortured, convoluted, but triumphant coming-out story? Learning what trust and betrayal between friends means in life? Countless, unbelievable and unpredictable variations. What one comes to learn is that in the most neurotic, idiosyncratic, and detailed personal story, when well told and well crafted, lies the universal. The story of my relationship with my mother, my father, my uncle, my friend, my lover, my enemy – the story of my fear, my triumph, my failure – is also your story. That's why stories are creative and cathartic.

What place does this personal storytelling work have in the field of education and in the field of learning? It is my opinion that too much time is spent in university on vocational training, on theoretical and academic issues, and/or on the mere acquisition and accumulation of knowledge. I know that's what my college education was about. It was not until I graduated from university that I started to look at and discover myself. I think I started too late, and that discovering who one is and what one wants to do in life is an essential part of anyone's education. Certainly the two can coexist: academic and/or vocational training along with self-discovery. However, finding the latter of the two sorely neglected in both my own university education as well in my observation of decades of students in my role as an educator, I have chosen my path to be that of educator of the 'self', ie how to look within oneself, discover one's own voice, and how to follow one's own unique path in life. It is what I teach in all my courses – self-expression and creativity. It's a crucial and essential part of 'learning'. Students are hungry for it.

Professor Eric Trules is an award-winning artist-educator, and lecturer at the School of Theatre, University of Southern California, USA. He was a 2002 American Fulbright Scholar and spent 8 months in Malaysia. He is an Allen Ginsberg Poetry Award winner, and in over 30 years as a professional artist he has been a modern dancer, actor, clown, screenwriter, theatre and film director, arts festival producer, poet, documentary filmmaker, and solo performer. He offers international workshops in self-expression and creativity.

Contact: trules@usc.edu See: www.erictrules.com; www.travels withtrules.com

Wisdom

Gardner (1993: 291), in his book on multiple intelligence, refers to four higher levels of cognitive work that goes beyond a straightforward notion of 'an intelligence'. These were common sense, originality, metaphoric capacity and lastly wisdom. Wisdom requires life experience and high levels of learning, considerable insight and experience, and a maturity that gives a strong ability to refuse to let the ego affect decision making and life choices.

Egan (2002: 19), referring to wisdom in the art of facilitation, remarks that 'helpers need to be wise, and part of their job is to impart some of their wisdom, however indirectly, to their clients'. He refers to two authors who define wisdom as 'an expertise in the conduct and meaning of life' or 'an expert knowledge system concerning the fundamental pragmatics of life'. Egan explores key characteristics that might usefully be developed in facilitator wisdom:

- self-knowledge and maturity;
- knowledge of life's obligations and goals;
- an understanding of cultural conditioning;
- the guts to admit mistakes and the sense to learn from them;
- a psychological and a human understanding of others; insight into human interactions;
- the ability to 'see through' situations; the ability to understand the meaning of events;
- tolerance for ambiguity and the ability to work with it;
- being comfortable with messy and ill-structured cases;
- an understanding of the messiness of human beings;
- openness to events that don't fit comfortably into logical or traditional categories;
- the ability to frame a problem so that it is workable; the ability to reframe information;

- avoidance of stereotypes;
- holistic thinking; open mindedness; open-endedness; contextual thinking;
- meta-thinking, or the ability to think about thinking and become aware about being aware;
- the ability to see relationships among diverse factors; the ability to spot flaws in reasoning; intuition, the ability to synthesize;
- the refusal to let experience become a liability through the creation of blind spots;
- the ability to take a long view of the problem;
- the ability to blend seemingly antithetical helping roles – being one who cares and understands while being also the one who challenges and 'frustrates';
- an understanding of the spiritual dimensions of life.

Conclusion

What does this knowledge about the nature of thinking, knowing and intelligence actually contribute to the practice of experiential learning? While the exact nature of intelligence remains controversial, it is clear that intelligence is more than just a range of cognitive abilities such as reasoning and problem solving. It is important to acknowledge the breadth of processes involved in thinking with the mind such as thinking with feelings, deep thinking and shallow thinking, fast and slow thinking. Such knowledge can support the development of deeper forms of experiential learning.

In order to understand experiential learning this broad ecology of thinking, knowing and intelligence must be explored in practice. All influence how we experience the world. Learning is not separated from the landscape of the body, of gut feelings or intuition, of emotions and spiritual feelings, nor is it separated from the outer landscape of our surroundings. There is still so much to learn about knowing and intelligence. What we discover will undoubtedly affect the future development of experiential learning. In considering the nature of intelligences in people, there is a further dimension of intelligence that is worthy of a brief mention in a final spirit of provocation. In Senge *et al*'s book *Presence* (2005), the authors note that 'the blind spot' of contemporary science is experience. They comment that David Bohm, a former colleague of Albert Einstein, said that 'the most important thing going forward is to break the boundaries between people so we can operate as a "single intelligence". Bell's theorem implies that this is the natural state of the human world, separation without separateness. The task is to find ways to break these boundaries, so we can be in our natural state' (Senge *et al*, 2005: 189).

Experience, learning and change
(The being dimension)

One must learn by doing the thing, for though you think you know it, you have no certainty until you try. ARISTOTLE

Introduction

In the last chapter, and in others, we have explored aspects of being, such as wisdom and the spiritual self. These topics could also have fitted well here in this last chapter covering the six dimensions of the model. Here, in covering the final tumbler of the learning combination lock model, we focus our investigation on the ways in which learning is connected with personal and organizational change. How people change as a result of experiential learning has clear links to previous chapters, particularly with the feeling and knowing dimensions of learning. Significant change and transformation often involve an intense emotional dimension and emotions can act as a bridge to personal change. There are many layers to change: the sensing self, the emotional self, the knowing self and the being self are just some of the aspects of change that we have explored in this book.

In Higher Education the changes involving our inner 'being' (the ontological self) are considered by some to be far more important than changes in the knowing self (epistemological self). When our very 'being' is transformed, changes can involve shifts in identity and the inner psyche, the development of wisdom and the letting go of the ego, the development of presence and authenticity, and the development of mindful states. The key to deep learning is of course self-awareness; the ability to know oneself.

In Western educational systems there are three core approaches to teaching and learning: namely transmission, transaction and transformation.

The latter emerges through the teacher facilitating student critical thinking and awareness about self and others so as to examine and challenge basic assumptions, values, belief systems and ways of acting in the world. Mälkki, a postdoctoral researcher from Finland, has developed the concept of the '*edge zone*', which is a helpful metaphor and this is explored in the Box below. Experiencing emotions in our comfort zone can seem less threatening to us as negative emotions can take us towards discomfort, to the 'edge' of the comfort zone. But this is where a perspective change can often occur (see Mälkki, 2010, 2011). This edge zone can be experienced as 'stretch' if moderate levels of stress are present, or generating 'panic' if the stress is excessive (for more on this see Palethorpe and Wilson, 2011).

Transformational change through learning is usually considered as developmental; as a moving forward. It is thus seen as a positive activity with positive results. Although the results are often desirable, the process nevertheless may involve unpleasant experiences and challenging phases as natural parts of it. In discussing transformation, it is often useful to consider what *form* is actually assumed to be trans*form*ed (Kegan, 2000; Illeris, 2007; Mezirow, 1991, 2000). The process of change, while enabling to acquire something new, involves having to give up something that used to be part of one's self and one's ways of understanding the world. Thus the change poses for us not only epistemological but also existential challenges (Mälkki and Green, 2012).

Whether it is a matter of our ways of knowing, our being or our acting in the world, being challenged often takes us out of our *comfort zone* (Mälkki, 2010, 2011). That is to say, when nothing questions our assumptions and we are able to interpret situations within the light of our previous experiences, we experience ourselves comfortable, in the *comfort zone*. Instead, when our beliefs, attitudes, values, relationships, or sense of understanding the world, for example, become questioned, we experience edge-emotions, ie discomfort and anxiety. These edge-emotions are, therefore, indicators of a threat to our meaning frameworks and current configuration of self (Mälkki, 2010, 2011).

Similarly, as emotions support survival by orienting us automatically to concrete action, such as fight, flight or freeze at the case of danger (Damasio, 1999, 2003), in the case of mental threat we are also automatically oriented towards returning to the comfort zone, so as to feel ourselves comfortable and safe again: we tend to avoid dealing with the unpleasant issues that question our ways of knowing or being and/or interpret the issues in a way that they no longer appear threatening.

At the basic level this mechanism supports the consistency of our meaning frameworks and identity, and, as such, is necessary for us. At the same time, however, it presents a challenge to efforts of learning and change: we have a natural resistance towards change and a tendency to cling to our current meanings.

If we wish to overcome some of the limitations to learning and change that the edge-emotions present, we need to recognize, in our thinking, this pattern of being automatically oriented towards the comfort zone. Often we wish to remove the unpleasant emotions out of our experience before we even have had time to actually live them through, digest them and hear what they wish to inform us. However, instead of being automatically oriented away from the unpleasantness at the edges of our comfort zones, we may aim to identify, accept and embrace the edge-emotions. With this kind of acknowledgement and tolerance of the edge-emotions that we inevitably encounter in life, we may be better suited to learning and change (Mälkki, 2010, 2011).

Kaisu Mälkki, Post-doctoral Researcher, Helsinki University, Finland.

An understanding of learning theories will enable us to select the appropriate elements from the various components of our holistic model. This will allow strategic choices regarding the manner in which we can encourage learning. The main theories of learning all involve experiential learning to some degree. In this chapter we will then progress to explore in detail the development and nature of reflective practice and action learning. These two practical forms of individual and organizational learning attempt to identify solutions to the challenges and problems that are faced and use the process of experiential learning.

Learning and change

> There can be no learning without action, and no action without learning.
>
> (Reg Revans)

When we as individuals learn something we add or change some of the neuronal connections within our brains. Similarly, when organizations learn something it may be through the knowledge employees possess or perhaps within work manuals or in electronic form. In both cases, whether individual or organizational, this repository of knowledge must be applied in practice for there to be a material difference.

This link between learning and change often only becomes apparent when we consider both elements more closely. A quotation by Charles Handy (1989) in *The Age of Unreason* brings the two more closely together:

> If changing is, as I have argued, only another word for learning, the theories of learning will also be the theories of changing. Those who are always learning are those who can ride the waves of change and who see a changing world as full of opportunities rather than of damage. They are the ones most likely to be

FIGURE 9.1 The learning gap or performance gap

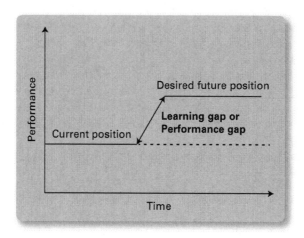

the survivors in a time of discontinuity. They are also the enthusiasts and the architects of new ways and forms and ideas. If you want to change, try learning one might say, or more precisely, if you want to be in control of your change, take learning more seriously.

Competition and the desire for improvement often highlight the need for change. In Figure 9.1 we can see how the *Current position* will remain the same and continue along the same trajectory unless circumstances change. This is exemplified by the saying, 'If you do what you have always done, you'll get what you have always got'. Thus, the *Desired future position* will not be achieved unless the *Performance gap* is bridged through learning and change.

Theories of learning: theories of change!

We are all unique and each of us has likes and dislikes, and effective and ineffective methods of learning. In this respect there is an almost endless list of individual learning theories. Take a moment to consider where and when you think best. Perhaps it is in the shower in the morning. Is it late at night just before you go to sleep? Individual variations such as these influence the success or failure of learning. In order to make the understanding of learning more manageable we need to provide some categorization of the main theories.

In essence, the main distinction involves the long-running debate about nature and nurture. The view of the authors is that there is an interactive dependency between the uniqueness of the individual and the specific influences that interact from the surrounding environment. It is the sum of these characteristics and the experiences that occur that shape the person. Wilson (in an article entitled 'Harsh words can deform children's brains for life' by Jason Burke, published in the *Observer* (London), 31 December 2000) stated, 'The nature versus nurture debate is being seen as increasingly outmoded. We are talking now about a complex interaction between genetic disposition and experience.'

The strategies that we use for our learning and that of others are based upon our conscious or subconscious philosophies about how people learn and their ability to learn. For example, if we believe that there is almost unlimited potential within human beings we may be encouraged to help them achieve their targets. If, on the contrary, we believe that some people are intelligent and others 'do not have it', we may be less inclined to support them. The influence of personal philosophies and more general ones is pervasive and can inhibit the learning process. It is important to be aware of the value of learning philosophies that can provide insights into the learning process but we should also understand the 'flip side' in that they can constrain our thinking and thus limit our potential to help people learn.

It is beyond the scope of this book to go into detail about the various learning theories that are noted in Table 9.1. More detailed information may be found by referring to the authors mentioned for each learning theory category. One important fact should be noted, which is that experiential learning would appear to be involved with all of these theories and thus provide a unifying theme. What is more, Handy's advice about the theories of learning being the theories of change illustrates the spectrum of possible approaches to learning and also those of change.

The development of reflective practice

While human beings have reflected on their actions for as long as we know, the circumstances described next are drawn from Kolb's writings about Lewin, and led to the formalization of the process of reflective practice. In 1946 Lewin and a number of colleagues worked on the development of training approaches in leadership and group dynamics for the Connecticut State Interracial Commission. Group discussion was encouraged between the participants and the staff, and records of the meetings were kept and later discussed by the staff without the involvement of the participants. However, the participants were concerned that they were not involved with this discussion and approached Lewin requesting permission to attend, and he agreed. Lippit, who was present, observed that a remark made by an observer was challenged by one of the participants who disagreed with the interpretation of events:

> At the end of the evening the trainees asked if they could come back for the next meeting at which their behaviour would be evaluated. Kurt [Lewin], feeling that it had been a valuable contribution rather than an intrusion, enthusiastically agreed to their return. The next night at least half of the 50 or 60 participants

TABLE 9.1 Learning theories

Learning theory	Description	Exponents
Action learning/ research	Theory and practice inform each other as the individual applies theories in the environment.	J Locke, J Dewey, R Revans, K Lewin, D Kolb
Cognitivist	A person perceives stimuli and consciously interprets them in relation to his or her own mental frameworks.	J Bruner, J Dewey, K Lewin, G Kelly
Cognitive development	Children pass through a number of stages of cognitive development.	J Bruner, J Piaget, L Vygotsky
Computational	The development of ICT has provided parallels with how the brain operates. Likewise, computers are being designed to operate more closely to the operation of the brain, eg parallel processing.	G Moore, R Kurzweil, A Turing
Conditioning – classical	The greater the frequency and recency of a stimulus, the stronger the bond between stimulus and response.	I Pavlov, J B Watson
Conditioning – reinforcement	Thorndike built on Watson's work but emphasized that after the response there was a satisfier or annoyer: thus S–R–S or S–R–A. The former encouraged and the latter discouraged behaviour.	E L Thorndike
Conditioning – operant	Skinner argued that although a stimulus produced some automatic responses (respondent behaviour), operant behaviour in response to stimuli is dependent to some extent on the individual or organism.	B F Skinner

Gestalt	Wertheimer used the term gestalt to indicate pattern or configuration. He maintained that we see the whole picture, eg the relationship of notes in music or the relationship between a figure and background in a picture.	W Köhler, M Wertheimer
Human development and self-actualization	People develop at particular rates and need to be supported and encouraged.	F Froebel, A H Maslow, M Montessori, J J Rousseau
Humanist	The belief that knowledge resides within the mind of the individual and that the role of the teacher is to question the student carefully and thereby draw out this knowledge.	Aristotle, Plato, Socrates, C Rogers
Hereditary	Our ability to change and our genes influence our development.	C Darwin, S Fraser, R Herrnstein
Neuroscience	The use of brain scanning of injuries, and operations on the brain illustrate how brain cells respond to stimuli.	R Carter, S Pinker
Theistic	Mental discipline is necessary to train the mind towards good rather than allowing evil to develop.	St Augustine, J Calvin

NB The concept of experience may be applied to all the theories above

were there as a result of the grapevine reporting of the activity by the three delegates. The evening session from then on became the significant learning experience of the day, with focus on actual behavioural events and with active dialogue about differences of interpretation and observation of the events by those who participated in them.

(Lippit, in Kolb, 1984: 9)

Kolb (1984: 9) stated that this incident demonstrated that 'learning is best facilitated in an environment where there is dialectic tension and conflict between immediate concrete experience and analytic detachment'. To put it rather less academically, the learner was freed to think about events that happened in order to make sense of them.

This leads us to the question, what do we mean by reflection? Dewey (1938: 9) defined reflective thought as, 'Active, persistent and careful consideration of any belief or supposed form of knowledge in the light of the grounds that support it and further conclusions to which it leads... it includes a conscious and voluntary effort to establish belief upon a firm basis of evidence and rationality.'

Using problems and challenges

In Chapter 2 we discussed Freire's (1982) concept of banking education in which the teacher 'narrated' and pupils were passive receptacles into which information could be poured. Freire was very critical of this approach, saying that not only did it dominate the pupils with a way of thinking but it inhibited them from thinking and learning properly.

To counteract the banking concept Freire (1982: 54) proposed 'problem posing education'. Rather than banking education with its anaesthetizing effect, 'problem posing education involves a constant unveiling of reality' and it 'strives for the emergence of consciousness and critical intervention in reality'.

Freire (1982: 54) stated that the teacher 'does not regard cognizable objects as his private property, but as the object of reflection by himself and the students. In this way, the problem posing educator constantly re-forms his reflections in the reflection of the students. The students – no longer docile listeners – are now critical co-investigators in dialogue with the teacher.' This approach involved the teacher and the pupils working alongside one another rather than being divided by desks and more importantly being divided by didactic and organizational barriers. By reflecting together he believed learning was best achieved through providing pupils with problems rather than solutions. Freire (1982: 54) stated:

> Students, as they are increasingly faced with problems relating to themselves in the world and with the world, will feel increasingly challenged and obliged to respond to that challenge. Because they apprehend the challenge as interrelated to other problems with a total context, not as a theoretical question, the resulting comprehension tends to be increasingly critical and less alienated. Their response to the challenge evokes new challenges, followed by new understandings; and gradually the students come to regard themselves as committed.

This approach to using problems to encourage reflection is a form of Socratic investigation. In effect, the recognition of a problem is the acceptance that there is a gap in performance. Through the process of challenge from either a problem or alternative perspectives from other people, reflection can lead to learning. This is a fundamental part of human nature, and Freire (1982: 56) maintained, 'Problem posing education bases itself on creativity and stimulates true reflection and action on reality, thereby responding to the vocation of men as beings who are authentic only when engaged in inquiry and creative transformation.'

Problems and problem solving are at the essence of human development, and this theme will be revisited in our consideration of action learning and also in the final chapter. The same principle of problem or challenge is incorporated in Chapter 4, 'Learning Environments', where we consider how different environments can be chosen for their impact on the learning objectives.

Reflection-in-action and reflection-on-action

One of the main books on the subject of reflection is *The Reflective Practitioner* by Donald Schön (1983). He distinguished between what he termed reflection-in-action and reflection-on-action as a means of investigating how people used their experience to analyse and frame problems, propose action and then re-evaluate the experience as a result of the action.

Reflection-in-action considers the consequences of action while one is within the process. This is what we term concurrent learning, and is discussed in Chapter 2. Reflection-on-action (Schön, 1987) involves thinking about previous personal experiences, analysing them and then developing personal theories of action; and this we call retrospective learning. The final chronological form of learning is prospective learning, ie exploring future possibilities, which is discussed in the next chapter.

Not only can reflection occur in a structured environment with formal support from the organization; it can also occur as a form of unstructured reflection where people gather together when they meet a challenging experience. This reflection occurs as managers attempt to make sense of the circumstances in which they find themselves.

Making sense of what is happening to themselves by professionals has been termed reflection-in-action by Schön (1983). This form of reflection occurs particularly where people face unusual and different experiences that they find difficult to structure and make sense of. Reflection-in-action does not necessarily require support or coaching because it happens spontaneously. However, for deep learning to occur there is a danger in relying on reflection-in-action happening, especially when time constraints put a premium on people making time to analyse what is happening. It is for this reason that many organizations have coaching, counselling and mentoring structures to support the development of their employees. Seibert (1999) called reflection-on-action coached reflection and illustrated the differences between the two (see Table 9.2).

TABLE 9.2 Reflection-on-action and reflection-in-action

Coached reflection (reflection-on-action)	Reflection-in-action
Planned intervention to support learning from an experience.	Spontaneous reflection that occurs as a result of a need to understand and respond to experience.
Learner(s) supported by a facilitator.	Learner(s) organize reflection themselves.
Is planned for specific times.	Can occur at any time but usually when understanding of the circumstances is necessary and when time is available.
Usually happens with learner(s) away from the immediate workplace.	Usually happens in the workplace.
Involves contemplation.	Reflection is an active process.

Single and double loop learning

Allied to the process of reflective practice is Kolb's learning cycle and also Argyris and Schön's (1974) single loop learning and double loop (or deutero) learning. They drew on the work of Bateson's (2000) *Steps to an Ecology of Mind*, which discussed single loop learning and deutero learning. Single loop learning involved planning the action, undertaking it, evaluating it and finally learning from the previous stages (see Figure 9.2). Essentially, it is not too different from the learning cycle and quality improvement cycle, which we saw in Chapter 2. What the learner asks is, 'Am I doing the thing right?'

Double loop learning or deutero learning is similar to single loop learning. However, in this case the learner steps out of the single loop in order to assess whether the activity he or she is involved with is appropriate and asks, 'Am I doing the right things?' (see Figure 9.3). For example, a traditional watchmaker might be operating within the single loop learning process and progressively improving what he does. However, it may be that he should have been asking himself whether he should consider digital technology. It was this single loop learning that caused the Swiss watch-making industry so much trouble until they asked themselves, 'Are we doing the right things?'

FIGURE 9.2 Single loop learning

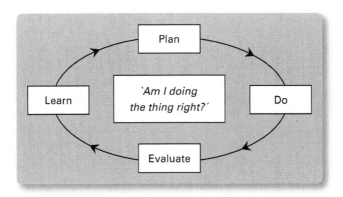

FIGURE 9.3 Deutero or double loop learning

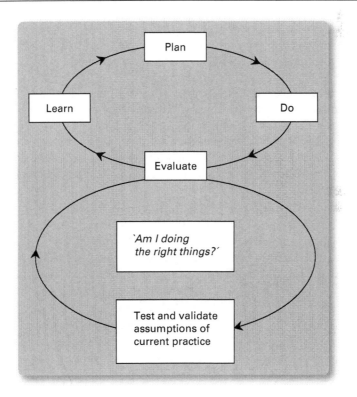

This may be a historical example, but when looking through the financial pages of newspapers it is not too difficult to find illustrations of industries and organizations that have failed to reflect more widely on what they are doing.

Encouraging conditions for reflection

Although reflection-in-action can occur spontaneously within an organization, the possibility of it happening is conditional upon the variety of factors occurring at the time, eg work pressures may minimize the opportunity for reflection. In the research conducted by Seibert (1999), one manager described how, owing to a heavy workload, his reflection was momentary. This does not necessarily minimize the potential for reflective learning from the experience since there may still be potential for profound insights. However, constraining the opportunities for reflection may also severely limit the degree and quality of the reflection and therefore the degree of learning. It is hard both to do and to reflect at the same time when the issues are complex and may not be related.

Five main factors that encourage reflection were identified by Seibert (1999) and are described below:

1 *Autonomy.* Where people work autonomously they are personally responsible for their actions and therefore must think things through and decide for themselves. Where people operate within the responsibility of others there is a danger that they will abdicate the responsibility for thinking and just follow instructions. The degree of autonomy is the responsibility of the organization. Seibert described a manager, Ted, who was given a considerable degree of autonomy while working on the launch of a new frozen food product. On his return from the assignment he experienced a very directive environment that allowed little opportunity for autonomy and reflection. It is easy to imagine the difficulties that could occur in terms of demotivation and a sense of lack of trust among his emotions.

2 *Feedback.* Feedback will also improve the quality of reflection, for without it there would be few ways of measuring performance and benchmarking what had or had not been achieved. For Ted feedback was received from his manager, marketing and sales staff, and retailers. It is not sufficient to know where you are going; you need also to know how well you are doing on the journey.

3 *Interactions with other people.* In his book *The Career is Dead, Long Live the Career*, Hall (1995) maintained that 'other people' were essential to supporting reflection-in-action. Seibert identified three types of interaction between the manager and others:

   – Access to others: a manager's work situation needs to provide interaction with others who have important information.

   – Connections to others: this category is not the same as 'access to others' since it concerns a 'meaningful supportive relationship' (Seibert, 1999: 60) in which bosses, peers, mentors and even spouses give emotional support.

- Stimulation by others: the need for others to provide information, new ideas and perspectives, which encourage the development of ideas.

4 *Pressure*. Promotive pressure is the situation in which managers have a high workload with little time in which to complete it. 'Not surprisingly, this reflection was highly concentrated and of brief duration, often lasting for only a few moments' (Seibert, 1999: 61). Directive pressure is related to the pressure people experience as a result of undertaking a highly visible assignment that focuses attention on their project.

5 *Momentary pressure*. This refers to those few occasions managers have when they can reflect on their work. These occasions are often when the person is involved with other activities such as walking to a meeting, waiting for an answer on the telephone, or even in the lavatory!

The categories described by Seibert above illustrate some of the circumstances when people reflect in the workplace. However, he does not discuss the quality of the reflective process and in particular how effective the insights are. The finding that managers have significant time pressures is nothing new and their limited time to reflect, sometimes only in the toilet, indicates that personal management of time and the creation of thinking time is an essential ingredient if reflection-in-action is to deliver satisfactory results.

The danger of formal education and training

It is only in the past 150 years that we have handed over the responsibility for learning to the educational system. Before then, individuals were more responsible for what they learnt. Today, the result of the abdication of responsibility is that there is a dependence on the teacher. Expressions such as, 'I have never been taught or attended a course so I can't do it', are far from uncommon. In many instances, 'I need to go on a course' provides an excuse to avoid learning. Attending a course is not the only way to learn. This mindset needs to be discouraged because deep and permanent learning is often more likely to occur in the workplace or the home rather than in formalized situations.

Research at the Centre for Creative Leadership and at Honeywell Inc indicated that managers learn more from structured and challenging work experiences than from sitting in the classroom (Seibert, 1999). Five types of experience were found to encourage learning among managers and these are regularly used intentionally by organizations to encourage the development of their managers:

- project or task force – temporary work on a project;
- increase in responsibility – significant increase in size of people, budget or job functions;

- transfer from line to staff responsibilities;
- start-up – creating and developing an area of responsibility from scratch;
- fix-it – resolving a problem in an organization.

The human resource development departments of numerous organizations, including PepsiCo, Hoechst Celanese and General Electric, took managers out of their work environment for workshop-based coached reflection. This reflection occurred both at fixed intervals during a period of work and at its conclusion. The learners were provided with formal tools and structured processes to stimulate reflection.

Critical reflection

The term critical reflection is not to be confused with reflection used in the individual or organizational context. Critical reflection emerged from the work of the Frankfurt School and is often known as critical theory, which encourages emancipation and the development of a just and democratic society. It is illustrated in the work of Habermas (1972), which challenges 'the dominant, science-influenced rationality which privileges means over ends, facts over values, and which perpetuates arid intellectualism at the expense of people's feelings' (Reynolds, 1998: 187). Critical reflection is concerned largely with social issues while reflective practice is predominantly concerned with individual and organizational learning.

Action learning

Action learning is a not dissimilar process to that of reflective practice. The main difference is that action learning is generally located in the workplace. It was originally developed by Reg Revans, a former Olympic long-jumper and Cambridge physicist, who began the process in 1938 while investigating the entry of women into the nursing profession. His main concern was with the divide that occurred between the consultants and administrators (scribes) and the nurses (artisans).

Revans, being a scientist, applied an evolutionary model to individual and organizational learning and stated that learning needs to be equal to or greater than the surrounding change:

Learning $\geq$ Change

Revans also stated that learning consisted of two elements: programmed knowledge (traditional teaching and instruction) and questioning insight:

Learning = f (programmed knowledge + questioning insight); $L = f(P + Q)$

There has been a significant amount of cross-fertilization among many of the contributors to experiential learning. In his book *Developing Effective Managers*, Revans (1971) described an approach to succeeding in managerial objectives, which he called System Beta. This approach he acknowledged was based on the scientific method that he used as a researcher at the Cavendish Laboratories:

1 a stage of observation;

2 a stage of hypothesis or theory;

3 a stage of experiment;

4 a stage of inspection;

5 a stage of consolidation.

Revans (1971: 105–06) explained that this System Beta was a cycle that contained the following elements:

1 an attention-fixing event occurring within a framework of experience;

2 a new constructive relationship perceived in or around this event;

3 an attempt to exploit this relationship for some desired purpose;

4 an audit or inspection of the results of this exploitation;

5 the incorporation (or not) of the relationship into the experience of the manager, namely, a process of learning.

This cycle is very similar to Kolb's learning cycle, which was published two years after a visit to Kolb at MIT by Revans and 21 Belgian managers in February 1969. In addition, illustrating this interconnection of ideas, Revans' early work on action learning has also been credited by Professor Naoto Sasaki, in his book *Management and Industrial Structure in Japan*, with being the foundation for the quality circle concept in Japan. Interestingly, the work of Deming paralleled that of Revans in the form of his quality circle.

In addition to System Beta, Revans developed a contrasting perspective called System Gamma, which considered the 'pre-disposing mental set', ie the subjective consciousness of the manager. Linking the objective System Beta and the subjective System Gamma is System Alpha, which involved personal values, the external environment and internal resources. It asked (Lessem, 1982: 11):

● By what values am I guided?

● What is blocking their fulfilment?

● What can I do against such blockage?

This consideration of values leads to the core of Revans' work. Pedler (1996: 91), in analysing Revans' writings, concluded:

> Revans is a radical and it is clear from his writings that he intends Action Learning to be a deeper, more revolutionary process than just a training

method for 'learning by doing'. Action learning, being about individual and organizational development, contains a *moral philosophy* involving:

- honesty about self
- attempting to do good to the world
- for the purpose of friendship.

One source of Revans' inspiration was the writings of John Locke (1968: 335). Locke argued in *Essay Concerning Human Understanding* that ideas originated from experience:

> Our observations may be employed either about external sensible objects, or about the internal operations of our minds. The former is the source of most of the ideas that we have, and, as it depends 'wholly upon our senses', is called 'sensation'. The latter is a source of ideas which 'every man has wholly in himself', and it might be called 'internal sense'; to it he gives the name 'reflection'.

Another writer to whom Revans referred was Piaget. Revans viewed the following quotation by Piaget (1977: 28) as a definition of action learning:

> Knowledge is derived from action, not in the sense of simple associative responses, but in the much deeper sense of the assimilation of reality into the necessary and general co-ordinations of action. To know an object is to act upon it, in order to grasp the mechanisms of that transformation as they function in connection with the transformative actions themselves. To know is therefore to assimilate reality into structures of transformation, and these are the structures that intelligence constructs as a direct extension of our actions.

This integration of the self and external reality is illustrated in the dialectic of what Lessem (1982: 11), in describing the work of Revans, called 'the interactions between thought and action, intellect and faith, scientific method and personal conviction'. These dualities are very similar to those identified by Dewey: person–nature, subject–object, knowing–doing and mind–body (see Chapter 2).

Defining action learning is not an easy task. Pedler (1996) explained that defining action learning was very difficult and he referred to the fact that Revans never provided a one-sentence definition. Pedler (1996: 13) stated, 'Although the idea may be essentially simple, it is concerned with profound knowledge of oneself and the world, and cannot be communicated as a formula or technique.' Revans (1982: 626–27) did in fact provide a long definition, part of which is reproduced here:

> Action learning is a means of development, intellectual, emotional or physical, that requires its subject, through responsible involvement in some real, complex and stressful problem, to achieve intended change sufficient to improve his observable behaviour henceforth in the problem field. 'Learning-by-Doing' may be perhaps a simpler description of this process, although action learning

programmes assume a design and organization unnecessary in the every day actions that supply the learning of young animals and of small children.

A clearer definition is given by McGill and Beaty (1992: 17):

Action learning is a continuous process of learning and reflection, supported by colleagues, with an intention of getting things done. Through action learning individuals learn with and from each other by working on real problems and reflection on their own experiences. The process helps us to take an active stance towards life and helps to overcome the tendency to think, feel and be passive towards the pressures of life.

McGill and Beaty (1992: 17) explained, 'We all learn through experience by thinking through past events, seeking ideas that make sense of the event and help us to find new ways of behaving in similar situations in the future.' They described how we all use reflection to connect past actions with improving our behaviour in the future. In addition, through the use of reflection we can improve action and 'learning from experience can be enhanced through deliberate attention to this relationship'.

The focus of action learning is mainly on the individual although, of course, the person is operating within an action learning set containing other people. Revans (1982: 632) argued, 'It is development of the self, not merely development by the self of what is known of the external world.' Through the process people actively challenge one another's ideas, encourage people to espouse theories and perceptions that they may not have voiced before and help people consciously to think about other ideas and concepts that might be applied.

Pedler (1996) built on these ideas and his interactions with Revans, and explained that the purpose of action learning was:

- Voluntarily to work on problems of managing and organizing.
- To work on problems that involve the set members.
- To analyse individual perceptions of the problem in order to provide other perspectives and identify courses of action.
- To take action after which it is reported back to the learning set to allow further reflection.
- To support and challenge members to encourage effective learning and action.
- To raise awareness of group processes and encourage improved team-work. The learning set sometimes has a facilitator who helps members develop the skills of action learning.
- To encourage three levels of learning:
  - about the problem;
  - about oneself;
  - about the learning process and 'learning to learn'.

The action learning set

Action learning may occur and be found in self-help groups, support groups, quality circles and learning sets. Learning sets provide a formalized structure within which to encourage learning. In essence there are four main elements in the action learning situation:

- the person – who joins the group voluntarily;
- the learning set – the group of people who meet;
- the problem(s) – which each person brings to the meeting;
- the action – which is taken and learnt from.

Many of the activities that occur within an action learning set also occur naturally in the work situation and it is not uncommon for people to say that they learn through discussing things with colleagues. The main difference is that action learning is formalized and thus legitimizes the process and provides a clear focus on a specific problem or group of problems. It also occurs with a specific group of people who meet on a regular basis and not in an ad hoc manner. The latter can lead to insufficient time and focus being given to the problems and learning opportunities.

Much of the reflection-in-action learning occurs through the dissection and examination of experience within the group and by the various individuals concerned. The 'action' part of the action learning is concerned with a project, the extent of which is decided by the group. This can be small and discrete, or as large and complicated as the group choose it to be.

There is no fixed duration for an action learning set or a project. On many occasions a project is brought to a group and may continue after the group has disbanded. In the reality of working life, problems are rarely completely solved; instead they change shape and/or lead into other related problems. As each issue is explored and addressed, so another surfaces ad infinitum.

Through reflection we are able to ensure that rather than having one year's experience 10 times, we have 10 years' experience where each year builds upon the learning that occurred in the previous year. That is to say, action learning enables us to build on what we have experienced.

It is not necessary in an action learning set that the people know each other, nor do they need to be experts on the subject in question. Their role is not to provide advice, albeit this can be of value; rather it is to act as devil's advocates and question and challenge the assumptions that underpin the reflections of others in the learning set.

The nature of the issues that are brought to the set can be placed on a spectrum from the very personal to those of concern to the organization. In order for the set to function effectively it is necessary for there to be trust and confidence among the members. Through this supportive environment, feelings and emotions can be explored, as well as practical issues, in a confidential environment. This takes time to establish and as confidence builds in the group so more will be shared. Action points may be minuted but the discussion is not normally included in any record of the meeting.

Although one objective of the meeting is the production of better action and results within the organization, probably the main purpose is the development of the individual. The impact of this learning is then likely to have a longer-lasting impact than the transitory influencing of a project. This reflects the adage, 'Give people a fish and they can eat for a day. Teach them to fish and they feed themselves for life.'

There are two roles in an action learning set: the presenter and the set member. While the presenter is providing information about the project, it is the 'contractual duty' of the other set members to explore the project and help the presenter to discover new insights and strategies with the intention of resolving the problem.

Some action learning sets have facilitators and this can provide a number of advantages. Facilitators normally possess much more experience than the other members of the set and thus ensure that the process is more effective and applied to achieving learning. The facilitator also does not have concerns of her or his own and can give more attention to the projects of the other members.

Members of the set are encouraged to use the word 'I' in order to indicate not only that it is the person him- or herself who is involved but also that the person is responsible for his or her actions. It also avoids confusion about the use of the words 'you' (indicating I or me) or 'one' (people in general).

It is important, too, that the members carefully analyse the project to identify the 'problems' of the presenter. It is not uncommon for the initial problem to be underlain by a more fundamental problem that is different from the original one. Likewise, the presenter may think he or she has a specific problem and depart from the meeting with a very different one. Feedback techniques such as rephrasing and gently probing can enhance the quality of the interaction between the presenter and the other members of the set.

As with counselling, there is much to be said for each presenter discovering his or her own solutions and new perspectives on the projects. To be provided with an answer dilutes the learning process and may result in the presenter not buying into the solution. The process may take much longer when the answer is not directly provided. Furthermore, an answer may not be the answer that is most appropriate to the situation since the presenter is often the most knowledgeable person about his or her situation.

Specific instances of the culture of learning hindering the learning of individuals include: providing answers too readily and allowing certain individuals to coast through the process without really examining their circumstances; allowing members to be too vague and not specific with their action plans and presentations; members receiving support when they make their presentations but not contributing to the process when others make their presentations.

In addition to the identification of more effective ways of working and also perceiving issues there are other benefits from undertaking the process of action learning. McGill and Beaty (1992: 190) stated that these include:

- enhanced effectiveness in working with the range of relationships at work, including teamworking, developmental roles such as mentoring, and working with and encouraging cultural and transpersonal change;
- capacity to learn, reframe and empower self and others;
- ability to live with uncertainty and ambiguity;
- enhanced capacity to undertake project management;
- developing skills of active facilitation that can be utilized to manage group processes.

In summary the basic elements of an action learning set are:

- Ground rules may be developed by the members.
- Ground rules may be changed following discussion by the members.
- Equal time should be allotted to each member.
- Action plans should be agreed.
- All members should make a commitment to attend.
- Each member's project is dealt with in turn.
- Members need to develop the skill of listening and receiving information.
- The presenter should clearly explain what he or she is looking for from the presentation so that the other members can focus their attention.
- Feedback should be conducted in a constructive and supportive spirit, which may require the development of these skills.
- Issues discussed in the set should be confidential.

The action learning set should also regularly review how effective it is in the process of encouraging development among its members. It should reconsider its ground rules and the culture that is operating in order to identify constraints and limitations that are holding back learning.

Timing and duration of learning sets

The frequency and duration of action learning set meetings is dependent on the particular circumstances and those involved. McGill and Beaty recommend that the presenter has half an hour to discuss his or her project, although more can be allocated. The frequency and duration may be dependent upon the organizational commitment to this learning process and many meetings occur on a monthly basis and continue for a period of between six months and a year.

Time needs to be dedicated and timetabled; otherwise other work pressures may squeeze out the time for the meetings. The use of the time should be carefully allocated in order that it is not wasted in general discussion and being sidetracked. A businesslike approach will provide momentum to the presentation and discussions, and ensure that people receive an equal consideration of their project.

Essentially, each meeting normally consists of a series of presentations from each of the members. This is likely to be the case even where all the people are working on the same project since they each have specific tasks and, more importantly, they all have different perceptions and feelings about the project and therefore will benefit from a personal examination of their own circumstances. The process for each individual at each meeting might be:

- action points from the last meeting;
- points completed and deferred;
- objectives to be achieved from this presentation;
- what the presenter learnt from completing and not completing action points.

Problems and action learning

The main starting point for action learning is for each member of the group to bring a problem to the meeting. It is only by being challenged and through engagement with the problem that people will find the opportunity for learning. For some people the word problem is a difficult one to use because of its negative connotations. Thus, it is quite satisfactory to call it a concern, an issue, an opportunity, a project or a task. The important thing is that this problem is the beginning of the investigation towards discovering solutions to the difficulty and identifying new personal perceptions about it and oneself.

Revans distinguished between what he called problems and puzzles. A puzzle is an issue about which there is already some knowledge or solution that might provide an answer. A problem is an issue to which there is no direct source to which we can go for an answer. He also identified three key questions (Pedler, 1996: 73):

1 Who knows about the problem?
2 Who cares about the problem?
3 Who can do anything about the problem?

Pedler emphasized the fact that much management education concentrates only on the thinking about the problem and very little on the emotional aspects of willingness and commitment to resolving the problem.

There are six main areas to consider in the identification of a problem:

1 It is valuable when identifying a problem to be used for action learning to be clear what it is about and what measures are going to be used to judge the level of achievement. One approach to this can be to write down the problem in one sentence. This will crystallize the issue and allow focus by yourself and the other members of the set.

2 Identify the benefits associated with addressing the problem. If you cannot identify any then there will be little motivation to resolving the issue and the energy will dissipate.

3 Choose a problem that is important to you and your organization. If the problem is perceived to be trivial then it will not occupy your attention and energies nor will it be something the organization will actively support in terms of time and resources.

4 Set yourself benchmarks to assess your progress in resolving the problem; this may also be done through consultation with other people who may have a vested interest in your quest.

5 Try to forecast possible difficulties that might arise, and work out strategies for overcoming these. One of the reasons the problem exists is probably that there are a number of difficulties that have previously prevented any action being taken on the problem.

6 Will the culture of the organization support action learning? Accepting that problems exist within an organization is an awkward one for some individuals and organizations since it may challenge the status quo and cast doubt on the abilities of people. It is not an easy situation to manage if notions of infallibility exist and egos are placed on the line. For this reason it is essential to the success of the action learning programme that there is commitment and openness across the organization and particularly from the top. Without support, attempts to address problems will be stifled and pushed to the periphery where they will be forgotten about. For action learning to be successful, as with almost all organizational development initiatives, there is a need for full organizational support in a trusting atmosphere, which is easy to talk about but difficult to deliver.

The action learning cycle is shown in Figure 9.4.

Strategies for learning and change

With the learning cycle there are four distinct stages, which involve: a concrete experience; thinking about the experience; generalizing and conceptualizing about the experience; and, finally, applying these ideas and thoughts to new situations. It can be argued that if we do not get as far as stage three then we have not really learnt from the experience. In stage three we make

FIGURE 9.4 The action learning cycle

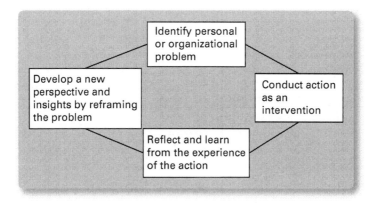

links and connections to our previous experience and knowledge held in our heads. Without the links the experience may have little value in learning.

The learning cycle is used by the Learning from Experience Trust (1987) to construct a learning approach. First, they recommend that we draw upon our life history and draw a life chart that chronicles all the major incidents in our life. The next step is to categorize the various experiences under headings such as education, work, relationships, travel, etc. By doing this, other experiences will emerge and these can be added to the categories.

The next stage is to ask who, what, when, where, why and how about one of the experiences. Also, did it involve someone else and did it happen as predicted? When this is done, describe your thoughts before, during, after and much later after the event. Then do a similar exercise with your feelings before, during, after and much later after the event. It may prove to be helpful to discuss the event with another person and reflect on how it changed your thoughts and feelings. What did you learn from the event and how have your expectations changed as a result of the experience?

The final stage is to analyse a subsequent event where your learning was applied. In what ways were you more able to deal with these circumstances as a result of your learning?

You may also project your thoughts forward and imagine the various scenarios that you might encounter and to which you might relate your previous learning. Consider how you might think and behave in this future event.

Essentially the four stages can be summarized as:

1 the experience;

2 main elements of the experience;

3 how the experience affected me and what I learnt;

4 situations where I have used, or will use, the previous experience to better effect.

Learning from experience is often more effective than traditional learning for children. At Raleigh Hunter Elementary School in the United States, children were not very successful in learning and the school was perceived to be a 'sink' school. As a result of a change in philosophy, greater emphasis was given to experiential and practical learning. This change had a major impact on the school – children's concentration levels increased, test scores improved and behavioural problems decreased. In addition, the turn-around in the overall school performance began to attract children from other families in neighbouring districts. The school is now perceived as a success and a role model for other schools.

It is not only in schools that experiential learning can improve performance. Universities, businesses, the probation service, etc also have problems in preparing students for work demands and difficulties in the real world. Hall *et al* (1978: 1) stated, 'Universities have trouble preparing their students for the job demands and problems they will encounter in the "real world"... most academic courses do a better job of providing theory than action.' To ameliorate this problem, Hall *et al* proposed redressing the balance between theory and action through the use of personal experience and action exercises.

Experiences in Management and Organizational Behaviour, written by Hall *et al* (1978: 2), consisted of many experiential exercises that were designed to encourage the transfer of learning from the university to the workplace. It is based upon a number of assumptions:

1 Learning is more effective when it is an active rather than a passive process.

2 Problem-centred learning is more enduring than theory-based learning.

3 Two-way communication produces better learning than one-way communication.

4 Participants will learn more when they share control over and responsibility for the learning process than when this responsibility lies solely with the group leader.

5 Learning is most effective when thought and action are integrated.

Being and presence

The successful application of the self in learning and development work, and in organizational development (OD) and coaching practices, is significantly dependent upon the ability to be present. Jung (1971) made reference to the self as 'total personality': it included the known and unknown. The known was referred to as the 'public persona', while the unknown and hidden was referred to as the 'shadow'. Presence is not manufactured, and self and other awareness of both the persona and shadow is vital. Tolbert and

Hanafin (2006) suggest the following six elements for cultivating presence in Organizational Consulting:

1 Continue to work unresolved issues and unfinished business.
2 Commit time and energy to active reflection.
3 Actively seek feedback from colleagues, clients and friends.
4 Live life fully.
5 Invest in a broad worldview.
6 Experiment with new ways of being.

Conclusion

Learning is a form of change, and the theories of learning can be considered as the theories of change. Through a focus on improvement or the solution of problems the learning gap between current position and desired future position can be addressed. This is precisely what happens with reflective practice and action learning in the development of individual and group learning through a consideration of problems and challenges. They can be used in the work situation but are equally effective in other circumstances. What becomes clear from the chapter is that it is experience that unifies these approaches to learning and gives us greater insight into how we can structure our own personal learning. Another factor arising from the chapter is the value of problems. They can be used to reflect on actions and oneself to develop new ways of thinking, behaving and being. Without problems it is unlikely that we would change what we do.

The other clear theme is that many of the developers of learning theories and learning strategies have drawn from one another. They have cross-fertilized their ideas, forming a rich, eclectic and collective whole.

PART THREE
Experiential learning and the future

Imagining and experiencing the future

10

Faith in the power of intelligence to imagine a future in which the projection of the desirable in the present, and to invent the instrumentalities of its realization, is our salvation. And it is a faith that must be nurtured and made articulate. DEWEY, 1917: 69

Introduction

The reflective process is an essential strategy for effective learning and in Chapter 2 we investigated the nature of reflection and how it was possible to consider it from three temporal perspectives: retrospective, concurrent and prospective. Retrospective reflection involves looking back on a past experience and learning from the events that occurred. This is what Schön (1983) termed reflection-on-action. Concurrent reflection involves a consideration of what we are doing in the present moment, eg adjusting our language and teaching style to accommodate children or adults who may not fully have understood what we had been saying. This is what Schön (1983) termed reflection-in-action.

Remarkably, Schön did not discuss the application of prospective reflection or reflecting on the future, which is an essential ingredient of almost all actions – if we do not have an intention, a plan that we have conceived, then actions will have little or no directive purpose. By imagining what might be possible we are then able to develop operational strategies that hopefully will deliver the concrete reality. In Chapter 7, which investigates emotions, it can be seen that these three forms of learning – retrospective, concurrent and prospective – are brought together in one of the trilogies by Wilkes (1999: 24), who described the need to: 'Revise the past. Revisit the present. Redirect the future.'

In this final chapter we will look at prospective learning and consider reasons why it has been largely overlooked. We will then examine imagination and look at the nature of problems and challenges, a recurring theme in this book, and how they are a necessary catalyst for change. We will then look at how the different parts of our brains can be in conflict with one another and thereby reduce our performance – we draw on examples from playing tennis.

Temporal limitations of Schön's reflective practice

Reflection-on-the-future, or reflection-before-action, would appear to be little discussed in spite of it appearing to be a natural human condition. There are a few acknowledgements in the literature, eg Van Manen (1991) who discussed the notion of 'anticipatory reflection' which involved consideration or planning of an event. Also, Greenwood (1998: 1049) wrote that: 'This Schönian model of reflective practice is essentially flawed in that it fails to recognize the importance of reflection-before-action.' The important practical application of this future reflection has application across all areas of life, particularly health care:

> To begin with, Schön's emphasis on reflection-in-and-on-action implicitly undervalues reflection-before-action. It is at least arguable, however, that much of the suffering in the world, including that caused by nurses' errors, could have been avoided had practitioners stopped to think about what they intended to do and how they intended to do it before they actually did it.
>
> (Greenwood, 1993: 1186)

Wilson (2008) identified five main reasons why it has been rarely discussed in the literature resulting in a lack of codification within reflective practice. First, reflecting on past and present actions has an inherent and tacit recognition that the purpose of this action is to improve future performance. That this is so obvious that it need not be considered might be considered as the 'reflective elephant in the room syndrome'. What is the purpose of reflection if not to improve subsequent performance or understand events? Thus, Moon (2000: 49) suggested that:

> Anticipation may imply a combination of reflection and imagination. In this combination, reflection-on-action – the revisiting of prior experiences of the same or similar events – is stretched into the future with the use of imagination. Imagination may work with the outcomes of reflection-on-action, but would not be considered to be part of reflection.

A similar perspective is illustrated by MacDonald *et al* (2005: 2) who stated:

> Two objectives drive student portfolios. One objective looks back and the other looks forward. Looking back involves reflecting on achievement and learning. Looking forward involves identifying gaps and future development opportunities based upon reflection... As with student portfolios, both past and future reflection is an element of teacher portfolios.

Moreover, Doncaster and Thorne (2000: 397) discussed reflection and planning as part of professional doctorates and stated: 'This task focuses heavily on the processes of planning. It is forward looking, but builds on both the research capability that candidates by this time must have demonstrated.'

Second, the semantic understanding of reflection suggests a consideration of what has happened rather than what might happen. It is not possible to reflect on something that has yet to happen without the use of imagination as (Moon, 2000: 97) argued:

> Reflection could be said to be involved in anticipation and planning, but it needs to be combined with imagination to extend its application into the future. The word 'reflection' has the connotation of a link to the past – going back over ideas and experiences or gathering current ideas so that thinking or learning may be progressed.

Third, reflection is generally considered to deal with concrete reality. We cannot address or change behaviour if something has yet to happen. Both reflection-on-action and reflection-in-action are rooted in the notion of experiential learning. That is, they both link theory and practice in a cycle. Theory informs and is tested by putting it into practice. The practice exposes the theory to intense scrutiny identifying what parts of the theory work and what don't work. Thus, the theory is refined and improved through practical application (Dewey, 1938). Dewey also defined reflective thought as:

> Active, persistent and careful consideration of any belief or supposed form of knowledge in the light of the grounds that support it and further conclusions to which it leads... it includes a conscious and voluntary effort to establish belief upon a firm basis of evidence and rationality.

> (1938: 9)

Another writer who emphasized the importance of developing knowledge through real interaction with the world was Freire (1982: 56) who maintained that: 'Problem posing education bases itself on creativity and stimulates true reflection and action on reality.'

A fourth reason for there being little emphasis on the future is that the very terms 'practice' or 'practitioner' both imply practice, ie the act of doing something. Thinking or reflecting about something ethereal is not doing.

Fifth, there may be a self-fulfilling prophecy in operation. Because there has been little exploration of the future temporal dimension it has not entered the mainstream of reflective practice. It is argued here that this reduced level of thought about the future constrains a holistic consideration of reflection and thereby inhibits the full development of professional practice.

A sixth point can be added. How can we use existing forms of reflection, ie reflection-on-action and reflection-in-action to help with new and original problems and randomness? (Taleb, 2007). We cannot depend solely upon reflection on past or even current events that are largely of benefit for incremental improvements. Creating new and innovative solutions to future challenges require us to speculate on the future, not rely upon the past.

Finally, if we accept the argument that reflective practice involves a consideration of the future then it should be made explicit. Reflection on the past and present is strongly emphasized in the literature but the future tends to be less considered. Given that the future is where we are all heading it demands more systematic consideration and this will now be considered in the next section.

Reflecting on the future

The third and final stage in this chronological consideration of reflection is to look at how we might reflect on the future. This is achieved by considering or imagining various possibilities and the strategies that are required to achieve them. By imagining or reflecting on what might be possible we are then able to develop operational strategies that hopefully will deliver the concrete reality.

When we reflect or speculate about ideas and the way things might be in the future, we are often exploring the potential to achieve them and their possible consequences (Markman *et al*, 2009; Bar, 2011). This speculation is often driven by desires and impulses to improve upon current circumstances and they have a clear purpose, eg to find a more effective way of achieving work targets; to plan a holiday that takes into account all the family's wishes; to examine what might be the best response when our boss asks why a certain task has not been undertaken, etc.

All these examples are testimony to a natural human condition, which is to speculate or reflect on what the future might bring and, importantly, be influenced. For example, Battista and Hodge (1999: 1464) considered what the turn of the millennium might bring and stated:

> For decision-makers at all levels in rapidly changing health care systems,
> reflecting on the future of health technology assessment is critical in an
> environment that is increasingly dominated by cost-effectiveness, evidence based
> medicine and changing ideas of accountability.

Although it is not possible to reflect on concrete experiences that have yet to happen, it is possible to give deep consideration to trends and future scenarios. One relatively successful application of scenario planning was that conducted in South Africa towards the end of apartheid. There was concern that the country might face serious civil disturbance and therefore the Mont Fleur scenarios were constructed and then discussed among all the main actors (Kahane, 2004). Four main pictures were painted of what the future might hold, including the continuation of apartheid, weak government, economic collapse, and inclusive democracy and economic growth. Through discussion and examination of future possibilities a consensus was developed which enabled a smoother transition to an open democracy.

Unlike the past, which cannot be changed, only reinterpreted, it is possible to have a variety of futures. There is not, as many people subconsciously believe, only one future but there are many possible alternatives unless one is a fatalist who believes that they have no real control over their destiny and that all is preordained. Many people, on the other hand, believe that they possess the power to influence their own future and that of their organization. In order to create a future we need first to be able to identify where we wish to go. Through reflection on current and former experiences we may project a variety of scenarios and examine what might happen. It is a form of future reflection and it allows us to examine pathways without the necessity of expending energy and other resources on inefficient or futile courses of action.

We are able to use our reflection to speculate about possible alternatives and we are able to select a course of action that can lead towards the achievement of our goals and objectives. Circumstances may intervene to hinder or prevent the achievement of our goals, not least our own limitations. But, at least we have the ability to weigh up the possibilities of success by taking into account our own strengths and weaknesses.

However, this line of reasoning is somewhat counterintuitive to much human behaviour as has been described above (eg Battista and Hodge, 1999). Greenwood (1993) maintained that human action was intentional, ie it was purposive and directional. In order to achieve an objective we first have to plan what needs to be done to achieve the objectives. She used the example of someone wanting to go to London. In order to get there one first had to catch a train; to catch the train one first had to get to the station, etc. In other words, our actions are determined from our intentions. Argyris *et al* (1985: 82) stated that people: 'do not just happen to act in a particular way. Rather, their action is designed; and as agents, they are responsible for the design.' This case was also presented by Greenwood (1993: 1186) who stated, 'Reflection-in-and-on-action, by contrast, requires the agent to reason from her actions to her intentions.' She also added that it was necessary for human beings to respond to action feedback in an iterative manner.

The case for reflecting on the future is well made by Greenwood (1993). Moon (2000: 49) too, appeared to warm to the concept, particularly later in her book. In spite of earlier scepticism suggesting that: 'Imagination… would not be considered to be part of reflection,' she (2000: 180) suggested a series of guided phases to encourage reflective practice, the last one being particularly pertinent.

Phase 1: Develop awareness of the nature of current practice.

Phase 2: Clarify the new learning and how it relates to current understanding.

Phase 3: Integrate new learning and current practice.

Phase 4: Anticipate or imagine the nature of improved practice.

Furthermore, later in the book Moon (2000: 207) once again returns to a consideration of the future by briefly discussing guided fantasy. She wrote, 'Leaders might be led to imagine themselves performing effectively in a situation that they fear, such as examinations or a difficult professional situation.'

By now it should be evident that reflecting-on-the-future should be a key component of reflection, therefore, to provide more precision a definition would be helpful:

> Future reflection is the act or process of reflecting on desirable and possible futures with the purpose of evaluating them as well as considering strategies intended to achieve the objective(s).

Imagination

Imagination is one of the most powerful mental tools we have at our disposal. Without this ability to speculate about what might be, we would be imprisoned in a world of fatalism waiting for whatever might befall us. We would be buffeted by whatever forces with which we came into contact and just react rather than attempting to shape our destinies at least to some degree.

Without the ability to project our thoughts into the future we would be like a ship without a rudder; there could be no direction other than drifting at the mercy of the tides. If we lacked the ability to imagine the future there could be no plans, no hopes, no aspirations, no wants, no dreams and no desires (Wilson, 2012b). There would only be ennui and a nihilistic approach to living life now with no regard to the consequences for the future. This would be a very negative existence and indeed it is hard to think how the human species could have survived without the power to investigate the myriad futures that might be possible.

Fortunately, the world is not as bleak as that which has been described in the preceding paragraphs. We are able to use our imagination to 'mental time travel' (Tulving, 1972); we can speculate about possible alternatives; and we are able to select a course of action that can lead towards the achievement of our goals and objectives. Circumstances may intervene to hinder or prevent the achievement of our goals, not least our own limitations, but, at least we have the ability to weigh up the possibilities of success by taking into account our own strengths and weaknesses. Sailing around the world like Ellen MacArthur may be a dream for those who are more adventurous, but the majority would recognize their limitations and fears, and opt for something more achievable such as sailing a dinghy on a relatively calm lake, or taking a sightseeing boat along the River Seine in Paris.

It is only through imagination that individuals and society have advanced and prospered. It enables us to learn from the future, and Dewey (1934: 267), recognizing this importance, stated:

> [Imagination] designates a quality that animates and pervades all processes of making an observation. It is a way of seeing and feeling things as they compose an integral whole. It is the large and generous blending of interests at the point where the mind comes into contact with the world. When the old and familiar

things are made new in experience, there is imagination. When the new is created, the far and strange become the most natural inevitable things in the world. There is always some measure of adventure in the meeting of mind and universe, and this adventure is, in its measure, imagination.

Our imagination is extraordinarily powerful and it provides us with the capability to explore possible options and potentially outline different future pathways. Indeed, Killingsworth and Gilbert (2010 argue that, "'stimulus-independent thought' or 'mind-wandering' appears to be the brain's default mode of operation." Given that the brain naturally spends a significant proportion of the day either consciously imagining or in absent-minded explorations, more attention should be given to building upon these natural processes. Organizations and the education system should encourage people to develop their skills of imagination, vision, creativity and foresight rather than criticising people for daydreaming.

There is a relatively clear process through which we investigate and act on our intentions. Dewey (1938) maintained that when we become aware of an impulse it becomes translated into a desire – something that we wish to achieve. However, neither an impulse nor a desire is the same thing as a purpose, which represents an achievement or outcome. Acting on an impulse or desire requires an examination of the potential consequences to determine whether they will have a positive or negative result. This examination requires the frontal cortex of the brain to assess whether desires and emotions that feed through the amygdala (which activates the emotional parts of the brain) are appropriate (Goleman, 1996). Dewey (1938) explained that a purpose is a complex operation and involves three main stages:

- Observation of the circumstances and environmental factors in operation at the time.
- Knowledge of what has occurred in similar circumstances in the past is applied to the observation of current factors. This knowledge is based upon personal experience and that of others together with advice and what we have read and learnt about second-hand.
- Application of judgement. This takes into account the observations and recollections to assess their importance and determine which is the most appropriate course of action. Judging what is realistic and achievable, and the potential consequences of a course of action, is a critical part of the process.

In 1938, Dewey was aware of the importance of thinking about a desire or impulse before acting upon it. This use of judgement was an important one from an educational perspective, and he (1938: 81) stressed, 'The crucial educational problem is that of procuring the postponement of immediate action upon desire until observation and judgement have intervened.'

The process of thinking about the consequences of a desire before acting upon it is increasingly important. We often talk about the difficulty of choosing between 'heart' and 'mind', ie the distinction between what our emotions are encouraging us to do and the more analytical reasoning of the brain. Drawing on neurological research, we now know that the emotions originate in the limbic system, while the neocortex allows us to think more rationally about the facts before responding. Evolutionary physiology suggests that it was the emotional parts of the brain that developed first, thus allowing us to respond with alacrity to threats from the likes of sabre-toothed tigers. However, as the threats diminished it became more important to think through a course of action about a possible threat before responding. For example, our boss attempting to bully us may cause an instinctive desire to punch him or her, but in most cases, hopefully, reason will take over and we will address the issue through more appropriate means, eg a grievance procedure. More significantly, the 9/11 Commission Report stated:

> There were failures of imagination, policy, capabilities, and management. The most important failure was one of imagination.

Imagination versus action

When people are accused of daydreaming it is usually in a pejorative sense, ie they are wasting time doing nothing or idly speculating about things that could never have any concrete reality. Of course, there is a danger that we can become lost in daydreams that are unattainable, as happened to Walter Mitty (Thurber, 1939) and Billy Liar (Waterhouse, 1959). In some respects this may be a waste of mental energy since the brain might be used for more constructive purposes. Indeed, perpetually wishing for things that are highly unlikely to materialize may be demotivating and harmful in its effects. Dewey (1938: 81) succinctly summed up this potential for wasting mental energy with the statement, 'If wishes were horses, beggars would ride.'

Alternatively, the process of daydreaming may be viewed more positively because it allows the brain to relax and enables it to structure, and store in the memory, information that might be used at a future date. Furthermore, daydreaming may be a means of energizing and exercising the brain when external stimuli are limited (Christoff *et al*, 2009).

The notions of daydreaming and imagination are not too disparate and may sometimes be interchangeable. However, on investigating them more closely it can be argued that daydreaming in its more negative sense implies futile speculation about unachievable objectives. Imagination, on the other hand, is perceived as being much more positive; hence the accusation that someone lacks imagination is seen as rather critical.

We saw earlier how the stages of an impulse may be translated ultimately into an action through a consideration of the requirements and demands needed to achieve an objective. Unfortunately, not all learning experiences are positive ones and these can mentally scar the individuals concerned.

We described in Chapter 2 three types of behaviour by people who have made a mistake: some people recognized the mistake, learnt new behaviour and so avoided the mistake in the future; some didn't learn and continued to make the same mistake time after time; and some were so traumatized by an experience that they avoided any potential of involving themselves in a similar experience again.

Staying within a safe and familiar comfort zone does have its benefits in the short term, but in the longer term it can also cause claustrophobia and stagnation. The lack of challenges minimizes the chances we have to learn new things and develop new conceptual frameworks. Failing to move from the comfort zone into the challenge zone removes most of the opportunities for learning. Postle (1993: 35) stated that:

> We often cling, with the intensity of addiction, to the comfort that comes from staying with our preferred mode and keeping away from the other modes.
> I remain convinced that this is usually because at some point in our history, one or another – or all – of the four modes of learning may have become debilitated or ruined. If this debilitation or damage was severe, whether locally or generally, then staying with the preferred mode may also successfully defend us against the feelings associated with that early hurt. If so, then our interest in action, *or dreaming up futures* [our emphasis], or caring, or arguing, whichever most keeps quiet our painful history, can indeed come to have the intensity of addiction.

It would appear, therefore, that we should add an element of caution to the use of imagination. While it fires our motivation it can also constrain our activity by locking us into idle speculation that may achieve very little. However, on the whole, the limitations of imagination are relatively small in comparison to the numerous benefits that can accrue from attempting to chart our future.

Mental fitness for the future

Have you ever broken an arm, leg or some other part of your anatomy and had it bound up in a plaster cast for a period of time? When the plaster was removed you would probably have noticed that the muscles surrounding the break were much weaker than before. Neurological researchers have discovered that not only are the muscles weaker but so too is the brain tissue associated with the movement of those muscles. The longer the body part is encased in plaster the greater the shrinkage of the brain.

As the development of scanning and imaging technology has grown so too has our knowledge of how the brain operates. In one experiment, research was conducted into the effect of physical and mental practice of tensing a finger in the left hand. During a four-week period involving five sessions per week, half the participants carried out physical exercises. The other people undertook a similar number of exercises but this was all done mentally. At the end of the period the ones who had done the physical exercises had increased their strength by 33 per cent. A control group who had done nothing showed no change. And the virtual exercisers improved their finger strength by 22 per cent! (Yue and Cole, 1992). The increase in strength had resulted from changes in the brain.

In another exercise, participants mentally rehearsed a five-finger piano exercise for two hours a day over five days (Pascual-Leone *et al*, 1995). Brain scans revealed that the area of the brain associated with the fingers had expanded over the period of the exercises. Thus, it becomes clear that if we project ideas into the future we are likely to increase the number of connections within the brain and thereby increase the chances of us being more effective. When we consider imagination in this light it is possible to view it as a form of mental exercise designed to increase the chances of success in a future activity.

Imagining the future

> Imagination is more important than knowledge.
> To raise new questions, new possibilities, to regard old problems from a new angle, requires creative imagination and marks a real advance in science.
>
> (Albert Einstein)

One of the main contributors to the subject of imagination was Gareth Morgan (1997b) in his book *Imaginization*. Morgan (1997b: 2) explained, 'Imaginization is about improving our abilities to see and understand a situation in new ways.' The book provided a number of strategies to develop the mind and encouraged the development of new perspectives and ways of thinking.

In the most basic sense, imaginization invites a way of thinking. It encourages us to become our own theorists and to feel comfortable about acting on the basis of our insights. It invites us to develop a skill that I believe we all have, even though we may not realize that this is the case. By recognizing this, and thinking creatively and intelligently about ourselves and our situations, we can 'push the envelope' on our realities and reshape them positively (Morgan, 1997b: 16).

To push the envelope on our realities and positively reshape them requires us to reflect and see past experiences in a new light – in other words this is a form of retrospective learning. It also requires us to place ourselves in new situations that present new challenges and opportunities for learning, ie prospective learning.

The difficulty is that we frequently fail to push the envelope and become entrapped in repetitious behaviour or habit, which Dewey described as 'the great flywheel of society' (Miettinen, 2000: 68). Revans expressed the danger of getting trapped in a particular routine or habit of which we were not aware and thus being unable to see or comprehend other ways of acting. Both our thought and language are closely interlinked and provide us with lenses with which we view the world. In this way our understanding is significantly influenced by the language we have at our disposal and the experiences that we have undergone. This perspective is endorsed by Sapir (1987), who maintained that 'language and our thought grooves are inextricably interwoven, [and] are, in a sense, one and the same'.

It would appear that our ability to comprehend is related to our use of language, which can liberate us or imprison us. The difficulty when we are trapped within a groove is that we are unable to recognize this and thus are unable to take action to remedy the problem. To avoid getting tramlined within a habit we need to be able to take a new and fresh perspective that allows us to learn in different ways. One of these approaches is through the use of metaphors, which Morgan (1997a) discussed in *Images of Organisations*. He (1997a: 4–5) stated, 'The use of metaphor implies a way of thinking and a way of seeing that pervade how we understand our world generally', and perhaps more significantly, 'all theory is metaphor'. Chapter 5 discusses the nature of storytelling and metaphors.

Through his research, Morgan identified a number of metaphors that allowed us to think about issues from a variety of perspectives. Each metaphor provided insights and also constrained our ways of thinking. For example, if we think of the organization as a machine and the people working in it as the cogs, then when there is a problem we may conclude that the best solution is to replace the cogs. On the other hand, if we envisage an organization as an organism then it is difficult to think of replacing parts of it through amputation. Rather, we will encourage the organism to grow, which might mean investing in educating and training the workforce. The types of metaphors Morgan identified were:

1 the organization as a machine;

2 the organization as an organism;

3 the organization as a brain;

4 the organization as a culture;

5 the political organization;

6 the organization as a psychic prison;

7 the organization as a flux and transformation;

8 the organization as an instrument of domination.

Through the use of metaphors we can gain different understandings on the world and ourselves. Aristotle in his *Rhetoric* (1946) was the first to discuss the value of metaphors and stated: 'midway between the unintelligible and the commonplace, it is metaphor which most produces knowledge' (cited in Morgan, 1997a: 379). When we use different metaphors they provide us with different perspectives, in other words different dimensions of the truth. As we discussed in Chapter 2, it is difficult to understand completely what we mean when we consider the concept of a chair. This dilemma about the nature of knowledge is discussed by Morgan (1997b: 279), who stated:

> Knowledge as objective or literal truth places too much emphasis on the object of knowledge and not enough on the paradigms, perspectives, assumptions, language games, and frames of reference of the observer. The challenge before us now is to achieve a better balance, by recognizing that all knowledge is the product of an interpretive process. To achieve this, we need fresh metaphors for thinking about the process through which knowledge is generated. Instead of placing emphasis on the need for 'solid,' 'literal,' 'foundational,' 'objective Truth,' we need more dynamic modes of understanding that show how knowledge results from some kind of implicit or explicit 'conversation,' 'dialogue,' 'engagement,' or interaction between the interests of people and the world in which they live.

The value of problems

> We cannot solve our problems with the same thinking we used when we created them.
>
> (Albert Einstein)

Problems, paradoxically, have both a negative and positive aspect. From a negative perspective a problem implies that we have a current state of affairs that is unsatisfactory and needs to be resolved. From a positive perspective, a problem provides us with the opportunity to improve upon the current situation. Without awareness of a problem we will continue with our unenlightened interaction with the world. Recognizing a problem allows us to advance and improve on the current circumstances. A problem might be that we are hungry and we need to eat; it might be that we want promotion at work, which encourages search activity to achieve this advancement; it might also be an argument we have had with a partner, which requires us to assess what we think and how we behave.

Revans talked about the notion of there needing to be a problem that exercises the mind to finding commitment to a solution. The presence of a problem indicates a challenge to the mental status quo. Morgan (1997b: 13) recognized the value of these challenges and stated:

> Ambiguity, uncertainty, questioning, instability, risk, chance encounter, crisis, openness, quest, challenge: these seem to be the characteristics of situations in which innovation thrives, and which systems of shared meaning need to support... One needs, in short, to encourage understandings that generate capacities for learning and continuous self-organization and an ability to deal with crisis and opportunity positively. Our capacities for imaginization can serve us well here, helping us to mobilize the power of shared understanding in fluid, creative ways.

In attempting to deal with problems we may have emotional blocks that prevent us from seeing things in a different way and thus from developing new schemas or conceptual frameworks. In Piaget's terms we reject a situation because we cannot incorporate it within our way of seeing the world. By not adjusting to the problem it continues to remain. These emotional blocks consist of various types, and Adams (1987: 42) includes the following:

1 fear that we may make a mistake, fail or risk;
2 inability to tolerate ambiguity; overriding desires for security or order; 'no appetite for chaos';
3 preference for judging ideas, rather than generating them;
4 inability to relax, incubate and 'sleep on it';
5 lack of challenge (problem fails to engage interest) versus excessive zeal (over-motivation to succeed quickly);
6 inability to distinguish reality from fantasy.

Facing up to problems

We can often solve problems we face if we are aware of our negative reactions. These negative reactions may constrain us within our comfort zones and restrict us from exploring and learning from new experiences.

Bransford and Stein (1984) described how a muscular friend went on a sports psychology workshop that was designed to address feelings about winning and losing. Initially the activities involved the use of power, eg arm and leg wrestling, most of which the friend won.

He explained that he was a 'humble winner' and that his ego would have stood up to losing.

Later, emphasis was given to coordination activities, one of which was dance instruction, which the friend found to be problematic. Indeed, he believed that he 'couldn't dance'. His frustration became so much that he exploded, 'This workshop has gotten ridiculous; I'm going to leave.' The instructor, who was alert to such concerns, encouraged the friend to remain and receive special classes with other people who felt challenged. Bransford and Stein (1984: 5) stated, 'According to our friend, this was a significant experience. It made him realize that he had been avoiding a number of situations because they were initially difficult. As a result of this experience, our friend resolved to increase his 'courage span' when dealing with uncomfortable situations.'

The next time you explode from frustration about an event, take time out to assess your thought patterns and whether they are inhibiting you from learning something new rather than trying to enforce your perspective of the world on someone else.

Revans argued that when we are in situations where we perceive that there is nothing really new we are just reliving an older experience. In effect, if we do not learn from something that we undergo then arguably it cannot be called an experience. We therefore have to look for differences that challenge our way of seeing things. In other words, we are looking for problems or challenges to our conceptual frameworks. Lumsdaine and Lumsdaine (1995: 37) offer advice on how to learn from the ordinary and mundane:

> If a new experience, fact, or situation is very much like something already in our memory, the mind will not pay much attention, and the new information will not be retained. Thus we must develop a habit of looking for differences, for something odd in the 'new' input, to prevent forgetting. In addition, attention comes from the outside through strong stimuli. Intense experiences are unforgettable. The classic example is the John F Kennedy assassination. People clearly remember what they were doing when they heard this shocking news: 'It was a hot, sunny afternoon and I was outside in the backyard, ironing this blue and white striped dress while listening to the radio.'

Imaginative strategies

Thinking perspectives

In order to break out of these habitual straitjackets a number of strategies can be used to view the world in different ways and thereby experience and learn so that we get closer to the truth about an object or concept. Edward de Bono (1986) recognized the limitations of the ways in which different people view the same issues and situations. He maintained that by putting on different metaphorical hats, conflict between individuals who see things in different ways would be minimized because the process would legitimize the way things were discussed. Moreover, it allowed a systematic approach to how the thought processes in meetings were organized.

He identified five main benefits from adopting this approach:

1 **Role playing.** In many cases the ego prevents one from seeing the other person's point of view and only defends its own perspective. Giving people the freedom of playing a role enables them to discard the egotistical posturing.

2 **Attention directing.** The hats enable us to direct our attention to a specific interpretation rather than being reactive to the views of others.

3 **Convenience.** It allows people to change perspectives in an efficient manner.

4 **Brain chemistry.** The chemicals that exist in our brains are neuro-transmitters, which enable thinking, and the creation of certain chemicals may encourage certain kinds of ideas.

5 Rules of the game. The hats procedure may be used with a group of people to enable them to operate in clear and understandable ways.

The six thinking hats have the following colours:

- **White hat.** This represents a neutral perspective, which only considers objective facts and information.
- **Red hat.** This symbolizes anger and allows people to express emotions.
- **Black hat.** This hat suggests negativity and allows people to discuss why a particular proposal is inappropriate or likely to be unsuccessful.
- **Yellow hat.** This symbolizes a bright and sunny view, which encourages people to think positively.
- **Green hat.** Like fertile vegetation, the green hat encourages the development of creative ideas.
- **Blue hat.** Like the sky, this hat provides an overview and enables the discussion to have order and control.

Experience and the inner game

The Inner Game of Tennis by Timothy Gallwey (1986), a tennis coach and former junior tennis champion in the United States, has become a classic. Through the medium of tennis, Gallwey has made a number of observations about the nature of learning and experiencing.

His first observation was that the secret of winning a game of tennis was not to try too hard, with the result that the mind became more relaxed and it became easier to make better shots. As a new coach he had also noticed some apparent anomalies when he tried to coach some pupils. Namely, some of the errors his pupils made seemed to correct themselves without his intervention or the pupils being aware of the improvement. Gallwey was also conscious of sometimes over-teaching his pupils and the fact that on occasions his attempts to improve a particular stroke resulted in a deteriorating performance from the pupil. Telling pupils to lift their shoulder might result in other errors creeping into their game with the result that they concentrated even more, causing further deterioration.

Gallwey theorized that there would appear to be two elements of the self involved with the game of tennis or other activities, ie the conscious self and the unconscious self. Self 1 is the part of the brain that is the conscious teller, which instructs the body and says such things as, 'Keep the racquet head closer to the ground in order to give the ball more topspin'. Self 2, the unconscious automatic doer, carries out the various movements needed to play a game of tennis. It is important to be aware that this part of the brain operates all the bodily functions that are needed to live – it ensures that our heart keeps beating and that our lungs keep breathing without us needing to be consciously aware of it. In many ways our brain is like an iceberg: the conscious brain is like the tip of the iceberg above the water; the unconscious brain, which conducts most of the processing and which we are rarely aware of, is like the greater part of the iceberg, which is under water.

Every time a person hits or doesn't hit a ball, Self 2 is gathering the information and storing this information in the memory. It is aware of how high the ball is bouncing, where the head of the racquet is positioned, where the feet are, how fast the ball is travelling and so on. For a beginner, the most effective way to learn is to experience hitting the ball and avoid detailed instructions that put Self 1 and Self 2 into opposition.

Gallwey suggests that the basic language of Self 2 is not words since we were learning as infants before we could speak. He maintains that an activity is learnt through feelings and visual images. This consists of stages:

1 **Observation.** In this stage, you see, feel and hear what is happening as you make a stroke.

2 **Programming.** You use visioning to see yourself serving and using supportive elements, such as the sound of the ball as it is hit, how smooth it feels to swing the racket, and the trajectory of the ball as it flies through the air and lands in the service box.

3 **Let it happen.** This stage is just to allow your body to do what is required without concentrating and using Self 1.

4 **Observation.** The cycle is complete and the server continues to be aware of what is happening from the various sources of sight, sound and touch that are available.

When sportspeople make several mistakes they evaluate their performance, recognize that it was weak and then sometimes call themselves bad players. You can see this phenomenon on tennis courts, golf courses, football fields, etc where people are talking and chastising themselves as they play. Not only does this self-criticism undermine their confidence but it also encourages Self 1, the conscious brain, to try to impose itself on Self 2, the unconscious brain, with destructive effect.

Gallwey recommended that we use Self 1 to support Self 2 by being alert and aware of what is happening. With a serve many muscles are used, and the coordination of all the elements is very complicated; it is extremely difficult for us to concentrate on all these elements at the same time. All Gallwey advised is that when we attempt to serve into the opposite court we are aware and note where the ball landed, ie was it long or short, and was it to the left or the right? Through just letting it happen rather than concentrating hard on what is going on and making it happen the serve will become fluent and accurate. This simple feedback of being aware then allows Self 2 to make the necessary corrections unconsciously, and our game improves. Gallwey (1986: 50) stated, 'It is important not only to understand intellectually the difference between letting it happen and making it happen but to experience the difference.'

The more we practise the easier it becomes to repeat the task because the neural connections have been increased and developed. Gallwey (1986: 67) described this in slightly different terms:

> One hears a lot about grooving one's strokes in tennis. The theory is a simple one: every time you swing your racquet in a certain way, you increase the probabilities that you will swing that way again. In this way patterns, called grooves build up which have a predisposition to repeat themselves. Golfers use the same term. It is as if the nervous system were like a record disk. Every time an action is performed, a slight impression is made in the microscopic cells of the brain, just as a leaf blowing over a fine-grained beach will leave a faint trace. When the action is repeated, the groove is made slightly deeper. After many similar actions there is a more recognizable groove into which the needle of behaviour seems to fall automatically.

Peak experience

One of the key skills in playing tennis is the use of concentration. By concentrating we are able to focus more clearly on what is happening within ourselves as well as what is happening around us. This develops our consciousness and allows us to experience even more deeply. Gallwey (1986: 85) explained:

> Whatever we experience on a tennis court is known to us by virtue of awareness – that is, by the consciousness within us. It is consciousness that makes possible awareness of the sights, sounds, feelings and thoughts that compose what we call 'experience'. It is self-evident that one cannot experience anything outside of consciousness. Consciousness is that which makes all things and events knowable. Without consciousness eyes could not see, ears could not hear, and mind could not think. Consciousness is like a pure light energy whose power is to make events knowable, just as an electric light makes objects visible. Consciousness could be called the light of lights because it is by its light that all other lights become visible.

Gallwey suggests that our focus can be developed in a progressive manner, moving from awareness, to attention, to concentration, to one-point concentration. The more we focus our attention the more we can experience. For instance, your concentration is on the words in this book, but if you disconnect from this stimulus and concentrate on what you can hear you may be able to pick out the sound of a bird or other sounds, and if you listen even more closely you may be able to identify what type of bird and where it is singing.

Similarly, concentrating on an experience and even reflecting on it will often provide us with a deeper and more satisfying sensation through increased understanding and increased awareness of the details that we might have overlooked when it did not fully occupy our consciousness. Thus concentration heightens the experience and enables us to benefit more significantly from events. Gallwey (1986: 125) asserted:

> What makes it possible to learn more from ordinary experience? Two people witness the same sunset; one has a deep experience of beauty, and the other, perhaps because his mind is preoccupied, has a minimal experience. Two people read the same lines in a book; one recognizes a profound truth while the other finds nothing worth remembering. One day we get out of bed and the world looks full of beauty and interest; the next day everything appears drab. In each case the difference lies in our own state of consciousness. In the final analysis it is our state of consciousness that is the determining factor in our appreciation of the beautiful, the true, or the loving.

Appreciation and recognition of beauty may lead to an advanced state of well-being. Most of us will have experienced occasions when we felt totally in tune with ourselves in some activity, perhaps at work, participating in a sport or being with another person. No major effort was required; there was no need to concentrate very hard because everything was very clear and understood. This heightened form of awareness is sometimes called peak experience and equates to Maslow's (1954) self-actualization. A good example of peak performance is given in Orlick's description of night-time skiing below.

Peak performance and skiing

One winter night, the sky was clear, the moon was full, the night air crisp. The snow sparkled like dancing crystals under the moonlight. It was a majestic evening as we set out to ski up the mountain trail to a small log chalet nestled in among the trees. We had a fire, had some wine, a bit of stew, joked a little and set out back down the mountain. As I skied down, I became one with the mountain, not knowing where it ended and where I started. I was so close to it, hugging it, it hugging me, as I flowed along that tiny snow packed trail. I moved in shadows and out of shadows as the moonlight darted through the trees. I was totally absorbed in the experience... it was novel, challenging, sensual, fun, exciting, physically demanding, a meaningful trip with nature... a peak experience, the kind that makes it great to be alive.

(Orlick, 1975: 12)

Orlick's description of being fully absorbed in the experience illustrates how he was fully aware of everything around himself and how he understood it so much that he became part of the mountain. In other words, he was learning to the fullest extent possible. Similarly, the inner game that Gallwey described is really a quest for the person on a journey of self-discovery and actualization. When we experience something very deeply we also know it to the maximum extent and this is a form of peak experience. It becomes very clear that if we wish to maximize learning we should involve people cognitively, affectively and behaviourally in the experiential learning event.

Imagination and the child

The power of imagination is strong, especially in children, who are sometimes unable to distinguish between fact and fantasy. As we saw in Chapter 5, the value of play enables children to rehearse skills and thoughts in a safe environment before venturing out into the real world where lessons are learnt in harder ways. Using their imagination allows children to project ideas into the future to test their viability. Imagination also allows the development of creativity. Developing the ability to imagine can unleash a powerful tool, as Alison Uttley (1943: 199), the children's writer, illustrated:

> 'Have you any toys? Toys! We play with anything, with sticks, stones and flowers, and we run about and look at things and find things and sing and shout. We don't have toys.'

> The fields were our toyshops and sweetshops, our market and our storehouses. We made toys from things we found in the pastures. We ate sweet and sour food of the wild. We hunted from hedge to hedge as in a market, to find the best provisions, and we had our wild shops in corners of fields, or among the trees.

The benefits of prospective learning or imagination can be very powerful for the child and far exceed the testing of ideas and the development of creativity. Cohen (1987: 136) summarized the cognitive benefits:

> The well-imagining child would learn to integrate experience, work out what was inner and outer, learn to organize information better, become more reflective, elaborate perceptions and cognitions, recognize mistakes quicker and develop better concentration... The 'social benefits of imagery' included becoming more sensitive to others, increased empathy, poise, acculturation, self-entertainment, reducing fear and anxiety, improved emotional well-being and self-control.

Parents encourage their children to become more mature. However, children have a great ability to live for the moment and experience the joy of just being, whereas adults often say that they will be happy when they own a new car or house, have completed a piece of work, etc. We need to remember as adults that this also means that we need to travel in the opposite direction and meet the child in us to appreciate fully the nature of being.

Tower and Singer's (1980: 36) perspective is very similar:

> When a child engages in imaginative play with a parent, a very special phenomenon is taking place: the child is generating and executing ideas based on its own experience in a context of mutual respect, interest and absence

of criticism. Parent and child are free to experience each other in terms of possibilities. Constraints inherent in the usual roles they play in relation to each other may be temporarily put aside. The give and take of laughter and of shared 'dangers' and 'rescues' may enhance a positive sense of communion. Parents often have lost touch with their own childhood joys in fantasy play and can regain some of that excitement through play.

A child's development begins at a very early stage, and the case study below demonstrates this clearly and shows how this may have significant implications for the future.

Case study: antenatal and post-natal development

During my pregnancy with twins we had an interesting experience. In one of my antenatal visits to the hospital I had an ultrasound scan, which showed that one of the babies was a girl. (We later found that the other was a boy.) Calum, the boy, was very active throughout the pregnancy while Eilidh, the girl, was quiet and slept a lot.

During the scan Calum was moving around and kicking vigorously while Eilidh was quite passive. As we were watching, Calum kicked out and came into contact with Eilidh who responded by spinning 180 degrees to turn her back on him, all the while continuing to suck her thumb.

Now that they are born I can observe them more closely and take note of their personalities. One year on, Eilidh still loves her sleep whilst Calum is a very early riser. Calum enjoys the rough-and-tumble of play while Eilidh likes more gentle play.

We tried to ensure that both babies were given equal care and stimulation, even alternating which parent put each baby to bed at night. They also shared the same toys. Despite this, both Calum and Eilidh are developing in quite different ways. Eilidh courts attention from others, especially adults. She treated me to her first real smile when she was less than four weeks old and learnt at a very young age that a smile would get the reaction and attention that she loves. Eilidh was first to recognize and sing along with her favourite songs. Calum, on the other hand, prefers things to people. He treats strangers with indifference, preferring to play with his toys. He quickly became very adept at recognizing and sorting shapes and exploring the mechanisms of his toys.

Although the twins were very close and became upset when they were separated, they behaved as if the other was an extension of themselves. They sucked each other's thumbs and toes but they did not interact with each other in the same way as with ourselves and other adults until one incident when they were around five months old. They were lying side by side on the floor and Eilidh had her hand in Calum's mouth. Calum sneezed and Eilidh pulled away, giggling. She put her hand back and he sneezed again, eliciting another giggle. For the next 20 minutes, both babies watched, smiled, touched and giggled with each other. It appeared to me that each baby suddenly recognized the other as a separate person. From that day, they became a team, interacted, played and communicated with each other, often sharing a private joke which nobody but themselves could understand.

One day I was teaching them to give me a kiss by kissing each of them in turn. A few minutes after the game was over, they started giggling and kissing each other. Since then, without any prompting from ourselves, they spontaneously give each other a kiss and cuddle every morning, as we do with them.

Although the only evidence I have is observing just two babies, from their behaviour I can only conclude that their learning is not driven solely by nature, nurture or environmental factors but a combination of all three.

(Rosie MacIntyre)

Conclusion

Throughout this book we have emphasized the importance of using the concept of experiential learning as a means of drawing together theory and practice. It is probably the single unifying feature that integrates the neurological processes of the brain with the various theories and strategies for encouraging learning. It involves action learning and reflective practice; it involves the emotional aspects of learning, and incorporates the various environmental factors that add to the learning experience.

The nature vs nurture debate has long been entrenched with protagonists making strong points from each perspective and, perhaps, the majority of people believing that both factors have an impact. Nurture, or experience, has a major impact as this book has emphasized and it would now appear to have an even bigger one. Remarkable evidence is beginning to accumulate that experience can influence gene activity without changing a person's genetic code. For example, research by Bygren *et al* (2001) in Sweden has revealed that the diet of ancestors after rich and poor harvests can impact on the longevity of succeeding generations. We do not have to wait for the human genome to evolve slowly over longer periods of time.

In this final chapter we have investigated the nature of prospective learning and the use of imagination to investigate future possibilities. We also discussed the value of problems that challenge our way of seeing the world. If we were not challenged we would tend towards inertia and gradually atrophy and fossilize. As a consequence we would fail to progress, and follow the route of the dinosaurs. We will leave the final words to Freire (1982: 57 — italics added), who linked problem solving with the development of our future and thus all our hopes:

> Problem solving education is revolutionary futurity. Hence it is prophetic (and, as such, hopeful), and so corresponds to the historical nature of man. Thus, it affirms men (*humans*) as beings who transcend themselves, who move forward and look ahead, for whom immobility represents a fatal threat, for whom looking at the past must only be a means of understanding more clearly what and who they are so that they can more wisely build the future.

REFERENCES

Abbot, C (1987) The good, the bad and the ugly: The role of outdoor programmes in working with young drug abusers, *Autumn School of Studies in Alcohol and Drugs*, proceedings of Seminar and Scientific Sessions, St Vincent's Hospital, Melbourne, Australia

Abram, D (1997) *The Spell of the Sensuous*, Vintage Books, New York

Adams, James L (1987) *Conceptual Blockbusting: A guide to better ideas*, Penguin, Harmondsworth

Adamson, John William (ed) (1911) *The Educational Writings of John Locke*, Edwin Arnold, London

Adler, H (2000) The missing link, *Achievement*, September Issue, Achievement Publishing, Kent

Adler, P S (1975) The transitional experience, *Journal of Humanistic Psychology*, **15** (4), pp 13–23

Agor, W H (1991) The logic of intuition: how top executives make important decisions, in *Creative Management*, ed J Henry, pp 163–76, Sage, London

Allison, P (2000a) Authenticity and outdoor education, *Values and Outdoor Learning*, Association for Outdoor Learning, Penrith, Cumbria

Allison, P (2000b) Research from the ground up, *Brathay Occasional Papers*, 1, Brathay Hall Trust, Cumbria

Amabile, T (1983) *The Social Psychology of Creativity*, Springer-Verlag, New York

Applebaum, S, Bregman, M and Moroz, P (1998) Fear as a strategy: effects and impacts within the organisation, *Journal of European Industrial Training*, **22** (3), pp 113–27, MCB University Press, Bradford

Argyris, C (1994) Good communication that blocks learning, *Harvard Business Review*, July–August, pp 77–85

Argyris, C and Schön, D (1974) *Theory in Practice: Increasing professional effectiveness*, Jossey-Bass, San Francisco, CA

Argyris, C, Putnam, R, & Smith, D M (1985) *Action Science*, Jossey-Bass, San Francisco, CA

Aristotle (1946) *Rhetoric*, Oxford University Press, Oxford

Arran, A (1998) Personal communication on the design of Spider Club awards

Assagioli, R (1980) *Psychosynthesis*, Wildwood House, London

Attard, P (2001) The use of drama-based training as a learning medium, Unpublished Master's thesis, Department of Continuing Education, Sheffield University, Sheffield

Attarian, A (1999) Artificial climbing environments, in *Adventure Programming*, ed J C Miles and S Priest, pp 341–45, Venture Publishing, Andover, MA

Bacon, S (1987) *The Evolution of the Outward Bound Process*, Greenwich Outward Bound, USA

Baddeley, A, Eysenck, M W and Anderson, M C (2009) *Memory*, Psychology Press, Hove, Sussex

Badger, B, Sadler-Smith, E and Michie, E (1997) Outdoor management development: use and evaluation, *Journal of European and Industrial Training*, **21** (9), pp 318–25, MCB University Press, Bradford

Bagshaw, M (2000) 17 tried and tested activities for understanding the practice and applications of emotional intelligence, *Using Emotional Intelligence at Work*, Fenman Ltd, Cambridgeshire

Baker, A C, Jensen, P J and Kolb, D A (2002) *Conversational Learning: An experiential approach to knowledge creation*, Quorum Books, Westport CT

Baldacchino, G and Mayo, P (1997) Adult education practice: alternatives to chalk and talk, in *Beyond Schooling: Adult education in Malta*, pp 85–88, Mireva Publications, Msida, Malta

Bandler, R and Grinder, J (1990) *Frogs into Princes: Neuro linguistic programming*, Real People Press, Utah

Bandura, A (1977) *Social Learning Theory*, Prentice-Hall, Englewood Cliffs, NJ

Bank, J (1994) *Outdoor Development for Managers*, 2nd edn, Gower, Aldershot

Bar, M (2011) *Predictions in the Brain*, Oxford University Press, Oxford

Barbalet, J (1998) *Emotions, Social Theory and Social Structure*, Cambridge University Press, Cambridge

Barbalet, J (ed) (2002) *Emotions and Sociology*, Blackwell, Oxford

Barnes, P (2000) *Values and Outdoor Learning: A collection of papers reflecting some contemporary thinking*, Association for Outdoor Learning, Penrith, Cumbria

Barrett, J and Greenaway, R (1995) *Why Adventure? The role and value of outdoor adventure in young people's personal and social development*, Foundation for Outdoor Adventure, Coventry

Bateson, Gregory (2000) The logical categories of learning and communication, *Steps to an Ecology of Mind*, pp 279–308, Essay written in 1964, University of Chicago, Chicago

Battista, R N and Hodge, M J (1999) The evolving paradigm of health technology assessment: reflections for the millennium, *Canadian Medical Association Journal, 18 May*, 1464–1467

Beard, C M (1996) Environmental awareness training: three ideas for greening the company culture, *Eco-Management and Auditing*, 3, pp 139–46

Beard, C M (1997) *The Future for Eco-design – new business products*, Conference Proceedings of Business Strategy and the Environment, 18–19 September, Leeds

Beard, C (1998) The outdoor leisure industry and the environment, *Horizons*, 2, Cumbria

Beard, C M (2000) *A brave new environmental vision for the millennium*, Euro Environment 2000 Conference: Visions, strategies and actions towards sustainable industries, 18–20 October, Aalborg Congress and Culture Centre, Denmark

Beard, C (2003) The circle and the square – nature and artificial adventure environments, in *Whose Journeys? Where and Why? The 'Outdoors and Adventure' as a Social and Cultural Phenomena: Critical explorations of relations between individuals, 'others' and the environment*, eds B Humberstone, H Brown and K Richards, pp 187–98, Fingerprints, Barrow in Furness

Beard, C (2005) The design of effective group-based training methods, in *Human Resource Development*, ed J Wilson, pp 342–64, Kogan Page, London

Beard, C (2010) *The Experiential Learning Toolkit: Blending practice with concepts*, Kogan Page, London

Beard, C (2012) Spatial ecology: learning and working environments that change people and organisations, in *Managing Organisational Ecologies*, eds K Alexandra and I Price, Routledge, New York

Beard, C (2013) *Sensory Intelligence*, Morphesus Learning Resources (audio book), Mumbai

Beard, C & Goode, M (2013) Contributing to a more sustainable world? Business product innovation and the development of an industrial ecology, in *Enhancing Education for Sustainable Development in Business and Management, Hospitality, Leisure, Marketing, Tourism*, eds R Atfield and P Kemp. The Higher Education Academy, York. ISBN 978-1-907207-69-3

Beard, C and McPherson, M (1999) Design and use of group-based training methods, in *Human Resource Development: Learning and training for individuals and organizations*, ed J P Wilson, Kogan Page, London

Beard, C and Price, I (2010) Space, conversations and place: lessons and questions from practice, *International Journal of Facilities Management*, 1 (2), pp 1–14

Beard, C and Price, I (2012) Learning spaces that change people and organisations, in *International Human Resource Development*, ed J P Wilson, pp 465–80, Kogan Page, London

Beard C and Price, I (2013) Room for Improvement, Journal of the Royal Society of Arts, Spring, pp. 38–41

Beard, C and Wilson, J (2002) *Experiential Learning*, Kogan Page, London

Beard, C and Wilson, J (2006) *Experiential Learning*, Kogan Page, London

Beard, C, Smith, K and Clegg, S (2007) Acknowledging the affective in higher education, *British Educational Research Journal*, 33 (2) April in press

Beard, C, Wilson, J P and McCarter, R (2006) Towards a Theory of eLearning: Experiential eLearning, *Journal of Hospitality, Leisure, Sport and Tourism Education*. 6 (2), pp 3–15

Becher, T (1989) *Academic Tribes and Territories: Intellectual enquiry and the cultures of disciplines*, Society for Research into Higher Education, Open University Press, Milton Keynes

Bee, F and Bee, R (1998) *Facilitation Skills*, Institute of Personnel and Development, London

Behuniak, S (2005) Finding solitude: the importance of silence and space for thinking, Paper presented to Design For Learning, the Twelfth International Conference on Learning, 11–14 July, Granada, Spain

Belbin, M (1981) *Management Teams: Why they succeed or fail*, Butterworth-Heinemann, Oxford

Benson, J (1987) *Working More Creatively with Groups*, Routledge, London

Bergenhenegouwen, G L (1996) Professional code of ethics for training professionals, *Journal of European Industrial Training*, 20 (4), pp 23–29

Berger, P and Luckmann, T (1985) *The Social Construction of Reality*, Penguin, Harmondsworth

Berne, E (1973) *Games People Play*, Penguin, Harmondsworth

Binstead, D and Stuart, R (1979) Designed reality into management learning events, *Personnel Review*, 8 (3), pp 12–19

Black, M (1979) More about metaphor, in *Metaphor and Thought*, ed A Ortony, Cornell University Press, Ithaca, NY

Black Mountain Ltd (1996) *Developing your human dimension*, Commercial publicity brochure

Block, P (2000) *Flawless Consulting*, 2nd edn, Jossey-Bass Pfeiffer, San Francisco

Bloom, B S *et al* (1956) *Taxonomy of Educational Objectives: The classification of educational objectives, Handbook 1: Cognitive Domain*, Longmans, Green & Co, London

Boler, M (1999) *Feeling Power: Emotions and education*, Routledge, London

Bolton, G (1985) Changes in thinking about drama in education, *Theory into Practice*, **24** (3), Summer, pp 151–57

Boniface, M (2000) Towards an understanding of flow and other positive experience phenomena within outdoor and adventurous activities, *Journal of Adventure Education and Outdoor Learning*, **1** (1), pp 55–68

Booth, B F and Moss, I (1994) *A Social History of Sport*, HPA Inc, Ottawa

Boud, D and Miller, N, eds (1996a) *Working with Experience: Animating learning*, Routledge, London

Boud, D and Miller, N (1996b) Synthesising traditions and identifying themes in learning from experience, in *Working with Experience: Animating learning*, ed D Boud and N Miller, pp 14–24, Routledge, London

Boud, D and Walker, D (1990) Making the most of experience, *Studies in Continuing Education*, **12** (2), pp 61–80

Boud, David and Walker, David (1993) Barriers to reflection on experience, in *Using Experience for Learning*, eds D Boud, R Cohen and D Walker, pp 73–86

Boud, D, Cohen, R and Walker, D (1993) *Using Experience for Learning*, Open University Press, Buckingham

Boydell, T (1976) *Experiential Learning*, Manchester Monograph 5, University of Manchester, Department of Adult Education

Bransford, John D and Stein, Barry S (1984) *The Ideal Problem Solver: A guide for improving thinking, learning, and creativity*, W H Freeman & Co, New York

Britzman, D P (1998) *Lost Subjects, Contested Objects: Towards a psychoanalytic inquiry of learning*, State University of New York Press, New York

Bronkhorst, A W (2000) The cocktail party phenomenon: a review on speech intelligibility in multiple-talker conditions, *Acta Acustica united with Acustica*, **86**, pp 117–28

Bryson, B (2000) *An Introduction, the English Landscape*, pp 1–2, Profile Books, London

Bull, N (1951) The Attitude Theory of Emotion, *Nervous and Mental Disease Monographs*, New York, Coolidge Foundation

Burns, G (1998) *Nature Guided Therapy: Brief integrative strategies for health and well-being*, Brunner/Mazel, Philadelphia

Butcher, G B (1991) Creating the right environment for training managers, *Training and Development*, **9** (6), pp 26–30, The Institute of Training and Development, UK

Buzan, T (2000 edn) *The Speed Reading Book*, BBC Worldwide Ltd, London

Bygren, L O, Kaati, G and Edvinsson, S (2001) Longevity determined by parental ancestors nutrition during their slow growth period, *Acta Biotheoretica*, **49** (1), pp 53–59

Cantor, J A (1997) *Experiential Learning in Higher Education: Linking classroom and community*, The George Washington University, Graduate School of Education and Human Development, Washington DC

Carlson, R (1998) *Don't Sweat the Small Stuff with Your Family*, Hyperion, New York

Cell, E (1984) *Learning to Learn from Experience*, State University of New York Press, Albany

Charlton, C (1992) Developing leaders using the outdoors, in *Frontiers of Leadership: An essential reader*, ed M Syrett and C Hogg, pp 454–61, Blackwell, Oxford

Chickering, A W (1977) *Experience and Learning: An introduction to experiential learning*, Change Magazine Press, New Rochelle, NY

Child, G (1993) *Mixed Emotions*, The Mountaineers, Seattle

Chisholm, A (2000) A time for change, *Achievement*, September, p 5, Achievement Publishing, Kent

Chopra, D (1996) *The Seven Spiritual Laws of Success: A practical guide to the fulfilment of your dreams*, Bantam Books, London

Christoff, K, Gordon, A M, Smallwood, J, Smith, R and Schooler, J W (2009) Experience sampling during fMRI reveals default network and executive system contributions to mind wandering, *Proceedings of the National Academy of Sciences May 26, 2009* **106** (21), pp 8719–24

CIPD (2012) *Learning and Talent Development Report 2012*, Wimbledon, CIPD

Clutterbuck, D (1998) *Learning Alliances: Tapping into talent*, Institute of Personnel and Development, London

Coffield, F, Moseley, D, Hall, E and Ecclestone, K (2004) *Learning Styles and Pedagogy in Post-16 Learning. A systematic and critical review*, Learning and Skills Research Centre, London

Cohen, David (1987) *The Development of Play*, New York University Press, New York

Collison, C and Mackenzie, A (1999) The power of story in organisations, *Journal of Workplace Learning*, **11** (1), pp 38–40, MCB University Press, Bradford

Consalvo, C (1995) *Outdoor Games for Trainers*, Gower, Aldershot

ContactBabel (2005) *The UK Contact Centre Operational Review*, ContactBabel, Sedgefield, Co Durham

Cooper, G (1998) *Outdoors with Young People: A leader's guide to outdoor activities, the environment and sustainability*, Russell House Publishing, Dorset

Cornell, J (1989) *Sharing the Joy of Nature*, Dawn Publications, California

Coursera [accessed 21 November 2012], https://www.coursera.org/about

Covey, Stephen R (1990) *The Seven Habits of Highly Effective People*, Simon & Schuster, New York

Cronon, W (1996) *Uncommom Ground: Rethinking the human place in nature*, Norton Publications, New York

Crosby, A (1995) A critical look: the philosophical foundations of experiential education, in *The Theory of Experiential Education*, eds K Warren, M Sakofs and J Hunt, Association for Experiential Education, Kendall/Hunt Publishing, Dubuque, IA

Crowder, R G (1976) *Principles of Learning and Memory*, Erlbaum, Hillsdale, NJ

Csikszentmihalyi, M and Csikszentmihalyi, I (eds) (1988) *Optimal Experiences*, Cambridge University Press, Cambridge

Cuffaro, Harriet K (1995) *Experimenting with the World: John Dewey and the early childhood classroom*, Teachers College Press, New York

Curriculum Corporation (1994) *Statements and Profiles for Australian Schools*, Melbourne, Australia

Dainty, P and Lucas, D (1992) Clarifying the confusion: a practical framework for evaluating outdoor development programmes for managers, *Management Education and Development*, **23** (2), pp 106–22

Dale, E (1969) *Audiovisual Methods in Teaching*, Dryden Press, New York

Damasio, A R (1995) *Emotion, Reason and the Human Brain*, G P Putnum's & Sons, New York

Damasio, A R (1996) *Descartes' Error: Emotion, reason and the human brain*, Papermac, London

Damasio, A R (1999) *The Feeling of What Happens: The body and emotion in the making of consciousness*, Harcourt Brace, New York

Damasio, A R (2003) *Looking for Spinoza: Joy, sorrow, and the feeling brain*, Harcourt, Inc, Orlando

Damasio, A (2004) *Looking for Spinoza*, Vintage Press, London

Darmer, P and Sundbo, J (2008) Introduction to experience creation, in *Creating Experiences in the Experience Economy*, eds J Sundbo and P Darmer, pp 1–12, Edward Elgar, Cheltenham

Darwin, C (1872) *The Expression of the Emotions in Man and Animals*, University of Chicago Press, Chicago

Daudelin, M (1996) Learning from experience through reflection, *Organizational Dynamics*, **24** (3), pp 36–46

Davies, W (1997) *One River: Science, adventure and hallucinogenics in the Amazon Basin*, Simon & Schuster Ltd, New York

Davis, B and Sumara D J (1997) Cognition, complexity, and teacher education, *Harvard Educational Review* **67** (1), pp 105–25

Davis-Berman, J and Berman, D (1999) The use of adventure-based programs with at-risk youth, in *Adventure Programming*, eds J C Miles and S Priest, pp 365–72, Venture Publishing, PA, USA

de Bono, Edward (1986) *Six Thinking Hats*, Viking, Harmondsworth

de Bono, E (1991) Lateral and vertical thinking, in *Creative Management*, ed J Henry, pp 16–23, Sage, London

DEEP [accessed March 1999] *Definitions, Ethics and Exemplary Practices (DEEP) of Experiential Training and Development (ETD)*, http://rogue.northwest.com/icg/deep.htm

Design Council (2005) *Kit for Purpose: Design to deliver creative learning*, Report of the Design Council, London

Desmond, B and Jowitt, A (2011) Stepping into the unknown: dialogical experiential learning, *Journal of Management Development*, **31** (3), pp. 221–30

Dewey, John (1916) *Democracy and Education*, Macmillan, New York

Dewey, John (1917) A recovery of philosophy, in *Creative Intelligence*, eds J Dewey *et al*, pp 3–69, Henry Holt, New York

Dewey, John (1925) *Experience and Nature*, The Paul Carus Foundation Lectures 1, Open Court Publishing Company, Chicago

Dewey, J (1933) *How We Think. A restatement of the relation of reflective thinking to the educative process* (revised edn), D C Heath, Boston

Dewey, John (1934) *Art as Experience*, Allen & Unwin, London

Dewey, John (1938) *Experience and Education*, The Kappa Delta Pi Lecture Series, Macmillan, New York

Dickinson, M (1998) *The Death Zone*, Arrow Books, London

Dillon, P (2007) A Pedagogy of Connection and Boundary Crossings: Methodological and epistemological transactions in working across and between disciplines, a paper presented at '*Creativity or conformity? Building Cultures of Creativity in Higher Education*', University of Wales and the Higher Education Academy, Cardiff, January 8–10.

Doncaster, K and Thorne, L (2000) Reflection and planning: Essential elements of professional doctorates, *Reflective Practice*, **1** (3), pp 391–99

Dunn, D and Chaput de Saintonge, M (1997) Experiential Learning, *Medical Education*, **31**(supplement 1) pp 25–28

Dybeck, M (2000) Commercial considerations, in *Values and Outdoor Learning*, ed P Barnes, pp 113–19, Institute for Outdoor Learning, Penrith, Cumbria

Egan, G (2002) *The Skilled Helper*, 7th edn, Brooks/Cole, Pacific Grove, CA

Elgood, C (1984) *The Handbook of Management Games*, Gower, Aldershot

Experience Creative Development (2000) Promotional leaflet, Leatherhead, Surrey

Falconar, T (2000) *Creative Intelligence and Self Liberation*, Crown House Publishing, Carmarthen

Feilden, R (2004) *The Impact of School Environments: A literature review*, The Design Council and the Centre for Learning & Teaching, University of Newcastle, February 2005

Feldman Barrett, L and Salovey, P (eds) (2002) *The Wisdom in Feeling: Psychological processes in emotional intelligence*, The Guilford Press, New York

Fenwick, T J (2000) Expanding conceptions of experiential learning: A review of the five contemplations of cognition, *Adult Education Quarterly*, 50, pp 243–72

Ferrucci, P (1982) The Visions and Techniques of Psychosynthesis, Turnstone Press, Wellingborough

Fineman, S (1997) Emotion and management learning, *Management Learning*, **28** (1), pp 13–25, Sage, London

Fox, Rebecca (1999) Enhancing spiritual experience in adventure programs, in *Adventure Programming*, eds J C Miles and S Priest, pp 455–61, Venture Publishing, Andover, MA

Frank, L S (2011) Maxine Greene: The Power of the Possible, in *Sourcebook of Experiential Education*, eds T E Smith and C E Knapp, Routledge, Oxford

Fraser, B (2001) Twenty thousand hours: editor's introduction, *Learning Environments Research*, 4, pp 1–5

Freire, Paulo (1982) *The Pedagogy of the Oppressed*, Penguin, Harmondsworth

Frijda, N and Mesquita, B (1994) The social roles and functions of emotions, in *Emotion and Culture*, eds S Kitayama and H R Markus, American Psychological Association, Washington, DC

Fritchie, R (1988) in *Working with Assertiveness*, BBC training video booklet, BBC Enterprises Ltd, London

Furedi, F (2004) *Therapy Culture – Cultivating vulnerability in an uncertain age*, Routledge, London

Gabriel, Y (1998) The use of stories, in *Qualitative Methods and Analysis in Organisational Research*, eds G Symon and C Cassel, Sage, London

Gagne, R M (1974) *Essentials of Learning Instruction*, Dryden Press, Hinsdale, IL

Gallagher, S (2005) *How the Body Shapes the Mind*, Oxford University Press, Oxford

Gallwey, Timothy (1986) *The Inner Game of Tennis*, Pan Books, London

Gardner, H (1983) *Frames of Mind: The theory of multiple intelligences*, Basic Books Inc, New York

Gardner, Howard (1986) Originally in conversation with Daniel Goleman and reported in Rethinking the value of intelligence tests, *New York Times Educational Supplement*, 3 November, and also in Goleman (1996: 37)

Gardner, H (1993) *Frames of Mind: The theory of multiple intelligences*, 2nd edn, Basic Books, New York

Gardner, H, Csikszentmihalyi, M and Damon, W (2001) *Good Work: When excellence and ethics meet*, Basic Books, New York

Gass, M (1992) WebCare international: using the Spider's Web with business populations, in *Book of Metaphors*, eds M Gass and C Dobkin, AEE, Boulder, CO

Gass, M (1995) *Book of Metaphors Volume II*, Kendall/Hunt Publishing, Dubuque, IA

Gass, M and Priest, S (1998) Using metaphors and isomorphs to transfer learning in adventure education, in *Outdoor Management Development*, ed C Loynes, Adventure Education, Cumbria

Gibson, J L, Ivancevich, J M and Donnelly, J H (1985) *Organisations: Behaviour, structure, process*, Business Publications Inc, Plano, TX

Gillis, H L and Thomsen, D (1996) quoted in Ringer, M (2000) Adventure therapy: a description, in *Therapy Within Adventure*, eds K Richards and B Smith, pp 19–20, Proceedings of the Second International Adventure Therapy Conference, University of Augsburg, Augsburg

Gilsdorf, R (2003) Experience-adventure therapy: an inquiry into professional identity, in *Therapy Within Adventure*, ed K Richards and B Smith, pp 51–75, Proceedings of the Second International Adventure Therapy Conference, University of Augsburg, Augsburg

Gladwell, M (2005) *Blink: The power of thinking without thinking*, Little, Brown, New York

Goffman, E (1971) *The Presentation of Self in Everyday Life*, Penguin, Harmondsworth

Gold, G (1996) Telling stories to find the future, *Career Development International*, 1st quarter, pp 33–37, MCB University Press, Manchester

Golding, B (2005) *Listening to Men Learning: An exploration of men's learning preferences in community contexts*, Paper presented to Design For Learning, the Twelfth International Conference on Learning, 11–14 July, Granada, Spain

Goleman, D (1996) *Emotional Intelligence*, Bantam Books, London

Gray, J (1993) *Men are from Mars – Women are from Venus*, Thorsons, London

Gray, J (1999) *Children are Heaven*, HarperCollins, New York

Greenaway, R (1993) *Playback: A guide to reviewing activities*, The Award Scheme Ltd, Duke of Edinburgh's Award and Endeavour, Scotland

Greenaway, R (1996) *Reviewing Adventures, Why and How*, NAOE, Sheffield

Greenaway, R [accessed 14 July 1999] http://www.users.globalnet.co. uk/-rogg/activities/outdoor_indoor.htm

Greenaway, R (2008) A view into the future, in *Other Ways of Learning*, eds P Becker and J Schrip, pp 347–67, BSJ, Marburg, Germany

Greenwood, J (1993) Reflective Practice: A critique of the work of Argyris and Schon, *Journal of Advanced Nursing*, 19, pp 1183–87

Greenwood, J. (1998). The role of reflection in single and double loop learning. *Journal of Advanced Nursing, 27*, pp 1048–53

Greenwood, R and Nagel, S (2008) *Inexperienced Investors and Bubbles*, NBER Working Paper, 14111, National Bureau of Economic Research, Cambridge, MA

Griffiths, J (2006) *Wild: An Elemental Journey*, London, Penguin Books

Gross, R (2001) *Psychology: The science of mind and behaviour*, 4th edn, Hodder & Stoughton, London

Gwilt, I (2013) Data-objects: sharing the attributes and properties of digital and material culture to creatively interpret complex information, in *Digital Media Technologies for Virtual Artistic Spaces*, ed D Harrison, IGI Global, Hershey, Pennsylvania, USA (forthcoming 2013)

Gwilt, I, Yoxall, A and Sano, K (2012) *Enhancing The Understanding Of Statistical Data Through The Creation Of Physical Objects*, The 2nd International Conference on Design Creativity (ICDC2012), Glasgow, UK, 2012. Proceedings published by the design society UK ISBN 978-1-904670-39-1

Habermas, J (1972) *Knowledge and Human Interests*, Heinemann, London

Hall, Douglas and Associates (1995) *The Career is Dead, Long Live the Career*, Jossey-Bass, San Francisco

Hall, D T *et al* (1978) *Experiences in Management and Organizational Behaviour*, St Clair Press, Chicago

Hall, E and Moseley, D (2005) Is there a role for learning styles in personalised education and training?, *International Journal of Lifelong Education*, 24 (3), pp 243–55

Hall, J (2004) *Phoenix House Therapeutic Conservation Programme: Underpinning theory*, English Nature Research Reports, no 611, English Nature, Peterborough

Handy, C (1989) *The Age of Unreason*, Business Books, London

Handy, C (1994) *The Empty Raincoat*, Hutchinson, London

Hardingham, A (1998) *Psychology for Trainers*, Institute of Personnel and Development, London

Hartmann, R and Beard, C M (2000) *Environmental training: a strategic tool in an organisation's environmental management*, Proceedings of the Euro Environment 2000 Conference: Visions, strategies and actions towards sustainable industries, 18–20 October, Aalborg Congress and Culture Centre, Denmark

Harwood, A (2005) Reaching the parts: the use of narrative and storytelling in organisational development, in *Organisational Development in Healthcare*, ed E Peck, pp 219–43, Radcliffe Publishing, Oxford

Hawking, Stephen (1988) *A Brief History of Time: From big bang to black holes*, Bantam, London

Heap, N (1993) Bridging the learning gap, *Training and Development*, January, pp 16–17

Heap, N (1996) The design of learning events, *Industrial and Commercial Training*, 28 (12), pp 10–14

Henry, J (1991) *Creative Management*, Sage, London

Heron, J (1990) *Helping the Client: A creative, practical guide*, Sage, London

Heron, J (1999) *The Complete Facilitator's Handbook*, Kogan Page, London

Higgins, P (1996) Connection and consequence in outdoor education, *Journal of Adventure Education and Outdoor Leadership*, 13 (2) pp 34–39

Higgins, P (1997) Outdoor education for sustainability: making connections, *Journal of Adventure Education and Outdoor Leadership*, 13 (4) pp 4–11

Hilton, I (2009) Tiananmen: The flame burns on, *The Observer*, 3 May, http://www.guardian.co.uk/world/2009/may/03/tiananmen-square-anniversary-china-protest, accessed 15 November 2012

Hochschild, A (1983) *The Managed Heart*, University of California, Berkeley

Holman, D, Pavlica, K and Thorpe, R (1997) Rethinking Kolb's theory of experiential learning in management education, *Management Learning* pp 135–48, Sage, London

Honey, Peter and Mumford, Alan (1992) *Manual of Learning Styles*, 3rd edn, Honey Publications, Maidenhead

Hong, H, Stein, J C and Yu, J (2007) Simple forecasts and paradigm shifts, *The Journal of Finance*, **62** (3), pp 1207–42

Hopfl, H and Linstead, S (1997) Learning to feel and feeling to learn: emotion and learning in organisations, *Management Learning*, **28** (1), pp 5–12, Sage, London

Hovelynck, J (2000) Recognising and exploring action-theories: a reflection-in-action approach to facilitating experiential learning, *Journal of Adventure Education and Outdoor Learning*, **1** (1), pp 7–20, Association for Outdoor Learning, Penrith, Cumbria

Hunt, C (1999) Reflective practice, in *Human Resource Development: Learning and training for individuals and organizations*, ed J P Wilson, pp 221–40, Kogan Page, London

Hunt, C (2005) Reflective practice, in *Human Resource Development*, 2nd edn, ed J Wilson, pp 234–51, Kogan Page, London

Hunt, J S (1995) Ethics and experiential education as professional practice, in *The Theory of Experiential Education*, eds K Warren, M Sakofs and J Hunt, pp 331–38, Association for Experiential Education, Kendall/Hunt Publishing, Dubuque, IA

Hunt, J and Wurdinger, S (1999) Ethics and adventure programming, in *Adventure Programming*, eds J C Miles and S Priest, pp 123–32, Venture Publishing, Andover, MA

Hurlburt, R T and Heavey, C L (2006) *Exploring Inner Experience: The descriptive experience sampling method*, John Benjamins Publishing Co, Amsterdam/Philadelphia, PA

Hutton, M (1989) Learning from action: A conceptual framework, in *Making Sense of Experiential Learning: Diversity in theory and practice*, eds S Weil and I McGill, Society for Research into Higher, Education & Open University Press, Milton Keynes, UK

Illeris, K (2002) *The Three Dimensions of Learning*, Krieger Publishing, Malabar, FL

Illeris, K (2007) *How We Learn: Learning and non-learning in school and beyond*, Routledge, London

Illich, Ivan (1973) *De-schooling Society*, Penguin, Harmondsworth

Ingleton, C (1999) *Emotion in learning: a neglected dynamic*, Paper presented at the HERDSA Annual International Conference, Melbourne, July

IPD (1998) *The IPD Guide on Outdoor Training*, Institute of Personnel and Development, London

Irvine, D and Wilson, J P (1994) Outdoor management development – reality or illusion?, *Journal of Management Development*, **13** (5), pp 25–37

James, T (2000) Can the mountains speak for themselves?, *Scisco Conscientia*, **2** (2), pp 1–4

Jarvis, P (1999) *International Dictionary of Adult and Continuing Education*, Kogan Page, London

Johnson, B (1996) Feeling the fear, in *Working with Experience: Animating learning*, eds D Boud and N Miller, pp 184–93, Routledge, London

Johnstone, K (1981) *Impro*, Methuen, London

Jones, L (2001) *Ethical issues for trainers*, Unpublished Master's thesis in education training and development, Department of Adult Education, Sheffield University, Sheffield

Jung, C G (1971) The collected works of C G Jung, in J Campbell (Editor) The Portable Jung, New York: Viking Press. (Original published work 1921)

Kahane, A (2004) *Solving Tough Problems: An open way of talking, listening and creating new realities*, Berrett-Koehler, San Francisco, CA

Kahneman, D (2011) *Thinking Fast and Slow*, Penguin Books, London

Kegan, R (2000) What 'form' transforms? A constructive-developmental approach to transformative learning, in *Learning as Transformation. Critical perspectives on a theory in progress*, eds J Mezirow *et al*, pp 35–70, Jossey-Bass, San Francisco

Kellert, S R (1993) The biological basis for human values of nature, in *The Biophilia Hypothesis*, eds S R Kellert and E O Wilson, Island Press, Washington, DC

Killingsworth, M A and Gilbert, D T (2010) A Wandering mind is an unhappy mind, *Science*, Vol. 330, 12 November, p 932

Kirk P (1986) Outdoor management development: cellulose or celluloid?, *Management Education and Development*, **17**, pp 85–93

Kirton, M J (1976) Adaptors and innovators: a description and measure, *Journal of Applied Psychology*, **61**, pp 622–29

Kitayama, S and Markus, H R (eds) (1994) *Emotion and Culture*, American Psychological Association, Washington, DC

Knight, S (2002) *NLP at Work*, Nicholas Brealey Publishing, London

Kolb, A and Kolb, D A (2008a) *Experiential learning theory bibliography: Volume 1 1971–2005*, Experience Based Learning Systems, Cleveland, OH, available from the Experience Based Learning Systems website, www.learningfromexperience.com

Kolb, A and Kolb, D A (2008b) *Experiential learning theory bibliography: Volume 2 2006–2008*, Experience Based Learning Systems, Cleveland, OH, available from the Experience Based Learning Systems website: www.learningfromexperience.com

Kolb A Y and Kolb, D A (2009) The learning way: meta-cognitive aspects of experiential learning, *Simulation and Gaming*, **40** (3), pp 297–327

Kolb, D A (1971) *Individual learning styles and the learning process* (Working paper #535–71), MIT Sloan School of Management, Cambridge, MA

Kolb, D A (1976) *The Learning Style Inventory: Technical manual*, McBer, Boston, MA

Kolb, David A (1984) *Experiential Learning: Experience as the source of learning and development*, Prentice Hall, Englewood Cliffs, NJ

Kolb, D A, Boyatzis, R and Mainemelis, C (2001) Experiential learning theory: Previous research and new directions, in *Perspectives on Thinking, Learning, and Cognitive Styles*, eds R Sternberg and L Zhang, pp 227–47, Lawrence Erlbaum, Mahwah, NJ

Kraft, U (2005) Unleashing creativity, *Scientific American Mind*, **16** (1), pp 16–23

Krakauer, J (1997) *Into Thin Air: A personal account of the Everest disaster*, Pan Books, London

Krouwel, B and Goodwill, S (1994) Achieving your aims in the outdoors, *Training Officer*, September, pp 220–21

Kuhn, Thomas S (1970) *The Structure of Scientific Revolutions*, University of Chicago Press, Chicago

Kull, R (2008) *Solitude: Seeking Wisdom in Extremes*, New World Library, California

Lackney, J and Fielding, A [accessed 09/04/2013] School Design Studio [online] http://Schoolstudio.typepad.com/school_design_studio/2007/01/12_design_princ .html

Lakoff, G and Johnson, M (1999) *Philosophy in the Flesh*, Basic Books, New York

Lamplugh, D (1991) *Without Fear: The key to staying safe*, Weidenfeld & Nicolson, London

Lave, J and Wenger, E (1991) *Situated Learning: Legitimate peripheral participation*, Cambridge University Press, Cambridge

Learning from Experience (2012) [accessed 14 November 2012] http:// learningfromexperience.com/

Learning from Experience Trust (1987) *Handbook for the Assessment of Experiential Learning*, LfET, London

Lessem, Ronnie (1982) A biography of action learning, in *The Origins and Growth of Action Learning*, ed R W Revans, pp 4–17, Chartwell-Bratt, Bickley, Kent

Lewin, K (ed) (1951) *Field Theory in Social Science*, Harper & Row, New York

Lewis, C S (1980) *The Chronicles of Narnia: The lion, the witch and the wardrobe*, Collins, London

Lin, T (2005) Information design for learning: A visual communication perspective, *International Journal of Technology, Knowledge, and Society*, **1**, Common Ground

Lindstrom, M (2005) *Brand Sense*, Kogan Page, London

Lippit, R (1949) *Training in Community Relations: A research exploration toward new group skills*, Harper & Brothers, New York

Locke, John (1968) *The Educational Writings of John Locke*, Cambridge University Press, London

Lombard, A (2007) *Sensory Intelligence: Why it matters more than IQ and EQ*, Metz Press, South Africa

Loynes, C (2000) The values of life and living: after all, life is right in any case, in *Values and Outdoor Learning*, ed P Barnes, Association for Outdoor Learning, Penrith, Cumbria

Luft, J (1961) The Johari Window, *Human Training News*, 5 (1) pp 6–7

Lumsdaine, Edward and Lumsdaine, Monika (1995) *Creative Problem Solving: Thinking skills for a changing world*, McGraw-Hill, New York

Macala, Joan C (1986) Sponsored experiential programs: learning by doing in the workplace, in *Experiential and Simulation Techniques for Teaching Adults*, ed Linda H Lewis, pp 57–70, Jossey-Bass, San Francisco

MacDonald, L, Liu, P, Lowell, K, Tsai, H and Lohr, L (2005) Graduate student perspectives on the development of electronic portfolios. Retrieved 1 March 2007, from https://uascentral.uas.alaska.edu/onlinelib/Spring-2005/ ED698-JD1/13705737.pdf

MacLennan, N (1995) *Coaching and Mentoring*, Gower, Aldershot

Maguire, E A *et al* (2000) Navigation-related structural change in the hippocampi of taxi drivers, *Proceedings of the National Academy of Science USA*, **97**, pp 4398–403

Malinen, A (2000) *Towards the Essence OF Adult Experiential Learning*, Jyväskylä University Printing House, Jyväskylä, Finland

Mälkki, K (2010) Building on Mezirow's Theory of Transformative Learning: Theorizing the Challenges to Reflection, *Journal of Transformative Education*, 8 (1), 42–62

Mälkki, K (2011) *Theorizing the Nature of Reflection*, Doctoral dissertation, University of Helsinki, Institute of Behavioural Sciences, Studies in Educational Sciences 238

Mälkki, K and Green, L (2012) Navigational Aids: The Phenomenology of transformative learning (Submitted)

Mallia, G (1997) The use of comic strips in adult education practice, in *Beyond Schooling*, eds G Baldacchino and P Mayo, Mireva Publications, Msida, Malta

Mallinger, A and De Wyze, J (1993) *Too Perfect*, HarperCollins, London

Margerison, C (1988) *Managerial Consulting Skills: A practical guide*, Gower, London

Markman, K, Klein, W M P and Suhr, J A (2009) *Handbook of Imagination and Mental Simulation*, Psychology Press, Hove, Sussex

Martin, A, Franc, D and Zounkova, D (2004) *Outdoor and Experiential Learning: An holistic approach to programme design*, Gower, Aldershot

Marton, F, Beatty, E and Dall' Alba, G (1993) Conceptions of learning, *International Journal of Educational Research*, 19 (3), 277–300

Maslow, A (1954) *Motivation and Personality*, Harper & Row, New York

Maslow, A H (1968) *Towards a Psychology of Being*, 2nd edn, Van Nostrand Reinhold, New York

Maslow, A (1971) *The Farther Reaches of Human Nature*, Viking, New York

Massaro, D W and Cowan, N (1993) Information processing models: microscopes of the mind, *Annual Review of Psychology*, 44, pp 383–425

McGill, Ian and Beaty, Liz (1992) *Action Learning*, Kogan Page, London

McLeod, J (1997) *Narrative and Psychotherapy*, Sage, London

Means, B, Toyama, Y, Murphy, R, Bakia, M and Jones, K (2010) *Evaluation of Evidence-Based Practices in Online Learning: A meta-analysis and review of online learning studies*, US Department of Education, http://www2.ed.gov/rschstat/eval/tech/evidence-based-practices/finalreport.pdf [accessed 21 November 2012]

Megginson, D (1994) Planned and emergent learning: a framework and a method, *Executive Development*, 7 (6), pp 29–32, MCB University Press, Manchester

Mezirow, J (1991) *Transformative Dimensions of Adult Learning*, Jossey-Bass, San Francisco/Oxford

Mezirow, J (2000) Learning to think like an adult. Core concepts of transformation theory, in *Learning as Transformation. Critical Perspectives on a Theory in Progress*, eds J Mezirow, J *et al*, pp 3–33, Jossey-Bass, San Francisco

Miettinen, Reijo (2000) The concept of experiential learning and John Dewey's theory of reflective thought and action, *International Journal of Lifelong Education*, 19 (1), January–February, pp 54–72

Miles, J (1995) Wilderness as a healing place, in *The Theory of Experiential Education*, eds K Warren, M Sakofs and J Hunt, Association for Experiential Education, Kendall/Hunt Publishing, Dubuque, IA

Miles, J and Priest, S (1990) *Adventure Education*, Venture Publishing, State College, PA

Miller, N and Boud, D (1996) Animating learning from experience, in *Working with Experience: Animating learning*, eds D Boud and N Miller, pp 3–13, Routledge, London

Mohawk, J (1996) A nature view of nature, *Resurgence*, **178**, pp 10–11

Moon, J (2000) *Reflection in Learning and Professional Development*, Kogan Page, London

Moon, J (2004) *A Handbook of Reflective and Experiential Learning*, RoutledgeFalmer, London

Morgan, G (1997a) *Images of Organisations*, Sage, London

Morgan, G (1997b) *Imaginization: New Mindsets for Seeing, Organising, and Managing*, Sage, London

Morris, D (1969) *The Human Zoo*, Corgi Books, London

Mortiboys, A (2002) *The Emotionally Intelligent Lecturer*, SEDA Publications, Birmingham

Mortlock, C (1984) *The Adventure Alternative*, Cicerone Press, Milnthorpe, Cumbria

Mumford, A (1991) Individual and organisational learning: the pursuit of change, *Journal of Industrial and Commercial Training*, **23** (6), pp 24–31

Neulinger, J (1974) *The Psychology of Leisure*, Charles C Thomas Publishers, Springfield, IL

Neulinger, J (1976) *The Psychology of Leisure: Research approaches to the study of leisure*, Charles Thomas, London

Neuman, J (2004) *Education and Learning through Outdoor Activities*, Duha Publishing, Prague

Newell, Allen (1990) *Unified Theories of Cognition*, Harvard University Press, Cambridge, MA

Nolan, R (2004) *Compatibility or Conflict: The sustainability of ecotourism consumerism*, Unpublished Thesis, MSc Environmental Management and Conservation, Sheffield Hallam University

Norris, J (2011) Crossing the threshold mindfully: exploring rites of passage models in adventure therapy, *Journal of Adventure Education and Outdoor Learning*, December 2011, 11(2) pp 109–126

Ogilvie, K (1993) *Leading and Managing Groups in the Outdoors*, NAOE Publications, Sheffield

O'Leonard, K (2012) *The Corporate Learning Factbook 2012*, Bersin and Associates, Oakland, CA

Orlick, Terry (1975) *In Pursuit of Excellence*, Human Kinetics Publishers/Coaching Association of Canada, Champaign, IL

Osborne, A F (1963) *Applied Imagination*, Scribners, New York

Palethorpe, R and Wilson, J P (2011) Learning in the Panic Zone: Strategies for Managing Learner Anxiety, *Journal of European Industrial Training*, **35** (5), pp 420–38

Palmer, J (ed) (2001) *Fifty Modern Thinkers on Education*, Routledge, London

Parkin, M (1998) *Tales for Trainers*, Kogan Page, London

Parr, J (2000) *Identity and Education: The links for mature women students*, Ashgate Publishing, Aldershot

Pascual-Leone A, Nguyet D, Cohen LG, Brasil-Neto JP, Cammarota A, Hallett, M (1995) Modulation of muscle responses evoked by transcranial magnetic stimulation during the acquisition of new fine motor skills, *Journal of Neurophysiology*, **74**, pp 1037–45

Pavlov, I (1927) *Conditioned Reflexes: An Investigation of the physiological activity of the cerebral cortex* (translated by G V Anrep), Oxford University Press, London

Peard, G (1999) Spirit of the Earth: Chief Seathl's speech, *Horizons*, **4** (4), pp 9–13

Pedler, Mike (1996) *Action Learning for Managers*, Lemos and Crane in association with The Learning Company Project, London

Petrick, J A and Quinn, J F (1997) *Management Ethics: Integrity at work*, p 43, Sage, London

Phillips, K and Fraser, T (1982) *Ethical and Professional Issues: The management of interpersonal skills training*, Gower Press, Farnborough

Piaget, J P (1927) *Conditioned Reflexes*, Oxford University Press, Oxford

Piaget, J P (1950) *The Psychology of Intelligence*, Routledge & Kegan Paul, London

Piaget, J P (1977) *Science of Education and the Psychology of the Child*, Penguin, Harmondsworth

Pinchot, G (1991) Conference Tapes, Institute of Personnel and Development Annual Conference, 23–25 October, Harrogate

Pine II, B J and Gilmore, J H (2011) *The Experience Economy*, Harvard Business School Publishing, Boston, MA

Pinkney, L (1999) *Sensory therapy*, available at www.sophp.soton.ac.uk/neuro/SENSORY.htm [accessed 20 May 2005]

Plato (1953) Laws, in *Plato's Modern Enemies and the Theory of Natural Law*, J D Wild, p 24, University of Chicago Press, Chicago, IL

Plutchik, R (1980) *Emotion: A psychobioevolutionary synthesis*, Harper & Row, New York

Pollock, L (2000) That's infotainment, *People Management*, 28 December, pp 19–23

Porter, T (1999) Beyond metaphor: applying a new paradigm of change to experiential debriefing, *Journal of Experiential Education*, **22** (2), pp 85–90

Postle, Dennis (1993) Putting the heart back into learning, in *Using Experience for Learning*, eds D Boud, R Cohen and D Walker, pp 33–45, Open University Press, Buckingham

Priest, S and Ballie, R (1995) Justifying the risk to others: the real razor's edge, in *The Theory of Experiential Education*, eds K Warren, M Sakofs and J Hunt, pp 307–16, Association for Experiential Education, Kendall/ Hunt Publishing, Dubuque, IA

Priest, S and Rohnke, K (2000) *101 of the Best Corporate Team-building Activities We Know!*, Kendall/Hunt Publishing, Dubuque, IW

Proudman, S (1999) Urban adventure in 1989 and reflections ten years after, in *Adventure Programming*, eds J C Miles and S Priest, Venture Publishing PA, USA

Rabin, M (2002) Inference by believers in the law of small numbers, *The Quarterly Journal of Economics*, **117** (3), pp 775–816

Rackham, N and Morgan, T (1977) *Behaviour Analysis in Training*, McGraw-Hill, London

Rae, L (1995) *Techniques of Training*, 3rd edn, Gower, Aldershot

Randall, R and Southgate, J (1980) *Co-operative and Community Group Dynamics*, Barefoot Books, London

Ray, M and Myers, R (1986) *Creativity in Business*, Doubleday, New York

Reed, C (1999) A weekend in the country: the outdoors, the earth and drama therapy, *Horizons*, **3**, pp 20–21

Reid, M and Barrington, H (1999) *Training Interventions*, IPD, London

Revans, Reginald W (1971) *Developing Effective Managers: A new approach to business education*, Longman, London

Revans, R W (1982) *The Origin and Growth of Action Learning*, Chartwell Bratt, London

Reynolds, M (1997) Learning styles: a critique, *Management Learning*, **28** (2), pp 115–33, Sage, London

Reynolds, M (1998) Reflection and critical reflection in management learning, *Management Learning*, **29** (2), pp 183–200, Sage, London

Robertson, I (1999) *Mind Sculpture: Unleashing your brain's potential*, Bantam Books, London

Rodwell, J (1994) *Participative Training Skills*, Gower, London

Rogers, A (1996) *Teaching Adults*, Open University Press, Buckingham

Rogers, C R (1969) *Freedom to Learn: A view of what education might become*, Charles E Merrill, Columbus, OH

Rogers, C R and Freiberg, H J (1969) *Freedom to Learn*, Charles E Merrill Publishing, Columbus, OH

Rose, C (1996) *The Greenpeace campaigning strategy: who we are, what we campaign for and why*, Greenpeace Business Conference: Brent Spar... and after, 25 September, London Marriott Hotel

Rosenberg, M (2003) *Nonviolent Communication: A language of life*, PuddleDancer Press, California

Royal College of General Practitioners (1993) *Portfolio-based Learning in General Practice*, RCGP, London

Saddington, (1992) Learner Experience: A rich resource for learning pp 37–39 in Mulligan, J & Griffin, C (Eds) *Empowerment Through Experiential Learning: Explorations of Good Practice*, Kogan Page, London

Salaman, G and Butler, J (1990) Why managers won't learn, *Management Education and Development*, **21** (3), pp 183–91

Salovey, P and Mayer, J D (1990) Emotional intelligence, *Imagination, Cognition and Personality*, **9**, pp 185–211

Samra-Fredericks, D (1998) Conversation analysis, in *Qualitative Methods and Analysis in Organisational Research*, eds G Symon and C Cassel, Sage, London

Sapir, Edward (1987) *Quoted in Conceptual Blockbusting: A guide to better ideas*, James L Adams, p 84, Penguin, Harmondsworth

Sasaki, Naoto (1982) Management and industrial structure in Japan, mentioned in Foreword, *The Origins and Growth of Action Learning*, R W Revans, Chartwell-Bratt, Bickley, Kent

Saunders, D (1988) Simulation gaming: three aspects, *Training Officer*, May pp 134–36

Schank, R C (1992) Story-based memory, in *Minds, Brains and Computers*, eds R Morelli *et al*, Ablex Publishing Corporation, Norwood, NJ

Schank, R and Childers, P (1988) *The Creative Attitude*, Macmillan, New York

Scheff, T (1997) *Emotions, the Social Bond, and Human Reality*, Cambridge University Press, Cambridge

Schein, E H (1992) *Organizational Culture and Leadership*, 2nd edn, Jossey-Bass, San Francisco

Schetter, M (1992) Comic strips in Belgium, in *Belgium, Economic and Commercial Information*, eds Borgerhoff Mulder *et al*, Belgium Foreign Trade Office, Brussels, quoted in Mallia, G (1997) The use of comic strips in adult education practice, in *Beyond Schooling*, eds G Baldacchino and P Mayo, p 89, Mireva Publications, Msida, Malta

Schoel, J, Prouty, D and Radcliffe, P (1988) *Island of Healing: A guide to adventure-based counselling*, Project Adventure Inc, Hamilton, MA

Schön, Donald (1983) *The Reflective Practitioner*, Basic Books, New York

Schön, Donald (1987) *Educating the Reflective Practitioner*, Jossey-Bass, San Francisco

Schueller, G (2000) Thrill or chill, *New Scientist*, **2236**, 20 April, pp 20–24

Schultz, G (1992) *Die Erlebnisgesellschaft: Kultursoziologie der Gegenwart*, Campus Verlag, Frankfurt am Main

Scott Peck, M (1997) *The Road Less Travelled and Beyond*, Rider, London

Seibert, Kent W (1999) Reflection in action: tools for cultivating on-the-job learning conditions, *Organizational Dynamics*, Winter, pp 54–65

Senge, Peter (1992) *The Fifth Discipline: The art and practice of the learning organisation*, Century Business, London

Senge, P M (1993) *The Fifth Discipline: The art and practice of the learning organization*, Century Business, London

Senge, P, Scharmer, C, Jawaorski, J and Flowers, B (2005) *Presence: Exploring profound change in people, organizations and society*, Nicholas Brealey Publishing, London

Sheets-Johnstone, M (2009) *The Corporeal Turn, An Interdisciplinary Reader*, Imprint Academic, Exeter

Siegler, R, Deloache, J, and Eisenberg, N (2006) *How Children Develop*, Worth Publishers, New York

Sinetar, M (1992) Entrepreneurs, chaos and creativity: can creative people survive large company structure?, in *Frontiers of Leadership: An essential reader*, eds M Syrett and C Hogg, pp 109–16, Blackwell, Oxford

Skinner, B (1974) *Adult Behaviourism*, Jonathan Cape, London

Smith, P K *et al* (1986) Play in young children: problems of definition, categorisation and measurement, in *Children's Play: Research developments and practical applications*, ed P K Smith, pp 37–54, Gordon & Breach, New York

Smith, R and Betts, M (2000) Learning as partners: Realising the potential of work-based learning, *Journal of Vocational Education and Training*, **52** (4), pp 589–604

Smith, T and Allison, P (2006) *Outdoor Experiential Leadership: Scenarios Describing Incidents, Dilemmas, & Opportunities*, Racoon Institute Publications/Learning Unlimited Publications, Wisconson, US

Smith, T E and Knapp, C E (eds) (2011) *Sourcebook of Experiential Education: Key thinkers and their contributions*, Routledge, Oxford

Snell, Robin (1992) Experiential learning at work: why can't it be painless?, *Personnel Review*, **21** (4), pp 12–26

Sterling, Stephen (2003) *Whole systems thinking as a basis for paradigm change in education: explorations in the context of sustainability*, unpublished PhD Thesis, University of Bath

Stouffer, Russell (1999) Personal insight: reframing the unconscious through metaphor-based adventure therapy, *Journal of Experiential Education*, **22** (1), June, pp 28–34

Strangaard, F (1981) *NLP Made Visual*, Connector, Copenhagen

Stringer, L and McAvoy, L (1995) The need for something different: spirituality and wilderness adventure, in *The Theory of Experiential Education*, eds Warren *et al*, pp 57–72, Kendall/Hunt Publishing, Dubuque, IA

Surtees, M (1998) *New frontiers in outdoor development: evaluating the personal development outcomes of expeditions*, Unpublished Master's thesis in HRD, Sheffield Business School, Sheffield

Swarbrooke, J, Beard, C, Leckie, S and Pomfret, G (2003) *Adventure Tourism: The new frontier*, Butterworth-Heinemann, Oxford

Taleb, N N (2007) *The Black Swan: The impact of the highly improbable*, Penguin, London

Taylor, H (1991) The systematic training model: corn circles in search of a spaceship?, *Journal of the Association for Management Education and Development*, **22** (4), pp 258–78

Terrell, C (2000) Cartoon review cards, *Horizons*, **12**, Winter, AfOL, Penrith, Cumbria

Thayer, R (1996) *The Origin of Everyday Moods: Managing energy, tension and stress*, Oxford University Press, Oxford

Thurber, J (1939) 'The Secret Life of Walter Mitty', The New Yorker, 18 March

Tolbert, M A and Hanafin, J (2006) Use of self in OD consulting: What matters is presence, in *The NTL Handbook of Organisational Development and Change: Principles, Practices and Perspectives*, eds B B Jones M Brazzel, Pfeiffer, San francisco, CA

Tolle, E (2006) *A New Earth: Awakening your life's purpose*, Plume, London

Tower, R B and Singer, J L (1980) Imagination, interest and joy in early childhood, in *Children's Humour*, eds P E McGhee and A J Chapman, Wiley, Chichester

Trules, A (2005) *Personal Storytelling Bridges the Great Divide: Changing the world one story at a time*, paper presented to the Twelfth International Conference on Learning, University of Granada, Spain, pp 11–14

Tulving, E (1972) Episodic and semantic memory, in *Organization of Memory*, eds E Tulving and E Donaldson, pp 381–403, Academic Press, London

Tumin, M (1976) Valid and Invalid Rationales, in *Experiential Learning*, eds Morris Keeton *et al*, Jossey-Bass, San Francisco CA

Turner, T (2005) *Video games as education and literacies: what we have to understand about video and computer games and technological environments to accomplish learning and literacies*, Workshop Presentation Abstract, Design For Learning, The Twelfth International Conference on Learning, 11–14 July, Granada, Spain

Ulrich, D (1974) Aesthetic and effective responses to natural environments, in *Behaviour and the Natural Environment*, eds I Altman and J Wohlwill, Plenum Press, New York

Ulrich, D and Hinkson, P (2001) Net heaps, *People Management*, pp 32–36, Chartered Institute of Personnel and Development, London

Uttley, Alison (1943) from *Country Hoard*, Faber & Faber, pp 199–201, in Jerome S Bruner, Alison Jolly and Kathy Sylva (1976) *Play*, Penguin, Harmondsworth

Van Manen, M (1991) *The Tact of Teaching*, The State of New York Press, New York

Van Matre, S (1978) *Acclimatisation*, American Camping Association, Martinsville, IN

Van Matre, S (1979) *Sunship Earth*, American Camping Association, Martinsville, IN

Van Ments, M (1994) *The Effective Use of Role Play*, Kogan Page, London

Vanreusel, B (1995) From Bambi to Rambo: towards a socio-ecological approach to the pursuit of outdoor sports, in *Sport in Space and Time*, eds O Weiss and W Schulz, Vienna University Press, Vienna

Vygotsky, L (1978) *Mind in Society: The development of higher psychological processes*, Harvard University Press, Cambridge, MA

Walker, R (1999) Fire in the sky: from big bang to big money, *Horizons*, **4**, pp 5–7

Walter, G and Marks, S (1981) *Experiential Learning and Change*, John Wiley & Sons, New York

Warner Weil, Susan and McGill, Ian (1989) *Making Sense of Experiential Learning: Diversity in theory and practice*, SHRE and Open University Press, Buckingham

Waterhouse, K (1959) *Billy Liar*, Michael Joseph, London

Whyte, W H (1960) *The Organisation Man*, Penguin, London

Wichmann, T (1995) Babies and bath water: two experiential heresies, in *The Theory of Experiential Education*, eds K Warren, M Sakofs and J Hunt, pp 109–19, Association for Experiential Education, Kendall/Hunt Publishing, Dubuque, IA

Wickes, S (2000) The facilitators' stories, *Organisation Development*, Brathay Topical Papers, **2**, pp 25–46, Brathay, Cumbria

Wildemeersch, Danny (1989) The principal meaning of dialogue for the construction and transformation of reality, in *Making Sense of Experiential Learning: Diversity in theory and practice*, eds Susan Warner Weil and Ian McGill, pp 60–77, SHRE and Open University Press, Buckingham

Wilkes, F (1999) *Intelligent Emotion*, Arrow Books, London

Williams, A (2012) Taking a step back: learning without the facilitator on solo activities, *Journal of Adventure Education and Outdoor Learning*, **12** (2), pp 137–55

Willett, J (1977) *Brecht on Theatre,* Eyre Methuen, London

Williams, S (1996) Uncovering the management training fraud, *Personnel Today*, p 21

Willis, A (2011) Re-storying wilderness and adventure therapies: Healing places and selves in an era of environmental crisis. *Journals of Adventure Education and Outdoor Learning*, December 2011, 11(2) pp 91–108

Wilson, J P (2008) Reflecting on the future: a chronological consideration of reflective practice, *Journal of Reflective Practice*, 9 (2), 177–184

Wilson, J P (2011) *The Routledge Encyclopaedia of UK Education, Training and Employment*, Routledge Falmer, Oxford

Wilson, J P (ed) (2012a) *International Human Resource Development: Learning, education and training for nations, organisations and individuals* (3rd edn), Kogan Page, London

Wilson, J P (2012b) *Dream: Your life, your future*, Burton in Kendal, Cumbria

Wilson, P (1997) *Calm at Work*, Penguin, London

Winston, R (2003) *The Human Mind*, Bantam Press, London

Woodruffe, C (2001) Promotional intelligence, *People Management*, 11 January, Chartered Institute of Personnel and Development

Yaffey (1993) The value base of activity experience in the outdoors, *Journal of Adventure Education*, 10 (3), pp 9–11

Yardley-Matwiejczuk, K (1999) *Role Play: Theory and practice*, Sage, London

Yerkes, R M and Dodson, J D (1980) The relation of strength of stimulus to rapidity of habit formation, *Journal of Comparative Neurological Psychology*, **18**, pp 459–82

Young, M (2008) *Bringing Knowledge Back In: From social constructivism to social realism in the sociology of education*, Routledge, London

Yue, G and K J Cole (1992) Strength increases from the motor program: Comparison of training with maximal voluntary and imagined muscle contracts, *Journal of Neurophysiology*, **67**, pp 1114–23

Zohar, Dana and Marshall, Ian (2001) *Spiritual Intelligence: The ultimate intelligence*, Bloomsbury, London

INDEX

NB: page numbers in italic indicate figures or tables